THE CLUNIACS
AND THE
GREGORIAN REFORM

THE CLUNIACS
AND THE
GREGORIAN REFORM

BY

H. E. J. COWDREY

OXFORD
AT THE CLARENDON PRESS
1970

Oxford University Press, Ely House, London W. 1

GLASGOW   NEW YORK   TORONTO   MELBOURNE   WELLINGTON
CAPE TOWN   SALISBURY   IBADAN   NAIROBI   DAR ES SALAAM   LUSAKA   ADDIS ABABA
BOMBAY   CALCUTTA   MADRAS   KARACHI   LAHORE   DACCA
KUALA LUMPUR   SINGAPORE   HONG KONG   TOKYO

PRINTED IN GREAT BRITAIN

PREFACE

AMONGST the friends and colleagues who have helped me in the preparation of this study, I must express an especial debt of gratitude to Dr. J. M. Wallace-Hadrill, who, at an early stage, attempted to clarify my mind on certain of the fundamental issues; to Dr. P. T. V. M. Chaplais and Mr. K. J. Leyser, who have criticized and commented upon particular sections; and to the advisers and staff of the Clarendon Press. Responsibility for such errors of fact and judgement as remain is entirely my own. I am most grateful to the staff of the Bodleian Library for their courteous service, sometimes under conditions of difficulty; my thanks are particularly due to Mr. D. H. Merry.

I should also like to acknowledge my debt to the continental scholars who specialize in Cluniac and Gregorian studies. I have too often referred to them in order to record dissent, and too seldom in order to indicate the true extent of what I owe. The names of H. Diener, G. Duby, Dom K. Hallinger, J.-F. Lemarignier, H.-E. Mager, C. Violante, and J. Wollasch come to mind with especial readiness. But, above all, it was the work of G. Tellenbach which first excited my interest in eleventh-century problems when I was an undergraduate, and to him my debt is greatest.

H. E. J. C.

St. Edmund Hall, Oxford
March 1969

CONTENTS

PART IV

THE CLUNIACS OUTSIDE FRANCE

ABBREVIATIONS

Abh. Berl.	*Abhandlungen der Deutschen (Berliner kgl. preuss.) Akademie der Wissenschaften, philosophisch-historische Klasse*
Abh. Gött.	*Abhandlungen der Gesellschaft der Wissenschaften zu Göttingen, philologisch-historische Klasse,* Neue Folge
A.U.F.	*Archiv für Urkundenforschung*
Becker, *Urban II*	A. Becker, *Papst Urban II.,* i (Stuttgart, 1964)
Bibl. C.	*Bibliotheca Cluniacensis,* ed. M. Marrier (Paris, 1614)
Bruel	*Recueil des chartes de l'abbaye de Cluny,* ed. A. Bruel, 6 vols. (Paris, 1876–1903)
Bull. C.	*Bullarium Cluniacense,* ed. P. Simon (Lyons, 1680)
D.A.	*Deutsches Archiv für Geschichte des Mittelalters* (1937–44); *für Erforschung des Mittelalters* (1950–)
D.H.G.E.	*Dictionnaire d'histoire et de géographie ecclésiastiques,* ed. A. Baudrillart, A. Vogt, and U. de Rouziès (Paris, 1909–)
E.H.R.	*English Historical Review*
Ep. Coll.	Gregory VII, *Epistolae Collectae, Bibliotheca rerum Germanicarum,* ed. P. Jaffé, ii (Berlin, 1856), 520–76
Esp. sag.	*La España sagrada,* ed. H. Flórez, 54 vols. (Madrid, 1749–1879)
G.C.	*Gallia Christiana,* i–xiii, new edn. by P. Piolin (Paris, 1870–8); xiv–xvi (Paris, 1856–65)
Hallinger, *Gorze–Kluny*	K. Hallinger, *Gorze–Kluny. Studien zu den monastischen Lebensformen und Gegensätzen im Hochmittelalter* (*Studia Anselmiana,* xxii–v, Rome, 1950–1)
J.L.	P. Jaffé, *Regesta pontificum Romanorum,* ed. W. Wattenbach, i, 2nd edn. (Leipzig, 1885)
J.E.H.	*Journal of Ecclesiastical History*
L'Huillier, *Saint Hugue*	A. L'Huillier, *Vie de saint Hugues abbé de Cluny* (Solesmes, 1888)
Mansi	J. D. Mansi, *Sacrorum conciliorum nova et amplissima collectio,* 31 vols. (Florence and Venice, 1759–93)

M.G.H.	Monumenta Germaniae Historica
— B.D.K.	Die Briefe der deutschen Kaiserzeit
— Const.	Constitutiones
— DD.	Diplomata regum et imperatorum Germaniae
— Dt. MA.	Deutsches Mittelalter
— Epp.	Epistolae
— Ep. Sel.	Epistolae selectae
— L. de L.	Libelli de lite imperatorum et pontificum
— Scr.	Scriptores
M.I.Ö.G.	Mitteilungen des Instituts für österreichische Geschichtsforschung
Neue Forschungen	Neue Forschungen über Cluny und die Cluniacenser, ed. G. Tellenbach (Freiburg, 1959)
N.A.	Neues Archiv der Gesellschaft für ältere deutsche Geschichtskunde (1876–1935)
P.L.	J. P. Migne, Patrologia Latina, 221 vols. (Paris, 1844–)
Q.F.I.A.B.	Quellen und Forschungen aus italienischen Archiven und Bibliotheken (Rome, 1898–)
Reg.	Gregory VII, Registrum, ed. E. Caspar, M.G.H. Ep. Sel. (Berlin, 1920–3)
R.H.F.	Recueil des historiens des Gaules et de la France, ed. M. Bouquet, 24 vols. (Paris, 1738–1904)
Sackur, Die Cluniacenser	E. Sackur, Die Cluniacenser in ihrer kirchlichen und allgemeingeschichtlichen Wirksamkeit bis zur Mitte des elften Jahrhunderts, 2 vols. (Halle, 1892–4)
Santifaller, Q.F.	L. Santifaller, Quellen und Forschungen zum Urkunden- und Kanzleiwesen Papst Gregors VII., 1. teil (Studi e testi, cxc, Vatican City, 1957)
SB. Berl.	Sitzungsberichte der Deutschen (Berliner kgl. preuss.) Akademie der Wissenschaften, philosophisch-historische Klasse
SB. Wien.	Sitzungsberichte des (kaiserlichen) Wiener Akademie der Wissenschaften, philosophisch-historische Klasse
S.G.	Studi Gregoriani, ed. G. B. Borino (Rome, 1947–61)
S.R.G.	Scriptores rerum Germanicarum in usum scholarum separatim editi
T R.H.S.	Transactions of the Royal Historical Society
Z.S.S.R. kan.	Zeitschrift der Savigny-Stiftung für Rechtsgeschichte, kanonistische Abteilung

INTRODUCTION

THE modern debate about the contribution of the Cluniacs to the Gregorian Reform began some seventy years ago with the work of Sackur.[1] Although the nature of this contribution has since been amongst the most-discussed problems of medieval history, no agreement about it has been reached, or has seemed likely to be reached. Sackur himself believed that, although the Cluniacs genuinely prepared the way for Gregory VII, they did so only indirectly and within narrow limits. Their overriding concern was with the reform of the monastic order in itself and for its own sake. As a kind of by-product, they did, indeed, also disseminate reform in the Church and in the world at large. But this was because they tended to draw their secular contemporaries into a close relationship with the higher and essentially self-sufficient

[1] Sackur, *Die Cluniacenser*. Sackur was the first scholar to draw a clear distinction between the objectives of the Cluniacs and of the Gregorians. The older view is well represented by the French historian Delarc. He considered that the Cluniacs were the initiators of Gregory VII's campaign for the moral purification of the Church and of his attempt to establish a new spiritual democracy. As Napoleon embodied and consolidated the principles of the French Revolution, so did Gregory those of the Cluniac Reform: O. Delarc, *Saint Grégoire VII et la réforme de l'église au xie siècle*, 3 vols. (Paris, 1889), esp. i, pp. x–xxxvii. Sackur's work is open to the general criticism that, in reacting too strongly against such a view, he used the name 'Cluniacs' too loosely and comprehensively, so that it became almost a portmanteau term for the monastic reform movements of the tenth and early eleventh centuries. By so doing, he obscured the peculiar features of Cluny itself and failed to bring out the varying degrees of subjection, filiation, and more indirect influence which marked Cluny's relationship with other houses. These are well discussed by D. Knowles, *The Monastic Order in England* (2nd edn., Cambridge, 1949), pp. 145–50, and *From Pachomius to Ignatius* (Oxford, 1966), pp. 10–15. The distinctive character of monastic life at Cluny itself has been well discussed by English-speaking historians, notably R. Graham, *English Ecclesiastical Studies* (London, 1929), pp. 1–45; J. Evans, *Monastic Life at Cluny* (Oxford, 1931); N. Hunt, *Cluny under Saint Hugh, 1049–1109* (London, 1967). K. J. Conant's studies of the architecture of Cluny, in *Speculum*, iv (1929) to xxix (1954), also serve to illustrate the special quality of Cluny's monastic life; for a summary, see his 'Mediaeval Academy Excavations at Cluny', *Speculum*, xxix (1954), 1–43, and 'Cluny, 1077–88', *Mélanges offerts à René Crozet*, ed. P. Gallais and Y.-J. Riou, i (Poitiers, 1966), 341–4.

life of the monastic order. They had no wider programme for the reform of the Church as such, and they looked for no transformation of the structure of the pre-Gregorian world. Accordingly, whilst they welcomed and co-operated with the reforming initiatives of the Papacy when the time became ripe for them to do so, they always solicited, accepted, and profited by the protection of the kings and great men, whose power over the Church was so pronounced a feature of tenth- and eleventh-century history. As a rule, they had no idea of promoting the wholesale emancipation of the Church from lay control. They belonged essentially to the pre-Gregorian order of Church and society.[1]

Sackur's conclusions have been broadly followed by a majority of subsequent writers. But it is well to remember that his own investigations did not extend beyond the time of Abbot Odilo of Cluny (994–1048) into that of Abbot Hugh (1049–1109). He thus barely touched upon the period after the reform of the Papacy in 1046 by the Emperor Henry III, which culminated in the decisive renovation of papal authority by Popes Gregory VII (1073–85) and Urban II (1088–99). Amongst the historians who have taken this later period into full account, there have for long been some who have come to very different conclusions from Sackur's. In a footnote to his *Kirchengeschichte Deutschlands*, Hauck implied that he would at least have modified Sackur's picture, by laying emphasis upon the development which took place in Cluniac objectives, as papal authority became more effective. He granted

---

[1] e.g. Sackur, *Die Cluniacenser*, ii. 440–9, 464–5. This view was also presented by A. Fliche, *La Réforme grégorienne*, i (Louvain and Paris, 1924), 39–60; and G. Tellenbach, *Church, State, and Christian Society* (Oxford, 1940), esp. pp. v–xvii, 42–7, 76–85, 93–5, 186–92. For a statement of it by an English historian, see L. M. Smith, 'Cluny and Gregory VII', *E.H.R.* xxvi (1911), 20–33. Miss Smith concluded that 'not until the time of Innocent II [1130–43] can the Cluniacs be said to have rallied as a body to the Gregorian standard'; and that 'from the lives of the first five abbots of Cluny we find no evidence for the connection of the Cluniacs with the reform of Gregory VII': ibid., pp. 31, 33. Miss Smith expressed a similar view in her book, *Cluny in the Eleventh and Twelfth Centuries* (London, 1930), pp. 66–82. Another statement of it occurs in N. F. Cantor, 'The Crisis of Western Monasticism', *American Historical Review*, lxvi (1960), 47–67. According to Cantor, 'the older view, now largely discredited, that the Cluniac movement directly inspired the Gregorian reform was not only naïve but also almost the complete opposite of the truth': ibid., p. 61.

that, in the earlier phases of the Cluniac Reform, the Cluniacs revealed no disposition to question the existing order of Church and
society. But he also believed that, from the middle of the eleventh
century when Sackur's study was broken off, they began to formu-
late and pursue more radical and comprehensive principles of
reform. Previously, they had aspired simply to reform the monastic
order by encouraging within it obedience to the Benedictine Rule;
henceforth, they also sought to reform the Church at large by
procuring a more general obedience to the canon law.[1] That is to
say, their perspectives became enlarged when the reform of the
Church was more energetically attempted by the reformed
Papacy. They thus responded to the new papal initiatives of
Rome, and gave them their assistance in a manner which was
appropriate.

Other, and more recent, writers have argued that, even from
the early days of their Reform, the Cluniacs deliberately and positively promoted the wider ends that Gregory VII was, in due
course, to pursue. For Brackmann the Cluniac and the Gregorian
Reforms were parts of a single and continuous development.
While the Papacy was, as yet, too weak to assume a position of
leadership in the Church, the Cluniacs worked on its behalf; they
prepared its way by subordinating monasteries to a central
authority and by strenuously upholding the superiority of the
spiritual to the secular power. In due course, under Gregory VII
and his successors, Cluny and its liberty provided the pattern for
a new ordering of the monastic world, and so for the dissemination of Gregorian principles in many lands. The Cluniacs were also
active on Gregory's behalf in a more practical way. Most notably,
during the crisis of the Investiture Contest, they assisted him in
southern Germany, especially through the Swabian monastery of
Hirsau; there Gregory used them in the very forefront of his
struggle with the Emperor Henry IV.[2]

---

[1] A. Hauck, *Kirchengeschichte Deutschlands*, iii (3rd and 4th edn., Leipzig, 1920),
495, n. 3. Sackur himself was well aware that Abbot Hugh's reign marked a new
stage in Cluny's development from a monastic point of view: op. cit. i, pp. vi–vii.

[2] A. Brackmann, *Zur politischen Bedeutung der kluniazensischen Bewegung*
(Darmstadt, 1955), esp. pp. 21–7; and 'Gregor VII. und die kirchliche Reformbewegung in Deutschland', *S.G.* ii (1947), 7–30. Brackmann's views were

Brackmann's conclusions about the external political significance of Cluny have been complemented by the theses which
Hallinger has propounded in his monumental work *Gorze–Kluny*.
In it he presented a comparative study of the different forms of the
monastic life itself during the tenth and eleventh centuries. He held
that, by contrast with German monasticism, Cluny always offered
a clear challenge to lay and episcopal authority over the monastic
order, in both the temporal and the spiritual spheres. At the very
outset of the Cluniac movement Cluny's Foundation Charter of
909 was already a manifesto of radical opposition to the incursions
of lay feudalism into the spiritual sphere, which took place especially by way of lay proprietorship and lay advocacy. Cluny did
not, indeed, openly challenge the existing world-order; it asserted
its claims within a purely monastic context and with an opportune
regard for the realities of the prevailing feudalism, against which
it never embarked upon open political action. Yet by vindicating
the principle of the absolute independence of the monastic order
from interference in temporal matters, it was a genuine fore-
runner of Gregory VII; thus Hallinger claimed that 'it safeguarded
the seminal ideas from which the struggles of the late eleventh
century were to grow'. It did so the more effectively because, from
its foundation, it shared with the Papacy a common dedication to
the apostles St. Peter and St. Paul. Like Brackmann, Hallinger
insisted upon the importance of Hirsau:

> It was Hirsau, one of Cluny's offshoots, that first became of strictly
> political significance. . . . Thus, it is permissible to speak of Cluny's
> political activity (*Wirkung*), even if its effects were produced somewhat
> indirectly. The Gregorian and the Cluniac movements diverged in
> their ultimate developments; but in their origins, they were closely
> akin. What they had in common was the frontal challenge that they
> offered to the feudal enslavement of the Church and of its domains.
> For centuries, opposition to the prevailing feudalism found sanctuary
> in monastic circles—long before Gregory VII took to their ultimate and
> radical conclusion the basic principles that he shared with the Cluniacs.[1]

criticized, and Sackur's upheld, by G. Ladner, *Theologie und Politik vor dem
Investiturstreit* (2nd edn., Darmstadt, 1968), pp. 46–7, 60–3, 140–2.

[1] Hallinger, *Gorze–Kluny*, p. 584; for Cluny's supposedly anti-feudal tendencies,
see esp. pp. 58, 548, 555–61, 573–97, 759–60.

In addition, Cluny's exemption from the spiritual authority of the bishops showed that the Cluniacs were determined to 'strip off the fetters of episcopal feudalism'.[1]

By its very nature, therefore, the Cluniac Reform was, in Hallinger's opinion, radically anti-feudal and anti-episcopal. Cluny stood for the principle of monastic autonomy under papal protection. At all stages of its history it accepted, at least in germ, the principles of the liberty of the Church which Gregory VII aspired to realize. It did so the more readily because, like the Papacy, it was exclusively dedicated to the service of St. Peter and St. Paul.[2]

Hallinger's conclusions, in particular, about the close connection of the Cluniac Reform with the Gregorian have met with widespread criticism.[3] No one, probably, would dissent from Tellenbach when, with Hallinger's work in mind, he insisted that the time is not yet ripe for an attempt finally to resolve the problem of the Cluniacs and Gregory VII; first of all, Hallinger's bold theses must be tested and modified by the systematic investigation of particular monastic personalities, houses, and developments.[4] But most historians, led by Tellenbach's own school,[5] undeniably stand much nearer to Sackur's position than to Hallinger's. Tellenbach's pupil, Mager, has well epitomized the prevailing opinion when he argued that, in implied contrast with the Gregorians, the Cluniacs were not revolutionaries in either ecclesiastical or political affairs; they were conservatives, who sought reform by evolution.[6]

Impressive support for this point of view has been provided by two inquiries into the attitude of Cluny towards the Proprietary

[1] Ibid., p. 558; on Cluny and exemption, see pp. 503, 557–73.
[2] See also Hallinger's article, 'Zur geistigen Welt der Anfänge Klunys', *D.A.* x (1953–4), 417–45. Hallinger's views have found recent support in H. Hoffmann, 'Von Cluny zum Investiturstreit', *Archiv für Kulturgeschichte*, xlv (1963), 165–209.
[3] e.g. T. Schieffer, 'Cluniazensische oder Gorzische Reformbewegung?' *Archiv für mittelrheinische Kirchengeschichte*, iv (1954), 24–44, and 'Cluny et la querelle des investitures', *Revue historique*, ccxxv (1961), 47–72; Tellenbach, 'Zum Wesen der Cluniacenser', *Saeculum*, ix (1958), 370–9; *Neue Forschungen, passim,* but esp. J. Wollasch's comments, pp. 116–20.
[4] *Neue Forschungen*, p. 10.
[5] Of which *Neue Forschungen* is the most important publication.
[6] Ibid., p. 194.

Church System and towards the bishops, which Tellenbach's pupils have published. Mager himself has indicated that, to judge by the proportion of churches and religious houses amongst the gifts to monasteries of which record survives in the charters of the tenth and eleventh centuries, Cluny in no way stands out as a champion of the movement to reduce the prevalence of lay proprietorship.[1] It did, indeed, benefit more and more from what was in fact a widespread and increasing tendency in France towards the transfer of churches and religious houses from lay into ecclesiastical hands.[2] Thus between 980 and 1049 only some 6.5 per cent of all gifts to Cluny were of this character. But during the reign of Abbot Hugh, while the total number of gifts of all kinds fell off, the proportion of gifts which were of churches and religious houses rose markedly: from 1049 to 1073 it was 16 per cent; and thereafter, until Hugh's death in 1109, it was 27 per cent.[3] This was, however, part of a long tendency towards the undermining of lay proprietorship, in which Cluny itself was far from being a leader. Mager analysed the gifts which were made to a number of Cluny's own dependencies, and showed that, in the acquisition of churches and monasteries, the dependencies often outpaced the mother house;[4] while the non-Cluniac houses of

[1] *Neue Forschungen*, pp. 169–217.

[2] Mager's arguments should be read in conjunction with an article which appeared in France just before Hallinger's *Gorze–Kluny* was published, and of which the contributors to *Neue Forschungen* did not take account: G. Mollat, 'La Restitution des églises privées au patrimoine ecclésiastique en France du ixe au xie siècle', *Revue historique de droit français et étranger*, lxvii (1949), 399–423. According to Mollat, the tendency for monasteries—both Cluniac and non-Cluniac—to receive gifts of churches which had been in lay proprietorship, was itself part of a widespread and increasing movement towards the transfer of churches from lay into ecclesiastical hands which began so early as the middle of the ninth century. The main impetus came, not from the monasteries, but from the bishops; in the eleventh century the popes added their encouragement to it. The transfer of churches from laymen to churchmen was thus evidence of a general willingness of the monasteries, the bishops, and ultimately the Papacy, to help each other; its origins antedated the foundation of Cluny. See also G. Schreiber, *Gemeinschaften des Mittelalters*, i (Regensburg and Münster, 1948), esp. 300–6.

[3] *Neue Forschungen*, pp. 173, 216.

[4] Ibid., pp. 174–7, 216; e.g. between 1050 and 1115, 35.3 per cent of gifts to the priory of Saint-Mont (Gascony) were churches; at Saint-Flour (Auvergne) during the eleventh century, the figure was 32 per cent; at Saint-Martin-des-

Redon (Brittany) and Conques-en-Rouergue were far ahead of it.[1] He concluded that Cluny was distinguished by no extraordinary zeal for the winning of churches from lay hands.[2] On the contrary, it was conspicuously tolerant of, and willing to make compromises with, the current forms of lay proprietorship. It was, for example, frequently content to accept gifts of part of a church while the remainder was left in lay hands.[3] It also willingly acquired gifts which were conditional upon certain of their rights being retained by former lay proprietors.[4] Mager's investigations thus tend to the conclusion that, far from maintaining the constant and conspicuous hostility to the incursions of lay feudalism into the spiritual sphere of which Hallinger spoke, Cluny showed a remarkable solicitude for the rights of lay proprietors.

Mager himself,[5] and still more his colleague Diener,[6] have also argued, with impressive documentation, that, in spite of their energetic campaign for the exemption of Cluny from episcopal jurisdiction, the Cluniacs in general enjoyed good relations with the bishops. Even with respect to exemption, they were, in practice, prepared to make large concessions to the episcopate so far as Cluny's dependencies were concerned; in return, they can be shown to have enjoyed friendly relations with a remarkable number of bishops, and to have been extensively favoured by them.[7] To such episcopal favour, indeed, they owed many of their opportunities for expansion in the time of Abbot Hugh.

In these studies by Tellenbach's school, a considerable weight of evidence has thus been brought to bear in support of the view that the Cluniacs were conservatives, whose aims and methods stand in contrast to those of the Gregorians, and who fitted in with the pre-Gregorian order of Church and society. Yet it is impossible

Champs (Paris), between 1059 and 1079, when it was given to Cluny, it was 50 per cent; although after it became Cluniac the proportion up to 1100 fell to 34 per cent, rising again to 53 per cent for the period 1100–25; at Romanmôtier (Burgundy) the proportion throughout the eleventh century was 40 per cent.

[1] Ibid., pp. 177–8, 216: Conques, 1000–50, 15 per cent, 1050–1100, 39 per cent, 1100–30, 50 per cent; Redon, 1000–1100, 37 per cent.
[2] Ibid., p. 178.   [3] Ibid., pp. 190–4.   [4] Ibid., pp. 194–200.
[5] Ibid., pp. 195–7, 208–11.   [6] Ibid., pp. 221–352.
[7] See Diener's conclusions, ibid., pp. 330–1.

to be satisfied that such studies point the way towards a balanced
account of Cluny's relationship to the Gregorian Reform, or that
they take proper account of all the evidence. In particular, they
wholly ignore the reiterated testimony of Gregory VII and of
many who stood nearest to him, that the Gregorians themselves
thought otherwise. For them the liberty of Cluny was a pattern
which found special favour in their eyes, and which they desired
to reproduce elsewhere in the Church; and Cluny itself was held
up as their valued ally in the cause of reform. They often proclaimed that there was, in fact, an underlying compatibility of
objectives between the Cluniacs and themselves: 'eadem enim via
eodem sensu eodem spiritu ambulamus', Gregory VII wrote of
himself and Abbot Hugh in 1080.[1] In an allocution at his Lent
Council of the same year, Gregory pronounced a remarkable
eulogy upon Cluny, which has been curiously neglected by historians, and in which he laid especial emphasis upon the exemplary
freedom of Cluny from all worldly subjection:

Although there are many monasteries beyond the mountains which
have been nobly and religiously founded to the honour of Almighty
God and of the holy apostles St. Peter and St. Paul, there is one in those
parts of the world that belongs to St. Peter and to this church by an
especial right as its own peculiar possession—I mean Cluny, which,
from the very first, was given over to the honour and protection of
this Apostolic See. By God's mercy, it has come to such a peak of
excellence and religion under its holy abbots, that it surpasses all other
monasteries that I know, even much older ones, in the service of God
and in spiritual warmth. I know of no other in that part of the world
to which it can be compared. For it has never had an abbot who was
not a saint. Its abbots and monks have never in any way dishonoured
their sonship of this church or bowed the knee to Baal [like] Jeroboam.
They have always exhibited the liberty and dignity of this holy see of
Rome, upon which they were founded from the beginning; and from
generation to generation, they have nobly upheld its authority. For
they have never bent their necks before any strange and earthly power,
but they have remained under the exclusive obedience and defence of
St. Peter and of this church.[2]

---

[1] *Reg.* viii. 3, 27 June 1080, p. 520.
[2] *Bull. C.*, pp. 21–2. For the text, see below, pp. 272–3.

The picture is certainly idealized, and when compared with such evidence as Mager has marshalled in his essay, it is at several removes from the kind of reality that is to be encountered in the everyday traffic of Cluny's charters. Yet the veritable mystique of Cluny which the eulogy of 1080 expressed had grown up at Rome even before Gregory VII became pope. Cardinal Peter Damiani's visit to Cluny in 1063 elicited a eulogy in terms which anticipated Gregory's own:

> From the very day of its foundation, the monastery of Cluny has been so eminently free by an innate and tranquil freedom, that it should be subject to no ecclesiastical or secular person save the Roman pontiff. God's mercy has ordained that, where the burden of earthly subjection has been done away, devotion to his service should be fullest; and that, where there is no liability to earthly service, the full dignity of the monastic profession should be completely revealed. O truly renowned and free-born service of God, which leaves no place for earthly service![1]

It was such an appreciation of the uniqueness of Cluny that led Abbot Bernard of Saint-Victor, Marseilles, in 1078, to advise Abbot William of Hirsau to adopt the Customs of Cluny:

> For there, the monastic life has grown to such a height of vigour and fame, because of the reputation of its excellent monks as well as because of its long continuance, that if the marks of sanctity seem nowadays to be found in other monasteries, there is no doubt that its individual streams have come from Cluny, as from a living and inexhaustible source.[2]

Next year, when Gregory VII wished to recompense the monks of Marseilles for Abbot Bernard's long absence in his service, he did so by communicating to Saint-Victor a relationship with the Apostolic See which copied that of Cluny:

> We trust . . . that St. Peter and St. Paul will guard and keep your house with especial care, since you have evidently suffered harm and trouble in their service. For we desire so to bind together the monastery

---

[1] *De Gallica Petri Damiani profectione et eius ultramontano itinere*, ed. G. Schwartz and A. Hofmeister, *M.G.H. Scr.* xxx. 1035.
[2] William of Hirsau, *Consuetudines Hirsaugienses*, *P.L.* cl. 928–9.

of St. Paul's [-without-the-Walls at Rome] and yours that, as Cluny has for so long done, you also may especially cleave to the Apostolic See and enjoy the special aid and blessing of this church.[1]

This relationship could be further reproduced. In 1080, when Gregory VII wished to confer upon the Swabian monastery of All Saints', Schaffhausen, a complete immunity from all outside interference in its temporal affairs, he prescribed that,

in order that the monks may more safely and readily fulfil their calling without vexation, and that they may constantly and gladly serve God with due devotion, we will and ordain by apostolic authority . . . that it may be as untroubled by any secular power, and as peaceful in the liberty of the Roman See (*Romanae sedis libertate*) as the monasteries of Cluny and Marseilles assuredly are.[2]

Again, in 1083, when Gregory conferred especial privileges upon the Spanish monastery of Sahagún, in León, his express intention was to set it up as the Cluny of Spain:

. . . we take this monastery into the safekeeping of our perpetual defence and of Roman liberty (*sub perpetuae defensionis et Romanae libertatis tutela*) and we lay down that it is to be free from the yoke of every ecclesiastical or secular power. . . . It is especially to cleave to the Apostolic See after the pattern and form of Cluny, which, in God's providence and under Roman liberty (*sub libertate Romana*), shines more clearly than the daylight through almost all parts of the world because of the fame of its religion, reputation, and dignity. It is likewise to enjoy a perpetual and inviolable security. Thus, like Cluny in France, Sahagún may be illustrious in Spain for its prerogative of liberty. As, by the grace of God, it will be its peer in religion, so let it be its equal in the confirmation of its rights by the Apostolic See.[3]

In due course these passages will be discussed in their historical context. For the present they suffice to indicate that, for Gregory VII and for many of the reformers who stood nearest to him, Cluny seemed to embody in an exemplary way the aspirations of the Gregorian Reform, and to have for long borne witness to

---

[1] *Reg.* vi. 15, 2 Jan. 1079, pp. 419–20; cf. vii. 7–8, 2 Nov. 1079, pp. 468–70.
[2] *Reg.* vii. 24, 8 May 1080, pp. 503–4.
[3] Santifaller, *Q.F.*, no. 209, pp. 244–5.

them with outstanding constancy. Cluny exhibited a pattern of
ecclesiastical liberty and of the monastic life as based upon it,
which it was eminently desirable to reproduce elsewhere. Such
day-to-day minutiae as the terms of gifts in the general run of
minor charters, were outside the consideration of those who built
up this picture; they were utterly overruled by the pre-eminent
position of Cluny itself which was based upon its prerogative of
liberty—the 'libertas Romana'.

Thus far, the explicit views of the Gregorians tend to bear out
Hallinger's opinion that Cluny exhibited a liberty which represented 'a frontal challenge to the feudal enslavement of the Church
and of its domain'. Yet—and here one of the weaknesses of
Hallinger's argument is revealed—Cluny's peculiar liberty, by
which the Gregorians set so great a store, was not simply, or even
mainly, the consequence of its Foundation Charter to which
Hallinger assigned such a crucial significance. It was not a mono-
lithic and largely unchanging phenomenon, but the outcome of
a long development. On the one hand, if it be studied against the
background of the longer history of the donation of monasteries
to St. Peter and St. Paul and of the exclusion from them of interference by other authorities than the Papacy, there was nothing
new or peculiar about the Foundation Charter of Cluny, nor,
indeed, about Cluny's position during the first hundred years and
more of its history.[1] On the other hand, the French historian
Lemarignier has recently indicated that the ascent of Cluny from
its originally undistinguished position to the pre-eminent liberty
that the Gregorians so fulsomely praised, was the outcome of
striking developments which were the result of the Papacy's zeal
in deliberately fostering and augmenting it. These developments
almost all came to a head within the eleventh century—indeed,
largely within the life-span of Gregory VII himself.[2] In particular,

[1] The best survey of the donation of monasteries to St. Peter and St. Paul
remains P. Fabre, *Étude sur le Liber Censuum* (Paris, 1892).
[2] J.-F. Lemarignier, 'L'Exemption monastique et les origines de la réforme
grégorienne', *A Cluny* (Dijon, 1950), pp. 288–340; 'Hiérarchie monastique et
hiérarchie féodale', *Revue historique de droit français et étranger*, xxxi (1953), 171–4;
'Structures monastiques et structures politiques dans la France de la fin du xᵉ et
des débuts du xiᵉ siècle', *Settimane di studio del centro italiano sull'alto medioevo, 1956*

Cluny was especially favoured by Popes Benedict VIII (1012–24) and John XIX (1024–32), whose significance as harbingers of reform has only lately begun to attract from historians the attention that it deserves.[1] It was in their time that Cluny's liberty began to assume a genuinely distinctive quality. It is also being increasingly appreciated that it was at much the same time—that is, in the second half of Abbot Odilo's reign—that many of the special characteristics of Cluniac monasticism at its apogee began to emerge. Examples are the constitutional position of the abbot of Cluny and the relations to the mother house of the dependent priories; and the claims of the Cluniacs to the exemption of their monks and monasteries.[2] By its origin the Cluniac Reform was much older than the Gregorian; but, so far as its coming to maturity is concerned, it was much more nearly contemporary with it.

If the second and later decades of the eleventh century were, indeed, so momentous for the development of both Cluny's liberty and its monastic life, it becomes necessary to reconsider the form in which the relation of the Cluniac and the Gregorian Reforms has usually been discussed. Hitherto, it has normally been assumed that these Reforms belonged to two different generations, if not to two different worlds: the Cluniac Reform had long since assumed a settled form, in most of its fundamental aspects, when the reform of the Papacy seriously began with the Emperor Henry III's intervention of 1046. The question which has been discussed has, therefore, been whether the Cluniacs did (Brackmann, Hallinger) or did not (Sackur, Tellenbach) largely anticipate certain of the principles and methods which the Gregorians later followed. But if much of what is most characteristic of

(Spoleto, 1957), pp. 357–400. The precise year of Gregory VII's birth is unknown, but it was probably between 1024 and 1029: see esp. R. Morghen, *L'origine e la formazione del programma della riforma gregoriana* (Rome, 1959), pp. 84–98.

[1] See e.g. the account of them by É. Amann in É. Amann and A. Dumas, *L'Église au pouvoir des laïques* (Paris, 1948), pp. 80–9; also the revised summary of John XIX's *Regesta*: L. Santifaller, 'Chronologisches Verzeichnis der Urkunden Papst Johanns XIX.', *Römische historische Mitteilungen*, i (1958), 35–76.

[2] See esp. Knowles, *The Monastic Order in England*, pp. 145–50, and *From Pachomius to Ignatius*, pp. 10–12; J. Hourlier, *Saint Odilo, abbé de Cluny* (Louvain, 1964), pp. 172–7.

Cluniac monasticism was formed during the eleventh century, it becomes necessary to change the form of the question, and to ask in what respects the Cluniac and the Gregorian Reforms developed together and reacted upon each other as an older and a younger contemporary, exercising a reciprocal influence upon each other's growth. It will be argued in the present study that, at least in large part, the evidence becomes most intelligible when it is interpreted after this fashion. As might be expected of an older and a younger contemporary—a Lanfranc and an Anselm, a Peter Damiani and a Hildebrand—there was not a complete unison between them; strains and tensions occurred, and, at times, even a certain divergence of objectives. Yet there existed an underlying harmony and compatibility which found their most eloquent and characteristic recognition in Gregory VII's conciliar eulogy of 1080. Seen through eleventh-century eyes and judged by eleventh-century standards, the Cluniac and the Gregorian Reforms were intimately bound up together, and served compatible ends. For the right understanding of both it is necessary to perceive how in essential respects they worked together continuously, intimately, mutually, and constructively.

Two further observations of a general nature may be made at this point. First, the evidence for the study of Cluny in the crucial second half of the eleventh century is very slight indeed. Only the barest handful of Abbot Hugh's letters has survived,[1] and they have little to say about his attitude to the wider issues of his time. The surviving 'Lives' of Abbot Hugh consist almost entirely of hagiographical material, and they yield only a few grains of evidence of other kinds.[2] The three surviving versions of the monastic

---

[1] Mostly printed in *P.L.* clix. 927–32; for other minor writings, ibid. 945–56.

[2] The earliest biography of Abbot Hugh, that by the monk Ezelo, *c.* 1115, is lost. The principal surviving 'Lives' are as follows: Gilo, *Vita sancti Hugonis* (*c.* 1120), L'Huillier, *Saint Hugues*, pp. 574–618; Hildebert of le Mans, *Vita sancti Hugonis* (1121), *P.L.* clix. 858–94; Hugh, monk of Cluny, *Hugonis abbatis Cluniacensis vita* (1122), *Bibl. C.*, cols. 437–48; Raynald of Vézelay, *Vita sancti Hugonis* (*c.* 1122), *P.L.* clix. 893–910: Anonymus primus, *Epitome vitae sancti Hugonis ab Ezelone atque Gilone monachis Cluniacensibus proxime ab obitu sancti scriptae*, *P.L.* clix. 909–18; Anonymus secundus, *Alia miraculorum quorumdam sancti Hugonis abbatis relatio*, *Bibl. C.*, cols. 447–62, cf. *P.L.* clix. 923–8. Both the anonymous 'Lives' were written soon after the others.

Customs of Cluny, again, have little to tell of Cluny's relations with the wider world.[1] The numerous charters of Cluny which survive provide invaluable evidence for the motives of Cluniac piety and for Cluny's relations with its feudal environment;[2] they are reinforced on a fairly generous scale by the charters of its dependencies. Yet Cluny's letters, Customs, and charters fail to illuminate, save at a few points, the question why the Gregorians had so high an estimate of Cluny. Such light as can be had on this question comes mainly from the privileges which earlier popes had conferred upon Cluny;[3] from the invaluable testimony of Peter Damiani;[4] from the letters and privileges of Popes Gregory VII,[5] Urban II,[6] and Paschal II;[7] and from such a reconstruction as is possible of the activities of the Cluniacs in the principal areas of conflict in the Gregorian period—Germany, Spain, and Italy. At every point the evidence is exceedingly slight, and it often fails completely on matters about which it would be most desirable to be informed. Sheer lack of evidence must leave a discussion at many points incomplete.

Secondly, and in part because of the insufficiency and ambiguity of the evidence, Cluniac studies bristle with problems which are unanswered, and at present unanswerable. For example, the tracing out of the expansion of Cluny, particularly the veritable explosion which took the number of its dependencies under Abbot Hugh from about sixty in 1049 to (on some computations)

---

[1] The *Consuetudines Farfenses*, in B. Albers, *Consuetudines monasticae*, i (Stuttgart and Vienna, 1900), compiled *c.* 1042–3, represent the Customs of Cluny in the latter part of Abbot Odilo's reign. From Abbot Hugh's time two versions survive: Bernard's *Ordo Cluniacensis*, in M. Herrgott, *Vetus disciplina monastica* (Paris, 1726), pp. 134–364, almost certainly is, at least in its original recension, the earlier, and was perhaps prepared *c.* 1075, with a new recension *c.* 1084–6; Ulrich's *Antiquiores consuetudines monasterii Cluniacensis, P.L.* cxlix. 635–778, was compiled *c.* 1079. For other details and for a discussion of the problems presented by the versions of Bernard and Ulrich, see Hallinger, *Gorze–Kluny*, p. 883, and 'Klunys Brauche zur Zeit Hugos des Grossen', *Z.S.S.R. kan.* xlv (1959), 99–140.

[2] Bruel.   [3] *Bull. C.*

[4] See principally the *De Gallica Petri Damiani profectione et eius ultramontano itinere, M.G.H. Scr.* xxx. 1034–46; and the material in *Bibl. C.*, cols. 477–90.

[5] Most of Gregory's surviving letters are printed in Caspar's edition of his Register; see also *Ep. Coll.* For his privileges, see Santifaller, *Q.F.*

[6] *P.L.* cli. 283–548.   [7] *P.L.* clxiii. 31–236.

about two thousand by the time of his death, has never been satisfactorily attempted.[1] Again, the solution of some of the problems of Hugh's reign will only be advanced when modern editions of the Customs of Cluny are complete. Much work in detail of this kind must be carried out before so large a question as the relation of the Cluniac Reform to the Gregorian can receive a confident answer. This discussion has of necessity the nature of a contribution to a continuing debate rather than of an attempt to make a definitive statement.

[1] For this expansion, see Knowles, *From Pachomius to Ignatius*, p. 11. The study by S. Berthelier, 'L'Expansion de l'ordre de Cluny', *Revue archéologique*, 6th ser., xi (1938), 319–26, has been subjected to damaging and justified criticism by Wollasch, *Neue Forschungen*, p. 116.

PART I

THE LIBERTY OF CLUNY

I

THE LIBERTY OF CLUNY TO 1032

Gregory VII and his like-minded contemporaries spoke of Cluny in terms of eulogy because for them it had an assured pre-eminence in respect of its monastic life. At the same time, they also praised it for what they called its 'libertas Romana'. The full significance of this phrase, as it was used in the case of Cluny, can be made apparent only when it is examined against the full background of the first two centuries of Cluniac history. But it was by no means used only of Cluny. It was, at the same time, of wide-spread occurrence in many other contexts in which it had both general and particular overtones. From these contexts the basic contemporary usage of the term is clear. In general, 'libertas Romana' was the attribute of the monasteries, as well as of the other institutions, that had received by formal grant a complete freedom under the protection of the Roman See from the claims, especially in temporal matters, of every kind of earthly lordship. Its primary effect was to extinguish lay lordship and secular proprietary rights; secondarily, it also implied a direct dependence upon the Apostolic See of St. Peter and St. Paul at Rome.[1] In Hildebrandine times the freedom from temporal obligations, which the 'libertas Romana' carried with it, was intended to have its complement in a correspondingly complete dedication to spiritual ends and to the purposes of the Papacy, as the reformers envisaged them. The quint-essence of this dedication was an unhindered service of God in direct obedience to St. Peter as the principal patron saint of the see of Rome.

The 'libertas Romana' was not, however, a generalized or an abstract concept. Every instance of it was marked by its own

---

[1] See esp. H. Hirsch, *Die Klosterimmunität seit dem Investiturstreit* (new edn., Darmstadt, 1967), pp. 33-4; E.T. in G. Barraclough, *Mediaeval Germany*, ii (Oxford, 1938), 137-8.

particular character, determined by the ends which each institution fulfilled and by the services which the men who comprised it performed. Thus, every monastery had its own distinctive style of the monastic life, which was manifest in its devotions and its wider activity. Inevitably, some monasteries which possessed the 'libertas Romana' in a general sense, realized more fully than did others the possibilities of growth towards Gregorian ideas that it opened up. In the eyes of Gregory VII and of the reformers who thought like him, Cluny enjoyed a special pre-eminence, for the reason that its monastic life and its wider service of God measured up uniquely to the demands that the 'libertas Romana' imposed upon it. As Gregory himself put it in his allocution of 1080, its abbots and monks had always proved that they were in no way untrue sons of the Roman Church. Cluny's pre-eminence in the monastic life was recognized as being the complement of the full realization there of the effective lordship of St. Peter, and of the liberty which that lordship conferred.

Cluny's uniquely articulated liberty and the reformers' appreciation of it, provide the key to the problem of the Cluniacs and the Gregorian Reform. An attempt to throw fresh light upon this problem may appropriately begin by examining the growth and eventual content of Cluny's liberty, as a particular example of the 'libertas Romana' in which the latent possibilities of subjection to the Apostolic See were realized with an altogether exceptional completeness.

I. THE FOUNDATION CHARTER OF CLUNY

At first sight, the proper and sufficient starting-point for a study of Cluny's liberty might seem to be the Foundation Charter that Duke William the Pious of Aquitaine gave it when he founded it in 909.[1] When it is considered by itself and apart from its historical context, the Charter indeed appears to have been far-reaching in what it laid down. In order that its monks might have autonomy in leading the monastic life, Cluny received a complete freedom

---

[1] Bruel, 112; E.T. in *Select Historical Documents of the Middle Ages*, ed. E. F. Henderson (London and New York, 1892, reprint 1965), pp. 329–33.

in temporal matters from all lordship, which was expressed in three principal provisions:

(a) As regards its proprietorship, Cluny was given to the highest authority that was available to safeguard it—to St. Peter and St. Paul, who were the apostles and patrons of the see of Rome. The duke made over to them the vill of Cluny and its appurtenances (*res iuris mei sanctis apostolis Petro videlicet et Paulo de propria trado dominatione*). Thus, he abandoned his own possession of, and right over, these things; he transferred the proprietorship of them to the two apostles (*dono autem haec omnia iam dictis apostolis*), in whose honour a monastery was to be founded.

(b) The monastery of Cluny was commended to the protection of the Apostolic See. In return for a quinquennial payment (*census*) of ten shillings, the monks were to have the protection (*tuitio*) of St. Peter and the defence (*defensio*) of the pope.

(c) While the actual word was not used, Cluny was to have a full immunity, in the technical sense. In all temporal matters it was to be subject to no outside yoke whatsoever. No authority at all, whether ecclesiastical or lay, not even the king or the pope, might intervene there.[1] The Papacy was to excommunicate anyone who invaded its lands or its goods.

The duke of Aquitaine in this way endowed Cluny with freedom to pursue the monastic life with no interference whatever from outside in temporal matters. Because of the apostles' proprietorship, its monks were to have, in following the Rule of St. Benedict, full power over (*possideant, teneant, habeant [atque]*)

---

[1] At about the time that Cluny was founded, the immunity of a monastery involved its complete freedom from taxation and levies in kind, in the sense that these were retained by the monastery itself and not exacted by an outside authority. The agents of all outside authorities were normally forbidden to enter its lands in the exercise of their office or jurisdiction. Immunities developed their own jurisdictional institutions, and, whether on a standing or an occasional basis, their advocates represented them in the public courts and oversaw their internal arrangements. At least in theory, the free men of an immunity were obliged to perform such public duties as military service and bridge-building; but they did so through the lords of their immunities. Bishops might exercise their spiritual rights and jurisdiction over immunities, but they might make no exactions of a financial or material kind. For contemporary definitions of immunity, see e.g. Pope John XI's privilege of 931 for Cluny: *Ep.* i, *P.L.* cxxxii. 1055–8; and King Lothar's confirmation of Cluny's immunity: Bruel, 980.

ordinent) the lands and goods that the duke assigned for their support. They and their possessions were placed under the authority and dominion (*sub potestate et dominatione*) of the abbot, Berno. After his death the monks were to have the right freely to elect his successor.

The eleventh-century reformers seem to have believed, as many modern scholars have also assumed, that Cluny's Foundation Charter marked a radically new departure in monastic history. Thus, Peter Damiani was to claim on Cluny's behalf that it could trace the exceptional liberty that he praised to the very day of its foundation; for it had always been subject to no ecclesiastical or secular person, save the Roman pontiff.[1] Gregory VII could say that Cluny had been 'ad honorem et tutelam huius sanctae et apostolicae sedis ab ipsis primordiis principaliter adsignatum'.[2] But, when it is placed in its historical context, the Charter was not, in fact, of such novel or such decisive significance in monastic history as would at first sight appear. It contained virtually nothing that was without clear precedent. The three matters of proprietorship, protection, and immunity with which its provisions dealt, all had a long history. Each of them was separately the outcome of slow developments which had already brought them substantially to the definition that they were given in 909. As they stood together in the Charter, they formed a characteristic example of how, since the second half of the ninth century, arrangements had already been made for the well-being of a number of monasteries.

Moreover, generous though its terms were, the Foundation Charter gave Cluny no more than an earnest of the developed liberty that it was to enjoy in the later eleventh century. This liberty was the cumulative outcome of developments at Cluny which had no close parallel elsewhere. Of these developments the Foundation Charter was no more than the starting-point; and they largely took shape under papal guidance. These developments were:

(*a*) The slow consolidation of Cluny's freedom from temporal claims upon it, as this freedom was initiated by the provisions of the Foundation Charter.

---

[1] See above, p. xxi. [2] *Bull. C.*, p. 21; see below, p. 272.

(*b*) The much later superimposing of Cluny's exemption; that is, of its freedom from all spiritual jurisdiction save that of the Apostolic See—a matter about which the Foundation Charter was silent.

(*c*) The Papacy's ultimate recognition and cultivation of Cluny as its own peculiar possession, which stood in an especially close relationship with itself.[1]

The outlines of this slow unfolding of Cluny's liberty only became complete in the early eleventh century under Popes Benedict VIII and John XIX and in no small measure by reason of their work. The developed liberty of Cluny owed at least as much to the actions of the tenth- and eleventh-century popes on its behalf, as it did to the original provisions of the duke of Aquitaine.

The Foundation Charter must, therefore, be assigned to a relatively undistinguished place in a long history of developments, both before and after it, that went to shape Cluny's liberty as the eleventh-century reformers praised it. Many of these developments had their origins far back in the past. They were bound up with the long and still insufficiently explored history of how, during Merovingian and Carolingian times and afterwards, outside agencies brought aid, in both temporal and spiritual matters, to monasteries; and of how the Papacy gradually emerged as the best safeguard of all for them. But the crucial happenings in the growth of Cluny's distinctive liberty took place during the first century and a quarter of its own history. It is thus appropriate to take as a framework of discussion the threefold development of Cluny's liberty during this period, making, in each case, such preliminary retrospects as are necessary to the earlier history of its constituent elements. The form that Cluny's 'libertas Romana' had assumed by the death, in 1032, of Pope John XIX, may thus be made clear. This in its turn may serve as the natural starting-point for considering the content and the high renown of Cluny's liberty in the Gregorian age, and the closeness of the bond which

---

[1] The three factors have been defined, in principle, by Lemarignier, *Histoire des institutions françaises au moyen âge*, ed. F. Lot and R. Fawtier, iii, *Institutions ecclésiastiques* (Paris, 1962), 59–60; I have ventured to give a somewhat different formulation of them.

in the reformers' eyes joined Cluny and its monks to the Gregorian Papacy.

II. THE FREEDOM OF MONASTERIES FROM TEMPORAL CLAIMS

a. *To 909*

The main purpose of Cluny's Foundation Charter was to ensure its freedom from interference by all manner of external authorities in temporal matters. The provisions regarding proprietorship, protection, and immunity by which the founder sought to do this all had a long history in relation to the monastic order, according to the changing circumstances of Merovingian and Carolingian times.

The last of them and the most important, Cluny's immunity, had the deepest roots in the past.[1] When Cluny was founded the term *immunitas* (*emunitas*) was a familiar and well-defined one. It had been in common use from ancient times, originally in relation to secular rather than to ecclesiastical lands. It was used under the Late Empire of the freedom that imperial lands enjoyed from certain taxes and burdens. Under the Merovingians it began to be conferred as a royal prerogative upon churches and monasteries.[2] How grants of immunity safeguarded monasteries from external claims of a secular nature may be seen, for example, in the Formulary of Marculf; their principal effect was to exclude

---

[1] Amongst the many discussions of immunity and protection, the following are especially useful: Fabre, *Étude sur le Liber Censuum*, esp. pp. 32–96; M. Kroell, *L'Immunité franque* (Paris, 1910); E. E. Stengel, *Diplomatik der deutschen Immunitäts-privilegien vom 9. bis zum Ende des 11. Jahrhunderts* (Innsbrück, 1910), and *Abhand-lungen und Untersuchungen zur mittelalterlichen Geschichte* (Cologne and Graz, 1960), esp. pp. 30–68; H. Hirsch, 'Untersuchungen zur Geschichte des päpstlichen Schutzes', *M.I.Ö.G.* liv (1942), 363–433; E. Lesne, *Histoire de la propriété ecclésiastique en France*, ii, fasc. 2 (Lille, 1926), 1–66; fasc. 3 (Lille, 1928), 83–102; A. Dumas, in É. Amann and A. Dumas, *L'Église au pouvoir des laïques* (Paris, 1948), pp. 341–56; T. Mayer, *Fürsten und Staat* (Weimar, 1950), esp. pp. 25–49; H. Appelt, 'Die Anfänge des päpstlichen Schutzes', *M.I.Ö.G.* lxii (1954), 101–11; F. L. Ganshof, 'L'Immunité dans la monarchie franque', *Les Liens de vassalité et les immunités* (*Recueils de la société Jean Bodin*, i, 2nd edn., Brussels, 1958), pp. 171–216; J. Semmler, 'Traditio und Königsschutz. Studien zur Geschichte der königlichen monasteria', *Z.S.S.R. kan.* xlv (1959), 1–34.

[2] See esp. Ganshof, art. cit., p. 190.

royal officials from monastic lands.[1] In Carolingian times grants
of immunity became at once more numerous and more effective.
With the waxing of royal power the negative aspect of excluding
outside interference was balanced by the positive capacity of
immune monasteries to develop their own institutions within their
own lands and generally to attend to their own affairs. These
distant beginnings of monastic immunity mark the starting-point
of the long quest by Frankish monasteries to seek freedom from
the temporal claims of outside authorities, which eventually
issued in such dispositions as those which the duke of Aquitaine
made for Cluny.

While this development of monastic immunity was happening
but independently of it, there may be observed the distant origins,
so far as the monastic order is concerned, of the second of the
provisions of Cluny's Foundation Charter—that which concerned
its protection. In early Carolingian times it was increasingly happening that monasteries were commended to the king's protection
(*tuitio, protectio, mundeburdium*).[2] The king, that is to say, took the
abbot, the monks, and the possessions of a monastery into the
peace that ruled in his own household. His protection provided, so
to speak, a protective shield which covered the persons and the
property of those who were commended to it. It served to guard
monasteries from at least some temporal claims upon them.
In this way monasteries began to enjoy the protection of an
exalted outside authority; although, until the waning of royal
power and the revival of the Papacy in the later ninth century,
such protection came, not, as was to be the case with Cluny, from
St. Peter and the Apostolic See, but from the kings and their
immediate agents.

Associated with it, there began to emerge the remaining provision of the Foundation Charter of Cluny—the deliberate vesting

---

[1] *Marculfi Formularium*, i, nos. 3–4, ed. K. Zeumer, *M.G.H. Formulae merowingici
et karolini aevi*, i. 43–5.

[2] For the formula which was usual from the early days of Pippin's reign, see the
Additamenta to the Formulary of Marculf, 2, *M.G.H. Form.* i. 111. Historians have,
perhaps, underestimated the extent to which these developments were anticipated
in the seventh century: see W. Schwarz, '*Jurisdicio* und *Condicio*. Eine Untersuchung
zu den *Privilegia Libertatis* der Klöster', *Z.S.S.R. kan.* xlv (1959), esp. pp. 73–5.

of proprietorship of a monastery in the authority that could best watch over it. Again, this authority was for the time being the king, not the apostles. During the reign of Charlemagne (768–814), with an increasing definiteness as the years went by, the handing over of a monastery to his protection was so understood that he was deemed to have exclusive lordship (*dominatio*) over it.[1]

By the heyday of Charlemagne, therefore, the origins of the three provisions of the Cluniac Charter of 909 can already be discerned. They were, however, directed towards royal authority because it was predominant. Furthermore, they did not yet fall into place as a single complex of provisions for ensuring the well-being of monasteries. On the contrary, up to and including Charlemagne's reign, grants of royal protection never became numerous; whereas grants of immunity were widely made. Indeed, with the characteristically Carolingian development of advocates, that is, of lay officials whose duty it was to attend to the secular affairs of immunities, immunities became a regular and integral part of the Carolingian system of government, so far as church lands were concerned. Royal protection of monasteries and the granting of immunity remained, therefore, wholly distinct matters.

But under Charlemagne's successors royal power receded. As a result, some fundamental changes took place with regard to the monasteries which, well before the end of the ninth century, caused proprietorship, protection, and immunity to come together, ultimately with the Papacy as their focus. Thus, in certain instances, the underlying pattern of Cluny's status in 909 already emerged.

To begin with, very soon after Charlemagne's death the former dissociation of protection and immunity came to an end, when the royal protection that had been the privilege of a few monasteries was made the right of all. When King Louis the Pious (814–40)

---

[1] See e.g. the charters for Saint-Calais (752), *M.G.H. DD. Karol.* i, no. 2, pp. 4–5; Hersfeld (775), ibid., no. 89, pp. 128–9; Ansbach (786), ibid., no. 152, pp. 205–7; Charroux (785–800), ibid., no. 194, pp. 260–1; Aniane (792), ibid., no. 173, pp. 231–3.

took it in hand to implement the monastic reforms of St. Benedict of Aniane, he extended his protection to all the monasteries of the empire. It rapidly became the normal practice for clauses conferring royal protection to be included in grants of immunity. In effect, royal protection became an integral part of them.[1] Protection and immunity, which had once been two distinct things, were now joined together. The standard formula for this was that the king took monasteries 'sub nostra defensione et immunitatis tuitione'.[2]

If royal authority had remained strong, the effect of this might well have been very greatly to heighten royal control of the monastic order. But this did not occur; at least so far as western Francia is concerned, the building up of protection and proprietorship in the king's hands, as it had begun to happen under Charlemagne, proved to be temporary. Throughout the later ninth century, as royal authority receded, more monasteries than ever before were subject to the proprietorship and protection of lesser lords, either because these lords appropriated existing monasteries, or more often because they made new foundations of their own. Such monasteries did not cease to have, and still less did they cease to desire, the immunity-under-royal-protection which had become a normal grant in the reign of Louis the Pious. But henceforth such royal grants, which became very numerous,[3] were supplementary to the protection that was mainly provided by the immediate lord. They naturally carried no implication of royal *dominium* or proprietorship, for they were essentially corroborative. If their frequency demonstrates how important the royal protection of monasteries remained, lay lords were, nevertheless, free to make such dispositions for their monasteries as they saw fit to make, or as the changing currents of opinion demanded.

The second half of the ninth century saw lay lords using this freedom, even to the extent of sometimes renouncing their own lordship. They were under increasing pressure to do this; for at

---

[1] See esp. Stengel, *Diplomatik*, pp. 553–77; Mayer, *Fürsten und Staat*, pp. 25–33.
[2] See e.g. *Formulae imperiales*, 4, M.G.H. *Form.* i. 290–1.
[3] See e.g. the large number in the reign of Louis IV of France: *Recueil des actes de Louis IV (936–954)*, ed. P. Lauer (Paris, 1914).

this time there began a widespread revulsion against the *dominium* which laymen exercised, as a result of the Proprietary Church System, over both the monastic and the secular orders of the Church. The clergy had for long emphasized the duties, rather than the rights, of the king, with regard to the churches that he protected. Now that lesser lords were advancing their position, the clergy were the better able to promote a movement against lay dominion. They were assisted by later ninth-century modifications in the institution of advocacy. As royal power was eroded, advocates ceased to be royal agents. Instead, they became quasi-independent feudal lords, and so the proprietors or founders of monasteries, for which they could make such arrangements as they saw fit. In obedience to the current trend amongst bishops and councils, they were sometimes willing to surrender their proprietorship and to confer liberty from their own lordship upon their monasteries or their new foundations. If, therefore, the years of Carolingian decline saw the establishment of many monasteries in lesser lay hands, they also saw lay lords from time to time becoming ready to surrender their proprietorship. Sometimes they did this, but retained the *tuitio* of their monasteries. Occasionally, however, they were willing to countenance a more radical arrangement.

The Carolingian decline was balanced by the building up of the authority of the Papacy under such active and capable popes as Nicholas I (858–67) and John VIII (872–82). In their day the founders and proprietors of monasteries sometimes sought the pope's protection where they might once have looked for the king's, and they found that it was readily forthcoming.[1] Like the

---

[1] It was not, indeed, altogether a novelty. Even in Charlemagne's day the founder of an Italian monastery might look to the Papacy for the protection which, north of the Alps, was sometimes sought from the king. Thus, in 790, at Lucca, the founder of the monastery of St. James and St. Philip laid down that it should enjoy papal protection, in return for furnishing oil to the annual value of ten shillings for a lamp at St. Peter's, to burn over the *confessio* of the apostle. If the religious life should ever fail there, it was to pass under St. Peter's direct authority and to be governed by the pope: L. A. Muratori, *Antiquitates Italicae medii aevi*, iii (Milan, 1740), 561–2. It was natural enough that, in due course, the crumbling of royal power to the north of the Alps should make papal protection seem the best available safeguard for a monastery in western Francia.

king's protection in the age of Charlemagne, the pope's protection might be conferred by itself. But it might also be associated with outright apostolic proprietorship of a monastery and its lands. That is to say, monasteries might be given to the Papacy, or rather to St. Peter and St. Paul, as the apostles of the Roman See, whose vicar the pope was. Contemporary endeavours to deliver churches and monasteries from lay dominion encouraged such a commendation of monasteries to the Apostolic See in full proprietorship, with a view to the creation of an immunity that was guarded by the keeper of the keys of heaven, and to the exercise of papal protection. The way lay open for the Papacy to harvest for itself, in the case of particular monasteries, the fruit of all the historical developments which had hitherto tended to the freeing of monasteries from temporal claims; and to do so in a coherent way on the lines of the Cluniac Foundation Charter.

But it was almost half a century earlier than the foundation of Cluny, in the time of Pope Nicholas I, that such arrangements for monasteries began to be made. Between 863 and 868 the foundation of Vézelay by Count Gerald of Roussillon provided a strikingly full example of how a monastery might now be entrusted to St. Peter and St. Paul.[1] In the principal documents relating to its foundation, which consist of a Foundation Charter, a letter from Count Gerald to the pope, and Nicholas I's privilege in return, all the provisions of the Cluniac Charter of 909 regarding proprietorship, protection, and immunity were substantially and conjointly present. In his letter to the pope, Count Gerald gave Vézelay to God and to the apostles of the Roman See (*haeredem ipsum Deum, beatosque apostolos Petrum et Paulum faceremus*). He said that he sought to provide for its defence and protection (*defensionem et protectionem*) by subjecting it (*subderemus*) to the city [*sic*] of St. Peter and St. Paul. To safeguard the rights of the monks, he committed it to the authority (*dominationi committeremus*) of the pope.[2] In his privilege Nicholas I recognized that

[1] Hugh of Poitiers, *Historia Vizeliacensis monasterii*, i, in L. D'Achéry, *Spicilegium*, ii (Paris, 1723), 498–503. At the same time, the count and his wife founded the monastery of Pothières on a similar basis; but the foundation documents have not survived.

[2] Ibid., p. 500.

the count had made the Papacy the proprietor (*haeres*) of Vézelay, and he secured it from all temporal exactions in terms that amounted to the guaranteeing of its immunity.[1] To complete the similarity with Cluny, the monks were to pay an annual *census* of two pounds of silver to Rome.[2]

The arrangements which were made in respect of Vézelay did not stand alone. The papal protection that they conveyed provided a model for Pope John VIII, when he issued privileges, in 878, for the monasteries of Saint-Gilles-du-Rhône[3] and Charroux.[4]

It was not the foundation of Cluny, but these events of some half a century earlier, that marked a new departure in monastic history. Following upon the precedent that was then set, monasteries were commended with increasing frequency to St. Peter and St. Paul, and so into papal protection. Sometimes, like the current form of royal protection, papal protection was afforded without a transfer of proprietorship to the apostles of the see of Rome.[5] But in a long series of instances of which Vézelay was the first, monasteries became the property of St. Peter and enjoyed his lordship in the fullest sense. Through his vicar he protected them and their possessions, while they were given immunity from temporal domination of every kind. Of St. Peter's lordship the payment of an annual *census* to provide lights to burn before

---

[1] '... subiungimus ... nullum de sacerdotibus, nullum de regibus,vel quemcumque fidelium per se suppositamve personam . . . de quacumque commoditate specialis aut temporalis obsequii, sive quibuscumque causis ad idem monasterium pertinentibus, audere in auro vel alia qualibet specie commodi vel exenii loco quidquam accipere . . .': ibid., p. 502.

[2] Ibid., p. 499. The immunity of Vézelay was immediately confirmed by King Charles the Bald: *R.H.F.* viii. 608–9.

[3] *Epp.* cxlvii, cxlix, *P.L.* cxxvi. 788–9, 792–5.

[4] *Archives historiques du Poitou*, xxxix (1910), 69–70. These privileges for Vézelay, Saint-Gilles, and Charroux were influenced by the letters of Pope Gregory I which foreshadowed the growth of monastic exemption. In so far as they were calculated to protect monasteries from the undue demands of bishops, they also served to support the aims of Nicholas I and John VIII, and to associate the name of Gregory I with the consolidation of immunity under papal authority. For a fuller discussion, see the articles by Hirsch and Appelt referred to above, p. 8, n. 1.

[5] See e.g. Montieramey (878): *Bibliothèque de l'école des chartes*, 3rd ser., v (1854), 281–3; Corvey (887): *P.L.* cxxix. 794–5.

his tomb was the symbolic recognition.[1] During the tenth and eleventh centuries such arrangements were made for many monasteries in France, Burgundy, the Spanish March, and Germany.[2]

So monasteries came by freedom from the temporal claims of all authorities. The Papacy emerged as the guarantor *par excellence* of such a freedom, because it had appropriated for itself the various ways of ensuring it which had developed, at first under royal authority, ever since Merovingian times; and because it was recognized as having in the sanction of excommunication a means of helping a monastery whose immunity was violated.[3] Royal protection, for all the frequency with which it was sought, took second place to it.

b. *Cluny*

Of this development Cluny is a good example; but so far as its foundation goes it is nothing more than an example.[4] There were other monasteries both before and after whose beginnings were similar. That Cluny became the centre of momentous developments in the future, was the result of no peculiarity in its origins; but rather of the special cultivation of its liberty by the popes, and

---

[1] For Vézelay, see the charters of Popes Nicholas I and John VIII in D'Achéry, *Spicilegium*, ii. 502–3. The relation between the *census* and apostolic proprietorship is clearly revealed in the accounts by Abbot Odo of Cluny of the foundation of Aurillac, in 884, by Count Gerald: *Vita sancti Geraldi Aureliacensis comitis*, ii. 4, 17, *Bibl. C.*, cols. 89, 95. These examples serve to rule out Sackur's view that protection by the Roman See did not imply proprietorship: *Die Cluniacenser*, i. 41; cf. Hirsch's views below, p. 16, n. 7. See also the discussions by Lesne, *Histoire de la propriété ecclésiastique en France*, ii, fasc. 3, 88–95, and Dumas, *L'Église au pouvoir des laïques*, pp. 346–8.

[2] See the list in Fabre, *Étude sur le Liber Censuum*, pp. 49–71.

[3] It is important not to underestimate the prestige of the Papacy as an institution in the tenth century, despite the personal inadequacy of the popes. See e.g. the discussions by Hauck, *Kirchengeschichte Deutschlands*, iii. 203–11, and Dumas, *L'Église au pouvoir des laïques*, pp. 342–3, 346–8.

[4] Cf. Hirsch's comment that 'in der Entwicklung des päpstlichen Schutzes bedeutet Cluny also eher einen Stillstand als eine Aufwärtsbewegung': art. cit., p. 410; and Schieffer's, that 'Cluny, à ses débuts, n'est pas un mouvement révolutionnaire, mais une étape tardive de l'époque carolingienne': art. cit., *Revue historique*, ccxxv (1961), 56.

of the unique renown in the monastic life which it was to win under the rule of its abbots.

The first signs of an exceptional development at Cluny are to be found in the sheer frequency of the early confirmations of its rights by the popes and by the kings of France. So far as the surviving evidence goes, and there is good reason for thinking that it is incomplete,[1] during the first fifty years of its history Cluny's rights as they were laid down by the founder in his Charter of 909, were confirmed three times by popes and three times by kings of France. Thus in 927 the succession of Abbot Odo was immediately followed by a charter from King Rudolf of France (923–36);[2] and in 931 Odo obtained from Pope John XI (931–5/6) the first surviving papal confirmation of Cluny's liberty.[3] In 938 John XI's privilege was renewed by Pope Leo VII (936–9),[4] and in 949 by Pope Agapetus II (946–55).[5] There were further royal charters in 939 from King Louis IV (936–54)[6] and in 955 from King Lothar (954–86).[7]

---

[1] Berno's will, which was drawn up before the first surviving royal charter for Cluny of 927, indicates that there were royal and papal confirmations of Cluny's immunity before those of 927 and 931 respectively. Berno besought temporal rulers that 'tam praelatos praedictos [i.e. Abbots Odo of Cluny and Guy of Gigny] quam et monachos et loca cum rebus ad ipsa pertinentibus, in eo statu quo et per regalia precepta, quin etiam et per apostolica privilegia dudum sancita sunt, et nunc a me decretum est, permanere consentiatis': *Bibl. C.*, col. 10.

[2] Bruel, 285.

[3] *Ep.* i, *P.L.* cxxxii. 1055–8.   [4] *Ep.* vii, *P.L.* cxxxii. 1074–5.

[5] *Ep.* ix, *P.L.* cxxxiii. 900–2.

[6] Bruel, 980.

[7] Bruel, 499. The confirmations of Cluny's immunity by Kings Rudolf and Louis IV both declared that its founder had subjected Cluny to the Apostolic See 'ad tuendum, non ad dominandum'; cf. Pope John XI's statement that Cluny belonged to the Apostolic See 'ad tuendum et fovendum'. Hirsch rightly used the former phrase as evidence that Duke William of Aquitaine at first committed Cluny to the protection, not to the proprietorship, of the Apostolic See: Hirsch, *Die Klosterimmunität seit dem Investiturstreit*, pp. 39–40; E.T. in Barraclough, *Mediaeval Germany*, ii. 143. At the same time, however, the duke also committed it to the proprietorship of St. Peter and St. Paul, the patron saints of the Apostolic See, and so established the basis of the future relationship between Cluny and the Papacy more firmly than Hirsch, in this passage, made clear. It may well have been the purpose of the French kings to emphasize that the Papacy exercised, in respect of Cluny, no more than the *tuitio* in the looser sense that the kings themselves had usually exercised over monasteries since the reign of Louis the Pious.

Apart from their frequency these documents, and especially the first two of them, are important because they show how, from a very early date, Cluny obtained in an exceptional way a clearer definition of the terms of its Foundation Charter, by turning to the help of outside authorities. Unlike the duke of Aquitaine, Pope John XI expressly granted Cluny an immunity (*immunitas*) from all claims upon its services and possessions. Again it is surprising to observe that the Foundation Charter provided for the liberty of Cluny without even once using the word 'libertas' or any of its cognates. But the Chanceries of King Rudolph and of John XI both made good the omission by freely using the adjective 'liber'. The king laid down that 'as [Duke William] has provided in his will, Cluny shall be altogether free (*liber*) from the interference and domination of kings, and of all princes, and of Duke William's relatives, and of all men'. He stated that the duke had intended Cluny to be 'ab omni saeculari dominatu liberum'. According to the pope, too, Cluny was to be 'liberum ab omni dominatu'; while its monks were to be left alone by the rulers of this world (*habeant liberam facultatem sine cuiuslibet principis consultu*) to order their affairs according to the Rule of St. Benedict. This explicit prescription of liberty, and especially its epitome in the neat phrase 'liberum ab omni dominatu' for which there seems to have been no precise precedent in a genuine source, appears to have been due to the initiative of Abbot Odo himself; for he obtained both documents. Yet the enunciation of it was the result of his collaboration with a king and with a pope. It was with the sanction of their authority that he naturalized at Cluny the terms regarding Cluny's liberty which were especially to strike the imagination of the eleventh-century reformers.

Henceforth, the popes, in particular, were to prove reliable upholders of Cluny's immunity. They showed that the canonical authority and the moral prestige which the Apostolic See owed to its bond with St. Peter, enabled them to direct both bishops and lay magnates in defence of a monastery that was placed under their protection. They are first known to have supported it in a dispute which arose between it and its sister monastery of Gigny, over a *curtis* called la Fracta which the abbot of Gigny violently seized

from Cluny.[1] In 928 Pope John X (914–28) intervened by sending
a letter to King Rudolf of France, to Archbishop Guy of Lyons,
to the bishops of Châlon-sur-Saône and of Mâcon, and to two
counts. He charged them to procure the return to Cluny of the
disputed lands; and he attempted to adjudicate fairly between the
two monasteries which were both subject to his protection. He
concluded by addressing a strong plea to the king of France and
to his vassals, that they should support the Holy See in its duty of
protecting the abbot and monks of Cluny.[2] Again, there survive
three privileges of Pope Leo VII, in which he confirmed Cluny in
the possession of certain *curtes* in the counties of Lyons and
Mâcon.[3] Pope Agapetus II's confirmation of Cluny's immunity
(949) explicity safeguarded it in the possession of certain tithes
which belonged to it.[4]

In the second half of the tenth century there followed a further
notable example of the Papacy's active vigilance on Cluny's
behalf, and also of its continuing readiness to invoke the bishops
in its support. Towards the end of his reign Pope John XIII
(965–72) wrote a letter to no fewer than fourteen bishops of
Burgundy, Provence, and the Auvergne, commending Abbot
Majolus to their closer care, together with Cluny and the other
monasteries that were subject to him. They were to act as their
protectors, and they were to excommunicate whoever invaded
their lands and rights. To this general duty the pope added two
specific directions: Bishop Stephen of Clermont was to compel

---

[1] La Fracta, which had formerly belonged to Gigny, was left by Berno in his
will to Cluny: *Bibl. C.*, cols. 9–10; and, in September 927, King Rudolf of France
confirmed Cluny in possession of it, in return for the payment of a *census* to Cluny:
Bruel, 285. But Abbot Guy challenged the legal validity of this clause of Berno's
will, and violently seized it back.

[2] 'Ceterum vobis, o fili Rodolfe, et fidelibus tuis, qui monasterio Cluniensi
prodesse valeant attentius, et abbatem et congregationem vestrae dilectioni
commendamus, utque locus ille, qui sanctae nostrae sedi commissus est, sese pro
amore apostolorum, mundi videlicet iudicum, atque paterna dilectione bene
gaudeat elegisse': *Ep.* xiv, *P.L.* cxxxii. 812–13. The conclusion of the matter was
that, in 935, Abbot Guy finally surrendered la Fracta to Cluny in return for a
census (an annual gift to Gigny of wax to the value of twelve pence), as had been
proposed in 927: Bruel, 425.

[3] *Epp.* iii, iv, xii, *P.L.* cxxxii. 1068–71, 1082–3; all date from 937.

[4] *Ep.* ix, *P.L.* cxxxiii. 901.

his *fidelis* Ambelard to restore to Cluny certain lands which he had seized; and Bishop Ado of Mâcon, in whose diocese Cluny lay, was to pay especial attention to its security: 'Cluniensis monasterii semper esto protector, sicut beati Petri es fidelis amator.'[1]

These interventions leave little room for doubting that the Papacy had the will to protect the temporal interests of a monastery, like Cluny, which was commended to it; and that, at least upon occasion, it could bring to bear on its behalf the support of bishops and of laymen. The advantage to Cluny of papal protection became the more apparent with the turn of the century, in face of added threats to its possessions which developed at about this time. It had been as a response to the crumbling of the central authority under the later Carolingians that the arrangements for the papal protection of particular monasteries, which were exemplified at Vézelay and at Cluny, had been devised. But for much of the tenth century the processes of feudal disintegration had still not greatly affected the *pagus*, the local unit of Carolingian administration in which the count had functioned as the local agent of the emperor. As oversight from above had come to an end, the count had merely consolidated and perpetuated his own local position. In many parts of France, however, at the end of the tenth century the *pagus*, too, broke up. This happened in the county of Mâcon during the time of Count Otto-William (982–1026). Effective power there became divided amongst some six holders of castles, besides the ecclesiastical immunities of the cathedral of Saint-Vincent, and of the monasteries of Cluny and Tournus. The count, who held the castle of Mâcon itself, was reduced to little, if anything, more than a position of equality with the other holders of castles in the county.[2]

The complaints which the monks of Cluny made at the Council of Anse, near Lyons, in 994, against the violence and rapine from which they were currently suffering, illustrate the dangers to which this further, and local, disintegration of public authority was

[1] *Ep.* xxvii, *P.L.* cxxxv. 990–1.

[2] For these developments, see G. Duby, *La Société aux xie et xiie siècles dans la région mâconnaise* (Paris, 1953), esp. pp. 102–14, 155–71; one aspect of these changes was the disappearance of references, such as had occasionally occurred in the tenth century, to the counts of Mâcon as advocates of Cluny; ibid., pp. 110–12.

increasingly exposing them. Their assailants were the holders of castles in the vicinity, against whom it was not easy to obtain defence.[1] Self-help, indeed, provided part of the remedy. Hitherto Cluny had only slowly developed its own system of justice.[2] At the Council of Anse the monks already began to look to their own security by requiring order to be kept in the valley of the Saône, and they themselves became responsible for punishing infringements of it.[3] At the same time they built up the institutions of their own local immunity and developed the jurisdiction of their own courts.[4] But, above all, they looked more earnestly than ever to Rome for protection against the increasing multitude of local lords who threatened their lands and their rights.[5]

They did not look in vain. In 998, at the request of Abbot Odilo and of the Emperor Otto III, Pope Gregory V (996–9) initiated the long series of papal confirmations of Cluny's liberties, according to the form which became customary after 1046: Cluny and its dependent monasteries and cells were listed with some completeness, and the rights and possessions of each house were specified in detail. Gregory included an emphatic assertion

[1] Bruel, 2255.

[2] Duby, 'Recherches sur l'évolution des institutions judiciaires pendant le x\u1d49 et le xi\u1d49 siècle dans le sud de la Bourgogne', *Le Moyen Âge*, lii (1946), 169–70.

[3] 'Violatores autem anathema maranatha dampnentur, nisi resipuerint et penitentiam egerint, aut ab abbatibus sanctissimi loci Cluniensis vel a fratribus ipsius loci absoluti quandoque fuerint': Bruel, 2255.

[4] For the emergence of a court which sat, usually under the presidency of the grand prior, though occasionally of the abbot, and with the assistance of small groups of monks and vassals, both clerical and lay, see Bruel, 1723, 1759, 1821, 1852, 1855, 1887, 1965, 1978, 2086, 2090, etc.

[5] With the succession of the Capetians, the series of royal confirmations of Cluny's immunity, which seems to have included most, if not all, of the French kings of the tenth century save the negligible Louis V (986–7), came to an end. For the weakness of the Capetians during the early decades of their rule, see Lemarignier, art. cit., *Settimane di studio del centro italiano sull'alto medioevo, 1956*, pp. 360–9. The Capetians were sympathetic towards Cluny, and Robert the Pious intervened to protect it against local lords; see e.g. his prohibition, in 1016 or 1017, of the building of castles or fortifications near Cluny: Bruel, 2800. This was particularly directed against Count Otto—William of Mâcon, who had lately built a castle at Lourdon, nearby: see Hourlier, *Saint Odilon*, pp. 83–4. For Robert the Pious's esteem for Odilo, see also Helgaud, *Epitoma vitae regis Rotberti pii*, 22, ed. R.-H. Bautier and G. Labory (Paris, 1965), p. 110.

of Cluny's immunity from temporal interference in respect of all
its lands.[1] In 1016 Pope Benedict VIII built upon the precedent
that had been set by John XIII, when, in reply to a plea from a
group of Cluniac monks who had the support of King Robert the
Pious himself, he wrote to nineteen bishops of Burgundy, Aquitaine, and Provence. He mentioned by name a number of laymen
who had molested the lands and possessions of Cluny, and he gave
details of their crimes. He called on them to repent and, on pain
of excommunication, to restore whatever they had wrongfully
taken. If they failed to do so the bishops were to reinforce the
papal sentence with their own, and a long list of lay feudatories
in the three provinces were to apply the sanction of force, if it were
called for.[2] Benedict's successor, John XIX, twice added his confirmation of Cluny's immunity to those which had gone before.
When John became pope in 1024, Abbot Odilo took advantage
of the occasion to obtain a new confirmation of Cluny's liberties;[3]
and in 1027, three days after Conrad II's imperial coronation at
Rome at which Abbot Odilo was present, they were confirmed
yet again.[4] On both occasions the definitions of Cluny's immunity
were brief but fundamental. They were not so much detailed
specifications of its rights, as forthright enunciations of Cluny's
utter freedom from the yoke of any external power and of its
sole dependence upon St. Peter and upon the Apostolic See.[5]

[1] *Ep.* xx, *P.L.* cxxxvii. 932-5.

[2] *Ep.* xvi, *P.L.* cxxxix. 1601-4. With it may be compared Benedict VIII's
letter to Bishop Stephen of Clermont, in which he called upon him for support by
excommunicating the despoilers of Cluniac possessions, naming especially two
brothers who had unjustly seized an allod which belonged to the monastery.
The letter began: 'Vobis notum est Cluniacum monasterium sanctae Romanae
ecclesiae a fundatore eiusdem ad defendendum contra insatiabilem cupiditatem
saecularium esse commissum. Unde, iustitiae regula dictante, admoniti, quoties-
cunque pressuram isdem locus a pravis hominibus patitur, scutum nostrae
defensionis debemus opponere': *Ep.* xxix, *P.L.* cxxxix. 1628-9.

[3] *Ep.* vi, *P.L.* cxli. 1135-7. For the date, see Lemarignier, art. cit., *A Cluny*,
p. 321, n. 3.

[4] *Bull. C.*, pp. 9-10, Santifaller, art. cit., *Römische historische Mitteilungen*, i
(1958), no. 44, pp. 55-6, see below, pp. 268-9. At the same time, John XIX also
confirmed Abbot Odilo and his successors in possession of land at le Champsaur,
in Lower Burgundy, which had previously been given to St. Peter at Rome:
Bruel, 2789.

[5] The privilege of 1024 said that Abbot Odilo asked the pope that 'praefatum

In the privileges of Gregory V, Benedict VIII, and John XIX, the Papacy fully and decisively made clear its purpose to uphold the complete immunity of Cluny and to provide for its defence by whatever means it could command. It acted far more strenuously on behalf of Cluny than of any other monastery which enjoyed its protection. In respect of Vézelay, for example, there is no history of papal favour during the years since its foundation, which is at all comparable with the history of papal support for Cluny. By 1032 Cluny was uniquely favoured. It already provided the quintessential example of 'libertas', as an utter freedom from temporal subjection under immediate papal defence, which was a ready-made pattern for the Gregorians to adopt in their own struggle for the freedom of the Church from temporal domination. Thanks in no small measure to papal action on its behalf, the first factor in the articulation of Cluny's liberty—the guaranteeing of its freedom from external claims upon it in temporal matters, and especially of its immunity—was, by 1032, fully and clearly established.

III. MONASTIC EXEMPTION AND ITS REALIZATION AT CLUNY

a. *To the time of Abbo of Fleury*

The consequences of the development of Cluny's immunity in the early decades of the eleventh century were the more momentous because Pope John XIX, in particular, introduced a new factor into the development of Cluny's liberty. He procured for it a further prerogative that was essentially novel in its own history: its exemption from the spiritual jurisdiction of its diocesan bishop, the bishop of Mâcon, and of all other bishops. Cluny was to be subject to the spiritual authority of the Apostolic See alone.

Like immunity, the exemption of monasteries had, by the

---

monasterium apostolicae auctoritatis serie muniremus, et omnia eius pertinentia perenni iure ibidem inviolabiliter permanenda confirmaremus, et absque omni iugo seu ditione cuiuscunque personae constabilire nostri privilegii pagina studeremus'. In 1027 the immunity of Cluny was simply expressed as follows: 'ad nullum alium respiciat locus ille sive habitatores eius, nisi ad Deum et sanctum Petrum et apostolicae sedis pontificem summum'.

eleventh century, a complex historical background which covered many centuries.[1] Yet it was by no means so clearly articulated a conception. Immunity had been from Roman times a current word with a clearly understood, although changing, meaning. But it was not until the twelfth century that the word *exemptio* came into general currency, or that it became familiar and well defined as a technical term meaning freedom from all spiritual jurisdiction save that of the Papacy. The early history of exemption must, therefore, not be studied by reading back into it the high medieval concept: to do so would be to fall into anachronism.[2] Rather, it should be regarded as a piecemeal process by which the Papacy occasionally exercised the function that it possessed by virtue of its Petrine authority, of protecting other churches and institutions from undue external interference of every kind. It was only at a very late juncture, in the 990s, that the securing of monastic exemption in anything that resembles the twelfth-century sense of the term, so much as began to be an objective to which the monks aspired with urgency. Even when it did so, Cluny was not at first a pioneer in the movement to promote it. However, by 1032 the newly won exemption of Cluny itself had come to the fore as the crown and climax of a hard-fought struggle in French monastic circles against the spiritual authority of the bishops.

That monastic exemption developed in the western Church so slowly and so late was, in part, owing to the Rule of St. Benedict. So far as immunity is concerned, the Rule envisaged as a basic

[1] On the subject of exemption, see, besides the literature mentioned above, p. 8, n. 1, W. Szaivert, 'Die Entstehung und Entwicklung der Klosterexemtion bis zum Ausgang des 11. Jahrhunderts', *M.I.Ö.G.* lix (1951), 265–98; W. Schwarz, art. cit., *Z.S.S.R. kan.* xlv (1959), 34–98.

[2] For the importance of Pope Urban II's use, after 1089, of a new formula, 'Ad indicium autem perceptae huius a Romana ecclesia libertatis, dilectionis vestrae dignum est [x] Lateranensi palatio quotannis exsolvere', into the privileges of monasteries which owed a *census* to Rome, in extending the exemption of monasteries and in preparing the way for the fully exempt orders of the twelfth century, see Fabre, *Étude sur le Liber Censuum*, pp. 94–6. It was, perhaps, unlikely that exemption should be widely sought by the monasteries until the Proprietary Church System had so far been transformed as to diminish their need for episcopal support against lay lords. (I owe this last suggestion to Mr. K. J. Leyser.)

postulate the autonomy and self-sufficiency of the individual
monastery. It therefore predisposed the monastic order to value
immunity from outside interference in temporal matters, as it
developed through its various phases. But the Rule also envisaged
the benevolent oversight, if not the formal spiritual jurisdiction,
of the bishop over the monasteries in his diocese. Thus it gave no
encouragement to a quest for exemption. Indeed, it tended to
inhibit it; for it designated the bishop as one of the authorities who
might intervene to set matters right, if, in the exercise of their
right of free election, the monks chose an unworthy man to be
their abbot.[1] In extreme circumstances the bishop might also be
invoked to discipline the priests of a monastery.[2] In view of such
provisions in the Rule, the eventual exemption of certain Benedictine monasteries can scarcely be regarded as a natural growth.

   Furthermore, from a very early date, church councils had
legislated in forthright terms to ensure that monasteries should be
straightly subject to the jurisdictional *potestas* of the bishops. In 451
the General Council of Chalcedon enacted canons to this end
which were quickly transmitted to the west in a Latin translation.[3]
A series of western councils afterwards legislated similarly. For
example, the Council of Orleans (511) provided that the bishop
was to oversee the abbot in his ruling of the monastic community
under his charge.[4] Such conciliar decrees as these firmly asserted
the principle of episcopal jurisdiction over monasteries. The
bishops of eleventh-century France remembered them and appealed to them, when the monks launched a radical challenge to
their spiritual authority over the monasteries of their dioceses.

   Whilst strong canonical precedents were thus being created in
favour of the bishops, a number of counter-precedents of a kind

[1] Cap. lxiv, *Saint Benoît, La Règle des moines*, ed. P. Schmitz (Maredsous, 1948),
p. 185.
[2] Cap. lxii, ibid., p. 179.
[3] Canon iv, Mansi, vii. 374: '... monachos vero per unamquamque civitatem
aut regionem subiectos esse episcopo ...'; cf. canon viii, ibid., col. 375.
[4] Canon xix, Mansi, viii. 354–5: 'Abbates pro humilitate religionis in episcoporum potestae consistat, et si quid extra regulam fecerint, ab episcopis cor-
rigantur: qui semel in anno, in loco ubi episcopus elegerit, accepta vocatione
conveniant ...'; for other examples, see Szaivert, art. cit., pp. 268–9; Schwarz,
art. cit., p. 44.

were also being established, which in due course could be
invoked by the monks. Of especial significance, in view of the
authority of his name in the Middle Ages, were some rulings of
Pope Gregory I (590–604). He was several times active in protecting monasteries from the exorbitant demands of their local
bishops. His Register contains a number of letters which, while
they cannot at all be said to have been grants of exemption, nevertheless tended to set limits upon the intervention of particular
bishops in the monasteries of their dioceses. To give two examples:
in a letter of 598 to Bishop Marinian of Ravenna, Gregory complained that the monastery of St. John and St. Stephen had suffered 'praeiudicia atque gravamina' at the hands of earlier bishops.
Marinian was to make them good, and he was to avoid providing
further occasions of complaint; the abbots of St. John and St.
Stephen were to be freely elected; they might appeal to Rome if
the rights of their monastery were again infringed.[1] Again, in 595,
the pope came similarly to the aid of the monastery of St. Andrew
and St. Thomas at Rimini. He wrote to Bishop Castorius, drastically curbing his right to say mass publicly in the monastery—
a provision which was to provide an important touchstone of
the rights of the monks as against the bishops in the eleventh
century.[2]

But the purpose of these letters was to deal with specific abuses
on the part of individual bishops; it was not to secure the complete
emancipation of monasteries from their spiritual authority. It has
commonly been held that the origin of monastic exemption in
the full sense may be traced to three papal privileges which were
given to prominent monasteries during the century and a half
after the death of Gregory I: Bobbio (628),[3] Fulda (751),[4] and

---

[1] Gregory I, *Reg.* viii. 17, ed. P. Ewald and L. Hartmann, *M.G.H. Epp.* i,
pt. 2, pp. 19–20.

[2] Ibid., v. 47, 49, pt. I, pp. 346–7, 348–9. For other letters concerning the
authority of bishops over monasteries, see ibid., vii. 40, pt. I, pp. 488–9; xii. 15,
pt. 2, pp. 361–2; xiii. 13, pt. 2, pp. 380–1.

[3] *Codice diplomatico del monastero di San Colombano di Bobbio*, ed. C. Cipolla, i
(Rome, 1918), no. x, pp. 100–3.

[4] *Codex diplomaticus Fuldensis*, ed. E. F. J. Dronke (Cassel, 1850, reprint Aalen,
1962), nos. 4 *a* and *b*, pp. 2–4.

Saint-Denis (757).[1] In line with these privileges the *Liber diurnus*, a formulary book of the Roman Church which was compiled during the seventh and early eighth centuries, is also widely held to embody material which related to monastic exemption.[2] The Bobbio privilege provided the basis of formula 77;[3] while formula 32, which appears in a privilege which is probably to be ascribed to Pope Gregory II or Pope Gregory III,[4] was to underlie the Fulda and the Saint-Denis privileges; and formula 86 was also of considerable later importance.[5] There is in addition some further material from other sources, which has been held to illustrate the beginnings of exemption at this time.[6]

Such is the generally accepted view of the origins of exemption. It has, however, lately been called in question. The suggestion has been made that the three privileges and the formulas of the *Liber diurnus* should be understood in the light of the antecedent conciliar legislation about monasteries which safeguarded the proper rights and functions of the bishops, and that they did not contradict it.[7] They were intended to prevent the abuse of episcopal authority over monasteries, and not its proper use. They were evidence of a prevailing concern to place a curb upon bishops who exceeded their legitimate *potestas* by exacting improper payments and services which did not spring from their rightful spiritual authority over the monasteries. The 'iurisdicio' of the pope to which monas-

[1] *P.L.* lxxxix. 1013–17.

[2] *Liber diurnus Romanorum pontificum*, ed. T. von Sickel (Vienna, 1889). See also the recent full edition of the surviving texts by H. Foerster (Berne, 1959), which has an important introduction; and C. R. Cheney, *The Study of the Medieval Papal Chancery* (Glasgow, 1966), pp. 23–4.

[3] *Liber diurnus*, ed. von. Sickel, pp. 82–4.

[4] The privilege was first published from a Manuscript in the Bibliotheca Barbariniana at Rome by P. Ewald, 'Zwei unedierte Briefe Gregors I.', *N.A.* vii (1882), 590–604, where it is accepted as a letter of Gregory I. In his edition of Gregory's Register, Hartmann expressed doubts, and was inclined to ascribe it to Gregory II (715–31) or Gregory III (731–41): Appendix iv, pt. 2, pp. 468–9.

[5] *Liber diurnus*, ed. von Sickel, pp. 23–4, 111–13.

[6] e.g. the supposed privileges of exemption for English monasteries: Appelt, art. cit., pp. 106–8; Schwarz, art. cit., pp. 65–70.

[7] See Schwarz, art. cit.; cf. the concepts which underlie the episcopal and royal privileges to monasteries which followed the first two texts in the Formulary of Marculf: *M.G.H. Form.* i. 39–43.

teries might be specially entrusted ensured their protection from such abuses; but it did not exempt them from all episcopal power whatsoever in spiritual matters. If this interpretation of the evidence be correct, the papal privileges for Bobbio, Fulda, and Saint-Denis may, like the Register of Gregory I, have provided later monastic propagandists with a fund of material which they could plausibly represent as providing ancient precedents for their latter-day claims against local bishops.[1] But they did not confer exemption in anything approaching the form which was characteristic of the later Middle Ages.

The problem of the origins of monastic exemption awaits a definitive survey. It may tentatively be concluded that the seventh and eighth centuries provided at most only very sporadic examples of it; and that they perhaps provided no true examples at all. At all events, there was little enough in the history of these centuries to which the monks could later appeal; while the bishops could confidently invoke the more ancient canons of Chalcedon and Orleans.

It is certain that if the evidence of the Carolingian age itself be examined, the prevailing insistence upon the bishops' authority over their dioceses, and the consolidation of the Proprietary Church System, did not provide a fertile soil for the seeds of monastic exemption to grow or to germinate. During the brief interval which elapsed between the papal privileges for Fulda and Saint-Denis, the Council of Verneuil (755) insisted that all bishops had a full *potestas* over the monks, as well as the secular clergy, of their dioceses, and that they should correct and reform them.[2] This provided the keynote of Carolingian policy as regards the monasteries in relation to episcopal authority, both under Charlemagne and under his ninth-century successors in eastern and western

---

[1] Either as they stood or by being revised to make their relevance to exemption seem more clear. See e.g. the eleventh-century version of Gregory I, *Reg.* viii. 17: *P.L.* lxxvii. 1340–2; cf. Lesne, 'Nicholas I et les libertés des monastères des Gaules', *Le Moyen Âge*, xxiv (1911), 333–45.

[2] 'Ut unusquisque episcoporum potestatem habeat in sua parrochia, tam de clero quam de regularibus vel secularibus, ad corrigendum et emendandum secundum ordinem canonicam spiritale . . .': *cap.* iii, *M.G.H. Capitularia regum Francorum*, i. 33.

Francia. Although the formulas of the *Liber diurnus*, and even of
Pope Gregory I's letters, sometimes appeared as a means of protecting the specific rights of individual monasteries, there was no
foreshadowing whatsoever of a general exemption in the twelfth-
century sense.

Thus, when Cluny was founded, monastic exemption was not
a live issue in the Church at large, neither was it anywhere an
aspiration of the monks. Nor did it immediately become one at
Cluny. The Foundation Charter of 909, like other comparable
contemporary documents, made no express reference to the jurisdiction of the bishop in spiritual matters. Its text did not rule out
at least such a measure of episcopal oversight of Cluny as the Rule
of St. Benedict itself envisaged; indeed, it can be construed as
having implied it.[1] The papal and royal confirmations of the first
fifty years of Cluny's history were likewise altogether silent about
the whole matter of exemption. Nor was it in strictly Cluniac
circles that the movements towards monastic exemption which
began in the tenth century were to have their origin.

These movements were twofold. First, during the fifth decade
of the century, the Emperor Otto I (936–73) wished to circumvent
the resistance of the German episcopate to his plans for the Church
in his eastern lands. He looked for allies against the bishops, both
at Rome and amongst the monasteries. He obtained from the
Papacy a series of privileges for imperial monasteries, which bor-
rowed the words of formula 32 of the *Liber diurnus*.[2] From this
starting-point there followed, during the tenth and eleventh

---

[1] '. . . habeant idem monachi potestatem et licentiam quemcumque sui ordinis,
secundum placitum Dei atque regulam sancti Benedicti promulgatam, eligere
maluerint abbatem atque rectorem, ita ut nec nostra nec alicuius potestatis contradictione contra religiosam duntaxat electionem impediantur . . . ': Bruel, 112.
In practice, however, it was to the archbishops of Besançon that the abbots of
Cluny usually turned for consecration: Diener, *Neue Forschungen*, pp. 282–3.

[2] For a summary account of Otto I's church policy, see R. Holtzmann, *Geschichte der sächsischen Kaiserzeit* (3rd edn., Munich, 1955), pp. 180–4. For detailed
discussions, see O. Lerche, 'Die Privilegierung der deutschen Kirche durch
Papsturkunden bis auf Gregor VII.', *A.U.F.* iii (1911), 125–232, esp. 150–60;
L. Santifaller, 'Die Verwendung des *Liber Diurnus* in den Privilegien der Päpste
von den Anfängen bis zum Ende des 11. Jahrhunderts', *M.I.Ö.G.* xlix (1935),
225–366; H. Goetting, 'Die klösterliche Exemtion in Nord- und Mitteldeutschland
vom 8. bis zum 15. Jahrhundert', *A.U.F.* xiv (1935–6), 105–87.

centuries, a long series of similar privileges for monasteries in Germany, France, Spain, and England.[1] These privileges had, however, no significance for the history of Cluny, save in so far as they accustomed the Papacy to the conferring of this kind of favour upon particular monasteries, and in so far as, particularly in the eleventh century, they gave widespread currency to the idea of monastic independence under the Apostolic See.

Secondly, certain disputes which occurred in France after the accession to the throne, in 987, of Hugh Capet, also began to pose there the issue of monastic rights as opposed to those of the bishops. In France the issue arose not, as in Germany, at the prompting of a strong royal power, but from a direct confrontation of the claims of the two sides. In the genesis of these disputes between monks and their bishops, Cluny was not itself involved; although the champion of the monks, Abbot Abbo of Fleury (988–1004), ruled a monastery which had once been deeply influenced by it.[2] Abbo first incurred the bitter enmity of his own diocesan bishop, Arnulf of Orleans, at the Council of Saint-Basle de Verzy (991), on a political issue. The Council met to try Archbishop Arnulf of Rheims, who had supported Duke Charles of Lower Lorraine against Hugh Capet. Abbo and his bishop took opposite sides, Abbo defending the archbishop against a charge of treason while the bishop of Orleans was prominent amongst his accusers. Abbo quickly brought in the question of papal jurisdiction; for he propounded the right of the Papacy to settle the matter of the archbishop's ecclesiastical status, as against the self-sufficiency of the Council to do so.[3] Soon afterwards, the question also arose of the rights of the bishops in relation to the monastic order; for Abbo and his bishop carried their political differences into their local

[1] For a list of examples, see Szaivert, art. cit., pp. 295–6. In Germany and Italy the policy of the Emperor Henry II (1002–24) led to a virtually complete cessation of grants of exemption, and Burchard of Worms allowed it no place in his compilation of canon law: P. Fournier and G. le Bras, *Histoire des collections canoniques en occident*, i (Paris, 1931), 390–1; Goetting, art. cit., pp. 125–6.

[2] For Cluny and Fleury, see Sackur, *Die Cluniacenser*, i. 186–204, 270–99; Wollasch, *Neue Forschungen*, pp. 106–16. For Abbo, see also Fournier and le Bras, op. cit., i. 320–30; and, above all, Lemarignier, *A Cluny*, pp. 301–15.

[3] For the Council, see esp. Gerbert, *Acta concilii Remensis ad sanctum Basolum*, *M.G.H. Scr.* iii. 656–86; cf. Sackur, *Die Cluniacenser*, i. 278–84.

relationship, and Abbo set himself to free Fleury from episcopal control so far as he could.

During the three or four years which followed the Council of Saint-Basle de Verzy, Abbo occupied himself in compiling his polemical *Collectio canonum*.[1] In it he endeavoured to sum up all the theses which he had hitherto been concerned to defend during his rivalry with his bishop. He propounded the universal authority of the Apostolic See as against the rights of the episcopate. At the same time he sought to promote the freeing of monasteries from the spiritual control of their local bishops, and to facilitate their subjection to papal authority. In support of his case he marshalled all the relevant letters from the Register of Gregory I, with the exception of the letter to Bishop Castorius of Rimini.

This monastic propaganda in the direction of papal authority and monastic exemption and the consequent quest for ancient authorities which could be pressed into service to support it, were matched by a lively reaction from the side of the bishops. They were well aware of such excellent authority for the episcopal control of monasteries as was to be found in the canons of Chalcedon and Orleans. Furthermore, when the French bishops assembled at the Council of Chelles (*c.* 993–4), they were so bold as to emphasize conciliar and episcopal authority by affirming that if the Roman pope were to do something which ran contrary to ancient canonical decrees, it was null and void.[2] Their forthright stand on behalf of episcopal rights brought into the open a radical conflict between the traditional prerogatives of bishops and councils, and the claim which the monks were beginning to advance on behalf of the Papacy that the Apostolic See had an active and immediate right to set aside these prerogatives. The French bishops thus posed fairly and squarely the wider issue of the nature of papal authority in relation to that of the episcopal order and of Church councils, which was to be so crucial in the time of Gregory VII.

That they did so was made still clearer in another controversy

[1] *P.L.* cxxxix. 473–508.

[2] 'Placuit quoque sanciri, si quid a papa Romano contra patrum decreta suggereretur, cassum et irritum fieri, iuxta quod apostolus ait: "Hereticum hominem et ab ecclesia dissentientem penitus devita" ': Richer, *Historiarum*, iv. 89, ed. G. Waitz, *S.R.G.*, pp. 169–70.

of about the time of the Council of Chelles, in which Abbo of
Fleury and Bishop Arnulf of Orleans again came into conflict,
this time over the monastery of Saint-Denis. When Abbo came
to the defence of its monks against episcopal complaints that they
had been usurping tithes, he encountered the bishop's counter-
allegations that he himself had fomented their resistance to legitimate episcopal discipline. This personal altercation broadened
into a wider conflict in which the bishops had recourse to
collective action against the monks. Meeting in a Council at
Saint-Denis, they excommunicated the monks of Saint-Denis and
placed their church under an interdict. The monks replied by
defiantly continuing to hold services; and they prevailed upon
Kings Hugh Capet and Robert the Pious to support them by
ordering Archbishop Gerbert of Rheims to come and celebrate
mass there. Gerbert complained of the dilemma in which he
consequently found himself. He said that on the one hand he was
being pressed to uphold on behalf of the monks, and against his
fellow bishops, claims based upon such papal privileges for Saint-
Denis as that of 757; on the other hand he must set the episcopal
thesis that nothing which was contrary to canon law might be
obeyed.[1] In the event, he refused the kings' command and did not
go to Saint-Denis; he did not allow himself to be the instrument
of a monastic challenge to the bishops' view of the rights of their
order.

Abbo, however, continued to be a strenuous protagonist of the
monks. From his point of view Gerbert's dilemma was one to
which Pope Gregory I's letter to Bishop Castorius of Rimini was
relevant; for it restricted episcopal rights of intervention in monasteries with especial stringency. He now included a citation of it

---

[1] 'Accusabamur quippe monachos beati Dionisii iniuste dampnasse. Urgebamur
coram dampnatis divina obsequia celebrare nec privilegiis Romanae ecclesiae
monasterio beati Dionisii factis contraire debere. Ad haec opponebatur nobis
privilegiis canonum auctoritate promulgatis nos assensum praebituros, nec, si
quid contra leges ecclesiasticas decretum sit, pro lege recepturos': *Die Briefsammlung Gerberts von Reims*, ed. F. Weigle, no. 190, *M.G H. B.D.K.* ii. 228; cf. the
translation, with notes, in H. P. Lattin, *The Letters of Gerbert* (New York, 1961),
no. 194, pp. 226–8. Gerbert made clear his own adherence to the episcopal thesis
in a letter of 995 to Archbishop Seguin of Sens: *Briefsammlung*, ed. Weigle, no.
192, pp. 230–3.

in a new condemnation which he drew up of exorbitant episcopal claims to interfere in monasteries.[1] He also put his principles regarding the exemption of monasteries from episcopal interference into practice at Fleury. He sought, and in 997 eventually obtained from Pope Gregory V, a papal privilege for Fleury which, while it neither embodied formula 32 of the *Liber diurnus* nor conveyed complete exemption in the twelfth-century sense, effectively met Abbo's desire to break the coercive power of the bishop of Orleans over his monastery. It provided that no bishop whatsoever might enter it to ordain or to celebrate mass without the abbot's leave. If any accusation were laid against the abbot, it was to be dealt with, not by the bishop of Orleans, but by a provincial council; or if the abbot preferred, it might be settled by the Apostolic See itself.[2]

The conflict between the monks of Fleury and the bishops of Orleans continued into the eleventh century. In due succession, Fulbert of Chartres fully upheld the pro-episcopal thesis of the Council of Chelles.[3] But the rights which, in close association with the Papacy, Abbo had won for his monastery in defiance of the bishops, now opened the way in France towards a kind of monastic exemption, which unambiguously looked forward to twelfth-century norms. The Papacy became fully and actively engaged in the controversy on the side of the monks against their bishops. It did so with a full awareness of the deeper issues of principle that were at stake with regard to the very nature of papal authority.

b. *Cluny*

It is at this juncture that Cluny at last comes into the centre of the picture. It was brought in by the pope. Following upon his

[1] *Ep.* xiv, *P.L.* cxxxix. 440–60, esp. 444–5. For Abbo and tithes, see G. Constable, *Monastic Tithes from their Origins to the Twelfth Century* (Cambridge, 1964), pp. 79–81.

[2] *Recueil des chartes de l'abbaye de Saint-Benoît-sur-Loire*, ed. M. Prou and A. Vidier (Paris and Orleans, 1900), no. lxxi, pp. 185–8. For its authenticity, see F. Lot, *Études sur le règne de Hugues Capet* (Paris, 1903), pp. 273–5.

[3] Thus, in 1008, a new dispute between the monks of Fleury and the bishop of Orleans provoked a new assertion of episcopal rights, in spite of Fleury's privilege from Pope Gregory V. For Fulbert of Chartres's contribution to it, see *Epp.* 16–17, *P.L.* cxli. 208.

recent privilege of 997 for Fleury, Pope Gregory V reinforced his detailed confirmation, in 998, of Cluny's immunity, by including in it an express provision that no bishop or priest might ordain or celebrate mass at Cluny unless it were by the abbot's invitation. He also allowed Cluniac monks to receive orders at the hands of any bishop of the abbot's choosing; while the monks of Cluny might themselves determine which bishop should consecrate their abbot.[1]

This was the first official and explicit step towards the emancipation of Cluny from the spiritual authority of the local bishop, which appears in any of the sources. It provided a precedent which was quickly followed elsewhere in Cluniac circles. It was imitated, amongst monasteries to which Abbot William of Volpiano, a former monk of Cluny,[2] was transmitting reform on a broadly Cluniac pattern, at Fécamp, in Normandy;[3] at Fruttuaria, near Turin;[4] and at William's own principal reforming centre of Saint-Bénigne, Dijon.[5]

It was left for Pope John XIX to complete this Cluniac progress towards exemption by making the monastery of Cluny itself absolutely free from all episcopal jurisdiction. When Abbot Odilo took advantage of John's accession in 1024 to secure a papal

[1] *Ep.* xx, *P.L.* cxxxvii. 932–5.

[2] For William, see Sackur, *Die Cluniacenser*, i. 239–56; W. Williams, *Monastic Studies* (Manchester, 1938), pp. 99–120; Amann and Dumas, *L'Église au pouvoir des laïques*, pp. 330–1; Lemarignier, *Étude sur les privilèges d'exemption des abbayes normandes* (Paris, 1937), pp. 27–43.

[3] Fécamp came under William's rule in 1001. In 1006 Duke Richard II of Normandy issued a diploma in which he laid down that Fécamp '. . . in restituendi abbatis electione . . . a nobis iuste collata utantur libertate, ita dumtaxat ut, in ipsa electione vel ordinatione abbatis, illa per omnia servetur consuetudo quae hactenus in Cluniaco cenobiorum servata est illu[s]trissimo, unde fons sanctae monasticae religionis, per multa iam longe lateque dirivatus loca, ad hunc usque Deo profluxit propicio . . ': *Recueil des actes des ducs de Normandie de 911 à 1066*, ed. M. Fauroux (Mémoires de la Société des Antiquaires de Normandie, xxxvi, 1961), no. 9, pp. 79–80.

[4] William reformed Fruttuaria in 1003. In 1026 the Emperor Conrad II confirmed that it should enjoy the same liberty as Cluny by then possessed: *M.G.H. DD.* iv, no. 70, pp. 87–8; cf. John XVIII's bull of 1006: *Ep.* viii, *P.L.* cxxxix. 1485–6.

[5] *Chartes et documents de Saint-Bénigne de Dijon*, ed. G. Chevrier and M. Chaume, ii (Dijon, 1943), no. 247, pp. 40–3.

privilege for Cluny, the new pope not only confirmed Cluny in all the benefits that his predecessors had ever conferred upon it; but he also provided that no bishop or priest might lay an anathema or an excommunication upon Cluny itself, and that Cluniac monks were to be secure from all episcopal censures and exclusively subject to the spiritual jurisdiction of the Apostolic See.[1] In respect of Cluny, he thus made a definition of monastic exemption in such absolute terms as had no parallel before or elsewhere. In 1024 Cluny became exempt in a thoroughgoing way.

Almost at once this newly defined exemption was put to the test. Abbot Odilo acted upon the concession, which Cluny first received in 998 and which John XIX confirmed in 1024, that the abbot might repair to any bishop whatsoever for the ordination of its monks. He invited Archbishop Burchard of Vienne to come and ordain some of his monks at Cluny. When this was done, the bishops of the provinces of Vienne and Lyons reacted vigorously to the withdrawal of a monastery from the spiritual authority of their order. At a Council which was held at Anse in 1025, the question of the rights at Cluny of the bishop of Mâcon came specifically into the open for the first time of which there is record. The bishop, Gozelin, obtained from the Council a firm condemnation of Archbishop Burchard's intrusion. The assembled bishops collectively reaffirmed the stand which had first been made by the Council of Chelles and which had been continued by Gerbert and Fulbert. They declared that the papal privileges upon which the Cluniacs and their supporters relied, ran counter to the ancient canons of Chalcedon and other councils,which set monasteries under the spiritual authority of their local bishop. These canons, it was forcibly contended, were not to be set aside by the latter-

---

[1] 'Non enim patitur sanctae sedis apostolicae auctoritas, ut ullius cuiuscunque personae obligatione proscindatur a se cuilibet concessa liberalis libertas: neque ipsius loci fratres ubicunque positi, cuiuscunque episcopi maledictionis vel excommunicationis vinculo teneantur astricti. Inhonestum enim nobis videtur ut sine nostro iudicio, a quoquam anathematizetur sanctae sedis apostolicae filius veluti cuiuscunque subiectae ecclesiae discipulus. Si qua vero competens ratio adversus eos quemquam moverit, et hoc aliter determinari vel definiri nequiverit, iudicium apostolicum, quod nulli praeiudicium praetendere patitur, super hoc patienter praestoletur et humiliter requiratur': *Ep.* vi, *P.L.* cxli. 1135-7.

day rulings of the popes.[1] Confronted by these arguments and by the united hostility of his fellow bishops, the archbishop of Vienne acquiesced in the findings of the Council of Anse. Abbot Odilo, for his part, was left without resource until he could solicit a new *démarche* from the side of the Apostolic See.

His opportunity to do so came in 1027 with his journey to Rome for the imperial coronation of Conrad II. Two days after the coronation John XIX issued four bulls in favour of Cluny, in which he energetically vindicated the prerogatives of the pope as the one source of ecclesiastical jurisdiction. In each of them he adamantly reasserted the exemption of Cluny as he had defined it in 1024. He wrote to King Robert the Pious calling upon him to give his fullest support to the papal ruling.[2] To Bishop Gozelin of Mâcon he addressed a sharp reproof for his aggression against a monastery which was reserved exclusively to the judgement of the Prince of the Apostles and of his vicar.[3] As metropolitan of the province in which Cluny was situated Archbishop Burchard of Lyons was to forbid his suffragan ever again to intervene in a monastery which belonged to the Apostolic See.[4] Finally, in a letter which he

---

[1] 'Surgens itaque domnus Odilo cum suis monachis, ostendit privilegium, quod habebant a Romana ecclesia, quod eis talem libertatem tribuebat, ut nulli, in cuius territorio degebant, nec alicui aliquatenus subiacerent episcopo: sed quemcumque vellent, vel de qualibet regione adducerent episcopum, qui faceret ordinationes vel consecrationes in eorum monasterio. Relegentes ergo sancti Chalcedonensis, et plurimorum authenticorum conciliorum sententias, quibus praecipitur, qualiter per unamquamque regionem abbates et monachi proprio subesse debeant episcopo, et ne episcopus in parochia alterius audeat ordinationes vel consecrationes absque licentia ipsius episcopi facere, decreverunt cartam non esse ratam, quae canonicis non solum non concordaret, sed etiam contrairet sententiis': Mansi, xix. 423–4; cf. *Cartulaire de Saint-Vincent de Mâcon*, ed. M. Ragut (Mâcon, 1864), no. dxviii, pp. 304–5.

[2] *Ep.* xi, *P.L.* cxli. 1145–6.

[3] '. . . coenobium Cluniacense, cunctis pene nationibus sanctitate praefulgens, nec non apostolicis privilegiis fultum et ab omnium ditione subtractum, solius principis apostolorum et vicariorum suorum iudicio reservatum, commoves, . . . apostolica privilegia cassare contendis': *Ep.* xii, *P.L.* cxli. 1146.

[4] Burchard was instructed 'ut eidem episcopo interdicatis, sicut nos litteris nostris fecimus, consecrationem, ordinationem vel aliquod ius in nostro monasterio quaerere, ne dum hoc iniuste appetit, quod iuste sibi licet pro sua inobedientia, iterata tantorum patrum querela, apostolica auctoritate careat': *Ep.* xiii, *P.L.* cxli. 1146–7.

addressed to all the faithful generally, the pope restated, in the most forthright terms, the unqualified exemption of Cluny and its exclusive subjection in spiritual matters to the Apostolic See.[1] Until after John's death Cluny's exempt status was not again challenged by the local upholders of episcopal rights.

Cluny's original immunity as the Papacy had repeatedly confirmed it had given it a complete freedom from temporal claims upon it. Now its newly realized exemption from the spiritual jurisdiction of the episcopate, which was the direct work of the pope, committed it more closely than ever to the Apostolic See. It added a new dimension to Cluny's liberty, and made Cluny more than ever the prime example of a monastery which enjoyed the benefits of exclusive subjection to St. Peter and his vicar; for it was so subject in spiritual, as well as in temporal, respects.

IV. CLUNY AS THE PAPACY'S OWN PECULIAR POSSESSION

Important though they were, the two developments in Cluny's liberty which have so far been considered, had a somewhat negative aspect. They effected Cluny's freedom from certain claims upon it: its immunity made it free from the claims in temporal matters of all ecclesiastical and lay lordship; while its exemption made it free from the spiritual jurisdiction of all ecclesiastical authorities save only the Apostolic See. In their negative aspect these developments, and more especially that of its immunity, indicate the highest common factor that Cluny was to have with the many monasteries and other institutions in the eleventh century which also enjoyed the 'libertas Romana'.

But there was also much differentiation amongst these institutions. Given medieval presuppositions about liberty as they were being formed in the eleventh century, it was possible for the

---

[1] 'Praeterea pervenit ad nos, quod quidam episcoporum temere et sine aliqua rationabili causa consultu pravo excommunicant sibi subiectos non solum saeculares perversa agentes, sed et religiosos sobriam et Deo placitam vitam ducere cupientes, quod de monachis Cluniacensibus omnino fieri prohibemus. Sed, si quaelibet querimonia episcoporum adversum illos exorta fuerit et aliter finiri non potuerit, apostolicae sedis examini reservetur, ut per eius iudicium quod iustum est decernatur': *Bull. C.*, pp. 9–10; Santifaller, art. cit., *Römische historische Mitteilungen*, i (1958), 56, see below, pp. 268–9.

concept of 'libertas Romana', in certain cases, to acquire a strongly positive connotation in terms of the special rights and services that were associated with a particular institution. Medieval man was not content to regard liberty as a merely abstract or negative condition. It was the correlative of lordship, without which it was impossible for a man or an institution to prosper. A vacuum of lordship was unthinkable; in order to be free, and as the only guarantee of freedom, any individual or corporate body must enjoy the protection and share the peace of a lord. To be free from the positive claims of one lordship, therefore, meant becoming subject to the positive claims of another and preferably a higher lordship. Until such claims were realized and articulated in specific ways, liberty was incomplete. But at the same time, the higher claims of higher lordship themselves enhanced the status of those upon whom they rested, and brought added honour to them. They intensified liberty and did not diminish it. The final criterion of liberty was thus not the negative one of what a man or an institution was free from, but the positive one of the service to which active subjection was due. The more exalted the lordship, the more excellent the freedom.[1]

Cluny was exclusively subject to the apostles of the Roman See, and the vicars of St. Peter actively exercised their duty of protection in order to give its liberty the greatest possible reality. In return, the Cluniacs performed services to the excellence of which the popes abundantly testified. In comparison with such a subjection, nothing could, by eleventh-century standards, be higher or better or more ennobling. It was, indeed, Peter Damiani who first made the point clearly in the next generation, when he praised Cluny because

where there is no liability to earthly service, the full dignity of the monastic profession [is] completely revealed. O truly renowned and free-born service of God, which leaves no place for earthly service![2]

[1] For the medieval conception of liberty, see esp. Tellenbach, *Church, State, and Christian Society*, pp. 12–25, 183–4. For other recent discussions, see H. Grundmann 'Freiheit als religiöses, politisches und persönliches Postulat im Mittelalter', *Hist. Zeitschr.* clxxxiii (1957), 23–53, esp. 26–30; and K. Bosl, *Frühformen der Gesellschaft im mittelalterlichen Europa* (Munich and Vienna, 1964), *passim*.

[2] See above, p. xxi.

But he was, in effect, anticipated by the popes themselves in the time of Benedict VIII and John XIX, in phrases which mark the complete unfolding, in principle, of Cluny's liberty. It was in the language of these popes that Cluny's 'libertas Romana' began to stand out conspicuously. Benedict was acutely aware that in upholding Cluny's immunity, he was exercising an especial stewardship on behalf of God and of St. Peter.[1] When John established its exemption he spoke of its 'liberalis libertas';[2] for him, Cluny was 'nostrum singulare monasterium',[3] and the 'singulare monasterium' of St. Peter himself.[4] Such phrases are evidence that the two popes were crediting Cluny with an especially intense liberty, in view of St. Peter's lordship as they understood it and of the services which the Cluniacs performed.

The superimposition of Cluny's exemption upon its immunity, in a manner that was peculiar to its own history, seems to have been of especial importance in prompting this positive filling out of its liberty. For Cluny's immunity had been in a sense restrictive, even with regard to the Papacy. When he founded Cluny, Duke William of Aquitaine defined its immunity so amply that he excluded even the pope from interfering in its temporal affairs;[5] if St. Peter was made the proprietor of Cluny, his vicar who was charged with its protection was, as it were, kept at a certain distance. But Cluny's exemption placed the Apostolic See in a new and more intimate relationship to it. For as John XIX made clear, although no other bishop might excommunicate a subject of the abbot of Cluny, the pope might and should do so, if a fair complaint were laid against him.[6] At least in principle, the terms

[1] 'Ego tamen ad quem, post Deum et sanctum Petrum, cura et providentia saepe supradicti loci [i.e. Cluny] specialiter pertinet, iuvamen et solatium auctoritatis apostolicae non desistam subministrare': *Ep.* xvi, *P.L.* cxxxix. 1602.

[2] See above, p. 34, n. 1.

[3] To the bishop of Mâcon: *Ep.* xii, *P.L.* cxli. 1146.

[4] To the archbishop of Lyons, *Ep.* xiii, *P.L.* cxli. 1147. The sense of the adjective 'singulare' is 'especial' or 'exclusive', rather than 'unique'; cf. its use in Pope Alexander II's privilege for the Spanish monastery of San Juan de la Peña (1071), in which monasteries placed in papal proprietorship are said to be 'in singulare patrocinium sanctae Romanae ecclesiae': Kehr, 'Papsturkunden in Navarra und Aragon, II', *Abh. Gött.* xxii (1928), 261.

[5] See above, p. 5.   [6] See above, p. 36, n. 1.

of Cluny's exemption gave the Papacy an active and immediate jurisdiction over it as well as over its enemies, which had no foreshadowing in the conditions of Cluny's immunity. The significance of this new function was reinforced by Cluny's utter dependence upon papal vigilance on its behalf, to protect it against the bishop of Mâcon and against the claims of the French episcopate which stood behind him.

Thus, from the second quarter of the eleventh century the liberty of Cluny could undergo its third, and positive, development, in terms of Cluny as the Papacy's own peculiar possession. The Papacy and Cluny began to be joined in an active and mutual bond of protection and service which had an intensity of its own. As it was made more and more effective, this bond filled out the liberty of Cluny by adding to the local prerogatives of the Burgundian monastery the prestige which attached to the especially active service and obedience of St. Peter at Rome. When the popes contemplated the liberty of Cluny, they saw reflected in it something of the inherent qualities of the Apostolic See itself into whose subjection it had been progressively brought: an exclusive acknowledgement of the lordship of the Prince of the Apostles and an unhampered dedication to his obedience. They saw these qualities as being uniquely expressed in the distinction of Cluny's monastic life and as bearing unique fruit in its service of God and of the Church at large.

In the time of Benedict VIII and John XIX, two things in particular illustrate the wholly exceptional place that Cluny was coming to occupy in relation to the Papacy by reason of its manner of fulfilling the demands of the 'libertas Romana'. One is the unique value that the popes began to set upon the services of the Cluniacs themselves to the Apostolic See and to the whole Church. A fuller consideration of these services will be made in a later chapter;[1] it is sufficient for the present to instance Benedict's high praise for the work of intercession for the whole Church, and for the salvation and peace of all the faithful, both living and departed, that Cluny performed by its unceasing prayers, masses, and alms. Benedict upheld this work as being of benefit to the

[1] See below, p. 162-71.

whole Church; therefore when the Cluniacs were assailed the whole Church was harmed. Cluny's pre-eminence in the monastic life imposed upon the Papacy an especial duty of caring for its liberty.[1]

Secondly, as a direct and express result of its building up, during the tenth and eleventh centuries, of support for the monastic order, and for Cluny above all other monasteries, the Papacy itself progressively grew in self-awareness. With increasing firmness it enunciated its own claims to hierarchical superiority in the Church and in society generally. This development had deep roots in relation to the monastic order. Ever since the ninth-century popes had begun to take monasteries like Vézelay into papal protection, visible examples were established of the freedom of the Church from temporal demands, which foreshadowed Gregorian ideas of the liberty of the Church. Again, up to the reigns of Benedict VIII and John XIX, the Papacy increasingly aspired to direct both bishops and lay authorities in defence of monasteries that were commended to it, in ways which, however tentatively, anticipated the claims upon their obedience of Gregory VII himself. In the case of Cluny, Pope John XIII's letter to the fourteen bishops in whose dioceses the principal possessions of Cluny lay, was a striking example of the way in which a pope could address the bishops as his local agents in the task of protecting monasteries.[2] Benedict VIII's letter of 1016 to the bishops of Burgundy, Provence, and Aquitaine was the climax of this movement towards concerted action on behalf of monastic immunity by the pope, the bishops, and, in this case, lay magnates.[3]

It was, however, when it began to vindicate the exemption of Cluny from the spiritual authority of the bishops of Mâcon that the Papacy became most articulate in insisting upon its own universal function and upon its title to general obedience. For in the episcopal resistance to monastic exemption, it faced a radical challenge to its own prerogatives. The opposition to papal jurisdiction by Bishop Gozelin of Mâcon and by the Council of Anse (1025), and the canonical precedents which were cited in its sup-

---

[1] *Ep.* xvi, *P.L.* cxxxix. 1601–2.   [2] *Ep.* xxvii, *P.L.* cxxxv. 990–1.
[3] *Ep.* xvi, *P.L.* cxxxix. 1601–4.

port, called into question the very foundations of papal authority in relation to that of bishops and councils. Might the bishops indeed rely upon ancient canonical precedents, including those of a General Council such as Chalcedon, to resist the latter-day rulings of the pope, when they stood in manifest conflict? Or did the pope have an immediate jurisdiction that bishops and councils must never resist?

These were the clear issues which confronted Pope John XIX at Cluny, to which his enthusiastic care for Cluny's liberty was the answer. His answer was unequivocal, and he strongly anticipated some of Gregory VII's theses in the *Dictatus papae*.[1] He proclaimed that the Roman Church was 'reliquarum ecclesiarum caput et cardo'.[2] It had the duty of hearing the petitions and meeting the necessities of all the faithful;[3] but it was particularly obliged to defend those who, like the Cluniacs, were directly committed to its care.[4] A monastery such as Cluny which was surrendered to the Roman Church was joined to it as the members of the body were joined to the head. An assault upon the members was tantamount to an assault upon the head itself, and it deserved the censures which were appropriate.[5]

To enable him to perform his appointed task of safeguarding such a monastery, the pope must act with an authority that was peculiarly his own. He judged the affairs of all the churches, while he himself was judged of none. His judgements were unique by reason of a certainty which was founded upon the steadfastness and authority of St. Peter.[6] Anyone of whatever order or dignity

---

[1] *Reg.* ii. 55a, pp. 201–8.

[2] To the bishop of Mâcon: *Ep.* xii, *P.L.* cxli. 1146.

[3] To the abbot of Cluny; '. . . omnium fidelium petitionibus et necessitatibus subvenire debeat apostolicae charitatis gratia': *Ep.* vi, *P.L.* cxli. 1135–7.

[4] 'Inhonestum enim nobis videtur ut sine nostro iudicio a quoquam anathematizetur sanctae sedis apostolicae filius, veluti cuiuscunque subiectae discipulus': loc. cit.

[5] '. . . qui profecto ipsum caput discerpere gestiunt, dum membra ab ipso separare volunt, et eos quos ut vernaculos habet iniuriis et contumeliis lacessere non desinunt, ignorantes utique miseri quod huius sanctae sedis decreta . . . pia fide a filiis matris ecclesiae accipienda sunt et veneranda . . .': *Ep.* xi, *P.L.* cxli. 1145–6.

[6] To King Robert, he spoke of the Apostolic See, 'quae de omni ecclesiaa fas habeat iudicandi, neque cuiquam liceat de eius garrire decreto, nec iudicare iudicio. Cuius iudicii sententiam eo magis oportet a nemine dissolvi, quo certius

in the Church who resisted him, went against the divine precepts
which the Church had obeyed and taught throughout the
centuries.[1]

Fortified by such principles as these, John XIX claimed that in
practice the pope had a title to the full and obedient collaboration
of the bishops. They were subordinate to his authority and not an
order apart. He praised the erring Bishop Gozelin of Mâcon because, for most of the time that he had been a bishop, he had been
a son and disciple of the Roman Church.[2] But now that he was in
rebellion against it, he called upon his metropolitan, Archbishop
Burchard of Lyons, to ensure for the future his obedience to St.
Peter.[3] John XIX addressed his requirement of dutiful support
still further than to the episcopate. With reference to Cluny, he
reminded King Robert the Pious that it is the duty of a king, as
well as of a pope, to devote his rule to the furthering of true
religion.[4] He thus acted as Benedict VIII had acted when he had
called upon the bishops and lay magnates of France to rally to
Cluny's defence in respect of its immunity;[5] but in respect of its
exemption his call was clearer still, and the nature of papal
authority was more sharply defined.

If it was the support of the Papacy in the early eleventh century
which enabled Cluny to achieve its full liberty, Cluny repaid the

apostoli constat illam Petri firmitate et auctoritate solidari. Ait enim in quodam
loco Leo papa . . .: "Non parvae insaniae est contra eum aliquem mutire, qui
clavigerum regni coelestis habet tutorem et patronum" ': loc. cit.; cp. *Dictatus
papae*, xviii–xxi, *Reg.* ii. 55*a*, p. 206.

[1] 'Quod si huic nostrae institutioni quilibet cuiuscumque ordinis vel dignitatis
contraire voluerit, timeat illud, quod meretur, qui contra divinum preceptum
catholicorum apostolicorum patrum terminos temerario ausu sive ambitionis
cupiditate transgredire presumpserit': *Bull. C.*, p. 10; Santifaller, art. cit., *Römische
historische Mitteilungen*, i (1958), 56; see below, p. 269.

[2] 'Ex quo ad episcopalem gloriam deductus es, Romanae ecclesiae filius et
discipulus visus es. . . . Nunc vero nescimus qua nova temeritate illectus, in-
exstinguibili cupiditate accensus, matri tuae repugnas, et contra nos, meritis
apostoli Petri magistrum tuum, levas calcaneum .. ': *Ep.* xii, *P.L.* cxli. 1146.

[3] *Ep.* xiii, *P.L.* cxli. 1146.

[4] 'His enim rei [i.e. the upholding of true religion] sacramentum non solum a
nobis exigitur, quibus pastoralis commissa est cura, verum etiam et a vobis, cui
credita est, cum usuris exigenda maxima pompa et regiae sublimitatis potentia':
Ep. xi, *P.L.* cxli. 1145–6.

[5] *Ep.* xvii, *P.L.* cxxxix. 1601–4.

debt by evoking this anticipation of Gregorianism when Gregory VII was not more than a babe-in-arms, and when the reform of the Papacy by the Emperor Henry III was, as yet, some twenty years in the future. The distant origins of Cluny's liberty had been in the direct line of late-Carolingian monasticism, and much of its development had its parallels elsewhere in the monastic order. But in the first third of the eleventh century Cluny decisively emerged as a focal point about which the aspirations of the monastic order for freedom from all kinds of external authority began uniquely to gather. Popes Benedict VIII and John XIX met them in its case, as in that of no other monastery. By 1032 Cluny had already become the most favoured subject of the Papacy within the monastic order, and the 'libertas Romana' was exemplified there with an altogether exceptional fullness and significance. At the same time, against the background of episcopal claims, Cluny's freedom in the leading of the monastic life had become inextricably bound up with the authority of the Apostolic See to rule the whole Church. The enunciation of the highest papal claims was the outcome of the meeting of Cluny's most urgent needs by papal aid. A bond of mutual and increasing dependence, service, and sympathy had been established between the Cluniacs and the Papacy, which was henceforth normally to be decisive for their relationship.

After a brief setback which only served to underline the indispensability to Cluny of active and permanent papal support against episcopal claims, this bond was sustained and developed during the ecclesiastical revolution of the later eleventh century.

II

THE LIBERTY OF CLUNY IN
HILDEBRANDINE TIMES

I. THE REACTION OF THE BISHOPS OF MÂCON

In its outline, the pattern of Cluny's liberty was complete by 1032. But the death, in that year, of Pope John XIX and the succession of Pope Benedict IX (1033–45), quickly led to an interlude of reaction which showed how vulnerable Cluny still was to the attacks of the church of Mâcon, and how serious these attacks could be. For throughout the twelve years of Benedict's reign relationships between Cluny and the Papacy were unwontedly cool. There is no evidence of contact between them, nor did the pope show any concern for the liberty of Cluny. In this his attitude reflected that of the Emperor Conrad II, to whose interests he was in general obedient. Conrad seems to have turned against Cluny during his struggle for the crown of the Burgundian kingdom, which became vacant in 1032.[1] From this time the imperial favour upon which Cluny had increasingly leant since the late tenth century was largely withdrawn.[2] It was not restored until well

[1] For the very obscure question of Cluny's policy at this time, see Sackur, *Die Cluniacenser*, ii. 236–7; Hourlier, *Saint Odilon*, pp. 103–5. Because two of Cluny's major dependencies, Payerne and Romanmôtier, lay within the kingdom of Burgundy, and because its kings had done much to augment and protect Cluny and its lands (e.g. Bruel, 1716, 2270, 2465), its future was a matter of great concern to Cluny. In the event, Conrad received the Burgundian crown at Payerne: Wipo, *Gesta Chuonradi*, xxx, ed. H. Bresslau, *S.R.G.*, p. 49; but there is no evidence that he later acted in any way on behalf of Cluny.

[2] The close relations which had prevailed between the Cluniacs and the empire had largely been owing to the Empress Adelaide: Sackur, *Die Cluniacenser*, i. 218–19, 223, 226–7, 341–2; ii. 451–3. Apart from lesser actions in favour of Cluny, Otto III had joined Abbot Odilo in soliciting Gregory V's confirmation of Cluny's liberties in 998; while Conrad II, on his accession, confirmed its possessions in Alsace: *M.G.H. DD.* iv, no. 1, pp. 1–2; and he took the place originally reserved for Henry II in obtaining John XIX's confirmation of Cluny's liberties in 1024: *Ep.* vi, *P.L.* cxli. 1135–7.

into the reign of the Emperor Henry III (1039–56),[1] when a *rapprochement* occurred between the empire and Cluny. It was partly a result of the emperor's marriage, in 1043, with Agnes of Poitou, daughter of the duke of Aquitaine, and partly of his final deposition, in 1046, of Benedict IX. The eighty-five-year-old Abbot Odilo hurried to Rome at the time of this last event. He was present on Christmas Day 1046 when the new German pope, Clement II, performed Henry's imperial coronation.[2] Odilo showed an enthusiasm on this occasion which was well grounded; henceforth Cluny could again count upon the favour of pope and emperor.

During the time that Cluny had been bereft of papal support, a new bishop of Mâcon, Walter (1031–62), had taken advantage of the opportunity to revive the claims of his see to spiritual jurisdiction over Cluny. Abbot Odilo early (c. 1033) provided him with a pretext for doing so. Relying upon Cluny's recent papal privileges, he invited Bishop Stephen of le Puy to come and consecrate an altar there. When Walter objected to this challenge to his position as bishop, Odilo had no alternative but to give way. According to an account of the matter which was preserved at Mâcon, Abbot Odilo found himself constrained to give Walter rich presents; he had to do penance in the cathedral of Saint-Vincent for all his past and present evasions of the bishop of Mâcon's jurisdiction; and he had to invite Bishop Walter to come and perform some ordinations at Cluny.[3] The clerks of Mâcon may well have exaggerated the humiliation to which Abbot Odilo was subjected. But the lesson of these events is clear. Without direct and effective papal support Cluny could not effectively enjoy the exempt status which papal action had lately conferred on it. On the other hand, it is no less clear that the Papacy could scarcely ignore for long the implicit challenge which was being made to its authority on behalf of the episcopal order; for

[1] The beginning of Henry III's reign significantly saw no confirmation of Cluny's possessions in Alsace and Burgundy.

[2] For Odilo's journey and enthusiasm about the coronation, see the additional chapter of Jotsald's *Vita Odilonis*, ed. Sackur, *N.A.* xv (1889), 119–21.

[3] For these events, see *G.C.* iv. 1060; *Cartulaire de Saint-Vincent de Mâcon*, ed. Ragut, nos. dxix–xx, pp. 305–6.

behind the resistance of the bishop of Mâcon, there lay all the arguments which the French bishops had used against papal authority ever since the Council of Chelles. What was at stake was the Papacy's right to intervene at will in the affairs of local dioceses, by giving privileges to monasteries which limited the bishops' spiritual authority over them.

Since the matter was so important both to Cluny and to the Papacy, the revival and reform of the Papacy after 1046, which was particularly effective during and after the energetic reign of Leo IX (1048–54) saw the popes coming speedily and often to Cluny's rescue. Clement II himself lost no time in renewing the support given by earlier popes. In 1047 he dispatched a circular letter to the bishops and lay magnates of France and Aquitaine, in which he urged them to safeguard Cluny, its lands, and dependencies from every kind of harm.[1] In 1056 the Council of Toulouse, which was held by the command of Pope Victor II, affirmed that Cluny and all its appurtenances were the property of St. Peter, and should therefore be inviolate.[2] Most important of all, the reforming popes resumed the series of papal privileges for Cluny, which had begun with those of Gregory V, Benedict VIII, and John XIX. Popes Leo IX (1049),[3] Victor II (1055),[4] Stephen IX (1058),[5] and Alexander II (1063)[6] successively confirmed its immunity and exemption in terms which, in sum, renewed all the rights that the three earlier popes had assured to it. Of the seven reforming popes who reigned between 1046 and 1073, all save

[1] *Bull. C.*, p. 12. This letter has never been reprinted, and has escaped the notice of historians. For the text, see below, p. 270. Clement's favour towards Cluny is referred to by Jotsald, *Vita Odilonis*, i. 7, *P.L.* cxlii. 902.

[2] Mansi, xix. 854–6.

[3] *Ep.* xii, *P.L.* cxliii. 607–9. For Leo's confirmation of Cluny's possessions of land at a place called *Raningas*, see *Ep.* xlvii, *P.L.* cxliii. 658–9.

[4] *Ep.* i, *P.L.* cxliii. 803–8.

[5] *Ep.* viii, *P.L.* cxliii. 879–94. This privilege laid especial emphasis upon the exemption of Cluny, and also illustrates the way in which the ideas of immunity and exemption now tended to merge into each other: 'Nec quovis modo quicunque episcopus aeu archiepiscopus locum ipsum vel monachos eius excommunicare vel iudicare audeat; sed semper sub tutela et immunitate Romanae sedis, soliusque Romanae pontificis iudicio consistentes omnipotenti Domino securi et quieti deserviant.'

[6] *Ep.* xiv, *P.L.* cxlvi. 1293–5.

the short-lived Damasus II and Nicholas II are thus known to have taken action of this kind on behalf of Cluny.

Furthermore, after 1046, the Papacy developed the practice of sending legates to perform tasks on its behalf, wherever it proved to be necessary. This had great significance for the continuing development of close relations between the Papacy and Cluny. The personal contacts between Cluny and the Apostolic See, which the visits to Rome of the abbots of Cluny had always fostered, were made of greater consequence than ever, when figures of importance at Rome came and saw Cluny at first hand, and were captivated by what they saw. Archdeacon Hildebrand himself came to Cluny as a legate, and the anecdotes concerning his visit which were later current at Cluny testify to the admiration which first-hand acquaintance induced in him for its monastic life, and, in particular, for the sanctity and wisdom of Abbot Hugh.[1] Moreover, the sending of legates gave the Papacy a far more effective way than it had hitherto possessed of helping Cluny against the bishops of Mâcon, and so of championing its own prerogatives as against episcopal ones.

In this connection the greatest importance attaches to the journey to Cluny of Cardinal Peter Damiani, whom Pope Alexander II dispatched as his legate in 1063.[2] In that year another acute crisis had broken out between Cluny and the see of Mâcon, to which a new bishop, Drogo (1062–72), had just succeeded. Like his predecessor, he made it his immediate concern to assert his rights at Cluny. Taking advantage of an absence of Abbot Hugh he demanded entry there; he sought to assert his jurisdiction as bishop by preaching and holding a council within the walls of the monastery. The monks, however, were successful in dispersing the armed band by which he was accompanied and in compelling him to withdraw. In retaliation, he laid an interdict upon them.

Once again a bishop of Mâcon was offering a frontal challenge to the exemption of Cluny, and therefore to the authority of the Papacy which was its creator and guarantor. Accordingly, when

---

[1] See below, pp. 148–50.
[2] See esp. *De Gallica Petri Damiani profectione et eius ultramontano itinere*, M.G.H. *Scr.* xxx. 1034–46.

he heard of it, Abbot Hugh hastened to Rome. At the Lent Council of 1063, he asked Pope Alexander II to intervene.[1] The pope commissioned Peter Damiani to go to France as legate. The decisive event in his busy journey was a Council which he held at Châlon-sur-Saône. At it he encountered the almost unanimous hostility of the bishops, not only to Cluny's exemption, but also to the fact and the theory of Roman intervention on its behalf. In face of it he asserted Cluny's exclusive subjection to the Roman pontiff, and he confirmed all the privileges that earlier popes had conferred upon it. When Bishop Drogo was thus confronted by a papal legate, he found himself compelled to do public penance. The earlier humiliation of Abbot Odilo was reversed, and the claims of both Cluny and the Papacy were upheld.

Peter Damiani's legatine journey of 1063 has a threefold significance. First, it provided tangible evidence that the Papacy now had a longer arm than ever before to act on Cluny's behalf, and at the same time to assert its own prerogatives. Whereas, in 1025, the provincial Council of Anse had compelled the Cluniacs to acquiesce at least temporarily in episcopal claims, and, in *c.* 1033, Abbot Odilo had been forced to do a humiliating penance at the behest of the Bishop of Mâcon, in 1063 the legatine Council of Châlon saw a signal vindication of the monks in face of the bishops and of the Papacy in face of conciliar claims. Secondly, on the other hand, however signal Peter Damiani's immediate vindication of Cluny may have been, it was manifestly not final. It is clear from the account of the Council of Châlon which was preserved at Mâcon, that Bishop Drogo did penance under protest and that he had no intention of accepting the situation once the legate had gone. Equally, it was the intention of his fellow bishops to resume, as soon as they had a chance, the campaign in favour of episcopal rights which for seventy years had punctuated the history of monastic attempts to shake off the bishops' spiritual authority.[2]

---

[1] *De Gallica Petri Damiani profectione*, 3, pp. 1036–7.

[2] For the Council, see ibid., 17–12, pp. 1044–6; Mansi, xix. 1025–8. The former source laid especial emphasis upon the corporate hostility of the bishops to Cluny and to Roman support for it: 'Paene omnes episcopi, qui tunc aderant, praeter archiepiscopum Bisuntinum . . . Cluniacensi monasterio invidebant eiusque causas, quantum caute poterant, conculcabant et, ut huius negotii magis infortunium

As the pontificate of Gregory VII approached, Cluny knew very
well that it remained utterly beholden to the Papacy for the defence of its liberty, in face of the smouldering hostility of the bishop
of Mâcon and of his fellow bishops. Equally, the Papacy could not
afford to relax its vigilance on behalf of Cluny, since the very
basis of its authority was being called in question by the French
bishops.

Thirdly, Peter Damiani's journey contributed greatly to the
growing spiritual bond between Cluny and the Papacy, and
to the Roman appreciation of Cluny and its exemplary liberty.
Following the earlier example of Archdeacon Hildebrand,
Peter Damiani, in 1063, became a devotee of Cluny with all the
enthusiasm of his impetuous nature. At first, indeed, the sometime
hermit of Fonte Avellana had his reservations about the lack of

quam triumphum abbas incurreret, occultis machinationibus fabricabant. Nam
unusquisque causam suam in iudicio agi credebat, cum coepiscopi negotium
Romana discussio ventilabat, quia, si abbati huius rei victoria proveniret, quilibet
episcoporum sibi amplius resistere non auderat.' Peter Damiani's judgement
accordingly laid a corresponding emphasis upon Roman jurisdiction and upon
the exemption of Cluny: 'Cluniacense monasterium Romanae ecclesiae esse
subditum nullus vestrum, fratres, ignorat, et, quod nulli aliae personae praeter
Romanum pontificem in eodem monasterio ius aliquod pertinet, nullus ad-
dubitat. Quod quidem supra omnia sibi pertinentia diligit monasteria, multis
quoque apostolicae sedis privilegiis constat esse munitum. Quae omnia domnus
Matisconensis episcopus parvipendens illud subiugare suaeque ditioni submittere
quasi temerarius studet invasor.' For the attitude of the church of Mâcon, see
Cartulaire de Saint-Vincent de Mâcon, ed. Ragut, no. dxxi, pp. 306–7; also the fragment of a version of the Council that Severt preserved from a manuscript of the
Church of Mâcon: '. . . synodus tredecim episcoporum apud Cabilonem est
habita, sub Petri Ostiensis episcopi Romanae ecclesiae legati praesentiam, prae-
dictum episcopum [i.e. Drogo] ad rationem misit, sicut per proclamationes
Cluniacensium monachorum in synodo Romana audierat. Dum autem episcopus optaret respondere, quod nihil eis intulerit, etc., nec ipsum coenobium
afflixerit, etc., aut Romana privilegia et papam spreverit, etc., sed versa vice plura
his ab ipsis pertulerit, nullatenus locus sibi datus est inde, sed tantum synodali
decreto purgavit se, scientes Romana privilegia non laesisse. Ipse vero legatus
coenobitis quorum obsequiis attractus advenerat favens, querimonias episcopi nec
ecclesiae eius suscepit: sed tantum quod praedecessores episcopi in ipso Cluniacensi coenobio eatenus habuerant, ipse laudavit et concessit. Privilegiis tamen
quae contra ius ecclesiasticum monachi collegerant, Matiscensis ecclesia prout
potuit ibidem contradixit, nec episcopus ea laudavit vel confirmavit, sed permanet
ut erat in querela, etc.': J. Severt, *Chronologia historica successionis hierarchicae
antistitum Lugdunensis archiepiscopatus* (Lyons, 1607), pp. 429–30.

austerity that he found there. But Abbot Hugh's tactful explana-
tions quickly satisfied him.[1] The account of his journey, which
was composed by a travelling companion who was also a hermit
of Fonte Avellana, and the copious letters that he himself afterwards wrote, testify to the unbounded admiration for all things
Cluniac that he came to display, and to his zeal on Cluny's behalf.[2]
In one of his letters, for example, Peter Damiani epitomized his
enthusiasm by rejoicing that he shared the merits of Cluny's
religion, because he had taken away the yoke of subjection that
the church of Mâcon had tried to fasten upon it in abrogation of
its liberty, and had seized from the clergy of Mâcon the club of
Hercules that they had brandished over it.[3]

It was, however, the sheer fact of Cluny's utter freedom from
every kind of earthly lordship, under exclusive papal protection,
that made the deepest impression upon him.[4] Reflecting his sentiments, his travelling companion congratulated Abbot Hugh
because, faced by Bishop Drogo's intolerable invasion, he had
wisely sought exclusive security in the bark of St. Peter.[5] In
general, Cluny's freedom from all outside obligations under the
Roman pontiff was the pattern of all Christian service; for it
created there the highest freedom which is the counterpart of the
highest subjection:

[1] *Bibl. C.*, cols. 460–2; *P.L.* clix. 925–6. St. Anselm, on the other hand, spoke of
the 'districtio ordinis' at Cluny: Eadmer, *Vita sancti Anselmi*, i. 5, ed. R. W.
Southern (London, 1962), p. 9.

[2] *De Gallica Petri Damiani profectione*, esp. 13, pp. 1041–3; for his letters,
Bibl. C., cols. 477–90.

[3] 'Ego etiam, ut spero, meritis me vestrae santitatis ingessi, dum Matiscensis
ecclesiae iugum, quod vobis imponi tentabatur, abegi; tuendumque me credo per
vos a versutiis daemonum, qui vibratam in vos clavam Herculis rapui de manibus
clericorum': *Bibl. C.*, col. 485. Peter Damiani especially prized the gift of confraternity with the Cluniacs, which he was given in 1063, and which served
thereafter to keep Cluny in the forefront of his mind: *De Gallica Petri Damiani
profectione*, 15, pp. 1043–4; *Bibl. C.*, cols. 477–9.

[4] 'Venerabilis itaque illa Cluniacensis congregatio, in qua nihil servitutis
vendicat Egiptus, nullum de triduo Pharao sibi retinet diem, quanto a iugo
terrenae dominationis est libera, tanto melius vivit devota': *De Gallica Petri
Damiani profectione*, 2, p. 1036.

[5] '. . . ut ex huius perturbationis gurgite ad quietae stationis portum per-
veniret incolumis, solam sancti Petri festinavit intrare naviculam': ibid., 3,
p. 1036.

From the very day of its foundation, the monastery of Cluny has been so eminently free by an innate and tranquil freedom, that it should be subject to no ecclesiastical or secular person save the Roman pontiff. God's mercy has so ordained that, where the burden of earthly subjection has been done away, devotion to his service should be fullest; and that, where there is no liability to earthly service, the full dignity of the monastic profession should be completely revealed. O truly renowned and freeborn service of God, which leaves no place for earthly service![1]

In the eyes of the reformers at Rome, the liberty of Cluny had now obtained the status of an ideal. At Rome as elsewhere, there grew up a mystique of Cluny which proved its power to captivate the reformers[2] and to sweep them further in praise of its liberty than the hard facts about it would necessarily have warranted; because they related it to the highest freedom in the service of God, which was made possible by Cluny's exclusive subjection to the Apostolic See. When the Gregorians aspired to achieve the liberty of the Church, Cluny above all other institutions henceforth provided a pattern of which they approved.

II. GREGORY VII AND THE LIBERTY OF CLUNY

When Archdeacon Hildebrand became pope as Gregory VII, he was no less zealous than his predecessors had been to protect the close relationship that had grown up between Cluny and the Papacy. In 1075 he confirmed its rights and possessions, as they had been built up in the past, by a privilege whose terms closely followed the model of Pope Stephen IX's.[3] Four years afterwards Gregory's zeal for Cluny was made clear in another crisis which broke out in the relations between Cluny and the church of Mâcon. The crisis was the more serious and dramatic because, at first, it seemed gravely to threaten Cluny's whole position in the Papacy's favour. But its character quickly changed; and it eventually came to its climax in Gregory's conciliar allocution

---

[1] Ibid., 1, p. 1035.

[2] For a discussion of Peter Damiani's reaction to Cluny and its spirituality, see J. Leclercq, *Saint Pierre Damien, ermite et homme d'église* (Rome, 1960), pp. 117–23.

[3] Santifaller, Q.F., no. 107, 9 Dec. 1075, pp. 95–100.

of 1080 which outdid even Peter Damiani in its eulogy of Cluny, its abbots, and its liberty.

The outbreak of the crisis saw Cluny at an initial disadvantage. Gregory was seriously, if temporarily, displeased with Abbot Hugh because he had lately admitted to Cluny as a monk Duke Hugh of Burgundy, whom Gregory valued as one of his very few really trustworthy supporters among the lay rulers.[1] So far as the evidence goes, the crisis began when Drogo's successor as bishop of Mâcon, Landeric of Berzé (1074–96),[2] went to Rome and complained in person that the monks of Cluny had violated certain purely temporal rights of the cathedral of Saint-Vincent. The initiative in making the complaints may well have lain, not with the mild and temporizing bishop, but with his turbulent chapter.[3] In any case the ground was carefully chosen: the complaints themselves merely concerned some local rights of the church of Mâcon; they in no way raised the old bones of contention about the exemption of Cluny, or about the respective rights of the Papacy and the episcopate.[4]

When the bishop put forward his church's case before the Roman Curia, many of his audience there appear to have been persuaded that Cluny was in the wrong.[5] Gregory himself was somewhat nonplussed by the allegations; but his letters show that he preserved a prudent detachment and trod with uncharacteristic

[1] See below, pp. 144–5.

[2] Landeric stood high in Gregory's favour because, in 1074, Gregory had successfully persuaded King Philip I of France not to persist in his simoniacal demands upon Landeric, and had himself consecrated him bishop: *Reg.* i. 35, 4 Dec. 1073, pp. 56–7; i. 76, 15 Apr. 1074, pp. 107–8; i. 85a, 28 June 1074, p. 123.

[3] See e.g. *Ep. Coll.* 37, pp. 564–5, where it was clearly Gregory's view of events during the crisis, that Landeric had been led astray by his clerks. The letter in *Cartulaire de Saint-Vincent de Mâcon*, ed. Ragut, no. xx, p. 17, purporting to be from Gregory VII to Bishop Hugh of Die, in which the pope urged him to take strong measures against Abbot Hugh, can scarcely be genuine as it stands; for it contradicts Gregory's attitude as revealed in other letters. It is marked as spurious by Jaffé: *J.L.* 5183. It is, however, evidence for the militancy and lack of scruple of the chapter of Mâcon. Landeric was represented as the innocent victim of the abbot's guile.

[4] This is clear from *Reg.* vi. 33, 14 Apr. 1079, pp. 446–7.

[5] The strength of the hostility to Cluny in the Curia at this time and his own consistent support for it, were referred to by Gregory in *Reg.* viii. 2, 27 June 1080, p. 518.

wariness. His first step was to seek further information by writing letters to Abbot Hugh and to his standing legate, Bishop Hugh of Die. In the first of these letters he informed the abbot of the allegations which had been made, and urged him to seek an agreement with his adversaries. If he could not do so by direct negotiations, the matter was to be settled by the mediation of Hugh of Die and 'the abbot of St. Paul's'.[1] In the second letter, Gregory wrote in similar terms of caution and detachment to Hugh of Die. It emerges from this letter that Bishop Landeric was supported by his archbishop, Gebuin of Lyons; and that the legate had also sent a report of his own to Rome, in which he had represented the dispute as being between Abbot Hugh and the archbishop. Gregory called upon his legate to do all in his power to reconcile them. In harmony with his letter to Hugh of Cluny, his tone in writing to Hugh of Die was restrained and conciliatory. He regretted that strife should divide two such religious men as Abbot Hugh and Archbishop Gebuin. They should be encouraged, rather than coerced, into agreement. Only if one of them refused to heed the way of righteousness, should severe steps be taken against him in order to recall him to it.[2]

Such was the genesis of the crisis, in which Cluny was at first placed very much upon the defensive. However, events quickly took a wholly different turn. Perhaps because Cluny's enemies at Mâcon were dismayed by Gregory's detachment and moderation, they rashly took a series of false steps which placed them hopelessly in the wrong.[3] They took the law into their own hands. Archbishop Gebuin of Lyons laid an interdict upon several of Cluny's churches; while Bishop Landeric of Mâcon excommunicated certain of its chapels and their chaplains. These steps

---

[1] *Reg.* vi. 33. The abbot in question was almost certainly Bernard of Marseilles: see below, p. 173.

[2] *Ep. Coll.* 32, pp. 559–60.

[3] The principal source for the events referred to in this and the following paragraphs is the *Charta Petri Albanensis episcopi et cardinalis Romani de immunitate Cluniaci, Bibl. C.*, cols. 511–14; thus, only the Cluniac version of the events is available. For discussions, see T. Schieffer, *Die päpstlichen Legaten in Frankreich* (*Historische Studien*, 263, Berlin, 1935), pp. 119–21; G. Miccoli, *Pietro Igneo. Studi sull'età gregoriana* (Rome, 1960), pp. 124–8.

by the bishops in effect threw down the gauntlet to Gregory VII; for they were acts of aggression which blatantly disregarded Cluny's papal privileges, including Gregory's own of 1075. They amounted to an uncompromising renewal of the old episcopal challenges to the growth of monastic exemption and to the direct exercise of papal authority in its defence. The circumstances of 1063 were now repeated; for by this challenge the bishops struck at the roots of Gregorian principles. Moreover, the challengers were not only the bishop of Mâcon, but also an archbishop, Gebuin of Lyons, upon whom Gregory himself had lately conferred primatial standing.[1]

The issue was thus transformed into an episcopal defiance of the Apostolic See, which Gregory would have been the last pope to ignore. It was now Abbot Hugh's turn to appeal to Rome. He quickly did so; and after a long inquiry in which he weighed the cases of both sides, Gregory came forward as Cluny's strenuous champion.[2] He took two immediate steps. First, he wrote to the Cluniac Archbishop Warmund of Vienne, instructing him to visit Cluny and to give visible proof of its exemption by ordaining there some of its monks.[3] Secondly, with a manifest intention of reviving the memory and renewing the consequences of Peter Damiani's journey of 1063, Gregory dispatched to Cluny Cardinal Peter of Albano. The cardinal, otherwise known as Peter Igneus, was, like Peter Damiani, a sometime hermit of Fonte Avellana, and a zealous partisan of reform.

Peter of Albano vindicated the cause of Cluny no less energetically than Peter Damiani had done. On Candlemas (2 Feb.) 1080 he solemnly confirmed its privileges in the name of the pope; he carefully defined the limits of its local immunity; he quashed the ecclesiastical sentences that the archbishop of Lyons and the

---

[1] The outbreak of the dispute coincided with Gregory's giving Lyons a primacy over the four provinces of Lyons, Rouen, Tours, and Sens: *Reg.* vi. 34–5, 20 Apr. 1079, pp. 447–52.

[2] Abbot Hugh sent his prior, Odo, to represent him at the papal Curia. It was upon this visit that Gregory promoted Odo to the cardinal-bishopric of Ostia, a move which does much to explain the favourable outcome of this dispute from Cluny's point of view: Becker, *Urban II*, i. 45–51.

[3] The letter to which Peter of Albano refers does not survive.

bishop of Mâcon had so rashly passed; and he prohibited them from so far exceeding their authority again. Four days later Peter of Albano held a Council at Anse with a view to setting matters finally at rest. At it the archbishop of Lyons still figured in support of the bishop of Mâcon, while Abbot Hugh was accompanied by Archbishop Warmund of Vienne. After Bishop Landeric had agreed to submit himself obediently to the judgement of the Pope and his legate, his offences against the liberty of Cluny were rehearsed. It further came to light that when Archbishop Warmund had travelled to Cluny in obedience to Gregory's instructions to carry out ordinations there, he had been set upon, at the instigation of the canons of Mâcon, by ruffians who cried, 'Ne vivat violator et adulterator sponsae sancti Vincentii'; and that when Bishop Landeric had been informed of this fresh affront to papal honour and authority, he had omitted to punish it. Peter of Albano, therefore, caused Gregory VII's privilege of 1075 to be read aloud; and he adjudged the bishop's contempt of papal decrees to deserve the sentence of excommunication. Landeric refused to acknowledge his guilt, weakly protesting that he had never heard, to that day, of the papal privilege of 1075. Peter of Albano suspended him from office until the pope himself might pass judgement upon him. The legate freed the churches that Archbishop Gebuin had laid under interdict. He also restored to Cluny the monastery of Pouilly, from which Gebuin had evicted Cluniac monks and into which he had intruded a community of nuns.

By his proceedings at Cluny and at Anse, Peter of Albano once again asserted the exemption of Cluny and vindicated against the bishops the Gregorian view of papal authority in the Church. When Gregory VII, who was at Rome, was apprised of the course of events, he fully upheld his legate's rulings. He wrote to Bishop Landeric rebuking him because he had dared to show delay in acknowledging the privileges of Cluny as Peter of Albano had directed. As a condition of his restoration to his episcopal office Landeric was to meet representatives of the monks of Cluny midway between Cluny and Mâcon, and there confirm their privileges. Gregory exhorted him for the future to heed the authority of the pope, not the promptings of his turbulent canons. He directed that the whole dispute between Cluny and Mâcon should be finally settled by Bishop Hugh of Die; but that, if necessary, it should be brought back to Rome for Gregory himself to determine.[1]

During his Lent Council of 1080 Gregory set the keystone upon his vindication of Cluny by pronouncing his remarkable eulogy of it. In it he gave the crowning expression to the unique relationship that had grown up, within his own lifetime, between Cluny and the Apostolic See. His allocution culminated in a full assertion of Cluny's absolute liberty under the tutelage of the Apostolic See:

We will and by our apostolic authority we affirm and urge, that no person whatsoever, great or small, and no authority whatsoever, whether it be archbishop or bishop, or whether it be king, duke, marquis, prince, count, or even my legate, may ever open his mouth against this place and monastery, or have any power there. In accordance with the privilege which we have issued, and with what our predecessors have with authority laid down, it is to possess fully and perpetually the immunity and liberty which have been granted to it by the Roman See. Covered by the wings of our apostolic protection, and by these alone, it is to breathe freely from all commotion and from every attacking storm. In the bosom of this holy mother church of Rome, it is to enjoy perpetual and pleasant peace, to the honour of Almighty God and of the blessed apostles Peter and Paul.

Gregory's allocution was far more than a vindication of Cluny within the narrow context of its controversy with the bishops of Mâcon. His assertion of its liberty was prefaced by a declaration in the most sweeping terms of his own enthusiastic devotion towards it. Gregory extolled the sanctity of Cluny and of its successive abbots, none of whom had failed to be a saint.[2] Under their rule it had won a pre-eminence in the monastic order

---

[1] *Ep. Coll.* 37, pp. 564-5. The immediate sequel is unknown; but when Hugh of Die had succeeded to the see of Lyons, he supported the bishops of Mâcon and Autun against the Cluniacs, perhaps in the disputes discussed below, p. 62: Ragut, *Cartulaire de Saint-Vincent de Mâcon*, nos. dlxxxi, dlxxxi *bis*, pp. 348-9.

[2] Gregory's words are reminiscent of his second letter to Bishop Hermann of Metz: *Reg.* viii. 21, 15 Mar. 1081, pp. 544-62, esp. pp. 558-9.

which set it above all other monasteries beyond the mountains. Gregory praised Cluny for its actions: it had never accepted the yoke of the princes of this world; its abbots had steadfastly been the courageous and obedient defenders of St. Peter and his church alone. But his fullest praise was reserved for what Cluny was in itself. It was the especial possession of St. Peter; it was, therefore, wholly devoted to the honour and defence of the Roman See. Its life was founded upon the liberty which was the mark of that see. By means of this liberty the abbots of Cluny had always nobly preserved the authority that their predecessors had won.[1]

In these terms Gregory extolled Cluny as being, in his eyes, the most perfect pattern of what the monastic order should be in relation to St. Peter and his vicar. It was the classic example of the true liberty in subjection to the lordship of St. Peter, which it was Gregory's purpose to foster in the Church. Gregory's allocution stands as his considered and final estimate of Cluny as an institution, and of its monks as partners with the Apostolic See in promoting the well-being of the Church. In this respect Cluny's liberty was an epitome of his reforming programme; its prayers and its actions throughout the Church made it his acknowledged ally. No praise could be too lavish when he expressed his sense of obligation to it.

[1] *Bull. C.*, pp. 21–2; see below, pp. 272–3.

III

CLUNY AND ITS LIBERTY UNDER
POPES URBAN II AND PASCHAL II

THE sixty years of Abbot Hugh's reign at Cluny continued
throughout the pontificate of Pope Urban II and well into that of
Pope Paschal II (1099–1118). Once the crisis of 1079–80 had been
settled, Bishop Landeric of Mâcon remained a quiet and friendly
neighbour of Cluny until his death in 1096; and there was no
further direct strife between Cluny and the church of Mâcon
during the remainder of Abbot Hugh's lifetime. Nevertheless, the
popes continued to praise the monastic life of Cluny and to bring
it their active support. For Urban II this was the discharge of
a personal obligation. During some ten years before 1080, when
Gregory VII raised him to the cardinal-bishopric of Ostia, he had
been a monk of Cluny and, for much of the time, its grand prior.
There is also a strong tradition that Paschal II had been a monk at
Cluny. Although it is still followed by some authorities,[1] it must
be regarded as improbable.[2] But Paschal's letters show that he
equalled Urban in his zeal for Cluny and its liberty. Gregory VII,
Urban II, and Paschal II were at one in their confidence that Cluny
was a principal bulwark of the Papacy in promoting the reform
of the Church. They showed a consistent purpose of upholding
Cluny's liberty, and they were all enthusiastic in their appraisal
of its services to the Church.

I. URBAN II AND THE LIBERTY OF CLUNY

Upon becoming pope, Urban II lost no time in confirming
Cluny's liberty. In 1088 he issued a privilege in which he confirmed

---

[1] e.g. A. Fliche, *La Réforme grégorienne et la reconquête chrétienne, Histoire de
l'église*, ed. A. Fliche and V. Martin, viii (Paris, 1946), 339.

[2] Haller's account of his early life is preferable to Fliche's: J. Haller, *Das Papsttum. Idee und Wirklichkeit*, ii (2nd edn., Darmstadt, 1962), 471–2, 619–20.

its enjoyment of the liberty, immunity, and authority that had
in the past been bestowed upon it. In the course of doing so he
made a clear and corroborative reference to Gregory VII's conciliar allocution of 1080.¹ He also strikingly acknowledged the
debt of the Apostolic See to Abbot Hugh, by conferring upon
him the right to wear the episcopal mitre in solemn processions,
and the dalmatic, gloves, and sandals on certain greater festivals
of Cluny's liturgical year.² He granted further general confirmations of its liberty on two occasions. In 1095 he visited Cluny and
consecrated the high altar of Abbot Hugh's third church.³ He also
issued a privilege in which he laid particular emphasis on Cluny's
temporal immunity.⁴ He reinforced it with a letter to Abbot Hugh
about Cluny's altar-dues and tithes.⁵ His final confirmation of
Cluny's liberty followed in 1097. He praised his former monastery because 'ut alter sol enitet in terris', and he especially emphasized its exemption, giving a detailed statement of what it implied.⁶

¹ *Ep.* ix, *P.L.* cli. 291–3. The following passage, with its use of the colloquialism
'buccam aperire', is a clear echo of Gregory's address of 1080: 'Praeterea de-
cernimus atque stabilimus ne quis ultra legatus Romani antistitis vices in vestris
partibus agens, absque ipsius licentia vel preceptione, buccam in vos, aut vestra
monasteria, audeat aperire, vel nisi ad ipsum specialiter dirigatur.'

² Ibid.; cf. *Ep.* cxxxvii, 1095, *P.L.* cli. 410–12. For earlier examples of such a
concession, see Lerche, 'Die Privilegierung der deutschen Kirche durch Papsturkunden', *A.U.F.* iii (1911), 148–57.

³ For his reception at Cluny, see *De adventu Urbani papae II ad monasterium
Cluniacense*, É. Baluze, *Miscellanea*, vi (Paris, 1713), 474–6. Abbot Hugh took the
opportunity to give Urban a fresh place in the devotions of Cluny: 'Pro his itaque
omnibus, necnon etiam et pro anteriori dilectionis familiaritate, postmodum
multiplicibus beneficiorum exhibitionibus erga nos luce clarius propalata, decretum est a supradicto patre nostro ut eius memoria quandiu vixerit ad generalem
missam specialiter agatur, post obitum vero, exceptis his quae illi pro communi
nostrae fraternitatis professione debentur, tricenario scilicet officiis, missis, psalmis,
atque elemosinis, anniversaria dies depositionis ipsius quotannis celebriter sicut pro
abbate huius coenobii recolatur resonantibus signis cum officio pleno et missa ac
XII pauperum refectione.'

⁴ *Ep.* cxxxvii, *P.L.* cli. 410–12; cf. Urban's address at the consecration, *P.L.*
cli. 563–4.

⁵ *Ep.* clxvii, *P.L.* cli. 441–2; cf. the privilege for Marcigny, *Ep.* clxviii, *P.L.* cli.
442–3.

⁶ *Ep.* ccxiv, *P.L.* cli. 485–8. The issuing of this privilege may have been occasioned by the death in 1096 of Bishop Landeric of Mâcon. He was succeeded by
Bishop Berard, who, in the time of Abbot Pons, was to provoke another crisis
with the Cluniacs on the issue of exemption.

Apart from these general confirmations, Urban II's letters provide ample evidence for his unceasing concern to uphold Cluny's rights in particular cases. For example, in 1097 he vindicated it against Duke Odo I of Burgundy and Count Aimo of Bourbon, who were vexing it.[1] Again, in a letter that seems to have had a wide circulation, he supported it against bishops who were trying to interfere in the affairs of some of its dependent priories.[2] He frequently confirmed its authority over houses which were already its subjects,[3] and he encouraged the donation to it of other monasteries.[4]

As he set about the task of rehabilitating the Gregorian Reform, Urban II thus confirmed and perpetuated the position that Gregory VII and his predecessors had granted to Cluny:

It beseems us [he wrote] to make provision for your future peace and to hold up the shield of apostolic protection against the assaults of your enemies on behalf of your monastery, both in its head and in its members.[5]

The only distinctive feature of his support for Cluny was a characteristically conciliatory gesture towards the bishops. He showed a certain willingness to safeguard legitimate episcopal prerogatives, rather than to ride roughshod over them, as earlier papal definitions of Cluny's exemption had done. Thus, in 1088, he laid down that

the bishops, within whose dioceses your possessions (*facultates*) lie, are altogether forbidden to pass judgement upon your monks or your

[1] *Ep.* ccxvi, *P.L.* cli. 488–9.
[2] *Ep.* ccxx, *P.L.* cli. 493–4. The letter was evidently disseminated to Cluny's dependencies; it was preserved at Auch: *Cartulaire du chapitre de l'église métropolitaine d'Auch*, ed. C. Lacave la Plagne Barris, no. clxx, pp. 210–11.
[3] Marcigny, *Ep.* clxviii, *P.L.* cli. 442–3; Montierneuf, *Ep.* clxxxviii, *P.L.* cli. 461–2; Saint-Martial, Limoges, *Ep.* clxxxix, *P.L.* cli. 462–4; Mont Saint-Michel, *Ep.* cxciv, *P.L.* cli. 465; Moissac, *Ep.* cxcvi, *P.L.* cli. 466–7; Saint-Orens, Auch, *Ep.* cxcvii, *P.L.* cli. 467–8; Beaulieu, *Ep.* cxcviii, *P.L.* cli. 468; Figeac, *Ep.* cxcix, *P.L.* cli. 469; Saint-Martin-des-Champs, *Ep.* cc, *P.L.* cli. 470–1, all of 1096.
[4] Saint-Bertin, *Ep.* cclviii, *P.L.* cli. 522; Saint-Germain, Auxerre, *Ep.* ccxxxvi, *P.L.* cli. 538–9.
[5] *Ep.* clxviii, *P.L.* cli. 441.

monasteries, saving, however, the canonical right that they have hitherto had over them.[1]

The last clause, which, as a general ordinance, has no parallel in earlier papal legislation on Cluny's behalf, left elbow-room for the reasonable claims of the bishops to be considered. It probably implied a measure of recognition of such rights as stemmed from the canons of Chalcedon and Orleans. It thus tended usefully to reduce the points of friction between the Cluniacs and the bishops.[2] It was a diplomatic gesture, and in no way a material qualification of papal lordship over Cluny or an abrogation of its liberty.

II. PASCHAL II AND THE LIBERTY OF CLUNY

Paschal II followed in the same tradition. In the part of his pontificate that elapsed before Abbot Hugh's death in 1109, he continued all the assistance that his eleventh-century predecessors had given to Cluny. Like them, he sent a notice of his election to Abbot Hugh.[3] He immediately issued a privilege in confirmation of Cluny's possessions and rights, in which he praised it for its exemplary devotion to the papal cause. In language which matched the eulogy of Gregory VII, he applauded its

zeal for the Lord; its pre-eminence in the religious life (*religionis praerogativa*) by which, in recent times, its congregation has been outstanding (*percelluit*) almost everywhere in the west; and the unshakeable unity by which it has adhered to the Apostolic See through all the storms of the past.

Paschal went on to renew his predecessors' acts in Cluny's favour.[4] In 1100 and 1107 he reinforced this privilege, by assuring Abbot Hugh personally of papal protection for his monastery.[5] In 1100 he

---

[1] *Ep.* ix, *P.L.* cli. 292; cf. Urban's ruling which is preserved in the *Collectio Britannica*, no. 31, P. Ewald, 'Die Papstbriefe der Brittischen Sammlung', *N.A.* v (1879), 361.

[2] Another characteristically peace-making gesture was Urban II's confirmation, in 1095, of the liberties of the church of Mâcon: *Ep.* cliv, *P.L.* cli. 428–9.

[3] *Ep.* i, *P.L.* clxiii. 31.

[4] *Ep.* xxxi, *P.L.* clxiii. 51–3, cf. *Ep.* xxxiv, *P.L.* clxiii. 56–8.

[5] *Epp.* xxxiv, cciv, *P.L.* clxiii. 56–8, 204–5.

also wrote to all the bishops of France, urging them to be vigilant for Cluny's interests throughout the land.[1] He was also, upon at least one occasion, forward to defend Cluny against the claims of local bishops. A record has survived of an agreement which was made at the Council of Mazille, in 1103, between Bishop Norgaud of Autun (1098–1112) and Abbot Hugh of Cluny. It relates how, in concert with Bishop Berard of Mâcon (1096–1121) Norgaud had infringed Cluny's rights in respect of certain churches. The Cluniacs had appealed to Paschal, who quickly sent Cardinal Milo of Palestrina to France, where he was to uphold Cluny's interests as well as to attend to certain other matters. Milo had gone to Cluny and had investigated Abbot Hugh's complaints; he now gave judgement against the bishop of Autun and fully confirmed Cluny's privileges as the popes had conferred them.[2]

Like his predecessor, Paschal also made clear his favour towards Cluny by his concern for the details of its interests. Thus, for example, in 1107 he prohibited the levying, within certain topographical limits, of the toll called 'pedaticum' on travellers to and from Cluny[3]. In 1100 he guaranteed papal protection for the Cluniac priory of Souvigny on the same lines as for Cluny itself.[4] In 1107 he vindicated Cluny's right to possess one of its cells against the claims of Abbot William of Saint-Père, Chartres;[5] and he entrusted the abbey of Saint-Wulmar to Abbot Hugh for its reform.[6] At an uncertain date he also made the abbey of Saint-Germain, Auxerre, subject to Cluny.[7]

These favours that Paschal II conferred upon Cluny and the enthusiastic terms in which he spoke of it, complete the evidence that, during the whole of Abbot Hugh's reign, the popes consistently praised Cluny for its services to the Papacy. They energetically

[1] *Ep.* xxxii, *P.L.* clxiii. 53–4.

[2] Mansi, xx. 1161–4, where the source is stated to have been a Cluniac cartulary; cf. Bruel, 3819, 3820. Milo died whilst in France, and was buried at Marcigny. The gratitude to Milo of the Cluniacs, 'quibus et notus erat et karissimus, atque in legatione commissa specialiter nobis directus', was recorded in Milo's mortuary roll, which is preserved at Padua, and printed by G. Morin, 'Rouleau mortuaire du Cardinal Milon de Palestrina', *Revue d'histoire ecclésiastique*, iv (1903), 241–6.

[3] *Ep.* cxcix, *P.L.* clxiii. 201–2. [4] *Ep.* xxx, *P.L.* clxiii. 49–51.

[5] *Ep.* ccxxiii, *P.L.* clxiii. 220–1. [6] *Ep.* ccxxix, *P.L.* clxiii. 225–6.

[7] *Ep.* ccxliii, *P.L.* clxiii. 235.

upheld its liberty, and they rewarded it, both in general terms and in detail, by protecting its interests. At all stages of the reform of the Church, beginning with its dim foreshadowing under such popes as Benedict VIII and John XIX, the popes eulogized Cluny and increasingly found in its liberty an expression of their ideal for the Church. This liberty was founded upon the bed-rock of Cluny's immunity: Pope Urban II might qualify its exemption by saving the legitimate spiritual claims of the bishops; but its freedom from all manner of temporal claims was always utterly inviolable. However, in the light of its momentous consequences for papal authority, its exemption greatly enhanced its liberty and brought it into a more intimate dependence upon the Apostolic See. The full quality of its liberty was disclosed in the especial favour that the Papacy accorded to it as its own peculiar possession, which was bound to it by a pre-eminence of duty and service.

For the greater part of the eleventh century, and constantly during the reign of Abbot Hugh, Cluny was thus straitly bound to the Papacy because it was the source and guarantor of its liberty. In the recurrent hostility of the church of Mâcon, it also had an ever-present reminder of its dependence upon papal support. At the same time, the Papacy knew full well that the debate with the bishops of Mâcon posed the general question of papal authority in the whole Church, and that it could not afford to let Cluny's case go by default. Because the liberty of Cluny was of such consequence for the Papacy, and because it epitomized its own aspirations for the Church, it was cultivated by the popes and eulogized by them as the quintessence of what the reformers were striving after.

PART II

CLUNY'S EXPANSION IN FRANCE AND THE PAPACY

I

THE SPREAD OF CLUNIAC MONASTICISM

So far, the discussion of Cluny's debt to the Papacy has been primarily concerned with the single case of the mother house. It has therefore only indicated the debt that the Cluniacs owed to the Papacy because it safeguarded and intensified the immunity and initiated the exemption of Cluny itself. But at every stage of Cluny's history the bond of obligation and interest between Cluny and the Papacy was reinforced by papal action to promote and safeguard Cluny's monastic expansion in France. From its early days the popes actively furthered its reforming work, and that of its abbots, in other monasteries; and they took steps to ensure the immunity of Cluny's dependencies as well as of the mother house. In the long run the exemption which the eleventh-century popes conferred upon the Cluniacs 'ubicumque positi', provided part of the background against which Cluniac monasticism assumed its distinctive constitutional forms in the days of Abbot Odilo and, still more, of Abbot Hugh.

Even in the early days of the Cluniac Reform, the popes supported the personal work of Abbot Odo. The monastic role of the first two abbots of Cluny, Berno and Odo, in particular, was old fashioned because it followed the lines of the late-Carolingian monasticism by which the beginnings of Cluny as an institution were so largely shaped. At Cluny, as at the other houses which they simultaneously ruled, Abbots Berno and Odo held an *abbatia*, in the Carolingian sense of a personal office with its attendant rights and duties which the king or some great man conferred upon a monastic figure. An outstanding person might well possess several such *abbatiae* at once. If so, the houses that he ruled would have no stronger common bond than arose from the circumstance of their concurrent subordination to the same abbot; and the bond would not necessarily persist for longer than the term of his life.[1]

---

[1] See Hourlier, *Saint Odilon*, p. 173. It is in this sense that the dispositions of

Nevertheless, in the case of so eminent a man as Abbot Odo,[1] the support of the Papacy, backed up by that of temporal rulers, conferred a peculiar importance upon the complex of *abbatiae* that he held; conversely, the abbot's own position itself testified to the authority of the pope by which it was guaranteed. Abbot Odo held, amongst others, the *abbatiae* of Cluny and of Bourg-Dieu, Déols, which were willed to him by Abbot Berno, and that of Fleury, which came to him later.[2] In all these three cases the abbot's special authority was determined by papal privileges. By virtue of them Abbot Odo was not only encouraged to sponsor the reform of other monasteries; but he was endowed with the hitherto unprecedented right of receiving from elsewhere monks who wished to transfer to a stricter observance. At Cluny this right was conceded in Pope John XI's privilege of 931.[3] At Déols Odo received a similar right in the same year;[4] and, in 938, Pope Leo VII gave him permission to receive monks from elsewhere at Fleury.[5] Because of these concessions Abbot Odo owed to papal authority a unique prerogative in promoting reform from three centres and not merely from one.[6] Cluny's importance during Odo's reign, when it was as yet new and small,[7] must be appreciated as part of this wider complex of its abbot's reforming activity in central and south-eastern France, which he undertook under

Berno's will must be understood. He held, during his lifetime, the *abbatiae*, not only of Cluny, but also of Déols, Massay, Gigny, Baume, and the unidentified monastery referred to as 'Aethicense'. He left the first three to Odo and the remainder to his kinsman, Guy: *Bibl. C.*, cols. 9–12.

[1] For Odo, see esp. the study by Wollasch: *Neue Forschungen*, pp. 88–142.

[2] For the Foundation Charter of Bourg-Dieu (917) with its close similarity to that of Cluny, see E. Hubert, 'Recueil historique des chartes intéressant le département de l'Indre', *Revue archéologique historique et scientifique du Berry* (1899), no. v, pp. 102–7. Fleury came to Odo *c.* 930. For his work there see, besides Wollasch, op. cit., Sackur, *Die Cluniacenser*, i. 88–93.

[3] *Ep.* i, *P.L.* cxxxii. 1055–8.

[4] Hubert, art. cit., no. viii, pp. 120–2.   [5] *Ep.* i, *P.L.* cxxxii. 1075–7.

[6] Wollasch, op. cit., pp. 88–116. That Odo made his three principal monastic centres the means of promoting reform in well-defined areas is suggested by the topographical limits in which they held possessions. Cluny's principal early development lay in the north of Burgundy; that of Déols along the valley of the Indre; and that of Fleury to the north of the Loire.

[7] Towards the end of Odo's rule, Bishop Berno of Mâcon could refer to the 'parvula . . . Cluniensium fratrum societas': Bruel, 408.

papal sponsorship. The pronounced *Romanitas* to which the Cluny of Abbot Odo was already giving clear expression,[1] bears witness to its indebtedness to the Papacy for this sponsorship.

Cluny also began, from an early date, to receive gifts of other monasteries which were entrusted to it for reform and which constituted the nucleus of its later family of subject houses. The Petrine proprietorship and papal protection of Cluny combined with its growing spiritual reputation to attract gifts of other houses, both from the Papacy and from lay magnates. In 932 the nearby monastery of Charlieu was entrusted to it in perpetuity by Pope John XI, in order that Cluny might watch over its immunity.[2] In 929 when Countess Adelaide, widow of Duke Richard of Burgundy, gave Cluny the ancient monastery of Romanmôtier, her motives were at once that it should share Cluny's dependence upon the Apostolic See, and also that it should be ruled by the abbot of Cluny and adopt the Cluniac way of life.[3]

In the first phase of their history, therefore, the Cluniacs were already in several ways indebted to the Papacy for the diffusion of their reforming work and for the growth of their monastic family.

During the latter half of the tenth century, under Abbots Aimard and Majolus, the distribution of Cluny's dependencies,

[1] See Hallinger, 'Zur geistigen Welt der Anfänge Klunys', *D.A.* x (1953–4), 417–45.

[2] *Ep.* ii, *P.L.* cxxxii. 1058–9. Cf. Pope Benedict VII's dictum that Cluny was given to the Papacy 'ad defendum et dilatandum': *Ep.* xiii (978) *P.L.* cxxxvii. 332.

[3] 'Predictus vero abbas [sc. Odo], dum advixerit, vel ipsi monachi idem monasterium ita possideant, ut quamvis apostolicae sedi, sicut et Cluniacus, delegatum sit, semper tamen velut una congregatio sub uno agant atque disponantur abbate, in tantum, ut cum iste decesserit, non illis aut istis liceat sine communi consensu abbatem sibi preficere, nec privatim (quod absit!) isti alium nisi ipsum quem illi habuerint substituere presumant; quoniam valde iniustum esset si illi qui forte velut filii Romanis monasterio succreverint, socialitatem Cluniensium, qui veluti patres locum resuscitant, aliquando disciderint. ... Monachi vero inibi consistentes modum conversationis istius, quae nunc ad informandum eos qui futuri sunt, de Cluniaco transfertur, ita conservent, ut eundem modum in victu atque vestitu, in abstinentia, in psalmodia, in silentio, in hospitalitate, in mutua dilectione et subiectione, atque bono obedientiae, nullatenus imminuant': Bruel, 379. In his confirmation of Cluny's immunity (931), Pope John XI included a reference to the gift of Romanmôtier to it: *Ep.* i, *P.L.* cxxxii. 1055–8.

lands, and possessions became progressively wider. As it did so papal surveillance became more and more requisite for it as a means of safeguarding its increasingly extended interests. In this connection Pope John XIII's letter of 968–71, in which he charged fourteen French bishops to protect Cluny and all its monastic dependencies in the secure enjoyment of their possessions, provides striking evidence of the help that the Papacy could bring to bear on Cluny's behalf wherever it had subject houses and lands.[1] In 998, early in the reign of Abbot Odilo, when the dissolution of the *pagus* in France was adding to the problems of the monasteries, John XIII's letter was followed by Pope Gregory V's confirmation of Cluny's immunity,[2] with its detailed specification of its subject monasteries and cells, and their local rights. Popes Benedict VIII and John XIX were to carry this protection of Cluny's widespread interests still further.

Such papal oversight of Cluny's immunity and freedom from lay depredations, not only in respect of the mother house but also of its dependencies and their possessions wherever they might be, was the first step towards the consolidation of Cluny's monastic dependencies in a single network of privilege. The Burgundian monastery was no longer an isolated house; all its interests were being treated by the Papacy as part of a single nexus, which was corporately endowed with the privileges and the claim to papal protection that had grown up on the basis of the Foundation Charter of the mother house.

But it was the subsequent growth, under far straiter papal oversight, of Cluny's exemption from episcopal control in spiritual matters, that did most to consolidate Cluny's subject houses under its own central authority; and in particular to establish its abbot in a position of exclusive personal rule over the Cluniacs, wherever they were. Such a development in a monastery with extensive reforming connections had, indeed,

---

[1] *Ep.* xxvii, *P.L.* cxxxv. 990–1. The bishops were those of Arles, Lyons, Vienne, Clermont, Valence, Besançon, Mâcon, Châlon-sur-Saône, Le Puy, Avignon, Geneva, Lausanne, Viviers, and one other (*Lurensis*), who cannot be identified. In 955 King Lothar had already confirmed the immunity of Cluny's possessions 'in omnibus ubi regnamus locis': Bruel, 980.

[2] *Ep.* xx, *P.L.* cxxxvii. 932–5.

been foreshadowed at Fleury under Abbo. In 997, when Pope Gregory V met Abbo's desire to throw off the supervision of his bishop, he endowed the abbot of Fleury with a general power of jurisdiction over all men and women under his rule, both at Fleury and elsewhere.[1]

It was, however, in the struggle over Cluny that the potentialities of such a provision were first realized, and that the importance of papal legislation for the internal development of a monastic body was first demonstrated. In 1024 Pope John XIX declared that the exemption of Cluny covered all its monks 'ubicumque positi'. No bishop anywhere might visit them with his malediction or excommunicate them.[2] For the first time in their history the Cluniacs now enjoyed, at least in principle, the full and explicit right to a thoroughgoing freedom from both spiritual and temporal interference of any kind. The growth of exemption had the negative consequence of freeing Cluny, its monks, and as time went on at least some of its dependencies, either absolutely or in part, from the jurisdiction of the bishops. It thus left a vacuum of spiritual authority which had somehow to be filled.

It has already been suggested that, in general terms, this vacuum was filled by the exclusive subjection of Cluny to the Apostolic See. As Gregory VII declared in his allocution of 1080, the Cluniacs 'have remained under the exclusive obedience and defence of St. Peter and of [the Roman] Church'. But it was alien to both the function and the resources of the Papacy to undertake the detailed spiritual oversight of the whole Cluniac body. To provide this oversight was necessarily the task of some agency within that body itself. The personal qualities of the successive abbots of Cluny pointed to the abbot as being, under the aegis of the Apostolic See, the natural centre of spiritual authority in the dependencies of Cluny as at the mother house itself. Such a general exercise of personal and paternal authority respected the spirit of the Rule of St. Benedict, that a monastic family should be a single

[1] '. . . solvendi et ligandi potestatem in viros aut feminas sui ordinis habeat . . .': *Recueil des chartes . . . de Saint-Benoît-sur-Loire*, no. lxxi, p. 187.
[2] See above, p. 34, n. 1.

community under the government of the abbot.[1] In harmony with this spirit, the papal granting to all Cluniac monks of exemption from the authority of the bishops, cleared the way for the abbot of Cluny to become, in all save purely sacramental matters, the bishop of the whole Cluniac body; and for the Cluniac body to be extended and consolidated by the subjection of other houses to the abbot's personal authority.

It would be anachronistic and against the evidence to express his role by importing a generalized idea of exemption of a twelfth-century kind into the eleventh-century constitution of the Cluniac body. Thus, in practice, the abbot's authority was full in respect of some of its houses, in the sense that he might have recourse to any bishop whom he saw fit for episcopal functions, and that the local bishop had no claim to ordain, preach, hold councils, or otherwise exercise jurisdiction. In other houses the abbot's authority was so modified by the rights of local bishops as the exigences of particular situations might dictate.[2] But whatever may have been the diversity of local practice, the principle of the freedom of the Cluniacs 'ubicumque positi' had been firmly enunciated; and it found its complement in that of the universal authority of the abbot of Cluny over all his personal subjects. The first consequence of this papal action on Cluny's behalf was to accelerate the growth of its monastic family during the rest of the eleventh century; for it was after the exemption of the Cluniacs had been thus conceded by Pope John XIX that the rapid expansion of Cluny's dependencies began.[3] This expansion was, of

[1] For this important point, see Hunt, *Cluny under Saint Hugh*, pp. 60–1.

[2] See Constable's comments: *Monastic Tithes from their Origin to the Twelfth Century*, pp. 6–7.

[3] It is very difficult to give accurate figures for the expansion of Cluny, a study of which is urgently needed. But even when Abbot Odilo died, the number of Cluny's dependencies, as recorded in the papal privileges which safeguarded their liberty, did not significantly exceed the number of houses which were governed by Abbot William of Dijon at the height of his power. Thus, Pope Victor II's privilege of 1055 named forty-five monasteries and cells which were subject to Cluny: *Ep.* i, *P.L.* cxliii. 803–8; William's reforming influence reached some forty houses: Ralph Glaber, *Vita Sancti Guillelmi abbatis Divionensis*, 24, *P.L.* cxlii. 715. In 1075, however, Gregory VII's privilege for Cluny named eighty-eight dependencies which fall into the categories of Victor II's: Santifaller, *Q.F.*, no. 107, pp. 95–100.

course, by no means simply a direct consequence of its exemption; but the prestige which Cluny enjoyed in the eyes of the reformers, in view of its developed liberty, did much to promote its spread. It was of still greater importance that the winning of exemption by the Cluniacs was followed by the clear emergence of so many of the most characteristic features of Cluniac monasticism. One of these was the Cluniac form of monastic subjection, whereby the abbot of Cluny was to all intents and purposes the abbot of its directly subject houses and ruled them through a prior who was his personal dependent.[1] The middle of the eleventh century, and, therefore, the era of the consolidation of Cluny's exemption by the Papacy, also witnessed the rise of the peculiarly Cluniac convention that all Cluniac monks, at whatever house they were, were deemed to have been professed at Cluny and to be directly the subjects of its abbot.[2] The abbot of Cluny accordingly began the frequent tours of visitation by which he sought to make effective his oversight of and jurisdiction over his subject houses.[3]

[1] The Romanmôtier Charter of 929 shows that the possibility of this development was present from an early date: above, p. 69. But the arrangements that Abbot Odilo was making for his dependencies between 1005 and 1011, still gave little evidence of the later institution of the subject priory: Hourlier, *Saint Odilon*, pp. 74-6. The increasingly frequent appointment of the prior of Cluny to rule one of its dependencies may have been a step towards it: M. Chaume, 'Les Grands Prieurs de Cluny', *Revue Mabillon*, xxviii (1938), 147-72; and, under Abbot Hugh, monks of Cluny were often sent to be priors of daughter houses: Hunt, *Cluny under Saint Hugh*, pp. 172-3. But the strongest evidence for the development of the dependent priory is, perhaps, provided by the series of Cluniac charters between 1064 and 1076, which either specify or imply the characteristically Cluniac arrangement: Bruel, 3402 (Saint-Felix et Saint-Licer, Tarbes, 1064); 3404 (Goudargues, 1065); 3409 (San Pedro d'Ager, 1066); 3425 (San Marco, Lodi, 1069); 3445 (*Vendrovia*, Toul, after 1070); 3454 (Lézat, 1073); 3469 (Figeac, 1074); 3490-1 (Beaulieu, 1076). The lack of explicit definitions in later charters suggests that, after *c.* 1075, it was a settled institution.

[2] There seems to be no direct evidence for the development of this convention; but Gregory VII's letter to Cardinal Richard of Marseilles in 1082, in which he described how Abbot Hunald of Moissac, one of Cluny's dependent abbeys, was overruled regarding certain of his monks 'iussu maioris abbatis Cluniacensis', indicated that it was by then well established: *Ep. Coll.* 39, p. 556.

[3] The journeyings of Abbot Odilo by which he kept in touch with his monastic empire and with Rome were an object of the satire of Bishop Adalbero of Laon, written at some time between 1022 and 1030: *Les Poèmes satiriques d'Adalberon*, ed. G. A. Huckel (Bibl. de la faculté des lettres à l'université de Paris, xiii, 1901),

74   *Cluny's Expansion in France and the Papacy*

Furthermore, it seems to have been when the abbot of Cluny began, in these ways, to make good his authority over his subject houses, that the Customs of Cluny began to develop in their mature form, with the abbot legislating on behalf of all his subjects.[1] All these things developed at Cluny in a striking way after the Papacy had given it a unique position of privilege; its new position did much to produce the salient features of Cluniac monasticism at its apogee, by clearing the ground for the special developments which characterized the Cluniac body.

In discussions of the milieu in which the eleventh-century constitution of Cluny took shape, two ideas in particular have rightly been insisted upon as having especially contributed to its formation. As they have recently been defined:

The Cluniac system . . . was a conflation of two ideas: the community of the Rule under an abbot, and the dominion and control of a king over his tenants-in-chief and sub-vassals . . . Cluny thus made use of the two most powerful ideas in early medieval society, that of the religious obedience of a monk to his abbot, and that of the fidelity and mutual obligations of vassal and lord. The pivot of the whole system was the abbot of Cluny, who was at once in his spiritual capacity the father and sovereign of all Cluniac monks and in his forensic capacity, as *persona* or lord of the church of Cluny, the overlord to whom all the churches linked to her owed fealty.[2]

These ideas explain much about the structure of the Cluniac body under Abbot Hugh. But, in the light of the foregoing discussion,

pp. 87–128. For the date, see Lemarignier, *Le Gouvernement royal aux premiers temps capétiens (987–1108)*, (Paris, 1965) p. 79, n. 53. The most recent study of Odilo's itinerary is to be found in chapters vi–xiii of Hourlier, *Saint Odilon*; his preoccupation with the visiting of his monasteries during the last months of his life is particularly noteworthy: pp. 113–17. For Abbot Hugh's much wider and more constant itinerary, see Diener, *Neue Forschungen*, pp. 355–417.

[1] See Abbot Odilo's regulations for the observance of 2 Nov.: 'Et ut hoc decretum perpetuum vigore obtineat, volumus et petimus, et precepimus tam in hoc loco, quam in cunctis locis ad istum locum pertinentibus, servetur . . .': *Cons. Farf.* i. 127, *Consuetudines monasticae*, i, ed. Albers, p. 125. In line with this prescription, grants of confraternity with Cluny came to emphasize the solidarity of the Cluniac body by conferring 'partem et societatem omnium bonorum quae fiunt in [Cluny] et in omnibus locis illi pertinentibus': see Cowdrey, 'Unions and Confraternity with Cluny', *J.E.H.* xvi (1965), 154, 160.

[2] Knowles, *From Pachomius to Ignatius*, pp. 12–13.

it is perhaps necessary to add a third idea: that of Cluny as being in principle exempt in head and members from all subjection to earthly authorities and utterly free in its service of St. Peter. By the privileges with which it helped the Cluniacs towards their liberty from external control, both temporal and spiritual, the Papacy performed an indispensable role by providing a kind of matrix within which the special characteristics of Cluniac monasticism in the later eleventh century might take shape. The Cluniac body in France thus owed a great debt to the habit of close collaboration with the Papacy.

At the same time, the special position of the Cluniacs bore witness to the prerogatives of the Papacy by which it was brought into being. By disseminating Cluny's own characteristics, the Cluniac expansion in France testified to the universal nature of papal authority and to its capacity to rule the Church both centrally and locally. In view of the inveterate tendency for the southern French bishops to stand upon the claims of their own order, the widespread Cluniac witness to papal prerogatives was of the utmost importance for their permeation of France, and for the defeat of ideas which were antagonistic to them.

The significance of these characteristics of the Cluniac body may be illustrated by examining such evidence as survives for the position of Cluny's individual dependencies in France.

II

THE VARIETY OF CLUNIAC INFLUENCE

It was in part owing to the special prerogatives with which the Papacy invested the Cluniac body that the abbot of Cluny was able to establish his authority over the large network of his subject houses in France, and over the dependencies which were associated with Cluny by various ties of a less binding character than outright subjection.[1] The general tendency of modern scholarship has, indeed, been to discount the significance of this network as a means by which the Gregorian Reform and its ideals were propagated in France. Thus Hallinger's over-rigid theory in *Gorze–Kluny*, of a consistent and articulated anti-feudal and anti-episcopal programme which the Cluniacs adopted from their earliest days, quickly received effective criticism in the well-documented studies by Diener and Mager in *Neue Forschungen*. They demonstrated how widely the Cluniacs sought reform by agreement with both bishops and lay magnates, and how little they challenged them in practice by a frontal assault upon their positions.

The very great extent to which the Cluniacs worked by such means is clear. Yet it is necessary also to appreciate and to take into fuller account than did the contribution to *Neue Forschungen* the profound changes that took place in the structure of Cluniac monasticism during the eleventh century, and the extent to which these changes bound the Cluniacs to the Papacy by ties of both duty and interest. The papal defence of the liberty of Cluny in its members as well as in its head, indissolubly linked the Cluniac body to the Papacy at the fullest extension of papal authority and jurisdiction. It is thus necessary to look again at as many of Cluny's French dependencies as the surviving evidence allows, in order to

[1] For a discussion of the constitution of the Cluniac body, see Knowles, op. cit., pp. 13-14.

see in what respects their history reflected that of the mother house.[1]

Two general points may usefully be borne in mind, in view of the very differing relationships of Cluny's dependencies with such external authorities as lay lords and bishops. First, given the disintegrated feudal structure of eleventh-century France on the one hand, and the emphatic claims of the French bishops to jurisdiction over monasteries on the other hand, it is antecedently likely that other Cluniac houses would tend to become microcosms of the mother house. They faced similar problems, and their problems were likely to have had similar solutions which were reached by similar means. It is to be expected that they would look for an immunity, on broadly the model of Cluny's own, from the temporal claims of outside authorities. Again, the model of Cluny's exemption and the rights of the Cluniacs 'ubicumque positi' were likely to lead some houses, at least, to aspire to the kind of exemption that Cluny itself enjoyed. In any case, it would become increasingly necessary to establish a *modus vivendi* with the diocesan bishop, which was compatible with the position of the abbot of Cluny as the immediate ruler of all its subject priories. As the examples which are about to be considered make clear, Cluny's dependencies tended, in fact, more and more to model their external relationships upon Cluny's own, and they inevitably sought a greater or less degree of the immunity and

[1] The amount of evidence which survives is not great, for the upheavals in France during the sixteenth and eighteenth centuries took a serious toll. I have endeavoured in this section to take account of all the relevant Cluniac material that is available in print to an English scholar. I do not think it likely that unpublished material would greatly alter the picture. In respect both of its constitution and of the significance of papal support, Cluny stands apart from other great French monasteries like La Trinité, Vendôme, and Saint-Victor, Marseilles, for which abundant records survive: *Cartulaire de l'abbaye de Saint-Victor de Marseille*, ed. B. Guérard, 2 vols. (Paris, 1857); *Cartulaire de l'abbaye cardinale de la Trinité, Vendôme*, ed. C. Métais, 5 vols. (Vannes, 1893-1904); although the Papacy was often active to bring help to French monasteries. A full comparative study of Cluny and other monasteries is badly needed. Some indication of the available evidence is given in F. Lot's articles, 'Liste des cartulaires et recueils contenant des pièces antérieures à l'an 1000', *Bulletin Du Cange*, xv (1940), 5-24; 'Liste des cartulaires et recueils contenant des pièces antérieures à l'an 1100', ibid., xxii (1953), 239-59.

exemption of which the Papacy was ultimately the most effective guarantor. They were drawn to emulate the 'libertas Romana' of the mother house which knew no lordship save that of the Apostolic See. Inevitably, the more they approximated to the pattern of Cluny, the more they became local demonstrations of the claims and aspirations of the contemporary Papacy at their fullest Gregorian expression.

Secondly, however, the very adaptability of the Cluniacs to the differing circumstances in which they worked, which Diener and Mager have rightly noticed, meant that, from place to place, they were likely to stand in very differing relationships to the local ecclesiastical and lay authorities. For example, on and near the Capetian demesne and, more generally, in France to the north of the Loire, Cluniac houses would be less likely to exhibit the conditions of immunity and exemption that marked Cluny itself. This is probably the principal explanation of Abbot Hugh's caution, especially during the first half of his reign, in expanding the Cluniac Reform to the north of the Loire.[1] But to the south and east, and especially in such regions as Burgundy and Aquitaine, there was a greater likelihood that Cluniac priories would tend to become microcosms of Cluny itself.

The probability that Cluniac priories sometimes did but sometimes did not stand in a relation to the Gregorian Reform which was similar to that of Cluny, may be illustrated by taking two extreme and contrasting cases.

I. TWO EXTREME CASES

a. *Saint-Mont*

The case of the priory of Saint-Mont illustrates, perhaps more clearly and fully than any other, how the local needs of a Cluniac priory, and the means by which they were met, served to put it into a relationship with the Papacy that made it in all essential respects a microcosm of the mother house itself.[2]

[1] For the Cluniacs and the Capetian demesne, see Lemarignier, *Le Gouvernement royal aux premiers temps capétiens*, esp. pp. 78, n. 40, 142–5, 199.

[2] *Cartulaire du prieuré de Saint-Mont*, ed. J. de Jaurgain (*Archives historiques de la Gascogne*, Paris and Auch, 1904); see also Schreiber, *Gemeinschaften des Mittelalters*, i. 93–9; A. Breuils, *Saint Austinde, archevêque d'Auch* (Auch, 1895), pp. 176–9.

Saint-Mont was the first Cluniac priory to be established in the Gascon archdiocese of Auch; it thus illustrates the circumstances of France to the south of the Loire. Its importance to Cluny and to the Papacy was the greater because of the position that it occupied on the routes to Castile and to the shrine of St. James at Compostela. A monastery was first founded there, quite independently of Cluny, *c.* 1050, by Count Bernard II Tumapaler of Armagnac (later of Gascony), who acted with the collaboration of a local knight, Raymond of Saint-Mont. It was at first dedicated to St. John the Baptist.[1] In 1055, however, Count Bernard gave it to St. Peter and St. Paul at Cluny. It became a Cluniac priory; lay proprietorship was totally extinguished; and the abbots of Cluny were given an unhampered right to rule it according to their will.[2] It was now necessary for Abbot Hugh to make good his authority.

He at once came up against the claims to spiritual jurisdiction of the diocesan, Archbishop Austindus of Auch (1042–68), who sought to establish his rights over the priory by holding a council and celebrating mass there. When he was rebuffed by the prior, Armannus (1052–62), he redoubled his hostility to its spiritual independence. Thus as Cluny itself was confronted by the claims of the bishop of Mâcon, so Saint-Mont was confronted by those of the archbishop of Auch. A similar problem found a similar solution. A charter which Count Bernard issued in 1062 shows that he took advantage of a personal visit to Saint-Mont by Abbot Hugh of Cluny to reaffirm that he had made his gift of the priory to Cluny without any kind of reservation.[3] The exemption of

---

[1] *Cartulaire*, ed. Jaurgain, no. i, pp. 3–8. This *Notitia fundationis* was written after Saint-Mont was given to Cluny, and the Cluniac influence under which it was compiled must be borne in mind. But the pattern of events is confirmed by the archbishop's account, which is preserved in the 'Black Cartulary' of the cathedral of Auch: *Cartulaires du chapitre de l'église metropolitaine Sainte-Marie d'Auch*, ed. C. Lacave la Plagne Barris, (*Archives historiques de la Gascogne*, Paris and Auch, 1899), no. xiv, pp. 15–17. The *Notitia* states that, from the start, Count Bernard envisaged that it would be subjected to Cluny; cf. *Cartulaire*, ed. Jaurgain, no. vii, pp. 15–17.

[2] Ibid., pp. xiii–xiv.

[3] Ibid., no. vii, pp. 14–20. At this time, Count Bernard travelled to Cluny with Abbot Hugh and was professed as a monk there. He returned to Saint-Mont,

Saint-Mont from the jurisdiction of the archbishop of Auch was publicly vindicated; and it subsequently received the confirmation of a series of papal legates who passed through.[1]

Its immunity, as well as its exemption, was established upon the Cluniac model. This was done by the direct action of a papal legate. In 1073, while he was passing through on his way to Spain, Cardinal Gerald of Ostia conferred upon Saint-Mont a charter of his own, which secured it on the pattern of Cluny itself from lawful and unlawful temporal claims. He asserted that, because it was a priory of Cluny, Saint-Mont had an especial claim to the defence of all those who exercised the authority of St. Peter in the Church:

> Since this place has been lawfully given and assigned to Cluny and is a recently acquired possession of St. Peter, and since we, though unworthy, are a legate of the Prince of the Apostles, we have been asked by its prior, Adhemar,[2] and the rest of the brethren, to set the protection and defence of St. Peter upon all the possessions of this monastery.

They were, therefore, placed under the *tuitio* of St. Peter as fully as was Cluny itself.[3]

Thus, both the immunity and the exemption of Saint-Mont came to be expressly guaranteed by means which included the intervention of a legate of the Apostolic See. In all essential ways the position of this Cluniac priory was a microcosm of that of

where he remained until his death in 1090: see esp. ibid., no. lxviii, pp. 92–4, and p. 3, n. 3.

[1] At the end of the document there appear the later confirmations of Hugh Candidus, Gerald of Ostia, Amatus of Oléron, and Bernard of Toledo, in their capacity as papal legates. Amatus of Oléron is described as 'Romanae ecclesiae cardinalis', a title which is not, to my knowledge, otherwise attested. But all four men functioned as papal legates in France and Spain. The charter was also confirmed by Archbishop Bernard of Auch (1118–26) and Bishop Bernard I of Lescar (1072–95).

[2] Prior c. 1068–79.

[3] *Cartulaire*, ed. Jaurgain, no. vi, pp. 12–14. Gerald also prescribed 'apostolica auctoritate' that the benefits of confraternity with the monks would accrue to those who, after due penance, obtained burial there. This well illustrates how a Cluniac house, dedicated to St. Peter, actively propagated the cult of the Prince of the Apostles and demonstrated the authority of his vicar upon earth.

Cluny itself; like Cluny, it was the property of St. Peter, and as Cluny testified to papal authority in Burgundy, so Saint-Mont testified to it in Gascony.

b. *Longpont*

At the other extreme stands the case of Longpont.[1] It was founded *c.* 1061, as a Cluniac priory, by Guy I, lord of Montlhéry, with the fullest support of Geoffrey, bishop of Paris (1061-95). It increased rapidly in wealth and importance. So far as its constitution is concerned, it was expressly laid down in the bishop's charter at its inception that it should remain under episcopal authority.[2] Situated near Paris and near the Capetian demesne,[3] it showed marked peculiarities which set it in contrast with Saint-Mont. Its sole dedication was to the Blessed Virgin; neither at its foundation nor afterwards did the names of St. Peter and St. Paul ever appear in the surviving documents concerning it. From the very first, the priory was not placed under papal protection; but it remained in the care of the bishop of Paris. In *c.* 1080, when it received the gift of the church of St. Martin in a vill called *Ordeacus*, the bishop's jurisdiction over the church was expressly reserved.[4] In the surviving evidence there is no hint that Abbot Hugh ever visited it,[5] nor that any papal legate had dealings on its behalf. Because of its proximity to the royal demesne, Pope Urban II did not visit it upon his journey in France.[6] It was not until 1152 that a papal privilege was issued in its favour, by Pope Eugenius III; and he scrupulously reserved the 'canonica iustitia' of the bishop of Paris.[7]

[1] For the documents, see *Le Cartulaire du prieuré de Longpont*, ed. J. Marion (Lyons, 1879).

[2] Ibid., no. li, pp. 97-9.

[3] For the marriage arrangement by which King Philip I, at the very end of his reign, added Montlhéry to the Capetian demesne, see Suger, *Vie de Louis VI le Gros*, viii, ed. H. Waquet (Paris, 1964), pp. 36-8.

[4] *Cartulaire*, no. cclvii, pp. 215-16.

[5] However, Odo, grand prior of Cluny, figured as a witness to one of its charters: ibid., no. clxvii, pp. 164-5.

[6] Urban's avoidance of the royal demesne and its vicinity was a consequence of King Philip I's marriage with Bertrada of Montfort: Becker, *Urban II*, i. 192-201.

[7] *Cartulaire*, no. i, pp. 59-61.

II. CLUNIAC DEPENDENCIES IN FRANCE
AND PAPAL SUPPORT

Saint-Mont and Longpont stand as extreme cases, whether for the closeness with which Cluny's priories were subjected to it, or for the extent to which they reflected its liberty, or for the ways in which they benefited by the exercise of papal authority. In every material respect Saint-Mont was essentially like Cluny, Longpont was unlike. Most of Cluny's dependencies fell somewhere between the two extremes. Next, therefore, the records of Cluniac houses will be examined, in the relatively few cases where they have survived, are readily available, and yield relevant evidence. Upon the basis of this evidence, an attempt may be made to draw some conclusions about how far Cluny's dependencies were themselves assimilated to the liberty of Cluny; how far they stood in need of and received papal support; and how far, in doing this, they served to demonstrate the nature of papal authority as the reformed Papacy understood it, and to propagate it in the various regions of France. Individual houses are considered in chronological order of their first association with Cluny.

a. *Sauxillanges*

Sauxillanges (dioc. Clermont)[1] was founded in 912 by Duke William of Aquitaine, the founder of Cluny itself.[2] When it was founded it was expressly placed under the *tuitio* of the Roman See.[3] In its Cartulary Abbots Odo, Majolus, and Hugh were all referred to as 'abbas Cluniacensis et Celsiniacensis'; and it is clear that, in Abbot Hugh's time, Sauxillanges was in every respect a dependent priory of Cluny.[4] His personal authority as its abbot was referred to,[5] and he visited it several times.[6] At least one donor bore eloquent testimony to his personal holiness and to the efficacy of his prayers.[7] Yet for practically the whole of the eleventh

---

[1] See *Cartulaire de Sauxillanges*, ed. H. Doniol (Clermont-Ferrand and Paris, 1864).

[2] *Cartulaire*, no. 146, pp. 135–7.   [3] *Cartulaire*, no. 14, pp. 51–2.

[4] *Cartulaire*, no. 566, p. 418.   [5] *Cartulaire*, no. 571, pp. 423–4.

[6] *Cartulaire*, no. 831, p. 578; no. 886, p. 601; no. 582, pp. 428–9; no. 801, pp. 563–4; no. 854, p. 588; no. 698, pp. 503–4; no. 628, p. 457; no. 569, pp. 421–2.

[7] *Cartulaire*, no. 569, pp. 421–2.

century there is no hint that the Papacy counted for anything positive in its history. In 1095, however, this state of affairs was changed. Urban II himself visited it to consecrate its monastic church; and to mark the occasion he conferred upon it extensive rights of immunity and exemption.[1] Thus, if at rather a late date, Sauxillanges came to enjoy privileges, conferred by papal action, which were comparable with those of Cluny.

b. *Paray-le-Monial*

Paray-le-Monial (dioc. Autun),[2] which became a Cluniac priory in 999, having earlier been under Cluniac influence, is another fairly well-documented priory, which owed much to Abbots Majolus, Odilo, and Hugh.[3] However, its records provide on evidence of any indebtedness to the Papacy for action upon its behalf at any stage of its history.

c. *Saint-Flour*

Saint-Flour (dioc. Clermont), in the Auvergne, is of especial importance; for it well illustrates the debt that, even before the Gregorian age, Cluny already owed to the Papacy in respect of the active oversight of one of its dependencies.[4]

The history of Saint-Flour began, so far as its relations with Cluny were concerned, during the local breakdown of the Carolingian order of society at the end of the tenth century, in face of which Cluny itself found effective help from the popes. The great county of the Auvergne had already become subdivided into six constituent counties; now these, in their turn, were disintegrating. A multitude of lesser feudal lords were jostling with each other for land and dependants. They were seeking to reduce their neighbours by force of arms to the status of their own sub-vassals. One of the counties that disappeared was that of Tallande, and the principal lord who filled the vacuum that it left was a certain Amblard,

---

[1] *Cartulaire*, no. 472, pp. 356–8; Urban II, *Ep.* clix, *P.L.* cli. 432–3.

[2] See *Cartulaire du prieuré de Paray-le-Monial*, ed. U. Chevalier (Paris, 1890).

[3] *Cartulaire*, no. 14, p. 12.

[4] The principal sources for the events summarized in this section are to be found in *Cartulaire du prieuré de Saint-Flour*, ed. M. Boudet (Monaco, 1910), nos. ii–vi, pp. 3–18; for their reliability, see Boudet's introduction, pp. ix–xxxi, xliii; and, for a full discussion of the foundation of Saint-Flour, pp. clxvii–clxxxviii.

lord of Nonette. His lordship included the rock of Indiciac, upon which there had long stood an oratory served by canons. In it rested the remains of St. Florus, whom legend held to have been one of Christ's seventy disciples and to have been present at the Last Supper. The immediate lord of Indiciac was Amblard of Nonette's uncle and vassal, Astorg of Brezons. He was a married clerk and had led a life of brigandage; but in *c.* 996, he decided to atone for his sins by endowing a monastery. So in two charters and with the eventual consent of his nephew, the count, he gave the church of St. Florus at Indiciac to Cluny.[1] Abbot Odilo took good care to seek papal protection for so new and vulnerable a gift. After its initial donation its name figures in Pope Gregory V's confirmation, in 998, of Cluny's possessions.[2]

It was, however, a long time before Cluny was able to derive any benefit from the gift. Astorg died soon afterwards and left his lands to a relative, Amblard of Brezons. Amblard of Nonette, for his part, did nothing to establish the Cluniacs in the oratory of St. Florus. Instead he destroyed the church and was the associate of Amblard of Brezons in years of successful local warfare. The latter made Indiciac his principal residence and built a castle there; from this time the place was known as Saint-Flour.

But by about 1025 Amblard of Brezons, in his turn, began to repent of his violent and disorderly life. He and his wife resolved to implement the gift of Saint-Flour to Cluny. At first Amblard of Nonette would have none of it; not even when he was reminded that, with the sanction of a papal privilege, it belonged to God and St. Peter. Then a judicial murder, by which he and his wife disposed of a kinsman, excited general horror amongst their neighbours and brought them to repent. Amblard of Nonette went to Bishop Stephen of Clermont,[3] who refused to absolve him but sent him to the Cluniacs' staunch friend, Pope John XIX. Both Amblards travelled to Rome together. The Pope absolved them; but he required them to establish the monastic life at Saint-Flour, which he gave to Abbot Odilo of Cluny. Soon afterwards

---

[1] Bruel, 2790 (incorrectly dated).
[2] *Ep.* xx, *P.L.* cxxxvii. 932–5.
[3] For the bishop and the Cluniacs, see above, p. 21, n. 2.

the two Amblards were in Rome again, and in Odilo's presence the gift of Saint-Flour to Cluny was effectually completed.

Abbot Odilo now spared no pains to make himself secure in the possession of Saint-Flour. He had the charter of donation published at Cluny and at Saint Flour,[1] and he quickly introduced monks from the Cluniac priory of Sauxillanges. He built a new church, increased its endowments, and established its immunity. The two Amblards formally delivered the town of Saint-Flour into the prior's possession.

The thirty years' process whereby Saint-Flour became securely established as a Cluniac priory illustrates the vicissitudes to which the anarchy of French feudal society in the early eleventh century subjected Cluny's dependencies. It indicates that when violence was rife and no trust could be placed in lay feudatories, the Papacy could, at least eventually, provide a real safeguard for monasteries and their property. With the pope's authority to support them, such bishops as Stephen of Clermont could bring spiritual sanctions to bear upon the likes of Amblard of Nonette, and so make good the results of even a temporary repentance. The abbot of Cluny could look to the pope with particular confidence because of the common dedication to St. Peter of the Apostolic See, of Cluny, and of many of its dependencies. It was also at least indirectly a gain to the Papacy that, after 1025, St. Peter took pride of place over St. Florus amongst the patron saints of Saint-Flour. For St. Peter's proprietorship was a reminder of all the claims and benefits that centred upon the Prince of the Apostles, and it established his name firmly in a new locality in France.

At Saint-Flour as at Cluny, the interests of the Papacy and of the Cluniacs were mutual. They were apparent in a bond that, as its charters illustrate, ensured the well-being of Saint-Flour through the remainder of the eleventh century.

d. *Vézelay*

In the eleventh century Vézelay (dioc. Autun), at which the dispositions of Cluny's Foundation Charter had been so largely

---

[1] Not without an attempt by Amblard of Nonette to withdraw at the last minute.

anticipated, came under the authority of the abbots of Cluny. It did not become a subject priory but remained an abbey with a large measure of autonomy.[1]

It was first commended to Abbot Odilo in 1026, when Count Landeric of Nevers expelled the abbot and monks, and introduced Cluniacs in their place.[2] He did this without consulting the bishop of Autun, who reacted by threatening to take back the monastery of Mesvres, which he had given to Abbot Odilo, and by excommunicating the Cluniac monks of Vézelay. The monks complained that this action contravened the liberty that Vézelay had always enjoyed by virtue of its own longstanding history of papal privileges.[3] They arrogantly trampled upon the bishop's letters to them and so scandalized many who would otherwise have been their supporters. Abbot William of Dijon was called upon to intervene. He acted as a peacemaker and approached Abbot Odilo in order to take counsel about the situation at Vézelay. The result was that Vézelay remained subject to Abbot Odilo. These events in which Cluny's interests were in jeopardy, formed part of the background to Pope John XIX's confirmation of its rights in 1027.

By the last decade of the eleventh century, Vézelay again stood in need of reform; and, in c. 1096, Abbot Hugh intervened to carry it out.[4] His activities once more raised the problem of the rights of the bishop of Autun. Under Pope Paschal II the Papacy twice intervened on behalf of the monks against the bishop. In 1102 Paschal wrote to Abbot Altardus of Vézelay a letter in which he safeguarded Vézelay's freedom to seek the consecration of its churches and the ordination of its monks and clerks from any

---

[1] Cf. its place in papal confirmations of Cluny's liberties, e.g. Stephen IX's of 1058, *Ep.* viii, *P.L.* cxliii. 883.

[2] See Abbot William of Volpiano's letter to Abbot Odilo, *P.L.* cxli. 869–72; also Sackur, *Die Cluniacenser*, ii. 38–9, and Hourlier, *Saint Odilon*, pp. 74–5.

[3] 'Ipsi vero, fidentes apostolicis privilegiis quibus libertas eiusdem loci ab antecessoribus provisa est, pro nihilo eius sententiam computaverunt, et nihil de interdictis dimittere curaverunt': William of Volpiano, *ubi supra*. For the papal privileges, see Hugh of Poitiers, *Historia Viziliacensis monasterii*, i, in D'Achéry, *Spicilegium*, ii. 498–505.

[4] Anonymous secundus, *Alia miraculorum quorumdam sancti Hugonis abbatis relatio, Bibl. C.*, col. 455.

bishop, subject to the counsel of the abbot of Cluny. The abbot of
Cluny was to have oversight of abbatial elections and the rights
of the bishops of Autun were strictly circumscribed.[1] In the
following year a settlement that was rather more conciliatory to
the bishop of Autun was made by Cardinal Milo of Palestrina
during his visit to Cluny. He negotiated an agreement between
Bishop Norgaud of Autun and Abbot Hugh of Cluny, according
to which the bishop might not exact a profession of obedience
from the abbot of Vézelay; but the monks were to receive holy
orders from him so long as he was canonically elected. If he were
not so elected they might have recourse to any canonically elected
bishop of their choice.[2]

The Cluniacs thus acknowledged a debt to the Papacy for the
longstanding privileges of Vézelay. They also twice had the
benefit of direct action by the Papacy on behalf of its rights in
face of the spiritual jurisdiction of the bishops of Autun; although
the final arrangement was based upon a compromise.

e. *Barbezieux*

The monastery of Notre-Dame de Barbezieux (dioc. Saintes)
was founded *c.* 1040 by Audoin, lord of Barbezieux, with the
consent of Archbishop Geoffrey of Bordeaux (1027–43). It was
built, during the next few years, on land which belonged to the
chapter of Saint-Seurin at Bordeaux. During travels in Burgundy,
Audoin fell gravely ill near Cluny. He thereupon gave Barbezieux
to it and became a monk at Cluny in anticipation of his death,
which probably followed soon afterwards.[3]

The gift was challenged by the dean and canons of Saint-Seurin,
and the Cartulary of the cathedral contains two accounts of the
steps that they took in order to frustrate it. The first account, dated
1060, described how Audoin's son, Iterius, had been brought to recognize tha this father had erred when he gave the church to Cluny.
In token of the rights of Saint-Seurin and of the archbishop,

[1] *Ep.* lxxxiii, *P.L.* clxiii. 102–4.   [2] Bruel, 3819.
[3] 'Barbezieux. Son prieuré aux xie et xiie siècles', *Archives historiques de la Saintogne et de l'Aunis*, xli (Paris and Saintes, 1911), no. i, pp. 1–2.

an annual tribute of ten shillings was to be paid to the saint in perpetuity.[1] The second and later account is more circumstantial.[2] It was drawn up in the name of Iterius himself. It describes how, when he succeeded to his father's inheritance, he found that the church of Notre-Dame was part of it. While he was vacillating as to whether it belonged to Saint-Seurin or to himself, the monks of Cluny presented their claim to it on the strength of his father's gift. When the canons of Saint-Seurin informed Archbishop Gozelin of Bordeaux (1059–86) of the Cluniac claim, he brought the matter before Bishop Amatus of Oléron at the Council of Bordeaux (1080). As a result, Iterius was persuaded that he should surrender Notre-Dame to the cathedral. He was, however, afterwards concerned to secure the fulfilment of his father's intentions. Prompted by the Cluniacs, he approached the chapter and secured from them a concession that he might give Notre-Dame to Cluny, in return for a single payment to Saint-Seurin of a hundred shillings, and an annual payment of five shillings.[3]

In the case of Barbezieux, Bishop Amatus of Oléron gave judgement against the Cluniacs, in circumstances which clearly called for him to do so. But the Cluniacs were quickly able to secure the church of Notre-Dame by a negotiated settlement. Amatus's judgement in no way hindered the proper prosecution of their claim to Barbezieux, or its eventually passing to them.

f. *Marcigny-sur-Loire*

Marcigny (dioc. Autun) was founded by Abbot Hugh himself *c*. 1055 on his own family lands, and it gradually acquired a large and far-flung endowment. It is the earliest instance of a double monastery under the authority of the abbot of Cluny which comprised both monks and nuns; Abbot Hugh devoted careful

---

[1] *Cartulaire de l'église cathédrale Saint-Seurin de Bordeaux*, ed. J.-A. Brutails (Bordeaux, 1897), no. xii, p. 13.

[2] The date must be 1080 or slightly later. The first date in the document, 1070, is before the pontificate of Gregory VII, during which it was written. The ninth year of Gregory VII, by which it was also dated, ran from 1081 to 1082. Amatus of Oléron's Council of Bordeaux, which is the *terminus a quo*, was in 1080.

[3] *Cartulaire de Saint-Seurin*, no. xiii, pp. 14–15.

attention to its affairs.[1] Its records suffered severe damage in the sixteenth and eighteenth centuries; but a careful attempt has recently been made to recover and edit the documents which remain.[2]

During Abbot Hugh's reign the close family link which he had with Marcigny seems usually to have ensured its security. But there were three occasions when the help of the Papacy was useful to him. The first was in its early days when, in 1063, during his legatine mission on behalf of Cluny, Cardinal Peter Damiani was present at Marcigny to support Abbot Hugh in settling the case of a knight, Bernard of Chavroches, who had repeatedly pestered the priory with his claims against it. In the legate's presenc ehe agreed to desist, in return for a payment of fifteen pounds in respect of the claims that he put forward.[3] The settlement seems to have been final, for Bernard later became a monk and gave a forest to Marcigny.[4] Secondly, in 1095, Urban II confirmed Marcigny's privileges as a Cluniac priory.[5] Thirdly, soon afterwards, a charter of Abbot Hugh's, addressed to his great-nephew, Count Geoffrey IV of Semur, provides evidence of hostility on his part, which Hugh used papal support to overcome. Geoffrey had added to a long series of vexations by unjustly arresting a citizen of the town of Marcigny. In 1102 Abbot Hugh dealt with him in the presence of Pope Paschal II's legate, Milo, cardinal-bishop of Palestrina, and Archbishop Raymond of Auch. Geoffrey swore before them to observe the rights of the town of Marcigny for the future, as well as the other rights of the Cluniacs. Milo then intervened on behalf of the pope and exhorted Geoffrey to keep his oath. He reinforced the sanctions of Abbot Hugh's charter by the authority of St. Peter and the Holy Roman Church.[6]

---

[1] *P.L.* clix. 947–52. For an account of it, see Hunt, *Cluny under Saint Hugh*, pp. 186–94; also J. Wollasch, 'Ein cluniasensisches Totenbuch aus der Zeit Abt Hugos von Cluny', *Frühmittelalterliche Studien*, ed. K. Hauck, i (Berlin, 1967) pp. 406–43, esp. 421–4.

[2] *Le Cartulaire de Marcigny-sur-Loire (1045–1144)*, ed. J. Richard (Dijon, 1957).

[3] *Cartulaire*, no. 121, pp. 90–1.   [4] *Cartulaire*, no. 83, pp. 60–1.

[5] *Ep.* clxviii, *P.L.* cli. 442–3.

[6] Richard, op. cit., no. 288, pp. 166–71. The charter contains an important statement by Abbot Hugh about the foundation and early history of Marcigny.

Even in the case of a priory which was so closely bound to
Abbot Hugh as was Marcigny, the Abbot thus found papal
support of great use at times of especial need.

g. *Saint-Martial, Limoges*

Saint-Martial, Limoges,[1] was given to Cluny in 1062 by
Adhemar II, *vicomte* of Limoges (1052–93). It had been founded
in Carolingian times, and had an unbroken succession of abbots
since 848. Its transfer to Cluny was resolutely resisted by its monks.

Evidence for the introduction of Cluniac monasticism survives
both from the Cluniac side and from that of the monks who
opposed it. According to the Cluniac charter which recorded the
transfer, Adhemar's gift was prompted partly by the laxity of its
monks in observing the Rule of St. Benedict, and partly by the
simoniacal practices which had invariably marred the election of
former abbots. These practices, it was said, had involved them in
a 'heresy' which St. Peter himself had condemned in the earliest
days of the Church,[2] and which Pope Leo IX and his successors
had more lately condemned. Adhemar fully resigned to Cluny all
his rights in the monastery, except an annual rent of two hundred
shillings and the right to the use of a sumpter-horse and its driver
in time of war. He also reserved certain rights to hospitality that
the counts of Poitou enjoyed there. His charter was drawn up
with the consent and by the authority of Bishop Iterius of Limoges
and the canons of the cathedral. It stated that the rights of the
Cluniacs at Saint-Martial were to be guaranteed by the bishops of
Limoges and by the Apostolic See.[3] In spite of this impressive
weight of local support, the transfer of the monastery to Cluny
did not, in fact, take place peaceably. Another source that is
favourable to Cluny, the narrative of Cardinal Peter Damiani's
French journey, describes how the monks of Saint-Martial

For the circumstances of Cardinal Milo's presence at Cluny, see above, p. 89.
Milo died during his visit to France, and was buried at Marcigny: see above,
p. 62, n. 2.

[1] For a study and documents, see C. de Lasteyrie, *L'Abbaye de Saint-Martial de
Limoges* (Paris, 1901).

[2] Cf. Acts 8 : 14–24.

[3] Bruel, 3383; de Lasteyrie, op. cit., no. vi, pp. 426–7.

refused to render obedience. They withdrew from the monastery, persecuted the Cluniac monks whom Abbot Hugh introduced, and were responsible for a fire that burnt the town of Limoges.[1]

That Abbot Hugh met with resistance on the part of the monks of Saint-Martial is confirmed, from their side, by an account of the course of events written by one of their number.[2] The monk maintained that the Cluniacs had wrongfully invaded his monastery: its full independence, he said, was guaranteed by a grant of immunity of King Louis the Pious;[3] and its liberty had been confirmed by Pope Leo IX.[4] He further complained that Abbot Hugh had for a long time been intriguing with the *vicomte* to secure Saint-Martial for Cluny. He had been working upon him through his friend, Peter, a knight of Limoges, who was *excausarius* of Saint-Martial.[5] Adhemar had refrained from acting on Cluny's behalf until the death, in 1062, of Abbot Mainard.[6] But then, primed, or so the monk alleged, by Abbot Hugh's gifts to him of a fine horse, called Miliscut, and of much gold, he acceded to Peter's promptings on Cluny's behalf. When the monks tried to elect a new abbot of their own, the *vicomte* resisted them so violently that they were forced to flee. With the armed support of the *vicomte* and his knights Abbot Hugh, who had himself hastened to Limoges, took possession and intruded his own monks.

---

[1] *De Gallica Petri Damiani profectione*, 14, M.G.H. Scr. xxx. 1043.

[2] De Lasteyrie, no. vii, pp. 426–9. For another statement that the *vicomte* acted 'per fraudem', see the version of Geoffrey of Vigeois, *Chronica Gaufredi prioris Vosiensis*, xiv, *Novae bibliothecae manuscriptorum librorum*, ed. P. Labbe, ii (Paris, 1657), 287–8. Geoffrey, however, approved of the results of the Cluniac reform at Limoges.

[3] See the spurious diploma of Louis the Pious, de Layesterie, op. cit., no. ii, pp. 420–1.

[4] There is no evidence that Pope Leo IX ever issued a privilege in favour of Saint-Martial.

[5] *Excausarius*: at Limoges, the title of an agent with certain powers of representing the monastery and its interests at law: C. du Cange, *Glossarium mediae et infimae Latinitatis*, s.v. The title may, however, already have become a family name: de Lasteyrie, op. cit., p. 84.

[6] All the documents seem to make it clear that Abbot Mainard died before Saint-Martial was given to Cluny, in spite of de Lasteyrie's interpretation of the Chronicle of Geoffrey of Vigeois, *Chronica Gaufredi prioris Vosiensis*, xiii, Labbe, p. 284: op. cit., pp. 82–4.

So [the monk concluded] the rightful monks were driven out by lay might and high-handed violence. Those who were responsible acted by their own sheer force, against law, against right, against what is good, against the canons of the church, against papal decrees and against all ecclesiastical order. In face of all protests, they utterly disregarded the law, by handing over the monastery to Abbot Hugh and setting him up as abbot in the seat of Saint Martial.

Such are the two versions of how Saint-Martial was given to Cluny. It is clear from them that, in 1063, the support of the bishop and the *vicomte* of Limoges was insufficient to enable Abbot Hugh to enjoy the gift of the monastery. Not only could the monks of Saint-Martial not be quietened; but they claimed a papal sanction for their independence which, however insecure it may have been, could only be overcome by a direct exercise of papal authority. In these circumstances the coming to France, in 1063, of Cardinal Peter Damiani provided Abbot Hugh with a timely opportunity. As the author of the *De Gallica Petri Damiani profectione* put it,

Unless the authority of Rome had been brought to bear and unless someone from the Apostolic See who inspired awe had come to its aid, the monastery [of Saint-Martial] seemed likely to be ruined and to suffer the gravest harm.[1]

He went on to relate how Abbot Hugh took advantage of Peter Damiani's ultramontane journey to solicit his intervention at Limoges. Peter Damiani at first hesitated;

but, because he had come for the safety of Abbot Hugh's monastery, he speedily acquiesced, and showed himself willing to help Cluny in its members, wherever they were situated (*ubicumque positi*).

Peter Damiani himself travelled to Limoges with Abbot Hugh. When they arrived the monks refused to confer with them. Peter Damiani therefore enlisted the aid of the bishop and the *vicomte*. He accused the monks before them of disobedience to a legate of the Apostolic See and to their rightful abbot; and he threatened

---

[1] *De Gall. Pet. Dam. prof.* 14, *M.G.H. Scr.* xxx. 1043.

them with excommunication, although he passed no definitive sentence.[1]

Peter Damiani's companion did not continue the story beyond this point. However, it is clear from the monk of Saint-Martial that Abbot Hugh's rule was now firmly established. Saint-Martial became a Cluniac dependency, although its head retained the title of abbot. Abbot Hugh installed there a conciliatory abbot named Adhemar who ruled it from 1063 until 1114.[2] So long as Iterius and his successor, Guy (1076–86),[3] were bishops of Limoges, Saint-Martial seems to have enjoyed a period of growth and calm.

It was broken with the advent of Bishop Humbald (1087–95), which introduced a troubled period when the value to the monks of papal protection was again made clear. As abbot of Limoges, Adhemar claimed that he had the right to take an active part in the election of the bishop. But he complained that he had not been present at Humbald's election, and he objected to Humbald because he was not personally well known at Limoges. An attempt by Humbald to take possession of the see led to violence between the citizens who supported the bishop, and the men of the *vicomte* who supported the abbot. Abbot Adhemar joined the abbots of Uzerche, Tulle, and Solignac in complaining to Archbishop Richard II of Bourges. They gave him their version of events and urged him to delay the consecration of Humbald.[4]

The result of this appeal to the metropolitan is not known. But soon afterwards, both Abbot Adhemar and Bishop Humbald appealed to Rome, and appeared there in person before Pope Urban II. The pope gave his sentence for the abbot; but, on his way home, the bishop forged papal letters, which purported to settle the matter in his own favour.[5] He found credence for them

[1] Ibid., 15, pp. 1043–4. It was Peter Damiani's zeal on this occasion which led the Cluniacs to grant him the confraternity that he so greatly prized.

[2] For his rule, see de Lasteyrie, op. cit., pp. 87–92.

[3] For his gifts to Cluny, see Bruel, 3490, 3491.

[4] For the letter, see de Lasteyrie, op. cit., no. viii, pp. 429–31. For an account of the events, see Geoffrey of Vigeois, *Chron. Gauf. prioris Vos.* xxvi, ed. Labbe, pp. 291–2, and xxviii, p. 295.

[5] They are printed by Baluze, *Miscellanea*, vi (1713), 407–9.

when he got back to Limoges, and it seems that Abbot Adhemar was persuaded to receive him publicly as bishop. In 1095, however, while he was making his progress through France, Urban II himself came to Limoges. He stayed at Saint-Martial and consecrated the new cathedral of Saint-Étienne[1] and the basilica of Saint-Sauveur, which Adhemar had just completed. During his visit the pope expressed surprise at finding Bishop Humbald in office. He asked by what right he had taken possession of his bishopric. The forged bulls were produced and inspected by Urban's chancery clerks. The forgery was detected, and Urban deposed and excommunicated Humbald.[2] In 1096 Urban issued a detailed privilege for Saint-Martial in which was included a lengthy account of its history as a dependency of Cluny. He confirmed its liberty fully and in great detail.[3]

In Peter Damiani's decision that he must help Cluny, not only in its head, but also in its members wherever they were situated, the value to the Cluniacs of papal defence of their interests elsewhere than at Cluny itself is particularly well illustrated. The whole history of Saint-Martial shows the multiplicity of threats that might face a Cluniac house: the hostility of monks who resisted reform; the threat of local factional strife between citizens and feudatories; the vagaries of local bishops; the uncertainty of help, whether from well-disposed local feudatories, or from bishops, or from Abbot Hugh himself; the danger of forged privileges by popes whether dead or living, which might be used against Cluniac interests. Direct papal intervention, either through a legate like Peter Damiani or, best of all, by the personal presence of the pope himself as in the case of Urban II, was the best assurance of security against the dangers that beset the Cluniacs. In addition to vindicating Cluniac interests, such intervention served as a visible demonstration of papal authority to the ecclesiastical and lay magnates who were in any way affected by it.

---

[1] *Chronicon Bernardi Iterii armarii sancti Martialis, s.a.* 1095, *Chroniques de Saint-Martial de Limoges*, ed. H. Duplès-Agier (Paris, 1874), pp. 49–50.

[2] *Chron. Gauf. prioris Vos.* xxvii, p. 294; cf. Baluze, *Misc.* vi, 409–10.

[3] *Ep.* clxxxix, *P.L.* cli. 462–4.

h. *Saint-Gilles*

The connection between Cluny and Saint-Gilles (dioc. Nîmes) was, in general, tenuous and uncertain.[1] The history of Saint-Gilles's relations with Cluny began, as it would seem, in 1066. Before this date it had been subject to the sole authority of the Roman Church.[2] In 1066, however, at a large assembly of bishops and lay lords in the church of Saint-Baudice, near Nîmes, the lately widowed Countess Almodis of Toulouse and her son, Count Raymond of Rodez and Nîmes, gave Saint-Gilles to Abbot Hugh and his successors. Because it was already an allod of the Papacy, papal rights and an annual *census* to Rome of ten shillings were duly safeguarded.[3] The immediate sequel to this grant is not clear. However, it seems likely that the monks resisted the attempt to commit them to Cluny. A new abbot, Berald, began his reign in 1067. He was consecrated by Pope Alexander II;[4] and in a letter of 1074 to Bishop Froterius of Nîmes, Pope Gregory VII vigorously defended Abbot Berald's independence of all external authority whatsoever, and was absolutely silent about any bond with Cluny.[4]

Within two years, however, Gregory's attitude to Berald had completely changed. He named the monastery of Saint-Gilles in his general confirmation of Cluny's possessions in December 1075;[5] and at his Lent Council of 1076 he excommunicated Berald.[6] In a letter to the monks of Saint-Gilles which was probably written soon after, he explained that he had entrusted them to Abbot Hugh of Cluny so that he might reform their monastery. But he disavowed any intention of permanently giving Saint-Gilles, which belonged to the Roman See, to the abbot of Cluny. Abbot Hugh was merely to hold authority while he reformed it

---

[1] See É. Goiffon, *Saint-Gilles, son abbaye, sa paroisse, son grand-prieuré* (Nîmes, 1882).

[2] St. Giles was believed himself to have given the monastery to St. Peter: see the spurious privilege of Pope Benedict II, É. Goiffon, *Bullaire de Saint-Gilles* (Nîmes, 1882), no. i, p. 3; and the privilege of Pope John VIII (878), ibid., no. iv, pp. 5–10.

[3] Bruel, 3410.   [4] *Reg.* i. 68, 22 Mar. 1074, pp. 97–9.

[5] Santifaller, *Q.F.*, no. 107, p. 98.

[6] *Reg.* iii. 10a, 14–20 Feb. 1076, p. 269.

once for all, and while, on the pope's behalf, he saw to the election of a new abbot. The monks evidently entertained fears that Abbot Hugh would act too drastically. Gregory reassured them by saying that he had instructed him to be gentle and fair; they might complain to the pope if his measures were unjust or oppressive. There was no question of Saint-Gilles being placed under any dominion save that of Rome alone.[1] The evidence suggests that Gregory did not know of the donation of Saint-Gilles to Cluny in 1066; that he sought to make temporary use of Abbot Hugh to reform Saint-Gilles after the disgrace of Abbot Berald; and that this provoked the unexpected fears of the monks. But in 1076 there was no intention on Gregory's part that it should be permanently subject to the abbot of Cluny.

The later history of Cluny's relations with Saint-Gilles is no less opaque. In 1096 Pope Urban II made a pilgrimage to it and issued a privilege in which he reiterated its sole dependence upon the Apostolic See and made no reference to Cluny.[2] But the malaise between it and Cluny went on. In 1098 Urban II wrote to the abbots of Cluny and of Saint-Gilles, urging them to seek a reconciliation, and saying that he had asked Archbishop Hugh of Lyons to mediate between them.[3] The immediate result of this intervention is not known; but, *c.* 1108, Pope Paschal II urged the monks of Saint-Gilles to be more unworldly and to be faithful in their observance of the ways of Cluny.[4] Only in 1132 did a letter of Pope Innocent II to Abbot Peter the Venerable of Cluny settle the 'lis et controversia' between his monastery and Saint-Gilles: he prescribed that if Saint-Gilles were ever to stand in need of reform, the abbot of Cluny was to intervene; otherwise it was to enjoy a complete liberty from outside intervention.[5]

The conclusion may be drawn that Cluny maintained some kind of a claim to superiority over Saint-Gilles, and that the Papacy never wholly conceded nor denied it. In so far as it was effective, it became so with the goodwill of the pope; while the

---

[1] Santifaller, *Q.F.*, no. 110, 1076?, pp. 104–5. For Bishop Anselm II of Lucca's stay at Saint-Gilles in 1075, when his biographers regarded it as definitely Cluniac in character, see below, p. 250, n. 5.

[2] Goiffon, *Bullaire*, no. xvii, pp. 35–6.   [3] *Ep.* cciv, *P.L.* cli. 477–8.

[4] Bruel, 3871.   [5] *Ep.* xc, *P.L.* clxxix. 128–9.

Apostolic See never abandoned its desire to preserve some kind of an association between Saint-Gilles and Cluny.

i. *Saint-Orens, Auch*

The monastery of Saint-Orens, Auch, which had been founded in the tenth century, was given to Cluny in 1068 by Count Aimeric of Auch and his brother, Bernard.[1] It became a Cluniac priory. When the gift to Cluny was made, Abbot Hugh was himsel fpresent. The count's charter expressed the wish that it should be confirmed by apostolic authority.[2] There was good reason for desiring this, for the Cluniacs inherited a dispute with the nearby cathedral of Sainte-Marie, in the prosecution of which the support of the Apostolic See would be of the utmost value to them.

There was a long history of conflict between the monks of Saint-Orens and the canons of the cathedral about their respective rights of cemetery. The fullest version of it is in a twelfth-century account, which came from the side of the monks.[3] The monks based their alleged rights to special privileges in the matter of the burial of the citizens upon the apocryphal early history of the see. According to this, the see had first been established not at Auch but at Éauze, some twenty-eight miles away; it was only transferred to Auch after four bishops had ruled there. When this happened, the bones of the four bishops were brought to Auch and buried, not in the new cathedral of Sainte-Marie, but in the older church of Saint-Jean-Baptiste. In due course St. Orens, a fifth-century bishop of Auch, was buried with them, and the dedication of the church of Saint-Jean-Baptiste was changed to Saint-Orens. When Saint-Orens became a monastery it retained the special cemetery rights that were appropriate to the church in which these burials had taken place. The monks complained that

---

[1] The principal source for Saint-Orens is the *Cartulaire du chapitre de l'église metropolitaine Sainte-Marie d'Auch*, ed. C. Lacave la Plagne Barris (*Archives historiques de la Gascogne*, Paris and Auch, 1899). Charters i–clx form the so-called 'Black Cartulary' of the cathedral, which was compiled early in the thirteenth century. Charters clxi–clxxiv were an addition to it, which appears to have been taken from a Cartulary of Saint-Orens. See also A. Degert, 'Auch', *D.H.G.E.* v (1931), 276–82.

[2] Bruel, 3414.   [3] *Cartulaire*, no. clxi, pp. 195–9.

in the eleventh century there had been episcopal attempts to violate their rights. In particular, Archbishop Raymond I (1036–42) had tried to establish a new cemetery in the city and so to deprive the monks of their rights and of the oblations of the faithful upon the occasion of burials.

During Raymond's time and that of his successor, Austindus (1042–68), who also opposed the Cluniacs at Saint-Mont, the dispute smouldered away. According to the garbled account preserved at Saint-Orens, Pope Leo IX himself came to the aid of the monks by issuing a privilege in defence of their rights.[1] From the side of the canons of the cathedral, it was stated that Archbishops Raymond I and Austindus, and also Bishop Boso of Saintes, all carried out burials in the new cemetery. The canons also recorded that while Austindus was archbishop the monks appealed to Rome and obtained a further papal ruling on their behalf; Austindus himself therefore travelled to Rome in the interests of the cathedral.[2]

Obscure as these events are, they indicate the need of Saint-Orens, when it became a Cluniac priory, to seek the support of the Papacy and its agents against its local adversaries. Such support was first provided in the year of its gift to Cluny. At the Council of Auch (1068), the papal legate, Cardinal Hugh Candidus, showed it great favour on the grounds that St. Orens was buried there. With Archbishop Austindus's concurrence, it was excepted from the legate's general ruling that the churches of Gascony should pay a quarter of their tithes to the cathedral of Auch, and all its existing customary rights were confirmed. The prior of Saint-Orens was allowed to exercise the rights of an archdeacon over the churches belonging to his priory and over the clerks who served them.[3] Nothing was said expressly about the cemetery

---

[1] *Cartulaire*, no. clxi, pp. 195–9. There is no other clear evidence of such a privilege, apart from that surviving at Auch; but cf. Leo IX's letter in support of the cemetery rights of Saint-Orens: *Ep.* xcviii, *P.L.* cxliii. 743.

[2] *Cartulaire*, no. lii, pp. 49–51. The date of this document is uncertain; the editor's ascription to *c.* 1080 is insufficiently supported. It may not have been drawn up until the death of Archbishop William in 1096. The Saint-Orens account knew of no interference by Austindus: *Cartulaire*, no. clxi, p. 197.

[3] *Cartulaire*, no. clxii, pp. 201–2. See Constable, *Monastic Tithes from their Origins to the Twelfth Century*, pp. 88–9.

rights of Saint-Orens.[1] But with the succession to the see of Archbishop William (1068–96), a Cluniac who had been named as the first prior of Saint-Orens, the priory embarked upon almost thirty years of peaceful development.[2] There is no reason to suppose that, for the time being, its rights were called into question.

William's successor, Raymond II (1096–1118), had also been prior of Saint-Orens. But the continuing peace which the monks anticipated when they promoted his election did not follow. The cathedral clergy used the opportunity to renew their claims.[2] There is conflicting evidence from the two sides as to the course of events. According to the canons, it was they who took the initiative by stating their case before Pope Urban II at the Council of Saint-Sernin, Toulouse (1096). Representatives of the monks of Saint-Orens replied by producing Pope Leo IX's privilege. After examining the seal, Urban II dismissed it as a forgery;[3] and he confirmed the canons in their right to have a cemetery.[4] The canons also placed it upon record that their rights were upheld by the Papacy on two subsequent occasions. At his Lent Council at the Lateran in 1099, Urban heard the canons' complaints that the monks were still molesting them, and he deferred the matter for private consideration in his own chamber. There he upheld the canons. In 1100, at the Council of Poitiers, the papal legates Cardinals John and Benedict confirmed this decision.[5]

But on the Cluniac side there survives from Saint-Orens a rather better-documented case that Urban II, in fact, showed favour to it, not the cathedral. According to the Cluniacs, in the

[1] According to the monks of Saint-Orens, the claims of their monastery were later strengthened when Prior Bernard, the future archbishop of Toledo, discovered in this church the tombs of the four bishops of Éauze: *Cartulaire*, no. clxi, p. 196.

[2] *Cartulaire*, no. clxi, p. 197.

[3] *Cartulaire*, no. lvi, pp. 55–6. The charter may have been that of which a copy survives in *Cartulaire*, no. clxvii, pp. 206–7. It was addressed to Archbishop Raymond I, who died some five years before Leo became pope. This reflects the confusion of *Cartulaire*, no. clxi, pp. 195–9. It should, however, be noted that in the documents referred to below, neither Urban II nor Paschal II ever doubted that Leo IX had issued a genuine privilege for Saint-Orens.

[4] *Cartulaire*, no. lvi, pp. 55–6.

[5] *Cartulaire*, no. lvi, pp. 56–7. For the Council of Poitiers, see Mansi, xx. 1117–26, where there is no reference to Auch.

course of his French journey when he was at Moissac, Urban wrote to Abbot Hugh a letter, in which he referred to the Papacy's special duty of preserving the peace of religious houses. He said that the prior and monks of Saint-Orens had appealed to him. In response he confirmed all their rights, and especially their rights of cemetery as they had been laid down by Pope Leo IX. The archbishop and canons of Auch were forbidden to start any new cemetery within the city of Auch or outside it, and they were to keep within their existing rights.[1] A year later Urban wrote from Rome to Archbishop Raymond II, warning him to obey the decrees of the Apostolic See. He was to punish the clerks who had violated the decrees of Leo IX and himself concerning the cemetery rights of Saint-Orens.[2]

There is no reason to doubt the authenticity of these two letters. It seems likely that Urban II's influence was, in fact, exercised to moderate the claims of the two sides; but that he laid particular emphasis upon the rights of the Cluniacs and upon the pope's duty to protect them. This also seems to have been the policy of Paschal II. It is, perhaps, to the early years of his pontificate that there belongs a letter to the monks of Saint-Orens from a papal legate, Cardinal-bishop Alberic of Ostia.[3] It recorded an agreement reached, under the legate's authority, at Limoges, between the archbishop of Auch and the prior of Saint-Orens. The archbishop agreed that he would 'love, honour, and maintain' the monks of Saint-Orens and renounce all exactions upon it. The question of cemetery rights and certain other matters which were not stated, were left open until Abbot Hugh of Cluny should have agreed to the terms of a settlement.[4]

---

[1] *Cartulaire*, no. clxviii, pp. 207–8; *Ep.* cxcvii, *P.L.* cli. 467–8. The date was 13 May, rather more than a week after the Council at Saint-Sernin: *Cartulaire*, no. lvi, p. 55.   [2] *Cartulaire*, no. clxvi, pp. 205–6; *Ep.* ccxxii, *P.L.* cli. 494.

[3] The name presents a difficulty, for there is no record of a cardinal-bishop of Ostia of this name. But there is a gap in the perhaps incomplete list in H.-W. Klewitz, *Reformpapsttum und Kardinalkolleg* (Darmstadt, 1957), pp. 115, 119, between Odo II († ? 1101) and his next known successor, Leo, who may not have taken office before 1106. Or there may be later scribal confusion with the Alberic who was cardinal-bishop of Ostia from *c.* 1137 to 1148, and who had been a monk and sub-prior of Cluny.

[4] *Cartulaire*, no. clxiv, p. 204; *P.L.* clv. 1631–2.

Whether a settlement was in fact reached, and if it was, on what basis, does not emerge. But probably at about the time of Cardinal Alberic's letter, Pope Paschal II himself reassured the prior and monks of Saint-Orens that their priory enjoyed the protection of the Apostolic See. He confirmed the measures of Popes Leo IX and Urban II about the monks' cemetery rights. He re-iterated Urban II's requirement that the archbishop of Auch and his canons were not to establish a new cemetery inside or outside the city, but that they were to respect the traditional arrangements.[1] At the very end of his reign, he wrote in a similar sense to Archbishop Bernard II (1118–26) when he succeeded to the see.[2] Once again it is in a Cluniac source that these letters survive. Yet there is no good reason to doubt their authenticity.

The history of Saint-Orens is at many points obscure. But like Saint-Mont it shows how the conversion of a monastery into a Cluniac priory raised local problems, in the meeting of which recourse to the Papacy and the aid of its legates were of the utmost value to the Cluniacs. Whatever truth there may be in the evidence from the cathedral of Sainte-Marie, its canons were well familiar with the technique of recourse to Rome. Whatever truth there may be in the evidence from Saint-Orens, which has the higher credibility because it includes papal letters which seem to be genuine, the monks consistently looked to the popes and their legates for support. These legates were represented as working in harmony with Abbot Hugh. Like Saint-Mont, Saint-Orens illustrates the pressing need of papal support that the Cluniacs had in Gascony, and the effectiveness with which this support could be brought to bear upon their behalf.

j. *Sainte-Foi de Morlaas*

The monastery of Sainte-Foi de Morlaas, near Pau (dioc. Lescar), was founded in 1074. It was given to Cluny in 1079 by Centullus IV, *vicomte* of Béarn, in token of his repentance for his marriage within the prohibited degrees to his first wife, Gisela.[3]

---

[1] *Cartulaire*, no. clxix, pp. 208–10.   [2] *Cartulaire*, no. clxv, p. 205.
[3] *Cartulaire de Sainte-Foi de Morlaas*, ed. L. Cadier (Pau, 1884), no. i, pp. 3–4; Bruel, 3546 *bis*.

In February 1079 Gregory VII had written urging him to set the matter right and to do penance, and to seek the counsel of Bishop Amatus of Oléron and Abbot Bernard of Marseilles, if they came to his part of France.[1] According to his charter, the *vicomte* made his gift to Cluny upon the advice of Bishop Amatus, Archbishop William of Auch, and of his uncle, Bernard Tumapaler, who was formerly count of Gascony and now a Cluniac monk at Saint-Mont.[2] It was also stated that, upon the advice of the archbishop of Auch and the bishop of Oléron, Gisela went to Cluny and became a nun at Marcigny.

Cluny was confirmed in its possession of Morlaas by Centullus's son, *vicomte* Gaston IV,[3] and became of considerable importance as a Cluniac house. Sainte-Foi thus provided another example of the assistance that Amatus of Oléron as papal legate gave with the establishment of Cluniac priories in south-western France.

k. *Figeac*

The monastery of Saint-Sauveur et Notre-Dame, Figeac (dioc. Cahors), which was first founded in 755, became a Cluniac priory in 1074. The circumstances are set out in the charter by which this was effected. It describes how the monks themselves, repenting their own slackness, desired to be subject to the abbot of Cluny. They had been encouraged in this by the former proprietor of the monastery, Hugh of Calmonte, who had taken the monastic habit. After his death the monks renewed their resolve with the authority and permission of Cardinal Gerald of Ostia and with the approval of Bego, the son of Hugh of Calmonte. Abbot Hugh accepted the gift of Figeac during a visit which he paid to it.[4] The charter included a request that Abbot Hugh should seek a confirmation of the gift by papal authority.

The foundation of Figeac as a Cluniac priory provides an

---

[1] *Reg.* vi. 20, 25 Feb. 1079, pp. 431–2.
[2] Abbot Bernard died on 20 July 1079.
[3] *Cartulaire de Sainte-Foi*, no. 2, pp. 7–8; Bruel, 3807, 3808.
[4] Bruel, 3469.

illustration of Cardinal Gerald of Ostia's encouragement of Cluny's expansion, and of the desire of donors to secure papal protection for their gifts.[1]

1. *Montierneuf*

The monastery of the Blessed Virgin Mary, St. John the Evangelist, St. Andrew, St. Simon, and St. Jude at Montierneuf was founded by Duke William of Aquitaine in a suburb of Poitiers.[2] He gave it to Cluny by a charter, dated 1076, in which he placed it under Abbot Hugh's authority.[3] At the same time he asked Gregory VII to confirm his gift. Gregory did this by a privilege which closely followed the formulas of his privilege for Cluny itself, and was probably issued at the same time.[4] In 1077 the duke issued a new charter in which he stated more emphatically than in 1076 that Montierneuf was fully subject to Abbot Hugh.[5] Urban II also issued a privilege for Montierneuf in which he emphasized that it was subject only to Cluny,[6] and he himself consecrated the monastery.[7]

Montierneuf illustrates the effectiveness of papal authority in securing for a dependent house the kind of subjection to the abbot of Cluny which excluded all temporal authority on the model of Cluny itself.

---

[1] For other examples of this desire, see Bruel, 3411 (*Ecclesia sanctae Geniverae*, 1067); 3454 (Lézat, 1073); 3523 (Saint-Pierre de Bexandum, 1078).

[2] For its foundation, see *Fragmentum historiae Monasterii Novi Pictavensis*, in *Thesaurus novus anecdotorum*, ed. E. Martène and V. Durand, iii (Paris, 1717), 1209–20; cf. *G.C.* ii. 1263–4.

[3] Bruel, 3495. The date presents a problem, if Bruel's text is correct; for this charter appears to precede Gregory VII's privilege of 1075.

[4] Santifaller, *Q.F.*, no. 108, pp. 100–3. Gregory's definition of the position of the bishop of Poitiers is noteworthy. So long as he was canonically elected and not a simoniac, the monks were to apply to him for such episcopal offices as consecrations and ordinations; if he were not, they might resort to any catholic bishop. This well illustrates Gregory VII's attitude to the spiritual authority of bishops over monasteries, and the sense in which, in practice, he modified the exemption of Cluniac and other houses.

[5] Bruel, 3506.

[6] *Ep.* clxxxviii, *P.L.* cli. 461–2.

[7] *Frag. hist. Monast. Novi, ubi supra*, col. 1219.

m. *Saint-Martin-des-Champs*

Saint-Martin-des-Champs (dioc. Paris)[1] was founded in 1060 by King Henry I of France; in 1079 King Philip I gave it to Cluny.[2] There was no change in its dedication, but donors to it were sometimes explicit in stating that their gifts were to 'beato Petro Cluniacensi', 'accclesiae beati Petri Cluniacensis', etc.[3] The gift of this monastery to Cluny thus tended to foster the cultus of St. Peter. There is, however, no evidence of any indebtedness to the Papacy for direct action on its behalf.

n. *Saint-Eutrope, Saintes*

The church of Saint-Eutrope, Saintes, was given to Cluny by Duke William of Aquitaine in 1081.[4] The duke personally delivered it into the hand of Abbot Hugh in the presence of the papal legates Hugh of Die and Amatus of Oléron. It already owed a *census* of five shillings to Rome and was, therefore, in apostolic proprietorship; as such, it was an especial concern of the legates. According to Duke William's charter it was by their counsel, licence, and authority that, having delivered it from lay hands and procured its liberty, he transferred it from his own hand into that of St. Peter of Cluny, so that Abbot Hugh and his successors should dispose of it in all respects, save that the *census* and due reverence should be paid to Rome.[5] The duke called upon the legates, 'qui vineae ecclesiasticae cultores vice beati Petri advenistis', to confirm the gift by adding their seal, which was the mark of apostolic authority. Amatus accordingly confirmed the gift as vicar of the Roman See and Hugh of Die did so as his associate.

The charter of 1081 demonstrates the close co-operation which could take place between Abbot Hugh and two Gregorian

[1] See *Recueil des chartes et documents de Saint-Martin-des-Champs*, i, ed. J. Depoin (Ligugé and Paris, 1912).

[2] *Recueil*, no. xviii, pp. 38–9.

[3] *Recueil*, no. xxii, pp. 44–5; no. xxv, pp. 50–1, etc.

[4] Bruel, 3580, dated 11 Jan. 1081.

[5] The charter claimed the concurrence of the bishop and canons of Saintes in the arrangements which it made.

legates, in freeing from lay control a monastery which properly belonged to the Apostolic See, and in vindicating the authority of St. Peter over it.

o. Saint-Denis de Nogent-le-Rotrou

Saint-Denis (dioc. Chartres) was founded *c.* 1028–9 by Geoffrey, lord of Nogent-le-Rotrou.[1] During its early years, it suffered from serious internal strife between factions of monks who wished to follow differing monastic customs. In *c.* 1078, Count Rotrocus of la Perche sought to procure strong rule by sponsoring the introduction of an abbot, named Hubert, and a group of monks from Saint-Père de Chartres. But upon his death soon afterwards, the new abbot have great offence to the new count, Geoffrey IV, and to his wife. They brought about the expulsion of Abbot Hubert and the monks from Saint-Père; and in 1081 they asked for monks from Cluny to come and reform Saint-Denis.[2] In 1082 Count Geoffrey gave it to St. Peter and St. Paul at Cluny and placed it fully under the rule of Abbot Hugh.[3] This was to all intents and purposes a new beginning in the history of Saint-Denis, which now took its place as a Cluniac subject priory. Abbot Hugh sent a Cluniac monk, also called Hubert, to be its prior, and a second monk to be his companion.

The Cluniacs soon found that they stood in need of outside help to maintain their position there. The deposed Abbot Hubert contested its gift to Cluny; in 1082 both he and Prior Hubert went to the Council of Meaux, where the papal legates Hugh of Die and Amatus of Oléron confirmed Cluny in its possession of the priory.[4] The monks of Saint-Père did not, however, abandon their claims. In 1094, at the Council of Autun, its abbot once more appealed to Hugh of Lyons to uphold them; but Count Geoffrey of la Perche vindicated the claims of the Cluniacs. Hugh of Lyons therefore confirmed them; but in doing so, he stipulated that the abbot of Saint-Père might go to Abbot Hugh of Cluny to

[1] See *Histoire et cartulaire de Saint-Denis de Nogent-le-Rotrou*, ed. C. Métais (Vannes, 1895).
[2] *Cartulaire*, no. cxvii, pp. 238–40.   [3] *Cartulaire*, no. vii, pp. 26–33.
[4] Baluze, *Miscellanea*, vi. 45, 428.

discuss the situation. If Abbot Hugh could be prevailed upon to relinquish Saint-Denis, Hugh of Lyons would confirm Saint-Père in possession of it; otherwise it must remain the property of Cluny. After negotiations between the two abbots, the abbot of Saint-Père gave up his claims.[1] Cluny was confirmed in possession of Saint-Denis, in 1095, by Urban II.[2] Saint-Denis thus provides an example of effective and reiterated intervention by the Papacy on behalf of the Cluniacs, both directly and through its legates.

p. *Saint-Bertin*

At the very end of the eleventh century Abbot Hugh made a major departure from his earlier practice of being reluctant to countenance the establishment of Cluniac priories to the north of the Loire. The principal reason for it was that the consort of Count Robert II of Flanders was Clementia, daughter of Duke William II of Burgundy. Clementia combined great religious fervour with a deep attachment to her homeland. In 1099 she persuaded Abbot Lambert of Saint-Bertin to commend his monastery to Cluny; in the succeeding years a family of Cluniac dependencies grew up in Flanders.[3]

Partly owing to the tactlessness and excessive zeal of Countess Clementia, the introduction of Cluniac Customs at Saint-Bertin and its subjection to Cluny did not take place without conflict. The initial gift of the monastery to Cluny was made secretly;[4] although the precaution was taken of securing from Urban II a privilege to confirm what had been done.[5] When the monks came to hear of the *fait accompli*, they showed great hostility to their abbot and tried to prevent his embarking upon a visit to Rome in the company of his bishop, John of Thérouanne. During his journey the abbot had the monks who were sent with him imprisoned; and he turned aside to Cluny in order to learn its Customs and to make his profession as a Cluniac. The monks of

---

[1] *Cartulaire*, no. xx, pp. 65–70.   [2] *Ep.* clxii, *P.L.* cli. 435–6.
[3] See the account of this reform by Hallinger, *Gorze–Kluny*, pp. 476–80. The principal source is *Simonis gesta abbatum sancti Bertini Sithiensium*, ed. O. Holder-Egger, 64–71, *M.G.H. Scr.* xiii. 648–50.
[4] Bruel, 3733.   [5] *Ep.* cclviii, *P.L.* cli. 522.

Saint-Bertin learnt of this when Bishop John returned from Rome, and twice sent envoys to demand Lambert's return. When he came, he at once encountered the violent resistance of the chapter. He therefore used his own knights to expel the monks by force and to disperse them to places of punishment elsewhere; and by licence of Abbot Hugh of Cluny, he imported monks from Cluniac houses to restore the monastic life. He was soon ruling a community of 120 monks.

Saint-Bertin was thus in a position to initiate the spread of Cluniac monasticism in Flanders. In doing this, it claimed papal sanction for its activity by asserting that it took place 'tam ex apostolica sanctione quam ex priscorum institutione'.[1]

Papal support was thus of the utmost importance to Abbot Hugh when he began the reform of Saint-Bertin.

III. CLUNIAC DEPENDENCIES IN THE KINGDOM OF BURGUNDY

In the eleventh century the regions to the east of the Rhone and the Saône up to the frontiers of Italy and Germany, and also a small area to the west of the two rivers, formed the kingdom of Burgundy and lay outside France. A small amount of evidence survives from Cluniac houses in Lower Burgundy which serves to complement that which has been reviewed from French sources.

a. *Vizille*

Vizille was a small Cluniac cell in the diocese of Grenoble, which had been given to Cluny by Bishop Humbert of Grenoble in 996.[2]

A letter from Pope Urban II to Bishop Hugh of Grenoble (1080–1132) survives, in which he referred to an earlier letter instructing the bishop to restore the cell to the monks of Cluny.[3] He now repeated the demand, explaining that, although he did not doubt the bishop's good faith in seizing the Cluniac cell, he himself

---

[1] *Gesta abbatum s. Bertini*, 71, p. 649.   [2] Bruel, 2307.

[3] *Cartularium sancti Theofredi*, no. ccci, in *Cartulaire de Saint-Chaffre du Monastier*, ed. U. Chevalier (Paris, 1884), pp. 143–44.

could provide the testimony of an eye-witness that it had once been in Cluny's possession. Whether this was just or unjust it was the province of the Apostolic See to determine. Urban therefore once again told the bishop to restore it to Cluny. Then he made provision for the rightful proprietorship of Vizille to be settled. An inquiry was to be made by the bishop of Maguelone.[1] Urban urged both parties to behave with fairness: the Cluniacs were not to use Abbot Hugh's absence as an excuse for delay, while the bishop of Grenoble was to act in such a way that the Cluniacs had no just cause to complain of him.

b. *Domène*

Domène was also in the diocese of Grenoble and founded in the time of Abbot Odilo.[2] While it was never actively defended by the Papacy or its agents, it is a good example of a priory whose charters testify to the cultus of St. Peter and St. Paul.[3]

IV. CONCLUSIONS

From this review of the relatively small number of Cluny's subject priories that it is possible to investigate in any detail, it may be concluded that quite apart from the over-all privileges in which the eleventh-century popes repeatedly confirmed Cluny's rights over its scattered dependencies, Cluny was deeply and increasingly indebted to the Papacy. The popes and their legates often took effective action to vindicate its rights and interests in its individual daughter houses. The more a Cluniac priory was, like Saint-Mont, a local microcosm of Cluny itself in respect of its characteristics and its problems, the more it needed and had the benefit of papal aid; the more it was like Longpont, the less it did so.

Of the houses that have been considered, a larger number shared some, at least, of the characteristics of Saint-Mont than of Longpont; few were so unlike Cluny itself, and so little beholden to the Papacy, as Longpont. Only Sauxillanges, Paray-le-Monial, and Saint-Martin-des-Champs are really comparable with it.

---

[1] Geoffrey (1080–1103).   [2] Bruel, 2801.

[3] See *Cartulare monasterii de Domina*, ed. C. de Monteynard (Lyons, 1854).

For the rest, the Cluniacs usually owed some debt to the direct action of the Papacy with respect to their subject houses, and they were sometimes deeply and repeatedly indebted to it. At Saint-Flour, Saint-Mont, Marcigny, Montierneuf, and Saintes there are clear examples of papal action to defend the Cluniacs, in one way or another, from the interference of lay magnates. At Limoges and Saint-Bertin the Papacy upheld the Cluniacs against monks who resisted the conversion of their monasteries to the status of a Cluniac dependency, and Cluny may also have had some papal support in its dealings with Saint-Gilles. At Nogent-le-Rotrou, the Cluniacs could count upon papal help against the abbots of Saint-Père de Chartres. They were also often helped by the Papacy against the general or the particular claims of local bishops; of this, Saint-Mont, possibly Saint-Gilles, Saint-Orens, Limoges, and Vizille serve as examples. At Saint-Flour, Limoges, and perhaps Saint-Bertin, the Papacy worked in harmony with bishops who were favourable to the Cluniacs. But it was especially by the local action of their legates that the popes brought effective aid. During Abbot Hugh's reign, Cardinal Peter Damiani intervened at Limoges and Marcigny; Cardinal Hugh Candidus at Saint-Orens and possibly Saint-Mont; Cardinal Gerald of Ostia at Saint-Mont and Figeac; Amatus of Oléron at Sainte-Foi de Morlaas and possibly at Saint-Mont; Hugh of Die and Lyons at Saint-Gilles and Nogent-le-Rotrou; Amatus and Hugh together at Saintes; Bernard of Toledo at Saint-Mont; Cardinal Alberic of Ostia (or another) probably at Saint-Orens; and Cardinal-bishop Milo of Palestrina at Marcigny and Vézelay. The Cluniacs also made direct appeals to Rome in the cases of Saint-Flour, Limoges, and Saint-Bertin. During the course of his travels in France Pope Urban II not only issued many privileges in favour of Cluniac houses, but he also acted directly in their favour in respect of the problems of Limoges and probably Saint-Orens. In sum, the debt of the Cluniacs to the Papacy was a notable one.

On the other hand, the collaboration between the Papacy and the Cluniacs and the spread of Cluniac monasticism did much to assist the gradual permeation of France by the ideals and the authority of the reformed Papacy. First of all, the Cluniacs performed a service to the Papacy by their wide dissemination of the cult of St. Peter and St. Paul, the apostles to whom Cluny and the Apostolic See had a common dedication. A glance at the charters of Cluny itself is sufficient to show how virtually every document of the abbey proclaimed and praised the lordship of the two apostles. If this was primarily done in relation to the abbey of Cluny, it is likely also to have awakened many to a fuller awareness of the apostles, and of their vicar at Rome who, in their name, was making ever larger claims to an effective and immediate authority over the whole Church. In many cases Cluniac priories, too, were dedicated to one or both of the Princes of the Apostles, or at least included them amongst their patrons: their charters, as well, testify to the spread of the cult of St. Peter. A wide range of possibilities lay open. As at Saint-Flour or Saint-Mont, priories might come under the outright proprietorship of St. Peter, just as did the mother house. Or, as at Sauxillanges, the name of St. Peter might stand at the head of a list of patron saints, without, however, seeming to evoke any special overtones of association with the Apostolic See. Again, as at Saint-Martin-des-Champs, St. Peter might not be a patron saint at all; but in this case, the record of gifts 'beato Petro Cluniacensi' is a reminder that there, too, St. Peter was brought especially near by the link with Cluny. Wherever Cluniac houses spread the cult of St. Peter and St. Paul, they placarded their names in regions where often they had earlier made little local impact. When these houses in addition sought and enjoyed the aid of the popes and their legates, they added to their dissemination of the cult of St. Peter the proof that his vicar disposed of effective authority which could and should be used in the government of the whole Church.

Secondly, the dedication of priories to the Blessed Virgin was sometimes characteristic of Cluniac houses: Abbot Hugh's own foundation of Marcigny and Longpont are examples; Paray-le-Monial, too, was dedicated to the Virgin and St. John the Baptist. In view of the increase of Marian devotion in the eleventh century, and especially of the place which Gregory VII assigned to the intercessions of the Virgin in connection with St. Peter's authority to bind and to loose, this was not without importance for the Papacy.[1] Cluniac devotion to the Virgin and the diffusing of her cult may be reckoned as one of the factors that tended to identify the Cluniacs with the work of Gregory VII.

Thirdly, Cluniac priories which were assimilated to the position of Cluny itself and which were helped by the intervention of the Papacy and its legates, also served to invest the ancient and widespread tendency to seek the freedom of churches from lay dominion with a specifically papal sanction. They thus tended to stand as propaganda for the liberty of the Church in the Gregorian sense just as did Cluny itself. The examples of Saint-Flour, Saint-Mont, Limoges, Marcigny, Montierneuf, and Saintes all, in various ways, indicate this. They did so both by their new freedom from external lordship, and because they looked to the Papacy to protect it. For whatever their precise dedication Cluny's priories, like Cluny itself, frequently needed a protection that the abbot of Cluny could not by himself provide. Only Rome disposed of the full range of censures to safeguard the lands, rights, and liberties of Cluny's possessions; and in its legates it came to have effective local agents who could implement them. By looking to the authority of Rome the Cluniacs necessarily became the disseminators of its claims.[2]

It is far from being the case that the evidence which has been reviewed in this chapter invalidates the conclusions of Tellenbach's collaborators in *Neue Forschungen*. The Cluniacs often took their colour from their surroundings, enjoyed the support of local bishops, and used the forms and conventions of lay feudal society. But it is clear that this is only part of the story. If the Cluniacs merged into local society at one end of the spectrum of their activities, so, at the other, they merged into the Gregorian Reform and its specific objectives. Especially in view of Cluniac devotion

[1] See esp. *Reg.* ii. 49, p. 190; iv. 2, p. 297; vi. 14, p. 419; vi. 29, p. 442; vii. 14a, pp. 483, 486; viii. 8, p. 526; viii. 22, p. 565; ix. 2, p. 572.
[2] Cf. R. W. Southern, *The Making of the Middle Ages*, (London, 1953), pp. 150-1. A striking illustration of the solidarity which Gregory felt to exist between the Apostolic See and those in France who brought help to St. Peter and St. Paul is provided by his letter of 1074-5 to Duke William of Aquitaine: Santifaller, *Q.F.*, no. 58, pp. 38-9.

to St. Peter and of the pressing need of Cluny in its head and in its members to have the active support of the vicar of St. Peter and all the resources at his command, the Cluniac body assisted the gradual permeation of French society, especially in the south of France, by Gregorian ideas and methods.

III

REFORM AT TOULOUSE

A FURTHER problem in the history of Cluniac expansion in France and its repercussions upon Cluny's dealings with the Papacy which deserves separate discussion, is that of the reform of the church of Toulouse.[1]

Cluny began to be a significant factor in the region of Toulouse in 1047–8, with the reform of the near-by abbey of Moissac (dioc. Cahors). The early history of this reform is obscure; but the up-shot of it was that Moissac became an abbey within the Cluniac family, owing subjection to the abbot of Cluny. It adopted Cluniac Customs and it received as its abbot a Cluniac monk, Durand of Bredon.[2] In due course Durand became bishop of Toulouse (c. 1057–71). The reforming policy that he initiated in the diocese was continued by his redoubtable successor, Bishop Isarnus (1071–1105). Both bishops enjoyed the active support of Cluny and of the count of Toulouse, William IV (1060–88).

If Isarnus was a reformer, he was also a strenuous upholder of a bishop's right to exercise unfettered control of his own diocese; in particular, he showed himself impatient of interference by the Papacy. However, at Toulouse as elsewhere, Abbot Hugh showed his willingness to work with men as he found them. In 1073, when Isarnus reformed the chapter of his cathedral of Saint-Étienne by introducing the 'vita canonica' according to the Rule of St. Augustine, he did so with the advice of Abbot Hugh and with the help of Abbot Hunald of Moissac.[3]

[1] See esp. E. Magnou, *L'Introduction de la réforme grégorienne à Toulouse (Cahiers de l'association Marc Bloch de Toulouse*, iii, Toulouse, 1958); and 'Le Chapitre de la cathédrale Saint-Étienne de Toulouse', *La vita comune del clero nei secoli xi e xii* (Milan, 1962), ii. 110–14. I have followed Mlle Magnou's account fairly closely, but offer a somewhat different interpretation of the evidence.

[2] See J. Hourlier, 'L'Entrée de Moissac dans l'ordre de Cluny', *Annales du Midi*, lxxv (1963), 353–61; *Saint Odilon*, p. 114.

[3] For the versions of the charter by which Isarnus carried out this reform, see

A few years later a similar reform was independently effected in the ancient suburban church of Saint-Sernin.[1] Its canons were afterwards at loggerheads with Bishop Isarnus. The precise origins and the early course of their quarrel are obscure; but it certainly involved disputes about property rights between the chapters of Saint-Étienne and Saint-Sernin.[2] The canons of Saint-Sernin sought to fortify themselves against their bishop by securing from Gregory VII a privilege which granted them papal protection and effected their direct subjection to the Roman See.[3] This privilege was quickly put to the test. For Gregory VII found it necessary to write to his legate, Cardinal Richard of Marseilles, a letter in which he referred to the vexation by laymen and the hatreds of churchmen (*sæcularium exagitatio et . . . ecclesiasticorum odia*) to which the canons were being subjected. Basing himself upon their allegations, he named four culprits. First, the canons of Saint-Étienne had induced a fugitive clerk from Saint-Sernin to make off with the privilege that the pope had lately granted to his church; they were also trying to deprive it of its ancient cemetery and to wrest away some of its churches. Secondly, the monks of Moissac were holding on to a church that Bishop Amatus of Oléron, as papal legate, had adjudged to belong to Saint-Sernin. Encouraged, as it was believed, by gifts from the monks of

Magnou, *Introd. de la réforme grégorienne*, pièces justificatives, no. 1, and her discussion, pp. 23–31. For Abbot Hugh's presence in south-western France in 1073, see Bruel, 3454.

[1] The date is uncertain, but, in 1082, Gregory VII said it had happened 'noviter': *Reg.* ix. 30, p. 615.

[2] See Magnou, op. cit., pièces justificatives, no. 3, pp. 14–15; *Cartulaire de l'abbaye de Saint-Sernin de Toulouse*, ed. C. Douais (Toulouse, 1887), no. 133, pp. 98–9.

[3] Cf. *Reg.* ix. 30, pp. 615–17. There survives in a seventeenth-century transcript a copy of a privilege of Gregory VII in which papal protection was given to Saint-Sernin in return for an annual payment of ten shillings. The principal difficulty which the text raises is that the privilege was stated to have been given at the request of Bishop Isarnus; it can be held to be genuine as it stands only on the supposition that forged letters from Isarnus were sent: Magnou, *Introd. de la réforme grégorienne*, pièces justificatives, no. 4, pp. 16–17; *Cartulaire de Saint-Sernin*, ed. Douais, appendix, no. 1, pp. 473–4. From the side of Saint-Étienne, there survives a statement that the privilege was fraudulently obtained from Rome, and that, when Isarnus heard of it, he successfully asked Gregory VII to annul it: Magnou, op. cit., pièces justificatives, no. 5, p. 18; G. de Catel, *Mémoires de l'histoire de Languedoc* (Toulouse, 1633), p. 867. In view of *Reg.* ix. 30, this cannot be true.

Moissac, Count William of Toulouse was, thirdly, using force on their behalf. Finally, Bishop Isarnus of Toulouse was vexing Saint-Étienne; and he was encouraging others whom he was in a position to restrain to do likewise.

Gregory VII went on, in his letter, to prescribe the steps that Cardinal Richard was to take in defence of Saint-Sernin's 'Romana libertas'. By sending letters and by all other means, he was to urge the clerks of Saint-Étienne, the monks of Moissac, and the count of Toulouse to withdraw from their evil courses and to act justly towards Saint-Sernin. He was also to admonish Bishop Isarnus to cease vexing it and to restrain those whom he was in a position to control. Finally, Gregory referred to the abbot of Cluny. Since the monks of Moissac were his subjects (*quoniam Cluniacensi abbatiae pertinent*), Gregory considered that Abbot Hugh should first be enjoined to curb the insolence of his subjects and to compel them to behave with righteousness (*iustitia*), if they could not be persuaded to do so. As a last resort Gregory would support his legate in imposing ecclesiastical sanctions upon any of Saint-Sernin's local enemies who persisted in their disobedience.[1]

Gregory VII's letter to Cardinal Richard is instructive for the light in which he regarded Abbot Hugh's position. Gregory VII assumed and scrupulously if tacitly acknowledged the abbot's detachment from the recent course of events at Toulouse. If they were, in part, his responsibility because the monks of Moissac were subject to his authority, they were in no way his fault. They were the misdeeds of local subordinates, of whose transgressions he might well be ignorant; for he was at a great distance from Toulouse. It was, therefore, necessary that he should be informed of what they had done and urged to impose upon them the discipline that was appropriate. The pope evidently expected the abbot's co-operation with every confidence.

However, while these plans for composing the affairs of Toulouse by agreement were being discussed, events there very quickly took a violent turn for the worse. Bishop Isarnus resolved to settle matters in his own favour without delay. In collusion with Abbot Hunald of Moissac and Count William of Toulouse,

---

[1] *Reg.* ix. 30.

he determined to seize Saint-Sernin and to expel its canons. He further had a charter prepared in which he gave it to Abbot Hugh of Cluny and Abbot Hunald of Moissac, in order that it might be converted to the monastic life. He defined his own rights over it as bishop in great detail, and secured the full and active compliance of the count.[1] Thus, in the course of the year 1082, the canons of Saint-Sernin were expelled and monks from Moissac were introduced to inaugurate the monastic life there on a Cluniac basis.

There is no evidence that Abbot Hugh had any foreknowledge whatsoever of this plan, let alone that he viewed it with approval or had any part in it.[2] It was a high-handed act for which Bishop Isarnus was chiefly responsible and which he undertook with only the local support of Abbot Hunald of Moissac, whose monastery was by now building up its own network of dependencies. Bishop Isarnus was, no doubt, in part animated by a genuine wish to promote reform by introducing Cluniac monasticism.[3] But his prior concern was to reassert his own episcopal rights over Saint-Sernin, which he did with a vigour that there is no reason to suppose would have met with Abbot Hugh's compliance. For he was making a frontal challenge to Gregorian principles regarding the authority of the Apostolic See, and therefore, by implication, to the very safeguards upon which Cluny's own liberty rested, in head and members.

There are two pieces of evidence that suggest how the immediate crisis was resolved.[4] A fragment of a further letter from Gregory VII to Cardinal Richard, probably of 1082, suggests that Abbot Hugh did, in fact, at once obey the pope's promptings. It establishes that he intervened decisively to secure the withdrawal of the monks of Moissac from Saint-Sernin. The same fragment also shows that Cardinal Richard had incurred the pope's dis-

---

[1] Magnou, op. cit., pièces justificatives, no. 7, pp. 21–2; de Catel, op. cit., pp. 873–4.

[2] There is no evidence to support Mlle Magnou's assertion that he did: op. cit., p. 6.

[3] Cf. his introduction of the Cluniac reform at la Daurade in 1077: Magnou, op. cit., pièces justificatives, no. 2, p. 13; de Catel, op. cit., pp. 871–2.

[4] Both Gregory and Hugh perhaps had in mind the lessons of the Spanish crisis of 1080: see below, pp. 230–7.

pleasure. He had gone so far as to excommunicate the intruded monks after they had been withdrawn; for this excess of zeal Gregory VII administered a sharp reproof.[1] In a second document that was preserved at Saint-Sernin, it is also recorded how, on 23 July 1083, Count William of Toulouse was brought to express his deep penitence for his part in the proceedings against Saint-Sernin. The document expressly records that he was urged to do this, not only by Gregory VII, but by Archbishop Dalmatius of Narbonne, Archbishop Hugh of Lyons, Abbot Hugh of Cluny, and Bishop Gerald of Cahors.[2] The count had fully restored the canons, had annulled his former charter to Bishop Isarnus, and had guaranteed the rights of the canons for the future. In what they indicate about the reaction of Abbot Hugh, both these documents very strongly suggest that when he was apprised of the forcible conversion of Saint-Sernin to Cluniac monasticism, he decisively condemned what had happened and collaborated closely with Gregory VII to set matters right.

The whole matter of the reform of Saint-Sernin well illustrates the extreme difficulty that was encountered by both the pope and the abbot of Cluny in controlling their respective subordinates who were acting at a distance. A headstrong local abbot or prior, and an over-zealous legate, could equally commit their principals by taking ill-considered initiatives. Thus by falling in with Bishop Isarnus's plan to turn Saint-Sernin into a Cluniac monastic house, Hunald of Moissac, as abbot of one of Cluny's dependent monasteries, acted in a way of which the cautious and diplomatic Abbot Hugh would probably never have approved and which he condemned when Gregory brought it to his knowledge. When Cardinal Richard went beyond his brief as papal legate by pursuing his vengeance against the monks of Moissac after they had abandoned their crime, he gravely offended Gregory by his intemperate zeal. Confronted by similar problems and placed far away from the theatre of the trouble and also from each other, Gregory and Abbot Hugh reacted in mutual understanding and

---

[1] *Ep. Coll.*, no. 39, p. 566.
[2] Magnou, op. cit., pièces justificatives, no. 9, pp. 24–5; *Cart. de S.-Sernin*, no. 290, pp. 204–5.

with no hint of recrimination. Each of them knew the value of the other's help when he was dealing with the affairs of a distant and turbulent locality, and counted upon it.

It remained to deal with Bishop Isarnus and Abbot Hunald and to confirm the liberty of Saint-Sernin. These matters were taken in hand by Pope Urban II. In 1090 and 1096 he twice confirmed the rights of Saint-Sernin on the lines that Gregory VII had laid down.[1] Bishop Isarnus seems gradually to have accepted the right of the Apostolic See to intervene in his diocese.[2] Urban II regarded Abbot Hunald, on the other hand, as a contumacious rebel, who had opposed the Roman Church. The pope himself saw to his deposition and to the consecration of his successor, Ansquelinus; he called upon both Bishop Gerald of Cahors and Count William of Toulouse to see that his directions were complied with.[3] Abbot Hunald died in 1095; a year later Urban II could issue a privilege in favour of Cluny with regard to its rights in the region of Toulouse, in which the past was tacitly overlooked and the restoration of religion at Moissac by Abbots Odilo and Hugh was praised.[4] By the time that Urban II made his French journey in 1095–6, the disputes that had vexed Toulouse under Gregory VII were laid to rest.

The problem of Toulouse was thus finally settled in a way that fully affirmed the respective claims of the Papacy and of Cluniac monasticism. It safeguarded the *vita canonica* at Saint-Étienne and Saint-Sernin. It secured the acquiesence of Bishop Isarnus in the new state of affairs. If events at Toulouse illustrate the points of friction that existed amongst all the parties concerned and the problems that confronted them, they demonstrate still more clearly the underlying compatibility and collaboration that characterized the dealings of Cluny and the Papacy. It emerges that at Toulouse, the popes and the abbot of Cluny acted with mutual understanding; and that their support for each other served to advance their respective interests.

---

[1] *Cart. de S.-Sernin*, ed. Douais, appendix, nos. 2–3, pp. 474–7. In 1096 Urban consecrated the new basilica at Saint-Sernin: *Chronicon sancti Sernani*, C. Devic and J. Vaissete, *Histoire générale de Languedoc*, v (Toulouse, 1893), 49–50.

[2] Cf. Magnou, op. cit., pièces justificatives, no. 12, pp. 28–9; *Cart. de S.-Sernin*, ed. Douais, no. 2, pp. 4–5.

[3] *Epp.* cxx–i, *P.L.* cli. 392–3.   [4] *Ep.* cxcvi, *P.L.* cli. 466–7.

PART III

ABBOT HUGH, CLUNY, AND
THE PAPACY

IT has emerged from the study of how Cluny's liberty grew and of how its monastic family expanded in France, that Cluny was deeply and continually indebted to the Papacy for protection against its rivals, both lay and ecclesiastical, and for the furthering of its interests. In return, the Papacy owed much to the Cluniacs because the character and the dissemination of Cluniac monasticism actively evoked the proclamation and assisted the spread of papal authority as the reformed Papacy understood it. But the Papacy's full debt to the Cluniacs has yet to be estimated. Its true magnitude will emerge from a consideration of how far the objectives of the Cluniacs and the Gregorian Papacy were, indeed, compatible; and of how far their practical collaboration for the welfare of the Church fulfilled the expectations of the Gregorians.

I

OBJECTIVES

I. THE SPIRITUAL CONCERNS OF THE ELEVENTH CENTURY

THE objectives of the Cluniacs and the Gregorians can be satisfactorily compared only in the light of the characteristic spiritual
needs which were generally experienced by eleventh-century
Christians. The essence of these needs was summed up in the
phrase 'remissio (absolutio, indulgentia) peccatorum' which was,
above all others, the epitome of eleventh-century Christian aspirations. No phrase was, at that time, of more frequent occurrence
or of more cardinal significance. In charters of donation to
churches and religious houses it was constantly used when stating
the motive of the donors. It ran as a leitmotif through the letters
of Gregory VII. In the documents that serve to illustrate why men
flocked to the First Crusade, it repeatedly appears at the heart of
Urban II's preaching and of the Crusaders' response: the belief
that the Crusade in some way availed for the remission of sins
goes far to explain why, in Gibbon's memorable phrase, 'a nerve
was touched of exquisite feeling; and the sensation vibrated to the
heart of Europe'.[1] The especial preoccupation of eleventh-century
Christianity with the 'remissio peccatorum' has never been satisfactorily explained by historians. But so far as its religious background is concerned, it seems to have been, in large measure, a
consequence of the state of the penitential system of the western
Church at this particular juncture.[2] An understanding of eleventh-
century penitential ideas and practice is, therefore, essential for an

[1] The quotation is from the last sentence of his fifty-seventh chapter: E.
Gibbon, *A History of the Decline and Fall of the Roman Empire*, ed. J. B. Bury, vi
(London, 1912), 268.

[2] For the penitential system, see esp. K. Müller, 'Der Umschwung in der Lehre
von der Busse während des 12. Jahrhunderts', *Theologische Abhandlungen Carl von
Weizsäcker gewidmet* (Freiburg-im-Breisgau, 1892), pp. 287–320; N. Paulus,
Geschichte des Ablasses im Mittelalter, i (Paderborn, 1922); B. Poschmann, *Der*

appreciation of the contemporary role of the monastic order in general and of Cluny in particular, and of the value that the Papacy set upon Cluniac monasticism, in the light of its own special objectives.

Eleventh-century ideas and practice regarding penance were alike remarkably archaic. This was not least true of the Rome of Gregory VII; for in matters of liturgy and discipline the medieval Papacy was ever distinguished by its conservatism. Whoever would understand the eleventh-century penitential system, must begin by divesting his mind of the later medieval, and *a fortiori* of the modern, Catholic pattern of contrition, confession, and satisfaction; for this pattern was settled in the twelfth and thirteenth centuries, largely by the work of Peter Abelard, Hugh of St. Victor, and St. Thomas Aquinas. Equally he must remember that, in the eleventh century, the later medieval system of indulgences, which cancelled some or all of the specifically temporal punishments due to sin whether in this world or in purgatory, was as yet little more than foreshadowed. A slow transition was taking place between the reforms which had been carried out in the penitential system by the Carolingian reformers of some two centuries earlier, and these later medieval developments which did not substantially begin until the twelfth century. It is by the light of the Carolingian past, not by that of the scholastic future, that it is necessary to understand what eleventh-century men were seeking when they looked so earnestly for the remission of their sins.

The ninth-century Carolingian reformers had been concerned to restore the ancient discipline of public penance. It had been largely superseded by the private penance that had become widespread on the Continent with the Celtic and Anglo-Saxon missions. While Carolingian legislation kept private penance for minor sins, it insisted upon public penance for such grave offences

---

Ablass im Licht der Bussgeschichte (Bonn, 1948); C. Vogel, 'Les Rites de la pénitence publique aux Xe et XIe siècles', *Mélanges Crozet*, i. 137–44. H. E. Mayer, *Geschichte der Kreuzzüge* (Stuttgart, 1965), pp. 31–4, gives a summary, and rightly insists upon the importance of the penitential motive, when understood against the background of current practice, as an incentive to the First Crusade.

as murder, adultery, perjury, and incest.[1] In its simplest outline these sins involved a person who was willing to submit to the discipline of the Church in a threefold process of making amends:

(i) confession, or acknowledging his fault and so placing himself under the discipline of a penitent;

(ii) satisfaction, or submitting to such a period of excommunication and appropriate penance as the bishop might appoint; and

(iii) reconciliation, or being restored to communion during the observances of Lent, with their culmination in the solemn reconciliation of the Maundy-Thursday rites.

Thereupon the restoration of the penitent to communion was complete. In their teachings about this penitential practice the Carolingian reformers drew no such distinction between the guilt (*culpa*) of sin and its punishment (*poena*) as St. Augustine of Hippo had drawn, and as was to be a commonplace in the later Middle Ages. For the Carolingians the forgiveness that this threefold process effected carried with it the cancellation of all the consequences of sin; and the reconciliation of the sinner at its conclusion was final.

The tenth and eleventh centuries saw much modification, erosion, and rehabilitation of the Carolingian pattern. For the most part the changes that took place were the outcome not of decisions by bishops and councils, but of the gradual pressure from below of current and local usage. Thus, the commutation of penances early became a common practice; and in the late tenth century, there appeared in penitential orders prayers for the absolution of the penitent, which added an intercessory element to their basically disciplinary character. But it was the eleventh century that saw the most striking modifications. From about 1000 there is evidence that the reconciliation of penitents might take place after the confession of sins and before satisfaction was made by the doing of penance.[2] In the long run this was to have

---

[1] See E. Amann, *L'Époque carolingienne* (*Histoire de l'église*, ed. A. Fliche and V. Martin, vi, Paris, 1947), pp. 346–52.

[2] e.g. Burchard of Worms, *Decretum*, xix. 41, *P.L.* cxl. 988; although the full rigour of the older rule was maintained in xix. 63, 143, ibid., cols. 998, 1010. See

momentous consequences which were the more decisive because they were not foreseen or intended by those whose day-to-day dealings brought them about. For it implied that being reconciled to the Church could no longer be regarded as a simple expunging of a sin and all its consequences. As men were later to say, it ended the guilt of sin but not the punishment. So far as punishment is concerned, it opened the way for the later medieval distinction between the eternal and the temporal punishments of sin.[1] It eventually gave rise to the view that the essential purpose of satisfaction was to discharge the temporal punishments that were due for sin, both in this life and in purgatory. The reconciliation of a penitent began to lose its old finality because it left him burdened with a satisfaction that had still to be completed.

The effect of these tenth- and eleventh-century developments was progressively to heighten the significance for Christians at large of the devotions of the monastic order. Since Carolingian times this significance had always been great.[2] One reason why, like Cluny itself, so many monasteries were founded during and after late-Carolingian times, and why churchmen and lay lords were alike so solicitous for the monastic order and for its liberty, was that in their minds the penitential system as the Carolingian reformers had rehabilitated it did not stand alone. Men felt the

also the early eleventh-century *ordo* from Arezzo, described by J. A. Jungmann, *Die lateinischen Bussriten in ihrer geschichtlichen Entwicklung* (Innsbruck, 1932), pp. 191–4. Some results of the eleventh-century modifications of penitential practice upon popular devotion are well illustrated by the Latin and vernacular *Orationes privatae* in the *Portiforium* of St. Wulfstan, of *c.* 1065–6: *The Portiforium of Saint Wulfstan*, ii, ed. A. Hughes (Henry Bradshaw Society, xc, 1960), pp. 1–24, esp. 17, 22–4. For the general conservatism of popular devotion between Carolingian times and the eleventh century, see R. W. Southern, *St. Anselm and his Biographer* (Cambridge, 1963), pp. 38–42.

[1] e.g. the influential treatise *De vera et falsa poenitentia*, which is probably of eleventh-century date and which was pseudonymously ascribed to St. Augustine, taught that the effect of confession was to turn mortal into venial sin, which could be purged by satisfaction in time: 10, 18, *P.L.* xl. 1122, 1128.

[2] For recent studies which cast much light upon the relations between monastic and secular devotion, with especial reference to Cluny, see K. Schmid and J. Wollasch, 'Die Gemeinschaft der Lebenden und Verstorbenden in Zeugnissen des Mittelalters', *Frühmittelalterliche Studien*, ed. Hauck, i. 365–405; J. Wollasch, 'Ein cluniacensisches Totenbuch aus der Zeit Abt Hugos von Cluny', ibid., pp. 406–43.

need for the resources of public and private penance to have their complement in the liturgical intercessions of the Church. Those who did penance always looked for such support. If like the founder of Saint-Flour they had for a long time postponed or evaded it, they often felt, in the hour of repentance or in old age or with the approach of death, a particularly urgent desire to be commended to God's mercy by the devotions of those who stood nearest to him by reason of their religion. In particular, they looked to the monks whose whole lives were given over to prayers and alms. The monastic order represented the highest form of the Christian life and the only really safe way of escaping from the perils of a sinful world. To reinforce their penances men must make haste to seek an assured part in its benefits. So they took the habit or they sought confraternity with the monks; or else they built or endowed monasteries, so that prayer might be offered on their especial behalf. By such means as these they wished to be assured of a part in the spiritual benefits of the monastic order of the Church, and so fully to secure the remission of their sins.

The penitential system and the monastic order at all times supported and complemented one another by their respective services to the penitent sinner. At least for the aristocratic classes, the monastic order satisfied the religious hopes and fears of men during the ninth to the eleventh centuries, no less importantly than did the secular Church.[1]

There were, indeed, other resources besides those which the monastic order alone supplied. New forms of religious expression also began to emerge, which helped towards the remission of sins and lightened the burden of a satisfaction which was still to be completed. Thus, the eleventh century witnessed a multiplication of formal absolutions, which were pronounced quite separately from penance. They expressed prayers for the remission of sins, either in general, or as a result of some particular action.[2] They

---

[1] For the monastic order and the lower classes, see esp. B. Töpfer, *Volk und Kirche zur Zeit der beginnenden Gottesfriedensbewegung in Frankreich* (Berlin, 1957), pp. 29–57.

[2] A good example, which well illustrates how the repercussions of changes in the penitential system, the activities of the reformed Papacy, and the monastic devotions of a Cluniac house, all interacted to further the remission of sins,

were more than simple prayers; but they were quite distinct from
the absolutions that were now appearing in the penitential orders.[1]
They owed their special significance to their being solemn prayers,
spoken by the authority of popes, legates, bishops, and others
with the power to bind and loose, which helped to lighten men's
burden. In the course of time, by a development for which the
widespread commutation of penance prepared the way, such
absolutions occasionally took the form of guarantees attaching to
certain religious acts, like almsgiving or military campaigns or
Crusades. They then had the practical effect of cancelling part, or
the whole, of outstanding penances. By so doing they gave rise
to the later system of indulgences.[2] But, in the eleventh century,
papal or episcopal measures which can properly be described as
indulgences, were very few and localized;[3] in 1100 their history
had hardly begun.

Until it had done so, until the Crusading movement had gained

without, in this case, anticipating the form of an indulgence, is provided by the
absolution which Cardinal Gerald of Ostia associated with the burial of a secular
person in the cemetery of the priory of Saint-Mont: 'Quicumque vero in prae-
dicti monasterii cimeterio sepeliri se fecerint et de peccatis suis puram confessionem
Deo obtulerint veramque poenitentiam susceperint et egerint, eos apostolica
auctoritate absolvimus et fraternarum orationum atque helemosinarum participes
esse laudamus': *Cartulaire du prieuré de Saint-Mont*, ed. de Jaurgain, no. vi, p. 14.
See also the formal absolutions which are frequently to be found at the end of
Gregory VII's letters.

[1] There was, however, an important similarity in that, until the thirteenth
century, absolutions in penitential orders were more often optative than declara-
tory in form, and there was no clearly defined view as to their effects.

[2] An early example of a papal statement which certainly contains an indulgence
is Alexander II's lifting of the penances of those French knights who took part in
the Barbastro campaign: 'Eos, qui in Ispaniam proficisci destinarunt, paterna
karitate hortamur, ut, quae divinitus admoniti cogitaverunt ad effectum perducere,
summa cum sollicitudine procurent; qui iuxta qualitatem peccaminum suorum
unusquisque suo episcopo vel spirituali patri confiteatur, eisque, ne diabolus
accusare de inpenitentia possit, modus penitentie imponatur. Nos vero auctoritate sanctorum apostolorum Petri et Pauli et poenitentiam eis levamus et
remissionem peccatorum facimus, oratione prosequentes': *Epistolae pontificum
Romanorum selectae*, ed. S. Loewenfeld (Leipzig, 1885), no. 82, p. 43. The date is
1063.

[3] The geographical distribution of indulgences during the eleventh century
was restricted to southern France and northern Spain: see Poschmann, op. cit.,
esp. pp. 52–3.

momentum, and until later medieval ideas about penance took shape, the Carolingian order of things was modified but not superseded. The growing distinction between the guilt and the punishment of sin, the sense of a burden of temporal punishments for sin that men carried, and the conviction that it might be lightened against the Day of Judgement by a part in the prayers and alms of the monks, made men look to the monastic order more insistently than they had ever done before, or than they would ever do again.

Faced with the burden of the temporal punishments for sin which had still to be borne after they were reconciled to the Church, and which were not complete on this side of the grave, the men of the eleventh century, in particular, stood in far greater need than ever of prayers on their behalf, that they might eventually have the full remission of their sins. More than ever, clergy and laity alike felt a crying need for the benefits of the monastic order. They had every incentive to find such an association with it as might stand them in good stead at the Day of Judgement. The eleventh-century religious climate, up to the turning-point of the First Crusade, impelled popes and bishops, kings and magnates and knights—those who promoted Gregorianism, those who abhorred it, and those who were indifferent to it—all to look for the devotions of the monastic order to stand them in good stead in the Day of Judgement and to help them find the remission of their sins.

It is the secret of the spectacular success of the Cluniacs under Abbot Hugh that they knew, better than any other part of the monastic order, how to meet these needs. Cluny's history is a history of development. Like its liberty, the full articulation of its spiritual objectives was, in essential respects, a product of the eleventh century. What the religion of the Cistercians was to the twelfth century and that of the Mendicants was to the thirteenth, that of the Cluniacs was to the eleventh. Cluny came to the height of its fame in response to strictly contemporary needs; and, with the changing of these needs in the twelfth century, it rapidly lost ground in the monastic order.

By what means, then, did it meet so well, in the especial circumstances of the eleventh century, the needs of those, from the popes

downwards, who sought the remission of their sins by means of
a close association with the monastic order?

II. CLUNY AS THE 'ASYLUM POENITENTIUM'

No Cluniac document from the time of Abbot Hugh throws
into clearer relief the objectives of Cluniac monasticism, as it was
directed towards meeting prevailing needs as experienced by the
world at large, than a letter which the Abbot wrote to King
Philip I of France, not very long before both of them died. Its
date is 1106, when Hugh was in his fifty-seventh year as abbot and
Philip in his forty-sixth year as king. Abbot Hugh urged the king
to resign his earthly kingdom and to end his life as a monk of
Cluny. Hugh recalled how Philip had once asked him whether
any king had ever taken the religious habit: he said that it was now
time for him himself to think of his own latter end and of the
supreme good which is God, and to consider how he might secure
eternal riches. Let him remember the sad fates and mournful
deaths of his brother-kings, William II of England and Henry IV
of Germany, who had lately met their respective ends by a sudden
hunting disaster and in lonely humiliation. Where were these two
kings now? Philip should study to avoid their fate by true repentance. Abbot Hugh urged upon him that there was no surer proof
of this than to embrace the monastic profession. Let Philip, therefore, come to Cluny:

Behold, St. Peter and St. Paul, the Princes of the Apostles, who are
the judges of emperors and kings no less than of the whole world, are
ready to receive you into this their house, which our fathers have
named the refuge of the penitent (*asylum poenitentium*). We ourselves,
as well, are willing to honour you as a king, to treat you as a king, and
to serve you as a king. We would devoutly intercede for you before
the King of Kings, that, as for his own sake he had called you from
being a king to be a monk, so he would graciously restore you from
being a monk to be a king—not, however, a king who ruled for a
brief season in some narrow and poverty-stricken corner of this world;
but a king who shared his own unending reign, in the boundlessly
rich and happy realms of heaven.[1]

[1] *Ep.* viii, *P.L.* clix. 930–2.

Hugh's letter illustrates how deeply the religious mind of Cluny, like that of the eleventh century in general, was preoccupied with the Last Judgement, which men universally believed was very near. It was at once a man's religious duty and his personal interest that he should fortify himself against the great and terrible Day, to bring whose solemnity home to Christians Cluny, in particular, marshalled all the resources of liturgy, visual art, and pastoral zeal. As Abbot Hugh planned it, the third church at Cluny was the supreme visible reminder of it. Its Christ was the Christ of the Revelation of St. John, close to whom at the Last Judgement would stand his apostles, St. Peter and St. Paul. It was the prerogative of Cluny, which was their house, that it could speak in their name and urge men to draw as near to them as they could, while there was yet time, by sharing in its observances. If they responded St. Peter and St. Paul would speak for, and not against, them before the eternal Judge. The two apostles would use the keys of heaven to open and not to shut.

In Crusading and in indulgences, and in a new penitential order that laid great emphasis upon personal contrition, the twelfth century was to find other ways of securing the remission of sins; in the eleventh, there was no way so sure as to have a part in the monastic observance of a house such as Cluny, which belonged to St. Peter and St. Paul.[1]

So Abbot Hugh and his predecessors defined their principal objective by naming Cluny the 'asylum poenitentium': the refuge of those who sought deliverance from their sins.[2] Apart from the few surviving letters to and from Abbot Hugh, evidence of what this implied is mainly to be found in Cluny's monastic Customs and in the enormous corpus of charters that conveyed gifts to it and its dependencies. The charters are a better source of evidence than is commonly appreciated. For they expressed the motives of

[1] Cf. Gilo's commentary upon the building of Cluny III, *Vita Hugonis*, L'Huillier, *Saint Hugues*, pp. 605–6.

[2] For similar phrases, cf. the references to Cluny as the 'cunctis patens azilium' in a charter of 1088 which recorded the intention of Regina, daughter of Count Cono of Otlingen, to enter religion at Marcigny: *Le Cartulaire de Marcigny-sur-Loire* (1045–1144), ed. Richard, no. 30 *bis*, p. 26; also Abbot Hugh's own statement, no. 288, p. 166.

the donors in the terms that the monks themselves suggested to them in the course of their spiritual dealings. Very occasionally, indeed, the authentic words and sentiments of a donor appear. But usually the charters express the religious themes that the monks themselves were propagating in the Church at large and in lay society. They were the current ideas of the age; yet even in the formal language of Cluny's charters they are repeatedly expressed with a force and conviction that they rarely have in other comparable sources. Thus, it is possible by their means further to explore the spiritual objectives of the Cluniacs, as they exercised their attractive power upon the world outside the cloister.

The Cluniacs fully shared the highly unfavourable contemporary estimate of the world and of life in it. They repeatedly expressed this estimate in their charters, by using the common eleventh-century simile of the world as a vast and treacherous ocean. Those who voyaged upon it were daily threatened by a shipwreck that they could avoid only by being brought into a close association with the monastic order:

Just as a man, who puts out into the deeps of the sea and sees boisterous storms about him, seeks to avoid shipwreck by reaching the shelter of a harbour, so we, who are placed upon the seas of this world, should avoid the currents of this life and always strive with haste to reach the shelter of the haven, where no one can suffer shipwreck. No one can come to it, unless he prepares the way here by giving generously of his substance to those who are labouring in Christ's vineyard, so that, by virtue of their prayers, he may avail to enter together with them into eternal joy.[1]

The Cluniacs were urgent in their insistence that every prudent man should take due thought about the multitude of sins which he had committed in this life and of which he still bore the burden. He should seek their remission by the sovereign means of adhering, in one way or another, to those whose prayers and good works availed to bring men near to the great mercy of the Creator.

To this end the Cluniacs sought to bring men to commit both themselves and their goods. As the Cluniacs represented it, the

[1] Bruel, 3111.

committing of a man's goods had itself a deeply religious significance. Such aspects of Cluny as the material magnificence of the monastic buildings and especially of the third church, the six enormous volumes of its collected charters, and the importunity with which gifts were solicited, should not lead the modern observer to the facile conclusion that the Cluniacs were preoccupied with corporate material wealth for its own sake; nor did they see in it nothing more than a reward for their own faithfulness in their monastic observance.[1] What they sought to achieve was a material splendour which, by its very richness and because it was founded upon the gifts of many men and women, was an integral part of their work of interceding for the living and the dead, in face of the Christ in majesty of the Last Day. Every part of Cluny's buildings, every embellishment of its worship, and every parcel of the endowments which sustained it, spoke of the glories of heaven and commended to St. Peter and St. Paul the souls of the benefactors for whose salvation the monastic round was performed. The apparent preoccupation of the Cluniacs with the seeking of lavish material gifts was, in fact, intended to bear witness to the quality of Christ's mercy: in view of the use to which the monks put it, every material gift was, as it were by his ordinance, a guarantee of effectual prayers on the donor's behalf.

The Cluniacs themselves expressed this point by teaching that although Christ had given his own self in the cause of human redemption, he did not afterwards disdain mercifully to accept a man's goods in order that he might have the remission of his sins.[2] As a common formula in Cluny's charters ran,

If a man desires to be made the heir of the land of which the Psalmist says, 'I believe that I shall see the good things of the Lord in the land of the living', he should not hesitate to give in exchange for it this land that we tread with our feet and that the worms inherit, in order that he may be cleansed from every stain of sin.[3]

The simple gift of churches, lands, or other property served to win a share in the benefits that the devotions of the monks

---

[1] See the remarks of H. Grundmann, *Religiöse Bewegungen im Mittelalter* (2nd edn., Hildesheim, 1961), p. 15.
[2] e.g. Bruel, 3052.   [3] Bruel, 3046, cf. 3056, 3064, 3109, 3318, 3345.

procured; for every such gift helped to sustain these devotions. Christ's difficult saying, 'Make for yourselves friends of the mammon of iniquity, that, when you fail, they may receive you into everlasting habitations',[1] was repeatedly interpreted as meaning that men should take some or all of the material possessions that bound them to a wicked world and to its destiny, and turn the tables by adding them to the endowments of the monastic order.[2] If their goods went to the support of Cluny's prayers and alms, they would speak for and not against their donors in the Day of Judgement.[3]

But as well as committing his goods, a donor must also in some way commit himself. Best of all, he might surrender himself as well as all he had, and become a monk. Such was Abbot Hugh's message to King Philip I. Again, a knight, Odo *de Segur*, spoke for many when he was taught to reflect that

while we live in the toilsome pilgrimage of this world, it is right that each of us should make haste to redeem his sins by giving alms from the goods that God has bestowed upon him. Thus, he may hope to find that Christ, the Creator of all things, is most merciful to him on the Last Day.

Odo accordingly both took the monastic habit and gave his goods to Cluny for the redemption of his sins, 'in order that Almighty God may give me part and society with his saints and with his elect in the kingdom of heaven'.[4]

Should a man not take the ultimate step of becoming a monk,

---

[1] Luke 16: 9.

[2] e.g. Bruel, 3014, 3045, 3108, 3210, 3267. The charters of Cluny rang the changes on a small number of biblical texts and echoes which linked almsgiving and the remission of sins; e.g. 'Date helemosinam et ecce omnia munda sunt vobis': Bruel, 3127, cf. Tobit 4: 11–12; 'Absconde elemosinam in sinu pauperis, et ipsa orabit pro te ad Dominum sedulo': Bruel, 2978, cf. Ecclus. 29: 15; 'Divitiae viri redemptio animae eius': Bruel, 2983; 'Date helemosinam et haec ipsa pro vobis orabit ad Dominum': Bruel, 3102, cf. Luke 11: 41; 'Sicut aqua extinguit ignem, ita helemosina extinguit peccata': Bruel, 2997.

[3] For the long persistence of this world-view, and for an interesting retrospect of Cluny's position in the eleventh century, see the letter which Peter, prior of the canons regular of Saint-Jean at Sens, wrote to Bishop Hato of Troyes in 1145, when he became a monk at Cluny: G. Constable, 'The Letter from Peter of St. John to Hato of Troyes', *Studia Anselmiana*, xl (1956), 38–52.

[4] Bruel, 3002.

he might commit himself in a lesser way, by establishing a monastery upon his lands and endowing it to stand as a token of his self-commitment. Then its monks might offer prayers and do alms, which availed for him because they were supported by his substance in a house which expressed his devotion to St. Peter. The words of another charter illustrate the ideas that Abbot Hugh propounded with good effect amongst the feudal classes of his day. Between 1049 and 1064 Count Roger of Foix and his wife addressed Abbot Hugh in these terms, when they converted the church of Frédelac, near Toulouse, to Cluniac monasticism:

It is well known to us, father and master and pastor of souls (*pater et magister animarumque pastor*), as we see how, day by day, human kind are everywhere dying off, that we, too, cannot live for ever in the body. So we have taken thought together for the remedy and salvation of our souls, and for the remission of the sins which we have committed. We have decided to give you part of the transitory inheritance that we now seem to possess, so that we may merit a perpetual reward with the Lord; and that after our mortal bodies are finished with, we may live happily in eternal rest. This we believe that we can gain in superabundance by the merits and the prayers of your order, through the merits of Christ's own mercy. . . . We confidently commend you to his mercy, and, along with you, ourselves and our gifts. In particular, for the benefit of our souls and for those of all the faithful, I, Roger, and my wife, for the gaining of eternal life, grant . . . the place of St. Antoninus, which is vulgarly called Frédelac, to our Lord God, to our Creator and Redeemer Jesus Christ, to his Mother the holy Virgin Mary, to the holy apostles of the monastery of Cluny, St. Peter and St. Paul, and also to you, Hugh, who are of holy life and of worldwide fame as abbot of Cluny. . . .[1]

Perhaps a man could neither become a monk nor found a monastery, where intercession might be made especially for him and his family. If not, a further possibility was for him to receive the confraternity of the monks. By this means, which the Cluniacs under Abbot Hugh seem particularly to have exploited,[2] clergy

[1] Bruel, 2991.
[2] See Cowdrey, 'Unions and Confraternity with Cluny', *J.E.H.* xvi (1965), 152–62. This point has recently been reinforced by Wollasch's discussion of Cluniac Necrologies, and especially by his identification of the Necrology Bibl.

and laity alike were admitted to an especially close association
with the prayers and alms of Cluny and its monastic family. As
Abbot Hugh himself put it when he admitted to confraternity
Bishop Peter of Pamplona (1084–1114): 'We take him as our
brother, desiring that in all things, whether in life or in death, he
may be as one of us'.[1] Lastly, and most frequently, the mere fact of
making an ordinary gift to Cluny expressed a personal commitment to seeking the saving efficacy of its prayers and alms.

In the eleventh century the secular Church with its old-
fashioned penitential system provided perilously few resources
for the sinner to meet his needs as he experienced them in face
of the overmastering prospect of the Last Judgement. By those
resources which it did provide, it only increased his sense of the
need for such help as the monastic order could abundantly offer.
In such circumstances this circle of ideas, which was nowhere so
effectively developed as at the Cluny of Abbot Hugh, was of incalculable appeal and potency.[2] To its proclaiming of these ideas,
and to the unique reputation for efficacy that its intercessions
possessed, Cluny above all owed its enormous following in the
Church and lay society.

Because of this following, Cluny had an increasingly widespread
influence outside the cloister. In line with the prevailing tendency
of western monasticism, it combined its doctrine of other-
worldliness and withdrawal with a desire to communicate to the
world at large religious standards that would raise the lives of clergy
and laity alike.[3] It did, indeed, give primacy to a call to repentance

Nat. Paris, nouv. acq. Lat. 348, with more than ten thousand entries, as that of
Marcigny, and therefore as standing in an intimate relationship with Cluny's own
lost Necrology: see the articles cited above, p. 124, n. 2. Wollasch reviews the
evidence provided by the five surviving Cluniac Necrologies of Saint-Martial,
Limoges, Saint-Martin-des-Champs, Notre-Dame de Longpont, Moissac, and
Marcigny, and concludes that the vast scale and systematic ordering of the
Cluniac system of liturgical commemoration made it of unique significance in
the eleventh century: see esp. his conclusions, *ubi supra*, pp. 397–401.

[1] J. Ramackers, 'Analekten zur Geschichte des Reformpapsttums und der
Cluniazenser', *Q.F.I.A.B.* xxiii (1931), no. xvii, pp. 48–9.

[2] For a valuable discussion of eleventh-century lay piety in its relation to the
monastic order, see G. Miccoli, *Chiesa gregoriana* (Florence, 1966), pp. 55–7.

[3] See esp. C. Erdmann's remarks, *Die Entstehung des Kreuzzugsgedankens*
(Stuttgart, 1935), p. 63.

and to seeking the remission of sins by way of association with the monastic round. Yet its rulers knew as well as anyone that prevention is better than cure. Its energies were therefore also directed to extirpating the causes of sin in the Church and, still more, in feudal society. It played an occasional, though not a leading, part in the struggle against such clerical offences as simony.[1] More characteristically, it sought to abate the disorders of lay society which were the occasions of sin through murders, plundering, and the oppression of the poor.[2] It was a pioneer of the movements for the Peace of God and the Truce of God.[3] Its readiness to act directly upon the world disposed it to welcome and to collaborate with other reforming movements which sought similar ends. This included collaboration with the Papacy. A common concern for the better ordering of Church and society reinforced the duty that Cluny owed to the Papacy as the guardian of its liberty and as the sole authority upon earth to which it owed subjection, and it enhanced the significance of the liberty of Cluny for the theory and practice of papal authority.

III. THE OBJECTIVES OF THE GREGORIAN PAPACY

To build up what the reformers called the liberty of the Church was the primary objective of the Gregorian Papacy. They meant

---

[1] See e.g. Odo, *Collationes*, ii. 6–7, iii. 1–3, *Bibl. C.*, cols. 190–2, 220–3.

[2] e.g. by disseminating the picture of an ideal Christian layman which Abbot Odo provided in his *De vita sancti Geraldi Aureliacensis comitis*, *P.L.* cxxxiii. 639–704; E.T. in G. Sitwell, *St. Odo of Cluny* (London, 1958), pp. 90–180.

[3] Thus, the Peace of God movement was foreshadowed at the Council of Charroux (989). It was quickly followed by other councils, including that of Anse (994), which was particularly concerned to protect the lands of Cluny and to bring peace to the neighbouring area of Burgundy: Bruel, 2255. In 1041 Abbot Odilo seems to have played a leading part in causing the bishops of Provence to legislate for the Truce of God: Mansi xix. 593. Of the many studies of the Peace and Truce of God, the following are of particular interest in connection with Cluny: Dumas, *L'Église au pouvoir des laïques*, pp. 492–500; R. Bonnaud-Delamare, 'Fondement des institutions de paix au xie siècle', *Mélanges d'histoire du moyen âge dédiés à la mémoire de Louis Halphen* (Paris, 1951), pp. 19–26; Töpfer, *Volk und Kirche zur Zeit der beginnenden Gottesfriedensbewegung im Frankreich*; Hourlier, *Saint Odilon*, pp. 108–9; H. Hoffmann, *Gottesfriede und Treuga Dei* (Stuttgart, 1964); Duby, 'Les Laïcs et la paix de Dieu', *I laici nella 'societas Christiana' dei secoli xi e xii* (Milan, 1968), pp. 448–69.

by this the freeing of the Church from the subjection of its episcopal sees, parishes, and monasteries to temporal lordship, and the full committing of it to the service of God under the full and unrestricted authority of the Apostolic See of Rome. For the reformers, Cluny in the time of Abbot Hugh stood out as an epitome of this liberty, and therefore as a conspicuous example of what they sought to achieve. So far as the liberty of the Church was concerned, the Papacy of Gregory VII and the Cluny of Abbot Hugh stood very close to each other. Yet especially under Gregory VII, the objectives of the Papacy itself underwent a striking development which requires to be explored further; for it tended to leave Cluniac objectives far behind, and suggests certain points of contrast with them. It might well have led to a serious divergence between Gregory and the Cluniacs, and it caused occasional tension.

The most significant point of contrast which emerged between the objectives of Cluny and the Gregorian Papacy turns upon the way in which devotion to St. Peter at Cluny tended to divert men from the affairs of this fallen world, and to set their minds instead upon the Last Judgement and upon what Abbot Hugh described in his letter to King Philip I of France as 'the boundlessly rich and happy realms of heaven'. The Cluniacs invited men, even if they remained in the world, to centre their lives upon the world-renouncing ends of the monastic order. It was, by contrast, the distinguishing mark of Gregory VII that he applied his daemonic energies to the task of making effective the claims of St. Peter and the Apostolic See over this world. The tendency has been for recent scholars to insist, with good reason, that he did not seek to foster flight from the world, but that he strove to effect its immediate reordering under the hierarchical leadership of the vicar of St. Peter, and to ensure its present subjection to the claims of righteousness (*iustitia*), as he enunciated them.[1]

He was essentially novel in this. Far more even than the seven reforming popes who had reigned since the Papacy was reformed by the Emperor Henry III, Gregory VII aspired to vindicate the

---

[1] For a statement of this view, see esp. Tellenbach, *Church, State, and Christian Society*. I hope to discuss it more fully in a future book on Gregory VII.

pope's unique function as vicar of St. Peter in directly and actively overseeing, judging, and ordering the whole of Christian society here and now.[1] In a classic article Caspar has laid emphasis upon the radical difference of his rule as he identified himself, more closely than any pope had done before, with St. Peter and with Rome.[2] Whereas his predecessors since 1046 were almost all from Germany, Burgundy, or Lorraine, and the only true exception, Alexander II, came from Lombardy, Gregory was an Italian: born at Soano in Tuscany he came to Rome at a tender age and had spent most of his life as a member of St. Peter's own household there. Again, his predecessors were aristocratic, even royal, in their family connections; they—like Abbot Hugh of Cluny—came from the established ruling circles of Europe and never entirely divested themselves of their outlook. Gregory was by origin plebeian. In 1073 Abbot Walo of Metz could hail him as 'virum de plebe' and as the new David whom God had raised up from amongst the sheepfolds to be the head of the people.[3] Politically and socially, therefore, he owed nothing to anyone; no ties whatsoever bound him, save those which he had with the apostle whose vicar he was. Moreover, Gregory was a monk;[4] whereas with one insignificant exception[5] his predecessors since 1046 were all seculars. In his case, the effect of monastic obedience and detachment was still more to accentuate his loyalty to the apostle in whose household he had been brought up. A monk with no ties to the world, and a poor man's son who was beholden to no one but who, because he was educated in the household of St. Peter,

---

[1] It is important to remember that, despite its occasional use since early times, 'vicarius Christi' was not often used as a papal title before the thirteenth century; indeed, in the eleventh century it was much more often used of the emperor. The usual papal title at this time was 'vicarius sancti Petri'. On the whole subject, see esp. M. Maccarrone, *Vicarius Christi, storia del titolo papale* (Rome, 1952).

[2] E. Caspar, 'Gregor VII. in seinen Briefen', *Historische Zeitschrift*, cxxx (1924), 1–30.

[3] *Pontificum Romanorum . . . vitae*, ed. J. M. Watterich, i (Leipzig, 1862), 740–2; cf. the sneers of Benzo of Alba: 'Quidam humuntio, ventre lato, crure curto . . . natus matre suburbana, de patre caprario': *Ad Heinricum imperatorem*, vi, ed. K. Pertz, *M.G.H. Scr.* xi. 659–60. [4] See below, p. 148, n. 4.

[5] The exception is Pope Stephen IX (1057–8). But he was a monk only briefly, after his election in 1055 as abbot of Monte Cassino; and he owed his promotion to the Papacy to the fact that he was the brother of the duke of Lorraine.

owed an eternal and exclusive debt to him, Gregory made clear in his letters the motives of zeal and love for his patron, which ruled his life:

I must diligently watch and consider how, by the help of God, I may proclaim and faithfully implement whatever makes for the furthering of the religion of the Church and the salvation of the flock of Christ. Before all else, I am impelled by the fear that negligence in the steward-ship that is committed to me may be my accuser before the eternal Judge; and by the love that I owe to the Prince of the Apostles, who has nourished me from my infancy with singular devotion, and who has favoured me in the bosom of his kindness.[1]

Like the Cluniacs, Gregory saw the world as set under the imminent judgement of God. But whereas their first objective was to call upon men to take refuge from it by associating them-selves as fully as they could with the world-renouncing life of the cloister, his was to call upon men to convert the world in order that it might be mastered and reordered by the pastoral authority of the vicar of St. Peter.[2] Where Hugh of Cluny bade men cast off the burden of this world, Gregory called on them to shoulder it. His function was, like that of the prophets of old, to announce to them the demands of truth and righteousness, so that they might actively do so.[3] His own words best convey the conviction and this-worldliness, with which he asserted his leadership:

Although we are a sinner and unequal to the bearing of such a burden, God has committed to our weak shoulders the care of all the churches. For our Lord Jesus Christ appointed blessed Peter to be the Prince of the Apostles, and he gave him the keys of the kingdom of heaven and

[1] *Reg.* i. 39, 20 Dec. 1073, pp. 61–2.

[2] See esp. Tellenbach, *Church, State, and Christian Society*, pp. x–xiv, 42–60, 162–8; 'Die Bedeutung des Reformpapsttums für die Einigung des Abendlandes', *S.G.* ii (1947), 125–49.

[3] Thus, some of his favourite biblical citations were from the greater prophets of the Old Testament; e.g. the following catena of Isa. 58 : 1, Ezek. 3 : 18, and Jer. 48: 10: '. . . in eo loco positi sumus, ut velimus nolimus omnibus gentibus, maxime christianis, veritatem et iustitiam annuntiare compellamur dicente Domino: "Clama, ne cesses; quasi tuba exalta vocem tuam et annuntia populo meo scelera eorum", et alibi, "Si non annuntiaveris iniquo iniquitatem suam, animam eius de manu tua requiram"; item propheta: "Maledictus", inquit, "homo, qui prohibet gladium suum a sanguine", id est verbum predicationis a carnalium increpatione': *Reg.* i. 15, 1 July 1073, p. 23.

the power of binding and loosing in heaven and upon earth. He also
built his Church upon him and entrusted to him the feeding of his
sheep. From his time, this principality and power have descended
through St. Peter to all his successors, and will descend to them until
the end of the world, as a divine privilege and by a hereditary right.
Because we have succeeded to it, we are compelled by an ineluctable
necessity to come to the aid of all the oppressed. We must fight with
the sword of the Holy Spirit, which is the word of God, to the death
if need be, in the defence of righteousness (*iustitia*) against the enemies
of God until they are converted.[1]

Because the pope exercised St. Peter's authority to bind and to
loose, the temporal rulers and the military classes to whom the
Cluniacs especially appealed, must obey him as loyally and
actively as must bishops. The obligation was more than a moral
one, and it was rooted in this world as firmly as in the next. In
Gregory's belief St. Peter's power to bind and loose on earth as
well as in heaven meant that, when his vicar spoke in his name,
he could not only give or withhold spiritual blessedness in the
world to come; he could also give or deny material prosperity and
military victory in the dealings of this world.[2]

Because St. Peter had such power over the affairs of men even
in this life and because his vicar was so straitly charged with the
proclamation and the fulfilment of righteousness here upon earth,
the pope necessarily looked to all men, and especially to those with
any kind of ecclesiastical, social, or political pre-eminence, for
active service in this world in the cause of St. Peter. It is at this
point, in particular, that Gregory's intention to divert the Church
from its old attitude of withdrawal from the world to one of
mastering it, has reasonably been interpreted as establishing the
sharpest possible contrast between the Gregorian Reform and the
monastic order, including Cluny.[3] For in order to recruit men for

[1] *Reg.* ix. 35, 1083, pp. 622–3. The letter is addressed to the bishops and lay
magnates of Flanders, and urges them to exhort Count Robert I to do penance
for certain wrongs which he had done with respect to the church of Thérouanne.

[2] For this important and recurring claim of Gregory's, see e.g. *Reg.* v. 14a,
Lent 1078, pp. 370–1; v. 15, 9 Mar. 1078, p. 376; vi. 1, 3 July 1078, p. 390; vii.
14a, 7 Mar. 1080, p. 486.

[3] e.g. Caspar wrote of Gregory VII that 'Sein scharfer Verstand und politischer
Herrschinstinkt bildete den cluniazensischen Reformgedanken: Freiheit der Kirche

active service in the world, Gregory radically reinterpreted the traditional conception of the 'militia Christi' as it had been understood, for example, by St. Paul[1] or in the Rule of St. Benedict.[2] Hitherto it had been regarded as an entirely spiritual warfare. It was waged most characteristically in the cloister; although, in a general sense, it comprehended the whole spiritual mission of the Church. In either case it stood in the sharpest contrast to the secular warfare of the knight.[3] In the letters of Gregory VII, however, the emphasis was changed. Gregory did, indeed, use 'militia Christi' and similar terms figuratively, to express the Church's spiritual warfare on behalf of Christ.[4] But he also extended the concept, sometimes ambiguously[5] and sometimes plainly,[6] so that it included actual warfare with earthly arms in the hierarchical service of the Church. The warfare of Christ was the warfare of knights upon an earthly battlefield.

Furthermore, he reinforced his new interpretation of the 'militia Christi' by giving wide currency to another and novel concept: that of a 'militia sancti Petri', with its associated idea that a Christian might be the 'miles (fidelis) sancti Petri'. These terms, too, might have a spiritual sense. But characteristically, they appear

von der Welt, unversehens weiter in den hierarchischen Gedanken: Herrschaft der Kirche über die Welt, als Garantie ihrer Freiheit von der Welt': art. cit., *Hist. Zeitschr.* cxxx (1924), 11.   [1] e.g. Eph. 6: 11–17.

[2] Prologue, ed. Schmitz, p. 3; *cap.* 2, p. 23; *cap.* 61, p. 177.

[3] For a particularly clear Cluniac statement of this contrast, see the charter in which, in 1088, a knight, Geoffrey III of Semur, renounced his secular knighthood, and, together with his wife, one of his sons, and two of his daughters, entered the religious life: '. . . ego Gaufredus de Sinemuro, audiens in evangelio Dominum dicentem, "nisi quis renunciaverit omnibus quae possidet, non potest meus esse discipulus", recognoscens quoque enormitatem et profundam voraginem peccatorum meorum, eligi in domo Dei abjectus esse magis quam habitare in tabernaculis peccatorum, et abjecto cingulo militiae saecularis, in quo Dominum graviter offenderam, militiae Dei, cui servire regnare est, me ipsum cum uxore mea nomine Ermengarde et uno filio ac duabus filiabus submittere, et ut hoc Deo sacrificium acceptabilius fieret, aliquid de haereditate mea in loco quem ad hoc opus elegerem conferre': *Le Cartulaire de Marcigny-sur-Loire*, ed. Richard, no. 15, pp. 15–17.

[4] e.g. *Reg.* i. 43, 25 Jan. 1074, p. 67; i. 75, 13 Apr. 1074, p. 107.

[5] e.g. *Reg.* iii. 15, 1076, p. 277; iv. 12, Jan. 1077, p. 312.

[6] e.g. *Reg.* i. 12, 29 June 1073, p. 20; i. 27, 13 Oct. 1073, pp. 44–5; ii. 37, 16 Dec. 1074, p. 173; vi. 17, 2 Jan. 1079, p. 423.

in Gregory's letters and in other Gregorian sources in relation
to the chivalric society of all lands. Gregory hoped and intended
that its obedience and earthly service might be available to the
vicar of St. Peter, in order that he might be able to enforce his
demands upon spiritual and lay powers alike by the temporal
sword and so to reorder this world according to the demands of
righteousness. As Gregory used the terms, they were used of lay
figures only, not of monks, prelates, or other secular clergy. They
did not ordinarily have any strict meaning in terms of formal
feudal dependence and obligation. They nevertheless proclaimed an overriding moral commitment to serve the cause of
St. Peter in the world with earthly arms, however and whenever
the pope might direct, in a way that stood superior to all merely
temporal loyalties and obligations. To such a 'servitium sancti
Petri',[1] Gregory sought, with varying degrees of success, to
commit kings[2] and magnates;[3] but above all it was to the lower
feudal classes that he appealed.[4] In all lands they were to rally and
devote their weapons to it. They were not to look away from the
world but to work for its conversion. By their means Gregory
sought to provide the pope with resources of military power, so
that the righteousness whose demands he proclaimed might be
enforced here and now upon all peoples.[5]

IV. CLUNY AND THE OBJECTIVES OF THE GREGORIAN REFORM

Given the novelty of Gregory VII's interpretation of the authority
of St. Peter and the duties of his vicar, and his zeal for the reordering and mobilization of the Church and of this world, there were

[1] e.g. *Reg.* i. 46, 2 Feb. 1074, p. 70; i. 57, 17 Mar. 1074, p. 84; ii. 3, 10 Sept.
1074, p. 128.
[2] e.g. *Reg.* i. 63, 20 Mar. 1074, p. 92 (Sancho II of Aragon); vii. 23, 24 April
1080, p. 500 (William I of England); ix. 3, Mar. 1080, p. 576 (the new anti-king
in Germany). [3] See above, p. 140, n. 6.
[4] e.g. *Reg.* ii. 49, 22 Jan. 1075, p. 190; ix. 4, Feb. 1080, p. 578. The Swabian
chronicler Bernold's use of the term 'miles sancti Petri' is particularly noteworthy:
Chronicon, s.a. 1078 and following, *M.G.H. Scr.* v. 435, 442–7, 450, 457, 461.
[5] In the last two paragraphs, I have drawn heavily upon Erdmann, *Die Entstehung des Kreuzzugsgedankens*, pp. 185–211.

manifest possibilities of a serious divergence, if not of a conflict, between Cluniac and Gregorian objectives. At first sight Cluny's way of promoting the service of St. Peter by drawing men into close association with the monastic order, was by no means readily compatible with Gregory VII's way of calling men to an active and this-worldly 'militia Christi'. There was even a tendency for Cluny at least implicitly to ignore and bypass the position of the Apostolic See altogether. The Cluniacs sought to help men to find the remission of their sins and to have favour with St. Peter on the Day of Judgement. But as it had its heart and centre in the monastic round at Cluny, such a service of St. Peter assigned no explicit function to his vicar at Rome, with his power to bind and loose upon earth, and with his claim to be the arbiter alike of heavenly rewards and of earthly prosperity. As it was exercised through Cluny and its monastic round, St. Peter's pastorate of souls might well seem to leave little place for his rule of the world as Christ had vested it in the Apostolic See and its jurisdiction; it might seem, instead, to provide a better way of salvation.[1] Nor did Cluny's concentration upon the fortunes of the individual at the Day of Judgement necessarily tend to promote attentiveness to Gregory's claims upon men's loyalty in his own struggle to reorder the world here and now.

Moreover, the splendour of Cluny could easily seem to make it a second and even a competing Rome. Its third church was planned to be larger than St. Peter's at Rome, and than all other churches in the west. It possessed relics of St. Peter, who could,

---

[1] Cf. Gilo's story of a pilgrim who found forgiveness of sins at Cluny more readily than at Rome: 'Quidam peregrinus limina apostolorum adiens, peccatorum remissionem ante beati Petri altare attentius implorabat; cui post longam precum instantiam revelatum est quod salutem, quam votis expetebat, in Cluniacensi monasterio paratius quam in urbe reperiret, si penes abbatem loci illius aditum impetraret. Cluniacum festinanter advehitur, sanctumque Hugonem Petri assecretum voce et animo passim requirit. Quem postquam videre meruit, fonte lacrymarum uberrime suffusus suppliciter exorat, ut ducatu ipsius patrie reddatur quam proprio excessu perdiderat. Narrat enim qualiter ad tantos ausus non presumptuose duceretur, immo magis animatus revelatione spirituali Rome sibi imposita. Tum vero pater piissimus commendatum sibi a Deo recipit, et in ovili Dominico constitutum habitu sacro induit regulariter informandum. Hic postea per aliquod tempus probabiliter vivens in bona confessione transivit': Gilo, *Vita Hugonis*, L'Huillier, *Saint Hugues*, p. 607.

therefore, be venerated there as he could be venerated at Rome.[1] It could even be said, by a bishop, that to come to Cluny was to come 'ad limina apostolorum'.[2] In so ardent a devotee of Cluny as King Alphonso VI of León-Castile, whose financial contributions largely made it possible for Cluny to undertake the building of the third church, devotion to St. Peter at Cluny could at times appear stronger than devotion to St. Peter at Rome.[3]

To this extent, there is a certain prima facie case for asserting that the Cluny of Abbot Hugh was not, in its own spiritual objectives, the supporter of Rome but its competitor, and that it tended to call men away from the kind of loyalty and service of St. Peter that Gregory was most concerned to recommend.

When certain episodes in the known dealings of Gregory VII with Abbot Hugh are considered, there can be no gainsaying that Gregory occasionally spoke as though Abbot Hugh were, indeed, neglectful of, or even antagonistic to, his own objectives. Upon occasion, Gregory expressly complained of Hugh's neglectfulness of matters outside the cloister. As early in his pontificate as the spring of 1074, he rebuked Hugh for his slackness in not visiting Rome, despite repeated requests that he should do so. Gregory complained that Hugh had not done the tasks with which he had charged him when he became pope. Hugh's words, said Gregory, were welcome and sweet; but he would have been better pleased if Hugh's love for the Roman Church had burned more brightly. He did not think that Hugh's remissness could be put down to the pressure of his other concerns. Was it not, rather, that he fled from toilsome duties and was prone to seek excuses for postponing business when the prospect of it wearied him?[4]

This querulous letter is not only evidence of Gregory's irritation with Hugh for seeming to neglect the claims that the pope reasonably made upon him. It is also a reminder that, in marked contrast to the normal custom of earlier abbots of Cluny, Hugh visited

---

[1] Bruel, 3540, cf. 3561. [2] Bruel, 3599, cf. 2984.

[3] See below, p. 244, n. 2.

[4] *Reg.* i. 62, 19 Mar. 1074, p. 90. For evidence that Hugh's reserve at this time was, in fact, prompted by a reasonable hesitation to follow Gregory in his extravagant demands in relation to the kingdoms of Spain, see below, p. 224.

Rome but seldom. He had, indeed, come three times to the
Apostolic See before Gregory became pope—a fact that makes
his later avoidance of it the more striking.[1] For under Gregory
VII, so far as is known he came only in 1076, when Gregory
is said to have absolved him from the excommunication that
resulted from his contact with the emperor;[2] and in 1083 when he
came to mediate between Gregory and Henry.[3] He does not seem
to have again visited Rome during the remaining twenty-six
years of his life.[4]

But the principal reason for suggesting that there was a divergence of objectives between the Cluniacs and Gregory VII which
made Abbot Hugh antagonistic to Gregory, at least in Gregory's
eyes, turns upon the question whether the truer service of St.
Peter was performed in the cloister or in the world. At Cluny
Abbot Hugh was particularly remembered in the twelfth century
for his concern to recruit as monks and to bring into the monastic
haven the very men of the feudal classes whom Gregory was
concerned to mobilize for the 'militia sancti Petri' in the world at
large. His biographer, Gilo, applauded him because

he shrewdly took note of men who had the makings of monks and
elicited monastic vows from them. . . . As men come from a raging
tempest into a haven, so, through him, the great of many ranks and
walks of life were converted from their turbulent and restless ways
into the calm of monastic peace.[5]

A notable case in point was Duke Hugh I of Burgundy (1075–8),
whom Hugh admitted to Cluny as a monk in 1078 upon the
death of his wife.[6] When Gregory heard of this he rebuked Hugh
for taking into 'the calm of monastic peace' one of the few lay

---

[1] In 1050, he was at the first Lent Council after he became abbot: Mansi, xix.
771; in 1058, he was at Stephen IX's Lent Council: *P.L.* cxli. 869; and, in 1063,
he sought Alexander II's aid against the church of Mâcon: above, pp. 47–8.

[2] Berthold, *Annales*, s.a. 1077, *M.G.H. Scr.* v. 289.

[3] See below, pp. 161–2. The anecdote in the *Dicta Anselmi*, no .vi, is too uncertain in its details to establish a third, and separate, visit: see below, pp. 149–50.

[4] See Mager's reconstruction of Hugh's itinerary in *Neue Forschungen*, pp.
357–76.

[5] Gilo, *Vita Hugonis*, L'Huillier, *Saint Hugues*, p. 582.

[6] He already enjoyed the confraternity of Cluny: Bruel, 3518.

rulers who were obedient to his own purposes. To do such a
thing was to jeopardize the salvation of Christian peoples;
Gregory insisted that Hugh should attend to the good of the
Church at large: 'dum satis intendis aulicos nutrire, de rusticis
parum tibi est curae'. He went on to accuse him of a grave lapse
of duty:

> Dearest brother, why do you not weigh or consider how great are
> the danger and the misfortune into which the holy Church has fallen?
> Where are the men who will gladly stand in the breach for the love of
> God and who do not fear to suffer death for the sake of righteousness
> and truth? Behold how those who seem to love or fear God flee away
> from the warfare of Christ and are heedless of the salvation of their
> brethren; loving only themselves, they seek out their own peace. The
> shepherds flee, as do the dogs who are the guardians of their flocks.
> Wolves and robbers ravage Christ's sheep while no one stops them.
> You have enticed, or at least admitted, the duke into the peace of
> Cluny. You are the cause of tens of thousands of Christians having no
> one to guard them. Perhaps our promptings have carried little weight
> with you. Perhaps the commands of the Apostolic See have not met with
> due obedience from you. If this be so, why have not the crying of the
> poor, the tears of widows, the desolation of churches, the mourning of
> orphans, and the complaining of priests and monks so moved you to
> fear that you no longer neglect the words of St. Paul: 'Charity seeks
> not her own', and that you remember your usual principle: 'He who
> loves his neighbour has fulfilled the law'?[1]

This outburst, in particular, lends colour to the view that on
Gregory VII's own showing Abbot Hugh was too preoccupied
with the monastic life and with promoting withdrawal from the
world for his own objectives to have been genuinely compatible
with those of the Gregorian Reform; if he well served St. Peter in
the cloister, he did not, by Gregory VII's standards, serve him
sufficiently in the Church at large.

There is, indeed, evidence in this letter of the possibility of
a serious divergence of aims and of at least occasional tension
and disagreement between Gregory and Abbot Hugh. But the
remarkable thing is that the divergence did not, in fact, ever develop,

[1] *Reg.* vi. 17, 2 Jan. 1079, pp. 423–4.

and that the tension was exceptional. Further, there is no evidence
for a conscious divergence of objectives to add to the little that has
already been given—just one letter of Gregory's which alleged
neglectfulness, and one which seems to imply a deeper antagonism;
and it would be wise to hesitate before placing too much weight
upon Gregory's rebuke, in the second letter, to Abbot Hugh
about the duke of Burgundy. Gregory addressed the letter
cordially to 'H. venerabili Cluniacensi abbati et carissimo fratri';
and he concluded it by referring to Hugh's habitual charity, and
by asking for the continuing support of his prayers and those of
his brethren.[1] Moreover, such a stricture as is contained in this
letter was no more severe than others that Gregory from time to
time addressed to his staunchest supporters, even to such as Hugh
of Die and Richard of Marseilles; for his attitude to his trusted
agents swung rapidly between praise and condemnation.[2] It is
important to view such a piece of evidence in a sufficiently wide
perspective to judge whether it is typical.

Thus, over against the case of Duke Hugh of Burgundy, there
must be set the praise that the Gregorian chronicler Bernold of
St. Blasien had for Abbot Hugh, because he was said to have refused to admit to the cloister, and so take out of the world, a far
greater figure than the duke—King Alphonso VI of León-Castile.
After referring to Alphonso's catholic faith and to his following
of the abbot of Cluny,[3] Bernold related how he had fought man-
fully and often against the pagan Almoravids.

He would [Bernold continued] lately have made himself a monk at
Cluny, had the lord abbot not thought it more in keeping with the
needs of the times, that he should remain where he was, in the world.[4]

---

[1] *Reg.* vi. 17, 2 Jan. 1079, pp. 423–4.

[2] See e.g. his rebukes of Hugh of Die: *Reg.* v. 17, 9 Mar. 1078, pp. 378–80;
ix. 5, 1081, pp. 579–80; of Abbot Richard of Marseilles, *Ep. Coll.* 39, 1082, p. 566;
and also his outburst against King Alphonso VI of Castile, *Reg.* viii. 3, 27 June
1080, pp. 519–20.

[3] '. . . in conversatione Cluniacensis abbatis obedientiarius . . .'.

[4] *Chron. s.a.* 1093, *M.G.H. Scr.* v. 457. Much later, in *c.* 1101–3, Abbot Hugh
sent encouragement to St. Anselm, as one who would rather have sat at Christ's
feet with Mary, but who, nevertheless, must follow God's will in serving with
Martha: St. Anselm, *Ep.* 259, *S. Anselmi Cantuariensis archiepiscopi opera omnia*,
ed. F. S. Schmitt, iv (Edinburgh, 1951), 172–3.

Whether or not the story be true, it shows that, after the incident of the duke of Burgundy, Abbot Hugh was to earn a good reputation, in one Gregorian circle at least, for leaving in the field those who were engaged in the warfare of Christ as Gregory propounded it; and that Abbot Hugh may have understood and furthered Gregorian objectives more positively than Gregory's letter about the duke of Burgundy might suggest.

So far as the rest of the evidence is concerned, both the personal relationship between Gregory VII and Abbot Hugh and, still more, the relationship between the two institutions of the Papacy and Cluny, are such as to suggest an underlying mutual understanding and compatibility of objectives: these were the rule, while Gregory's strictures were the exception.

Gregory's own letters and privileges yield ample evidence that so far as his personal relationship with Abbot Hugh is concerned, his habitual praise of him and his work was no less eloquent than his occasional blame. In 1075, he wrote to him as 'karissimo sanctae Romanae ecclesiae filio reverentissimo videlicet Cluniacensis coenobii abbati'.[1] Just after his conciliar allocution of 1080, he asserted, in a letter to King Alphonso VI of León-Castile written at a time of crisis, that Abbot Hugh and he were at one in their service of God: 'eadem enim via eodem sensu eodem spiritu ambulamus'.[2] At the same time he congratulated Abbot Hugh himself upon his long and active zeal for the Apostolic See:

> You have given long-standing proof of our confidence that you think exactly as we think about the honour of the Holy Roman Church, and that you have kept to the liberty of the right path as regards the keeping of righteousness (*iustitia*), which, as love grows cold, has now departed from almost all lands.[3]

It is not surprising in view of this sense of common purposes that, in Gregory's Register, Abbot Hugh was the only correspondent, apart from Countess Matilda of Tuscany, to whom the pope wrote with any hint of personal warmth and feeling:

---

[1] Santifaller, Q.F., no. 109, p. 104.   [2] *Reg.* viii. 3, p. 520.
[3] *Reg.* viii. 2, 27 June 1080, pp. 517–18. For a fuller discussion of these letters, see below, pp. 232–6.

'Wearied by the pressure of all manner of people and by pondering many matters of business, I am writing a little to one I love much.'[1]

A similar sense of common purposes and of mutual affection also existed between the two men according to the oral traditions of Cluny. This is illustrated by the general tone of the six anecdotes about Gregory which are preserved amongst the *Dicta Anselmi*.[2] These anecdotes were quite widely recorded in variant forms,[3] and four of them expressly mention Abbot Hugh. They were current at Cluny during the abbot's last years, and may be taken to reflect faithfully his own memories of Gregory. The first three of them concern Abbot Hugh's dealings with Hildebrand before he became pope. According to the first anecdote, when Archdeacon Hildebrand came to France as a legate, he greeted the abbot with especial warmth and friendship; for, as it related, Hugh was dear to him on account of their early residence together and of Hugh's well-known goodness.[4] That Hildebrand

---

[1] *Reg.* v. 21, 7 May 1078, p. 384; cf. ii. 49, 22 Jan. 1075, pp. 188–90.

[2] For the *Dicta Anselmi*, see F. S. Schmitt, 'Neue und alte Hildebrand-Anekdoten aus den *Dicta Anselmi*', *S.G.* v (1956), 1–18; for an English translation and commentary, see A. Stacpoole, 'Hugh of Cluny and the Hildebrandine Miracle Tradition', *Revue bénédictine*, lxxvii (1967), 341–63. In Schmitt's opinion the Hildebrandine anecdotes were told at Cluny during the second exile of St. Anselm of Canterbury, probably in 1105. They were then noted down by a monk of Christ Church, Canterbury, Alexander, who accompanied the archbishop. Alexander wrote them in their final form some ten to fifteen years later.

[3] For the parallels, see Schmitt, art. cit., pp. 6–7.

[4] Ibid., pp. 9–10. This anecdote, together with the third, is evidence for Hildebrand's own monastic profession. The two anecdotes add to the improbability that Hildebrand was actually professed at Cluny after the death of Pope Gregory VI, a story that first occurs in Bonizo of Sutri, *Liber ad amicum*, ed. E. Dümmler, v, *M.G.H. L. de L.* i. 587, a very unreliable source. Gregory VII never referred to his profession as a monk; but it is improbable that he became one during his exile. While Gregory VI lived, Hildebrand's presence with him and his familiarity with the German court tell against a conversion of life: Reg. i. 19, 1 Sept. 1073, p. 32; ii. 44, 10 Jan. 1075, pp. 180–1. Gregory VI's death cannot have been before Christmas, 1047, and may have been some months later: Anselm, *Gesta archiepiscoporum Leodiensium*, ed. R. Koepke, 65, *M.G.H. Scr.* vii. 228–9. The time between it and Hildebrand's return to Rome with Pope Leo IX, who was elected pope in December 1048, hardly admits of the year's novitiate required by the Rule of St. Benedict (*cap.* 58) and by the Customs of Cluny at the time: *Cons. Farf.* ii. 2, ed. Albers, p. 139. It is more likely that Hildebrand became a monk

held Hugh in high esteem is also clear from the third anecdote, which again concerns his legatine activity in France: when he visited Cluny and was present at the monastic chapter of faults, he had a vision of Christ himself standing at the abbot's left hand while he presided.[1] In the first anecdote, Abbot Hugh was tempted to think Hildebrand proud. The story told of Hugh's secret anim-adversions upon Hildebrand's sudden rise in the world and his zealous and busy service of St. Peter;[2] it well illustrates the social and temperamental distance between the conservative and aristo-cratic Burgundian monk and the low-born familiar of St. Peter whose tendency to magnify his office knew no restraints. But, in the second, Hugh recognized in Hildebrand the spirit of prophecy, and so held him thereafter in great veneration.[3] The sixth anecdote is of Gregory as pope, and it casts a rather surprising light upon the pastoral dealings of Gregory and Hugh at Rome.[4] During a journey from the city, Gregory learned in a vision that a close Roman

before 1046 in the Roman monastery of St. Mary's-on-the-Aventine, with its Cluniac associations: Paul of Bernried, *Vita Gregorii VII*, 9, *Pontificum Romanorum . . . vitae*, ed. Watterich, i. 477. The statement in the first anecdote, that Abbot Hugh was dear to Hildebrand' ex antiqua cohabitatione', strongly suggests that Hildebrand stayed at Cluny for a time during his exile, although it in no way implies that he was professed there. As a monk, Hildebrand's place in chapter would perhaps be explicable if he had been admitted to the confraternity of Cluny: *Cons. Farf.* ii. 58, Albers, p. 199. For recent discussions, see esp. G. B. Borino, 'Quando e dove si fece monaco Ildebrando?' *Miscellanea Giovanni Mercati (Studi e testi,* cxxv, Rome, 1946), pp. 218–62; Schmitt, art. cit., pp. 5–6; A. Stacpoole, 'Hildebrand, Cluny and the Papacy', *Downside Review*, lxxxi (1963), 142–64, 254–72; C. N. L. Brooke, *Europe in the Central Middle Ages* (London, 1964), p. 250, n. 1; Wollasch, 'Die Wahl des Papstes Nikolaus II.', *Adel und Kirche*, *Festschrift für Gerd Tellenbach*, ed. J. Fleckenstein and K. Schmid (Freiburg, 1968), pp. 205–20, an article which, upon the evidence of Cluniac Necrologies, makes it virtually certain that Hildebrand was not a Cluniac monk.

[1] Schmitt, art. cit., pp. 11–12.

[2] Ibid., p. 10. The anecdotes of Hildebrand and Hugh which are preserved by Paul of Bernried have a similar character: *Vita Gregorii VII*, 18–20, 119, *Pontificum Romanorum . . . vitae*, ed. Watterich, i. 481, 543–4.

[3] Schmitt, art. cit., pp. 10–11: 'Ab illo igitur die praefatus valde venerabilis vitae vir eundem HILDEBRANDUM in magna veneratione habuit, quem prophetiae spiritum habere in duobus iam signis evidenter agnovit.' Cf. the fourth, fifth, and sixth anecdotes: ibid., pp. 13–16.

[4] Ibid., pp. 15–16. For the problem of the date and place, see Stacpoole, art. cit., *Revue bénédictine*, lxxvii (1967), 361–2.

supporter of his who was also well known to Hugh, had committed
fornication. He employed Hugh as his agent in gently bringing
him to repentance, and the anecdote ends on a note of praise for
Gregory on account of his mild and paternal conduct.[1]

Taken as a group, these anecdotes from Cluny give credibility
to Gregory's own assertion about his dealings with Abbot Hugh,
that 'eadem enim via eodem sensu eodem spiritu ambulamus';
just as they testify to Hugh's own regard for Gregory. The two
men differed in temperament and, especially in the early days
of their relationship, the contrast between them could become
apparent. Yet this was the exception; the rule was one of co-
operation and mutual affection.

But perhaps the most instructive of all the evidence for the
personal relations between the two men is Gregory's habitual
nickname for Abbot Hugh which was remembered at Cluny in
the twelfth century:

> When he was made pope, [Gregory] used to call [Hugh] 'the
> urbane tyrant' (*blandum tyrannum*); for to the fierce he showed himself
> a lion, but to the meek he was a lamb. He knew well how to spare the
> humble and to rebuke the proud.[2]

Each word of the nickname is significant. 'Blandus', which refers
to Hugh's skill in handling men, suggests approval and an admiration that was the sharper because of Gregory's own frequent
want of this very skill. 'Tyrannus' indicates Gregory's recognition
that while Hugh might be asked and urged to do things, he might
never be commanded. Within his vast sphere of influence, both
inside and outside the cloister, his authority must be acknowledged.
Yet as the interpretation of the nickname shows, it was approving
and even affectionate. Abbot Hugh was urbane to the Papacy
as well; and he was bound to it by Cluny's need of the Papacy
to defend its liberty and by the obligation of service that this
defence created. Abbot Hugh had a fundamental obligation to
the Apostolic See, even if he occasionally showed a prudent

---

[1] For the approval with which Gregory's pastoral dealings with individuals
met at Cluny, cf. the fifth anecdote: Schmitt, art. cit., pp. 14–15.

[2] Gilo, *Vita Hugonis*, L'Huillier, *Saint Hugues*, p. 583; *Epitome vitae ab Ezelone
atque Gilone . . . excerpta*, 3, P.L. clix. 912.

calculation in its discharge. If Gregory and Hugh sometimes treated each other with a certain mutual wariness, they habitually respected each other and their purposes.

It is, however, when the eleventh-century popes' appreciation of the monastic objectives of Cluny as an institution is added to Gregory's approval of Abbot Hugh as a person and as an ecclesiastical figure, that Cluny and the Papacy are most clearly revealed to have had outlooks and objectives which, even apart from the question of Cluny's liberty, were basically compatible and complimentary. For it stands out in the evidence that, despite all the changes in papal policy during the eleventh century, the popes themselves in fact understood and set the highest value upon the objectives of Cluny. This was above all the case with Gregory, the most revolutionary of them all. His occasional strictures upon Abbot Hugh were invariably addressed *ad hominem*; of Cluny, as an institution, Gregory never spoke save in terms of honour and approval. It has already been seen how, even when he had carried his interpretation of his vicariate of St. Peter to its fullest development, he upheld the liberty of Cluny, in his conciliar allocution of 1080, as a pattern of the liberty which he sought to propagate in the Church. It is no less important to notice that the eleventh-century popes, including Gregory, always valued and applauded the services to the Papacy, and to the Church at large, which it has been shown that Cluny's devotions were understood to provide; and, in particular, that they warmly approved of Cluny's chosen role as the 'asylum poenitentium'.

The popes themselves felt to the full the contemporary need for intercessory support in life and in death. They looked as did everyone else to the monastic order, and to Cluny in particular, for such support, in order to secure the remission of their sins and the salvation of their souls. Cluny accordingly met the need by assigning to the popes a regular and special place in its masses for the departed.[1] At Rome, it was Popes Benedict VIII and John XIX who first appear to have set an especial value upon the penitential and intercessory work of the Cluniacs. When Benedict VIII wrote

[1] *Ordo Cluniacensis per Bernardum*, i. 42, Herrgott, *Vetus disciplina monastica*, pp. 232–3, and i. 73, p. 266; Ulrich, *Consuetudines*, i. 7, *P.L.* cxlix. 652.

in 1016 to the bishops of Burgundy, Provence, and Aquitaine, he explained how the masses and alms of the Cluniacs brought bene- fit to the whole Church.[1] When Benedict died it was believed that it was the intercessions of the Cluniacs that opened the gates of heaven for him.[2] As their intercessions opened heaven for Benedict, so, it was later believed, those of Abbot Hugh performed a similar service for Stephen IX: Hugh was present at his death- bed in Florence, and according to a widely circulated anecdote, it was only by the power of his intercessions that the demons who vexed the pope were kept at bay.[3]

So far as Gregory VII himself was concerned, he was not so little of a monk that, in his preoccupation with the reordering of this world, he did not value Cluny's intercessions both for the salvation of sinners and in all the contingencies of his own life. In particular, he desired the Cluniacs' prayers for himself as pope. The abbot of Cluny was one of those to whom he wrote upon his election.[4] Almost a year later he reminded Hugh of the request for Cluny's prayers that he then made; he said that, without their continual support, he could not hope to avoid the dangers which menaced both himself and the Church.[5] In January 1075, when all the plans of his early months as pope seemed in ruins, it was Abbot Hugh to whom Gregory poured out his soul. He desired the prayers of his monks on the very grounds that their withdrawal from the world assured their nearness to heaven; and he contrasted his own immersion in worldly matters with the excellence of the Cluniac life:

Because praise is not seemly in the mouth of a sinner, whose way of life deserves [little] praise and whose doings are worldly, and because

[1] *Ep.* xvi, *P.L.* cxxxix. 1601–4.

[2] Jotsald, *Vita Odilonis*, ii. 14, *P.L.* cxlii. 927–9.

[3] Gilo, *Vita Hugonis*, L'Huillier, *Saint Hugues*, p. 583; Hildebert of le Mans, *Vita Hugonis*, Bibl. *C.*, col. 418; Hugh, *Vita sancti Hugonis*, ibid., col. 439. For Stephen's own appreciation of Cluniac devotion, see *Ep.* vii, *P.L.* cxliii. 879. For a strong argument that Stephen made a *professio in extremis* as a Cluniac monk, and that Abbot Hugh played an important part in the election of his successor, Nicholas II, see Wollasch, art. cit., *Adel und Kirche*, ed. Fleckenstein and Schmid, pp. 205-20.

[4] *Reg.* i. 4, 28 Apr. 1073, p. 7. However, he wrote to the abbot of Monte Cassino some days earlier: *Reg.* i. 1, 23 Apr. 1073, pp. 3-4.

[5] *Reg.* i. 62, 19 Mar. 1074, p. 91.

the prayer of such a man, with its hasty intercessions, lacks the mark of holiness, I pray, beg, and beseech you to implore those who deserve to be heard for the excellence of their lives, that they will pray to God for me with the charity and the love that they owe to [the Apostolic See], their universal mother.[1]

Even the sharp letter that Gregory addressed to Abbot Hugh after he admitted Duke Hugh of Burgundy to Cluny, ended with an exhortation that Hugh should offer Gregory the hand of prayer and stir up his brethren to pray the more earnestly for him.[2] Gregory's letters thus leave no doubt that, however revolutionary some aspects of his rule may have been, he nevertheless set a high value upon the intercessions of Cluny, on the very grounds of its monastic withdrawal from the world.[3]

As might be anticipated in a former grand prior, Urban II, too, desired the intercessions of the Cluniacs. Like Gregory, he at once announced his election to Abbot Hugh, whom he described as being 'satis avidum exaltationis Romanae ecclesiae'. He appealed to Hugh to visit Rome, and he urged Hugh to pray for the return of the Church to its pristine condition: 'noveris enim omnibus specialius hoc negotium super te pendere'.[4]

Most significantly of all, the popes were consistently concerned to commend and uphold Cluny's place as the 'asylum poenitentium', and they were glad to make use of it as such. They made this abundantly clear from a very early date. In 1024, when John XIX confirmed Cluny's liberty, he spoke of its services to the penitent in one of the fullest and most laudatory appraisals of Cluny's place in the eleventh-century Church that are to be found in a non-Cluniac source:

On behalf of the apostle whose vicar we, though unworthy, are, we appoint and ordain that [Cluny] and all places that are subject to it shall be a haven of mercy and a harbour of all grace and salvation to everyone who flees to it in order to be saved. May the righteous man

[1] *Reg.* ii. 49, 22 Jan. 1075, p. 190.   [2] *Reg.* vi. 17, 2 Jan. 1079, p. 424.
[3] Cf. the estimate of the monastic life which is ascribed to Gregory VII in *Cartulaire du chapitre de l'église métropolitaine Sainte-Marie d'Auch*, ed. la Plagne Barris, no. clxxiv, p. 216.
[4] *Ep.* ii, 1088, *P.L.* cli. 284–5.

find a place there and may the unrighteous man, who wants to do penance, never be turned away. May the charity of brotherly love be extended to the innocent and may the hope of salvation and the mercy of pardon never be denied to the guilty. If someone who is bound by the anathema of some authority or another seeks out this place, either for burial there or for some other means to his good and salvation, may he in no way be shut out from the pardon and mercy that he seeks. Rather let him be comforted by the medicine of salvation and kindly admitted. For it is right that, in a house of religion, the righteous man should be greeted with the love of holy brotherhood, and the sinner who is fleeing for pardon should not be denied the healing of mercy and salvation. To all who come there, may it be an aid to salvation, both here and in eternity. May it be a refuge of God's mercy and pity, and a guardian of apostolic blessing and absolution.[1]

In due course Gregory VII was to value Cluny for such services to the Church as John XIX had praised. He required a Flemish knight, Gerbod, who in 1071 had murdered his liege lord, Arnulf, heir to the count of Flanders, to do penance there; Gerbod, indeed, eventually became a monk of Cluny.[2] Gregory also encouraged Count Warin of Rosnay, late in his life, to take the monastic habit at Cluny, and so win the remission of his sins.[3] Cluny was one of the monasteries to which in 1080 Gregory prescribed that Archbishop Manasses of Rheims must retire, pending the settlement of the accusations that Gregory had made against him.[4] In his third confirmation of Cluny's liberty,

---

[1] *Ep.* vi, *P.L.* cxli. 1135–7.

[2] Giselbert, *Chronicon Hanoniense, M.G.H. Scr.* xxi. 492; *Chronicon sancti Huberti Andaginensis,* 24, *M.G.H. Scr.* viii. 582–3.

[3] At the Council of Meaux (1081), the count's intention was expressed as follows in a charter, witnessed at the Council, in which he declared his purpose of becoming a monk, and gave a church to Cluny: 'Ut ergo praedictam ecclesiam ex integro haberent Cluniacenses monachi, consilio habito cum domno apostolico Hildebranno nomine, in papatu autem dicto Gregorio, ut morerer mundo et viverem Deo, in remissionem omnium delictorum, et ad salutem antecessorum meorum, cum benedictione apostolica . . . dedi me cum allodiis meis principibus apostolorum Petro et Paulo . . .' The charter was witnessed, amongst others, by Gregory's legates, Hugh of Die and Amatus of Oléron: Mansi, xx. 585–6. Warin of Rosnay had earlier received the confraternity of Cluny: Bruel, 3377 (1061–73).

[4] *Reg.* vii. 20, 17 Apr. 1080, pp. 495–6. Cf. the Hildebrandine anecdote in Paul of Bernried, *Vita Gregorii VII,* 119, *Pontificum Romanorum . . . vitae,* ed. Watterich, i. 543–4.

Urban II included an almost verbatim repetition of John XIX's description of Cluny as a place of refuge for the innocent and for the guilty, which showed that the reformed Papacy had in no way abated its support for Cluny's objectives as the 'asylum poenitentium' in spite of the revision of its own objectives which had taken place during the intervening sixty years.[1]

The eleventh-century reforming popes thus consistently regarded the objectives of the Cluniacs as basically compatible with and complementary to their own. Had they not done so, they would not have been men of their age. As the eleventh century regarded the matter, this compatibility was more than sufficient to hold in check the tendencies to divergence which were manifest when Gregory VII dedicated the Papacy to the task of reordering the Church and the world of his day, and which occasionally found passing expression in his letters. In such evidence as survives, a divergence of objectives is the exception, and a compatibility is the rule. The words and actions of the eleventh-century reforming popes, and not least of all Gregory VII, the most revolutionary of them, show that they regarded their own lives and work for the Church as having an indispensable and incomparable support in the monastic devotions and the penitential work for all men, in life and in death, which Cluny set itself to sustain. Even had the Cluniacs done nothing more for the Papacy, the support of Cluny's prayers and alms would have been no unworthy repayment of its debt to Rome. That they were the fruit of what Peter Damiani praised as a 'truly renowned and free-born service of God, which left no place for earthly service' made them the more acceptable, for it associated them inseparably with the Gregorian ideal of the liberty of the Church.

For the Gregorians the fundamental harmony of objectives between the Cluniacs and themselves was assured by their estimate of Cluny's liberty. The alleged contrast between Cluniac and Gregorian objectives has too often been drawn in such terms as that, whereas the Cluniacs sought the reform of the Church, the Gregorians sought its liberty.[2] In so far as the Cluniacs kept

---

[1] *Ep.* ccxiv, 1097, *P.L.* cli. 485–8.
[2] See e.g. Caspar's statement above, p. 139, n. 3.

a prudent reserve in face of the more extreme, novel, and impracticable elements of Gregory VII's own attempts to enforce the hierarchical lordship of the Papacy upon the Church and upon lay society, for example, by his sponsorship of an armed 'militia sancti Petri', there are, indeed, grounds for distinguishing Gregorian from Cluniac objectives. But Cluny itself, by reason of its own freedom from all temporal lordship and from all spiritual jurisdiction save that of the Apostolic See, was deeply committed to the Gregorian ideal of liberty. In all essential respects Cluny stood for the liberty of the Church no less than did Gregory VII, and the popes themselves spoke of it as the archetype of that liberty. For this reason a decisive divergence of objectives between Cluny and the Gregorian Papacy was unthinkable.

II

COLLABORATION

THE evidence which was examined in the last chapter suggests that Cluny's intercessions on behalf of the whole Church and its self-appointed role as the 'asylum poenitentium', already went far to satisfy the practical obligations which papal protection imposed upon it. It also suggests that the eleventh-century Papacy fully and consistently acknowledged that this was so. But the Cluniacs also provided the reformed Papacy itself with several kinds of more tangible service which, despite the sparseness of the evidence, provide added testimony to the close bond which existed between them.

I. ABBOT HUGH AS MEDIATOR BETWEEN GREGORY VII AND HENRY IV

Abbot Hugh's position in the bitter struggle between Gregory VII and Henry IV provides a first illustration of how, although pope and abbot occasionally stood at a certain distance, they were basically striving in close liaison with each other and for compatible ends.[1] Hugh's actions in the course of the struggle appear to have been determined by three factors. The first and overriding factor was the commitment to the Apostolic See that was imposed upon Cluny, both morally and in practice, by its debt to Rome for papal protection of its liberty. This commitment, as it has already been shown, became increasingly strong in the course of the eleventh century.

Secondly, however, Abbot Hugh was also the heir to a long history of close relations between Cluny and the empire. Because Cluny had acquired dependencies in the kingdoms of Italy and

---

[1] For a recent assessment, which, if the present argument be sound, goes too far in stressing Cluny's neutrality and superiority to parties, see Mager, *Neue Forschungen*, pp. 418–19, 422.

Burgundy, it had become dependent upon the emperors to protect them. In return, Abbot Hugh's two predecessors, Majolus and Odilo, had demonstrated their active toleration of the imperial control over the Church which it was Gregory VII's purpose to break down; and they had normally enjoyed high favour at the German court. Odilo's biographer went so far as to say of him that he was 'one in heart and mind' with the Emperors Henry II, Conrad II, and Henry III.[1] It has, however, already been noticed that, during the latter part of Conrad's reign, Cluny became estranged from the empire as well as from the Papacy, and that royal grants of protection for its Burgundian possessions came to a temporary end. In 1046 the aged Abbot Odilo took advantage of the reform of the Papacy to re-establish Cluny's relationships with the empire, as well as with the Papacy, upon their old footing.[2] He sent his prior, Hugh, to the German court; when Hugh succeeded him as abbot, Henry III confirmed Cluny's rights over its possessions which lay within the empire.[3] But things were never again quite as they had been in Odilo's day. Abbot Hugh never, in the evidence which survives, gave expression to such an active toleration of imperial control over the Church as his predecessors had shown. He was, indeed, concerned to see that Cluny's link with the German court should never again suffer such a break as was made good when he became abbot. Thus, in 1051, he accepted the emperor's invitation

[1] 'Principibus et potestatibus Christianis secundum apostolicam sententiam in nullo restitit, sed ita amicabilem et officiosum se reddidit, ut tanquam alter Joseph ab omnibus amaretur et celebriter veneraretur. Concurrat in hunc amorem Rotbertus rex Francorum; accedat Adeleida mater Ottonum; veniat Henricus imperator Romanorum; intersint Conradus et Henricus . . . : quorum omnium amicitiis, officiis et imperialibus muneribus ita magnificatus est, ut sibi et illis cor unum et anima fuerit'; Jotsald, *Vita Odilonis*, i. 7, *P.L.* cxlii. 902–3. A good example of Odilo's views is the letter, edited by Sackur, *N.A.* xxiv (1899), 734–5, in which, while Odilo urged the emperor to show a certain restraint, his claim to oversee church affairs in collaboration with the bishops was freely conceded. Sackur and many later writers, including Tellenbach, *Church, State, and Christian Society*, p. 174, have related this letter to Henry III's intervention at Rome in 1046. But Erdmann, 'Das ottonische Reich als Romanum Imperium', *D.A.* vi (1943), 436–7, has adduced strong reasons for referring it to Henry II's Italian expedition of 1014 and to affairs at Ravenna.

[2] See above, pp. 44–5.

[3] *M.G.H. DD.* v, no. 244, 4 Dec. 1049, pp. 326–8.

to stand godfather to his son, the future Henry IV;[1] he thereby
founded a personal bond of such tenacity between himself and
Henry, that Henry could appeal to it in the last crisis of his reign.[2]
Yet from Hugh's side, Henry's miserable and impenitent death
stood as a stern warning to other rulers.[3] During his lifetime there
is no suggestion that Hugh ever acknowledged the close commitment to the emperor that had marked the reigns of his predecessors.
He had good reasons for not doing so. If Cluny stood in need of
imperial favour to protect its dependencies in Burgundy and
Italy, this need declined with the relaxing of Henry's power there
during the Investiture Contest. By this time the relatively novel
issue of exemption made Cluny's need for papal support against
the bishops of Mâcon far more pressing than its need for imperial
support to protect its dependencies within the empire. Thus, if
Hugh was still committed to seeking the well-being of the
emperor, his commitment to the pope was more insistent, both
morally and prudentially.[4]

Thirdly, however, subject always to the priority of duty and
interest which held him to the Papacy, Abbot Hugh had a desire,
which sprang from Cluny's spiritual objectives, to keep such a
measure of contact with all parties and groups as would serve to
lead them towards reconciliation and to advance their common
salvation. His zeal to be profitable to all men was emphasized at
Cluny after his death:

His counsel was desired, not only by his neighbours, but from the
very ends of the earth. He was sought out both by ordinary people and

[1] For Henry's request, see *Ep.* vi, *P.L.* clix. 931-2.
[2] C. Erdmann, *Die Briefe Heinrichs IV.*, no. 37, 1106, M.G.H. Dt. MA. i. 46-
51; cf. no. 38, 1106, pp. 51-2; also no. 31, 1102, pp. 39-40, in which Henry referred to the long breach of contact between himself and Abbot Hugh: 'Diu est,
domine et pater, quod infirmum vestrum, sicut solebatis, non visitastis et quod
adhortationum et consolationum fomentis contritum vestrum non curastis.'
[3] See his letter to King Philip of France, above, p. 128.
[4] It is significant that, when he was confronted by Pope Paschal II's concessions to the Emperor Henry V in 1111, Abbot Pons, the designated and
unanimously elected successor of Abbot Hugh and his great admirer, came out
strongly on the side of the high Gregorians: Ordericus Vitalis, *Historiae ecclesiasticae libri tredecem*, xii, ed. A. Le Prévost, iv (Paris, 1852), 6; *Simonis gesta
abbatum S. Bertini Sithiensium*, 97, M.G.H. Scr. xiii. 654.

by those in high places—kings and emperors, and bishops of the
Roman and of many other sees. He answered them with such prudence
and equity, that he succeeded at once in putting God first in all respects
and in showing that he was of good will to all men. This was especially
clear in the case of the Emperor Henry's schism from the Roman
Church.[1]

Hugh did not desire, nor was he in a position, to act in complete
detachment from either side or without an overriding concern
for papal interests. His purpose was to use his relations with
both pope and emperor to reconcile the emperor to the pope, not
vice versa; and to work towards a solution which was, above all,
acceptable to Gregory.

So far as the very fragmentary evidence goes, he twice tried
actively to mediate between Gregory and Henry. The first occasion was in the events which led up to Canossa. His endeavours
began in the autumn of 1076, when he was with Henry in
Germany. According to one source his contact with the excommunicated emperor made it necessary for him to receive absolution from the pope when he visited Rome before the end of the
year.[2] This indicates that Hugh may initially have acted without
Gregory's knowledge or antecedent consent. However, it was
negotiations that Hugh conducted in concert with the staunch
Gregorians, Countesses Matilda of Tuscany and Adelaide of Turin,
that finally brought pope and emperor face to face at Canossa.[3]
According to Gregory himself, the same three persons acted together when Henry's submission was confirmed.[4] It is, indeed,

[1] Raynald of Vézelay, *Vita Hugonis*, iv. 25, *P.L.* clix. 903.

[2] Berthold, *Annales, s.a.* 1077, *M.G.H. Scr.* v. 289. An anecdote about Abbot
Hugh, which is preserved by the Saxon chronicler Bruno, indicates, however,
that in the early summer of 1076, Abbot Hugh's attitude towards the Henrician
bishops in Germany was coloured by strong disapproval. After the death, on 28
April 1076, of Bishop William of Utrecht, the most loyal of Henry IV's supporters, but before the news of it reached Abbot Hugh, the bishop appeared to
him in a vision and said, 'Non sum vivus, sed vere defunctus et in inferno sepultus':
Bruno, *Saxonicum bellum*, 74, ed. H.-E. Lohmann, *Deutsches Mittelalter*, ii (*Kritische
Studientexte der M.G.H.*, Leipzig, 1937), pp. 76–7.

[3] Berthold, loc. cit.

[4] *Reg.* iv. 12, Jan. 1077, p. 313; cf. v. 7, 30 Sept. 1077, p. 357: see also Arnulf,
Gesta archiepiscoporum Mediolanensium, v. 8, *M.G.H. Scr.* viii. 30; Lampert of Hersfeld, *Annales, s.a.* 1077, ed. O. Holder-Egger, *S.R.G.*, pp. 290, 294: Lampert's

also the case that, when the emperor took his oath to the pope, Hugh's name appeared in the Roman version of the list of those who stood by 'ex parte regis'; and it did so in such company as the names of Archbishop Liemar of Bremen and Bishop Benno of Osnabrück.[1] But this demonstrates, not that Hugh was specially committed to the emperor's party, but that all sides were glad to make use of Hugh's position as godfather of the penitent emperor. That Gregory VII and Countess Matilda of Tuscany in fact viewed with full favour Hugh's part in the events of Canossa was made abundantly clear when, immediately afterwards, Gregory himself entrusted Hugh with the reform of the monastery of Polirone, near Mantua, which Matilda's grandfather had founded, and which, after Canossa, she committed to papal protection.[2] It would be difficult to imagine a more signal proof that both the pope and the countess approved of Abbot Hugh's actions in the winter of 1076–7.

After Henry's second excommunication in 1080, Hugh again figured in the role of mediator between pope and king. This time he certainly did do at the pope's direct instance. He arrived at Rome while, during June and July 1083, Henry, who had captured the Leonine city to the north-west of the Tiber, was besieging Gregory in the castle of San Angelo. Hugh at once gravely offended Henry by avoiding any meeting with him. He went so far as to omit the customary reverence to the tombs of the apostles which visitors to Rome paid immediately upon their arrival, because he could only have done so by passing through ways which the emperor controlled. Instead, he went straight to Gregory. When Henry protested that he had failed in his religious

statement that Henry IV associated Abbot Hugh with Countess Matilda, Countess Adelaide of Turin, and Count Azzo of Este, as intermediaries 'quorum auctoritatem magnum apud eum [Gregory] momenti esse non ambigebat', is noteworthy; Donizo, *Vita Matildis*, ii. 1, *M.G.H. Scr.* xii. 381.

[1] *Reg.* iv. 12a, 28 Jan. 1077, pp. 314–15.

[2] Santifaller, *Q.F.*, nos. 125–6, early 1077, pp. 125–7; see below, pp. 249–50. At about the same time, Gregory also paid tribute to Hugh's complete personal integrity. In a letter to Hugh of Die about French affairs, he declared: 'Confidimus enim in misericordia Dei et conversatione vitae eius, quod nullius deprecatio nullius favor aut gratia nec aliqua prorsus personalis acceptio eum a tramite rectitudinis dimovere poterit': *Reg.* iv. 22, 12 May 1077, p. 333.

duty out of regard for a mere man, Hugh replied that he would more quickly be forgiven by the apostles for going straight to so severe a man as the pope in the interests of peace, than by the pope if he had acted otherwise. Hugh added that it would not have done for him to have used the pretext of saying his prayers, to give talks with the king first place over talks with the pope. Hugh's prudent answer somewhat softened Henry's anger and he eventually agreed to see him; but in view of Henry's strong position it is not surprising that nothing came of Hugh's attempts at mediation.[1] What seems quite clear from Hugh's concern to reach Gregory is that, in 1083 as in 1077, his attempts at mediation were made from a standpoint that was nearer to that of the pope than to that of the emperor; and that, because this was so, he enjoyed Gregory's approval.[2]

II. CLUNIACS AS AGENTS OF THE REFORMED PAPACY

Besides the intercessions which it offered for the well-being of the Church at large and the services which it performed as the haven of the penitent, Cluny and its monks performed many duties of a more active and tangible kind in support of the reformed Papacy. The Cluniacs themselves were ready and willing to perform such services. An early twelfth-century Cluniac writer said that, in the days of Abbot Hugh, Cluny had been the source

to which practically the whole world had recourse, as if to a common sanctuary of religion (*tanquam ad commune pietatis asylum*), for the spiritual replenishment of its localities. For its own inhabitants who

---

[1] Rainald, *Vita Hugonis*, iv. 26, *P.L.* clix. 903–4. Hugh did induce Henry to punish Bishop Ulrich of Brixen for obstructing his negotiations with Gregory.

[2] Gregory's approval of Abbot Hugh in the year 1083 is confirmed, if confirmation were needed, by his letters regarding Count Robert of Flanders, in which he referred to Hugh as 'venerabilis abbas' and 'gravis et illustris vir': *Reg.* ix. 33–4, pp. 620–1; and by the language of his privilege for Sahagún: Santifaller, *Q.F.*, no. 209, pp. 243–6; see below, pp. 241–2,. Bonizo of Sutri names Abbot Hugh as regarding the emperor as an excommunicate after his capture of Cardinal Odo of Ostia in Nov. 1083: *Liber ad amicum*, ix, *M.G.H. L. de L.* i. 614. Gregory's biographer, Paul of Bernried, also called Abbot Hugh to witness concerning the righteousness of Gregory's cause: *Vita Gregorii VII*, 58, *Pontificum Romanorum . . . vitae*, ed. Watterich, i. 505–6.

fought a continual spiritual warfare to subdue the flesh to the spirit, truly (as the Apostle says) to live was Christ and to die was gain. But many of them were chosen and claimed for the edifying of the Church, some as popes, some as cardinals, others as bishops, abbots, and pastors. When the balsam of their spiritual virtues was poured abroad, the whole world was filled like a house with its perfume; while the fervour of monastic religion, which at this time had all but grown cold, kindled again from the exemplary zeal of these men.[1]

Such a balance of practical achievement in the monastic order and in the Church at large was by no means out of line with what Gregory looked for in the monasteries; and, as this passage suggests, the Cluniacs, in fact, provided him with some of his most loyal and effective collaborators.

Gregory VII's letters show that, from his side, he was well aware of the claims upon Cluny that papal protection entitled him to make and of the resources which lay to hand for him there, as in the rest of the monastic order. Especially during the last ten years of his pontificate, he developed what may fairly be described as a new policy of papal action in the Church at large, which depended to an altogether novel degree upon the monastic order. He sought to use, mould, and fashion certain parts of the monastic order as the chosen instruments of his purposes for the reordering and conversion of the world, and to use monastic figures as his agents. The first enunciation of this policy can be seen in the letter that Gregory addressed to Abbot Hugh early in 1075, when all the plans of his early years as pope seemed to be falling in ruins.[2] He complained that all those, whether churchmen or laymen, to whom he had hitherto looked for help, had failed him. Amongst the bishops there were scarcely any who had come by their office without simony and who lived in obedience to the law of the Church. Gregory knew of no one amongst the secular princes who preferred God's honour to his own and righteousness (*iustitia*) to money. Gregory's own near neighbours, the Romans, the

---

[1] *Vita sancti Morandi confessoris, Bibl. C.*, col. 506.

[2] *Reg.* ii. 49, 22 Jan. 1075, pp. 188–90. This letter should be compared with his appeal to Duke Rudolf of Swabia and other German laymen: *Reg.* ii. 45, 11 Jan. 1075, pp. 182–5; and his earlier letter, probably to Count Albert of Calw: *Reg.* ii. 11, 26 Oct. 1074, pp. 142–3.

Lombards, and the Normans, were worse than Jews and pagans.
If temporal princes would not restrain the fierceness of wicked
men, then the pope himself must safeguard the lives of the godly.
For his allies he turned to the monks: he besought the aid of the
Cluniacs, first of all by their intercessions. But he also asked Abbot
Hugh to assist him in his endeavours to call upon the middle
ranks of feudal society to rally in defence of righteousness, and, in
general, to marshal all men in the hierarchical service of St. Peter:

> We beseech you in brotherly charity to be zealous and vigilant, so
> far as in you lies, in extending your hand to those who love St. Peter,
> and to implore, ask, and exhort them not to hold the princes of this
> world dearer than they hold him. For the princes of this world barely
> provide paltry and perishable rewards; St. Peter promises the for-
> giveness of all our sins and blessed and eternal rewards; and he leads
> men, by the power which has been committed to him, to the heavenly
> country. I want to know more plainly than the daylight who are
> indeed his faithful followers; and who love St. Peter as their heavenly
> prince, for the sake of glory in heaven, no less diligently than do those
> who have put themselves into subjection for some paltry hope in this
> world.

Where bishops and magnates had failed, monks and lesser laymen
were to contend together, under the hierarchical direction of the
Papacy, in the defence of righteousness: the monks, by the round
of the monastic life, by inciting men to zeal for St. Peter in this
world, and, although, Gregory did not explicitly refer to it in this
letter, by active service as legates and as bishops; laymen, by such
directly military and political action as was called for, in order
to give effect to Gregory's demands as the vicar of St. Peter.

What Gregory had particularly in mind was, clearly, the in-
ducing of the middle ranks of lay society to find their primary
moral loyalty, not in the service of temporal princes, but in his
new conception of the 'militia sancti Petri'; and the monks were
to encourage them to do so. The prudence of the Cluniacs and
their superior understanding of the mind of lay society in general
restrained them from promoting the 'militia sancti Petri' in
the extreme Gregorian sense. In other ways, however, they
followed Gregory's call by encouraging clergy and laity

alike in the cause of reform, and in the pursuit of righteousness and obedience. The consequences of Gregory's decision, in 1075, to turn for help to the monastic order, and especially to Cluny, can be seen writ large upon the later history of his pontificate.

The first illustration of this collaboration is the use which Gregory henceforth made of Abbot Hugh himself; for in spite of the occasional and, upon examination, unimportant personal differences that tended to set them apart, Abbot Hugh must be numbered amongst Gregory's most consistently trusted agents. After 1075 Gregory repeatedly used him, whether as a legate or in some less formal way, to deal with French affairs. He often employed him to collaborate with his energetic standing legate, Bishop Hugh of Die. In 1076 the abbot was already associated with him in Hugh's first recorded legatine dealings since 1072.[1] King Philip I of France had driven Count Simon of Crépy from his county;[2] and Simon had appealed to Gregory at Rome. Hugh of Die and Hugh of Cluny were charged with the task, which they successfully fulfilled, of reconciling the king and the count.[3] The two men also collaborated in the case of Bishop Rainer of Orleans[4] who after 1076 was under attack by Gregory for simony and for disobedience to the Roman Church.[5] In 1078 Gregory called upon him to appear before a legatine Council, which was to be held by Hugh of Die, Hugh of Cluny, and Roger, a sub-deacon of the Roman Church.[6] In the same year the bishop and the abbot were once again to be associated in hearing charges against Archbishop Evenus of Dol.[7] In 1083 Gregory intended

[1] Abbot Hugh had occasionally been used as a papal legate, or had performed specific tasks for the Papacy, before 1073. In 1051 or 1052 he had gone to Hungary, on behalf of Pope Leo IX, to mediate between the Emperor Henry III and King Andrew I: Hildebert of le Mans, *Vita sancti Hugonis*, ii. 7, P.L. clix. 864. In 1072, when he was at Worms in the company of the Empress Agnes, he brought letters from Pope Alexander II, in which he excommunicated Abbot Robert of Reichenau on grounds of simony: Lampert of Hersfeld, *Ann. s.a.* 1072, S.R.G., p. 138.

[2] Simon was a benefactor of the Cluniacs: Bruel, 3477.

[3] R.H.F. xiv. 38; Bruel, 3493. Simon soon after entered Cluny as a monk: Bruel, 3499.

[4] For his good will towards Cluny, see Bruel, 3438, 3547.

[5] *Reg.* iii. 16–17, Apr. 1076, pp. 278–80; v. 8, 6 Oct. 1077, pp. 358–9.

[6] *Reg.* v. 20, 24 Apr. 1078, pp. 383–4. The Council did not take place.

[7] *Reg.* v. 22, 22 May 1078, pp. 385–6.

them to go to Anjou to strengthen the hand of Archbishop Ralph of Tours in face of the vexations which he was suffering at the count's hands.[1] In 1083 Gregory similarly referred Bishop Lambert of Thérouanne's complaints against Count Robert of Flanders to a Council which Hugh, by now archbishop of Lyons, was to hold.[2] Hugh was to associate the abbot of Cluny with his actions, because he was himself *persona non grata* to the king of France; and the count of Flanders might accordingly be prejudiced against him if he acted alone.[3] Gregory also commissioned the two men to investigate further complaints by Bishop Lambert against Count Eustace of Thérouanne.[4]

Leaving aside, for a moment, their dealings with Archbishop Manasses of Rheims, the long history of collaboration between Hugh of Die and Hugh of Cluny, which is likely to have been more considerable than the scanty surviving evidence records, demonstrates the reliance that Gregory placed upon the abbot. The two legates provide a contrast in character. By temperament and policy the bishop was an ultra-Gregorian and fanatically committed to the cause of reform. Yet he was given to an exaggerated zeal that sometimes led him to exceed Gregory's own wishes.[5] Upon occasion he could so far antagonize those with whom he had to deal that his usefulness as a negotiator was diminished. Abbot Hugh was especially fitted to serve in double harness with him because of his moderation and skill in handling men. It was because he was on good terms with laymen like Count Simon of Crépy and bishops like Rainer of Orleans and because he was almost universally acceptable throughout the feudal and the ecclesiastical hierarchies of France, that Gregory so greatly valued him as a medium of diplomacy. He could be relied upon to promote Gregorian ends; and his personal detachment, integrity, and moderation were qualities that commended him

[1] Ramackers, art. cit., Q.F.I.A.B. xxiii (1931), no. vii, pp. 40–1; cf. no. vi, pp. 38–40. For the dates, see Schieffer, *Die päpstlichen Legaten in Frankreich*, p. 109, nn. 116–17.

[2] Hugh of Die became archbishop of Lyons in 1082.

[3] *Reg.* ix. 33, 1083, pp. 619–20, cf. ix. 34, 1083, pp. 621–2.

[4] *Reg.* ix. 31, 1083, pp. 617–18.

[5] See above, p. 146, n. 2.

to Gregory as a colleague for his standing legate, whom he was well qualified to counterbalance and to restrain.[1]

Abbot Hugh's long concern with Gregory's most notorious opponent amongst the French bishops, Manasses of Rheims (1069–80), fully bears this out.[2] As early as 1073 Gregory called upon Hugh to intervene on his behalf at Rheims, where Manasses was invading the property of the monks.[3] By 1077 Manasses had fallen so deeply into Gregory's disfavour that Gregory told Hugh of Die to summon him before a Council at Autun. Gregory instructed Hugh of Die to associate Hugh of Cluny with what he did.[4] That Gregory had been prudent in associating a milder man with his standing legate, was apparent when, almost certainly in the abbot's absence, Hugh of Die peremptorily deposed and excommunicated Manasses. This proceeding was of such undue severity, even in Gregory's eyes, that at his Lent Council of 1078 Gregory provided for the restoration of Manasses to his see in return for an oath of obedience.[5] Gregory later wrote another letter to Manasses requiring him to appear before Hugh of Die and Hugh of Cluny;[6] but his case was still not settled in 1080, when Gregory added Cardinal Peter of Albano to the number of his legates and

[1] For Hugh's activity with regard to Germany, see below, pp. 194–6.
[2] See Diener, *Neue Forschungen*, pp. 239–45; also J. R. Williams, 'Manasses of Rheims and Gregory VII', *American Historical Review*, liv (1949), 804–24, where Manasses is presented in a less unfavourable light than usual.
[3] *Reg.* i. 14, 30 June 1073, pp. 22–3.
[4] *Reg.* iv. 22, 12 May 1077, p. 333.
[5] That Hugh was absent is implied by Hugh of Flavigny's statement that Hugh of Die visited him at Cluny after the Council: *Chron.* ii, *M.G.H. Scr.* viii. 417–18; and by the phrase 'quem eidem synodo [i.e. Lyons, 1080] interesse speramus', which implies that he had not been at the earlier council: *Reg.* vii. 12, p. 476. For Gregory's ruling, see *Reg.* v. 17, 9 Mar. 1078, pp. 378–9.
[6] *Reg.* vi. 2, 3, 22 Aug. 1078, pp. 391–6. The attitude of Archbishop Warmund of Vienne, a Cluniac and always a close associate of Abbot Hugh, is also instructive. Soon after he became archbishop in 1076, he intervened directly at Rheims, by first deposing and then reinstating several clerks. This elicited from Manasses a sharp protest to Gregory VII that he was arrogating to himself the functions of a papal legate: *R.H.F.* xiv. 611. Gregory did nothing to restrain or to rebuke Warmund, but placed the affairs of Rheims in the hands of Hugh of Die and Hugh of Cluny: *Reg.* vi. 2. Archbishop Warmund's zeal for reform at Rheims, and the confidence in him of both Gregory VII and Abbot Hugh, tell against the complete neutrality and detachment of Cluny in the matter of the church of Rheims.

prescribed that Manasses should appear before them at Lyons.[1] In a long letter to Hugh of Die, Manasses made his excuses for not obeying his summons to it, which was issued in Hugh of Die's name alone. One was that Gregory had conceded that he might be judged by Hugh of Cluny and he would not attend while he was denied his proper judge.[2] After all due allowance has been made for the delaying tactics of this letter, Manasses's insistence upon having Hugh of Cluny amongst his judges testifies to the abbot's reputation for fairness. In the rest of his dealings with Manasses Gregory was careful to see that he was involved.[3]

Apart from the history of his long collaboration with Hugh of Die, the veil that hides the relationship between Gregory VII and Abbot Hugh is scarcely raised, save in German and Spanish affairs which form the subjects of later chapters.[4] But there are occasional hints that the two men were often in touch about matters of wider importance. In one of his letters Gregory reveals that Hugh had written to him about the eucharistic teachings of Berengar.[5] He sent his answer verbally by Cluniac monks, whose presence at Rome demonstrates that direct contact existed between Gregory's Curia and Abbot Hugh.[6] A further curious

---

[1] *Reg.* vii. 12, 3 Jan. 1080, pp. 475–7.   [2] *R.H.F.* xiv. 781–6.

[3] Thus in 1080, after Hugh of Die had deposed Manasses at Lyons and the pope had confirmed this action, Manasses was given a last chance to purge himself, supported by the oaths of six other bishops, by the following Michaelmas. Meanwhile he was to withdraw either to Cluny or to la Chaise-Dieu. His judges were to be Hugh of Die and Hugh of Cluny, or, if the latter were unable to be present, Bishop Amatus of Oléron: *Reg.* vii. 20, 17 Apr. 1080, pp. 495–6.

[4] Gregory's Register, as edited by Caspar, raises many difficult and unsolved problems. It is still open to question whether it was an original register; see the denial of this by L. Santifaller, 'Beschreibstoffe im Mittelalter', *M.I.Ö.G.* Ergänzungsband xvi, Heft i (1953), pp. 94–114. Its status as an original register has been defended against Santifaller by A. Murray, 'Pope Gregory VII and his Letters', *Traditio*, xxii (1966), 149–202. But even if Murray's view be correct, it remains likely that many letters escaped registration and that, even together with Jaffé's *Epistolae Collectae*, the Register may not provide anything like a complete record of Gregory's letters concerning Cluny.

[5] *Reg.* v. 21, 7 May 1078, p. 384. There is an apparent reference to Abbot Hugh's dealings, as Gregory's legate, with the Berengarian heresy in Ramackers, art. cit., no. v, *Q.F.I.A.B.* xxiii (1931), 38–40.

[6] *Reg.* v. 21, 7 May 1078, p. 384. For this contact, see also the opening sentence of *Reg.* vi. 17, 2 Jan. 1079, p. 423.

detail of Hugh's dealings with Gregory is that they appear to have
taken counsel together for the conversion of the Saracens in Spain.
In the life of a Cluniac monk named Anastasius, it is related how,
at the command of Gregory which was supported by the threefold
entreaties of Abbot Hugh, he went to Spain, and for a time
abortively attempted to preach to them.[1]

If Abbot Hugh can be shown to have been thus active in his
collaboration with the Papacy, his monks performed notable
services to it at the Curia itself. At Rome a particular importance
attached to the cardinal-bishopric of Ostia, whose bishop was the
senior cardinal, and as such played the leading role in the event of
a papal consecration. Of the three bishops who held the see under
Gregory VII and Urban II, two, and perhaps all three, were
formerly monks of Cluny. They were also loyal and effective
servants of the popes. Gerald, cardinal from 1072 until his death
in 1077, had once been Hugh's grand prior. He not only served
Gregory well at Rome, but was also repeatedly active as a legate
in France, Spain, and Germany. After Canossa he was one of the
two envoys whom Gregory sent to Milan, where they preached to
the citizens and absolved many people from their sin of resisting
the Papacy during the long train of events which had led up to the
emperor's submission.[2] He was followed by Odo I (1080–8),[3]
who had also been grand prior of Cluny. Odo, too, did good

---

[1] *Vita sancti Anastasii auctore Galtero*, 5, P.L. cxlix. 429. Abbot Hugh's concern
for the conversion of the Saracens, as well as for the abolition of the Hispanic rite,
is also expressed in his letter to Abbot Bernard of Sahagún, below, p. 243, n. 2;
see also Hildebert of le Mans, *Vita Hugonis*, ii. 9, P.L. clix. 867; Gilo, *Vita Hugonis*,
L'Huillier, *Saint Hugues*, pp. 584–5.

[2] Gerald succeeded Peter Damiani (1057–72): Klewitz, *Reformpapsttum und
Kardinalkolleg*, p. 115. His frequent employment as a legate may be illustrated
from *Reg.* i. 6, 30 Apr. 1073, pp. 8–10; i. 16, 1 July 1073, pp. 25–6; i. 51, 14 Mar.
1074, pp. 77–8; i. 55, 14 Mar. 1074, p. 82; i. 62, 14 Mar. 1074, p. 90; i. 64,
19 Mar. 1074, p. 94; ii. 23–5, 16–18 Nov. 1074, pp. 155–7; v. 7, 30 Sept. 1077,
p. 357; vii. 18, 12 Apr. 1080, p. 493; see also Paul of Bernried, *Vita Gregorii VII*,
58, *Pontificum Romanorum . . . vitae*, ed. Watterich, i. 505–6. At the beginning of
his pontificate, Gregory asked Gerald to secure a better understanding between
Cluny and Cardinal Hugh Candidus: *Bibl. C.*, cols. 467–8. For Gerald at Milan,
see Arnulf, *Gesta arch. Mediolan.* v. 9, M.G.H. Scr. viii. 31.

[3] For Odo as cardinal, see Becker, *Urban II*, i. 51–90. Becker gives reasons for
supposing that he did not become a cardinal until 1080.

service to Gregory as his legate. During Gregory's last winter as pope, he went to Germany in an endeavour to rally the wellnigh desperate Gregorian cause there.[1] He was one of the three persons whom Gregory himself designated as being suitable to succeed him as pope; after the brief reign of Victor III, he was elected to the see of St. Peter on 12 March 1088,[2] and dedicated himself to the task of renewing Gregory's work.[3] The next cardinal-bishop of Ostia, Odo II, was a monk, and possibly a Cluniac; he may have been Urban II's nephew, and he seems to have served him well.[4] Cluniac monks are known to have been active at Rome in other ways. Under Urban II, Abbot Hugh made available the administrative skill of his monks to help with the reorganization of the finances of the Apostolic See; under Urban and Paschal II the remodelled papal treasury was in the hands of a *camerarius* named Peter, who was a Cluniac monk.[5]

Gregory VII's predilection for Cluniac monks as occupants of the senior cardinal-bishopric at Rome may well be evidence of a more general intention to fill episcopal sees with Cluniacs. When recording how Abbot Hugh dispatched Odo I to Rome for the papal service, the *Historiae Tornacenses* commented that he was only one amongst others, whom the abbot sent in response to Gregory's call for a number of his monks who were suitable to become bishops[6]. It is, however, possible to cite only one likely instance,

[1] See below, pp. 210–11.

[2] Hugh of Flavigny, *Chron.* ii, *M.G.H. Scr.* viii. 466; see Becker, *Urban II*, i. 78–82.

[3] 'De me porro ita . . . credite, sicut de beatissimo patre nostro papa Gregorio; cuius ex toto sequi vestigia cupiens, omnia quae respuit respuo, quae damnavit damno, quae dilexit prorsus amplector': *Ep.* i, *P.L.* cli. 283–4.

[4] Klewitz, op. cit., pp. 115, 160; Becker, *Urban II*, i. 213.

[5] See D. B. Zema, 'Economic Reorganization of the Roman See during the Gregorian Reform', *S.G.* i (1947), 147–9; K. Jordan, 'Die päpstliche Verwaltung im Zeitalter Gregors VII.', ibid., p. 128; J. Sydow, 'Cluny und die Anfänge der apostolische Kammer', *Studien und Mitteilungen zur Geschichte des Benediktordens und seiner Zweige*, lxiii (1951), 45–66, esp. 55–8. Zema's references (art. cit., p. 148, n. 33) are insufficient to support his statement that in 1088 Urban addressed appeals for financial help to Cluny, although this is not impossible; it was for the intercessions and the counsel of the Cluniacs that Urban asked.

[6] 'Cumque [Odo] ibi [Cluny] per aliquot annos religiossime vixisset, et dominus papa Gregorius VII eidem Hugoni mandasset, ut sibi aliquos de monachis suis

apart from Odo I of Ostia, of Gregory's directly appointing a Cluniac monk to a bishopric. In 1078 he wrote to Abbot Hugh that he had given an unspecified Spanish see to an abbot whom Hugh had himself commended for the episcopate.[1] Perhaps Gregory intended the Cluniacs, to whom the *Historiae Tornacenses* referred, for imperial sees which did not, in fact, come into his control because the fortunes of the emperor revived.[2] There were, however, also a number of Cluniac monks who occupied sees otherwise than by papal appointment, and who served the reformed Papacy well. In France these include Archbishop Warmund of Vienne (1077–81), who served Gregory as a legate in Flanders; Archbishop William of Auch (1068–96); and Bishop Peter of Aire (*c.* 1061–92). In Spain the first archbishop of Toledo after its reconquest was the Cluniac Bernard of Agen (1086–1124), and Bishop Dalmatius of Compostela (1094–1100) was also a Cluniac.[3]

The collaboration of Abbot Hugh and of other monks of Cluny in the government and reform of the Church thus emerges sufficiently clearly from the evidence which survives, to demonstrate that the primary service of intercession which the Cluniacs discharged on behalf of the Papacy was reinforced by effective services of a more practical kind. They thus did much to fulfil the tasks that Gregory VII sought to impose upon the monastic order in 1075. They complemented and collaborated with the activity of the Gregorians, and were not in any fundamental way antagonistic to it. There are no good grounds for supposing that either Gregory VII or Urban II regarded them as being in any way deficient in the practical services that the 'libertas Romana' called for on their part.

---

viros sapientes transmitteret, quos competenter episcopos ordinare posset, ei inter ceteros praefatum Odonem transmisit . . .': *Hist. Torn.* iv. 11, *M.G.H. Scr.* xiv. 340–1; cf. Orderic Vitalis, *Ecclesiastical History*, iv, *The Ecclesiastical History of Orderic Vitalis*, ii, ed. M. Chibnall (Oxford, 1969), 298–300.

[1] *Reg.* v. 21, 7 May 1078, p. 384.

[2] Although Orderic Vitalis commented that 'Alios quoque monachos papa prout ratio dictabat promovit, et diversarum ecclesiarum tutelae digniter praefecit': loc. cit.

[3] Diener, *Neue Forschungen*, pp. 322–3.

III. GREGORY VII AND THE DISSEMINATION OF CLUNY'S LIBERTY

But the most interesting development of Gregory VII's monastic policy after 1075 remains to be considered. No one more eloquently idealized than did Gregory VII the liberty of Cluny as the crowning example of the freedom of the Church from all external domination. In his eyes its exemplary liberty, which was so largely the creation and gift of the Apostolic See, provided a pattern that invited reproduction in other Gregorian monasteries. It formed the basis of what was, perhaps, the most characteristic of all the developments that Gregory foreshadowed in his letter to Abbot Hugh of January 1075.[1] In 1079 and 1080, in face of the reviving fortunes of Henry IV, Gregory began to use the special bond which had grown up between Cluny and the Apostolic See, the liberty of Cluny, and the reciprocal obligations to which it gave rise between the Papacy and the monastic order, as a pattern to be reproduced in a number of other monasteries. He chose ones which were well placed either to be the centres of opposition to the emperor, or else to build up the pope's authority in areas of especial importance. In no case had these monasteries been directly subject to Cluny, nor did they become so. Their place in the Gregorian scheme of things did not depend, and was not intended to depend, on such a subjection. Instead, upon the analogy of Cluny itself, it was to be based on their immediate and unqualified subjection to St. Peter and to his vicar at Rome.

The first of these monasteries was Saint-Victor, Marseilles. Saint-Victor had formerly come under the influence of Abbot Odilo of Cluny,[2] and a monastic union existed between the two societies;[3] but Saint-Victor was never in any way subject to Cluny

---

[1] *Reg.* ii. 49, 22 Jan. 1075, pp. 188–90: see above, pp. 152–3.

[2] Saint-Victor rose to prominence as a result of the work of Abbot Isarnus (1022–47). For a general study, see P. Schmid, 'Die Entstehung des Marseiller Kirchenstaats', *A.U.F.* x (1928), 176–207. For Isarnus's relations with Odilo of Cluny, see Gilo, *Vita Hugonis*, L'Huillier, *Saint Hugues*, p. 581.

[3] *Ordo Clun. per Bern.* i. 74, Herrgott, *Vetus disciplina monastica*, p. 274; see V. Saxer, 'Les Caldendriers liturgiques de Saint-Victor et le sanctoral médiéval de l'abbaye', *Provence historique*, xvi (1966), 489–91, for further details of a liturgical bond with Cluny.

or its abbots. Since 1077 the abbot of Saint-Victor, Bernard, had served Gregory well in Germany, where he had enjoyed the support of Abbot Hugh and the Cluniacs.[1] Early in 1079 Gregory wrote a letter to the monks of Saint-Victor, in which he praised their abbot as one of the few men who were without any doubt wholly devoted to the cause of God and of St. Peter. St. Peter and St. Paul would assuredly reward the community of Saint-Victor for the inconvenience that it had sustained in their service by the long absence of its abbot. Gregory accordingly purposed to unite their abbey with that of St. Paul's-without-the-Walls at Rome, and to confer upon both of them that special link with the Roman See from which Cluny had for so long derived help and blessing.[2] Gregory therefore soon afterwards conferred upon Saint-Victor privileges that were similar to those of Cluny.[3] When later in the same year Bernard was succeeded as abbot by his brother, Cardinal Richard, Gregory confirmed the union between Saint-Victor and St. Paul's at Rome.[4] Now that Saint-Victor was endowed with the same liberty as Cluny, it was henceforth to be an extension of St. Peter's authority in regions where the Papacy stood in especial need of support. With its own situation inside the kingdom of Burgundy and with its relatively compact network of filiated houses in Provence and Catalonia, it was well placed to complement Cluny in pursuing Gregory VII's purposes.[5]

Very soon afterwards the policy of explicitly reproducing the liberty of Cluny in other strategically vital monasteries was further implemented by Gregory in Germany and in Spain. In 1080 Gregory conferred the same liberty that Cluny enjoyed

[1] It is important to insist that, despite occasional differences, there was never a prolonged or an endemic hostility between Cluny and Saint-Victor. Thus, before 1079, Cluny supported Abbot Bernard in Germany; afterwards, as will be shown later, Abbot Richard worked closely with the Cluniacs in Spain.

[2] *Reg.* vi. 15, 2 Jan. 1079, pp. 419–20.

[3] Santifaller, *Q.F.*, no. 173, 4 July 1079, pp. 199–206.

[4] *Reg.* vii. 7–8, 2 Nov. 1079, pp. 468–70. In the former of these letters, Gregory confirmed Richard's mission to Spain. In the latter, he referred to his intention of using Bernard, if he had lived, in Italy as well as in Spain.

[5] Cf. the terms in which Gregory confirmed the privileges of la Chaise-Dieu (dioc. le Puy) on 27 Mar. 1080: Santifaller, *Q.F.*, no. 181, pp. 210–12.

upon the Swabian monastery of All Saints', Schaffhausen;[1] three years later, he did so in favour of the Leónese monastery of Sahagún, in order that it might become the Cluny of Spain.[2]

In the latter years of Gregory's pontificate when so many of his policies fell upon disaster and ruin, this communication of Cluny's liberty to other chosen monasteries was a principal part of his strategy and, perhaps, the part in which he had the most marked success. For like Cluny itself the three monasteries of Saint-Victor, Schaffhausen, and Sahagún remained unaffected by Gregory's reverses. At the time of his death they continued to stand as visible proclamations to the empire and to Spain of his programme for the liberty of the Church. The two of them which lay within the empire were a legacy to Urban II which, although he allowed Gregory's arrangements to be modified, still afforded invaluable outposts in the continuing struggle against Henry IV. Sahagún stood as a witness to the opening up of north-western Spain to papal authority and to Roman usages.

Cluny was therefore of the greatest significance for Gregory VII as providing a pattern of ideal liberty which he was able to disseminate after he turned in 1075 to the monastic order with especial insistence as a means of promoting his objectives in the Church at large.

IV. CLUNY, URBAN II, AND THE CRUSADE

As Urban II sought and valued the intercessory support of the Cluniacs, so too he followed Gregory VII by using them in practical ways; and they did him good service. His use of them differs from that of Gregory VII according to the contrast which in general, distinguished the two men. Urban was deeply committed to consolidating Gregory's work. But where Gregory's character was ardent and enthusiastic, Urban's was cool and calculating. Gregory had an unmeasured zeal which had, as its complement, a liability to be driven in moments of disappointment into moods of no less unmeasured condemnation; Urban's whole tenor of life and expression was temperate and measured.

---

[1] See above, p. xxii, and below, p. 202.   [2] See below, pp. 241-2.

Preoccupied with his clear-cut principles of reform which were essentially the result of his understanding of canonical precedents and requirements, Gregory was a poor judge of men; Urban was diplomatic and accommodating and he shared with Abbot Hugh an ability to win men by persuasion to collaborate in his purposes. For too long underestimated by modern historians as the mere 'pedisequus' of Gregory VII which his detractors in his own day called him,[1] Urban's stature as a pope has recently been accorded the recognition to which he is entitled.[2] He successfully consolidated the reform which Gregory had begun but of which, in the events which led up to his death in exile at Salerno, he had seen the apparent ruin. By refraining from Gregory's extravagances and by never acting beyond his resources, Urban established a broad and assured basis of support in the Church and in lay society for the reformed Papacy and its aims. It has been suggested that he was, perhaps, at bottom more Cluniac than Gregorian.[3] Such a suggestion at once underestimates his insight into the changing circumstances of the decade in which he was pope,[4] and sets Cluniac and Gregorian in too stark an antithesis. But he was Cluniac in his temper and in his skill at taking all men as he found them and at leading, rather than commanding, them to serve his ends; and in his ability to understand men as they actually were and then to guide them to where he would have them be.[5] Where, in the days of Gregory VII, the Cluniacs had prepared

[1] Beno, *Contra Gregorium VII et Urbanum II scripta*, ii. 2, ed. K. Francke, *M.G.H. L. de L.* ii. 375. On the other hand, twelfth-century writers who favoured reform rated Urban highly in comparison with Gregory; cf. Kuttner's comment that 'to the authors of the twelfth century the great reform pope was Urban II rather than Gregory VII': S. Kuttner, 'Urban II and Gratian', *Traditio*, xxiv (1968), 504, citing P. Classen, *Gerhoh von Reichersberg* (Wiesbaden, 1960), p. 55.

[2] Becker, *Urban II*, reviews the historiography of Urban (i. v–ix, 1–17), and himself does him justice, as do Erdmann, *Die Entstehung des Kreuzzugsgedankens*, esp. pp. 285–325, and Fliche, *La Réforme grégorienne et la reconquête chrétienne* (Paris, 1946), pp. 199–337.

[3] 'Vielleicht war er im Grunde doch mehr Cluniazenser als Gregorianer': J. Haller, *Das Papsttum. Idee und Wirklichkeit* (new edn., Darmstadt, 1962), ii. 435. Haller underestimated Urban's achievement as pope.

[4] See Becker, *Urban II*, i. 16.

[5] Urban's diplomatic skill, and its limitations, are apparent in his achievement in rallying the city of Milan to the papal cause: Cowdrey, 'The Papacy, the Patarenes,

the ground for the spread of Gregorian ideals and methods, Urban showed political tact in so building upon their work as to further his general purpose of realizing what was soberly practicable in the Gregorian programme.

His tactics were already evident during the brief pontificate of Victor III, which was little more than an interregnum between the two great popes.[1] In March 1087 a Council met at Capua to consider whether to proceed with the election to the Papacy of

and the Church of Milan', *T.R.H.S.*, 5th ser., xviii (1968), 43–8; and 'The Archbishops of Milan in the Time of Pope Urban II', *E.H.R.* lxxxiii (1968), 285–94. Cf. his dealings in south Italy: Klewitz, 'Studien über die Wiederherstellung der Römischen Kirche in Süditalien durch das Reformpapsttum', *Reformpapsttum und Kardinalkolleg*, pp. 137–205.

[1] For events between the death of Gregory VII and the election of Urban II, see Becker, *Urban II*, i. 78–96. Tellenbach has drawn attention to the link which for long persisted between Abbot Hugh of Cluny and the conservative reformers who were connected with the abbey of Monte Cassino: 'Zum Wesen der Cluniacenser', *Saeculum*, ix (1958) esp. pp. 377–8; cf. W. Wühr, 'Die Wiedergeburt Montecassino unter seinem ersten Reformabt Richer von Niederaltaich', *S.G.* iii (1948), 369–450. For Hugh's presence at the deathbed of its sometime abbot, Pope Stephen IX, see above, p. 152. In his *Dialogues*, *P.L.* cxlix. 963–1018, Abbot Desiderius, Stephen's successor, combined approval of the reformed Papacy with a desire to mediate between pope and emperor. In 1082 he incurred excommunication during his endeavours to this end: Hugh of Flavigny, *Chronicon*, ii, *M.G.H. Scr.* viii. 467. In 1083 Hugh of Cluny visited Monte Cassino in the course of his own attempts to mediate, and concluded a monastic union between the two communities of Cluny and Monte Cassino: *Chronica monasterii Cassinensis*, iii. 51, *M.G.H. Scr.* vii. 741. When Desiderius became pope, he alienated the extreme Gregorian party; he excommunicated Archbishop Hugh of Lyons and Abbot Richard of Marseilles in 1087: ibid., iii. 72, p. 752. Abbot Hugh also parted company with the extreme Gregorians, and Hugh of Lyons reproached him bitterly for allowing the Good Friday liturgical prayers for the emperor to be recited at Cluny: Mansi, xx. 634–5. By contrast, after the excommunication of the extreme Gregorians, the monks of Cluny received favourably the injunction that they should refrain from communion with them: ibid., cols. 635–6. Tellenbach regards this history of contacts between Cluny and the reformers of Monte Cassino, which was particularly apparent between 1082 and 1087, as evidence that, although Abbot Hugh was 'ein zuverlässiger Freund der Reformpäpste', he succeeded 'Cluny aus den zeitgebundenen theologischen und politischen Spannungen weitgehend herauszuhalten'. But it does not weigh heavily in the scales against all the evidence for collaboration between Cluny and the Gregorian Papacy; it should be interpreted as showing that in pursuing this collaboration, the Cluny of Abbot Hugh maintained all the contacts that were possible with the monastic and reforming worlds, and that it showed prudence and reserve in face of the extremer manifestations of Gregorianism.

Abbot Desiderius of Monte Cassino.[1] An extreme Gregorian opposition party then emerged under the leadership of Archbishop Hugh of Lyons and Abbot Richard of Marseilles. When Desiderius, who had the strong support of the Norman princes, agreed to accept election, Cardinal Odo of Ostia at first associated himself with this opposition. Then he veered to the support of Desiderius; and in May 1087 he took the leading part in his consecration. His change of front elicited from Archbishop Hugh the bitter reproach of the Psalmist: 'Conversus est in die belli';[2] in August, Hugh and Richard suffered excommunication at the Council of Benevento. Odo thus came out on the winning side. In so far as the obscure events of 1087 can be penetrated, Odo's course of action seems to have been determined less by any real confidence in Desiderius, with whom there is no clear evidence that he collaborated when he became pope, than by his intention at all costs to preserve the greatest possible unity of the anti-imperial party and, still more, to provide for the government of the Church to be carried on. The predominance of the Norman princes and the lack of general support for the ultra-Gregorians, left no alternative but to accept Desiderius as pope, once his resolve to accept election was made clear. Certainly, the effects of Cardinal Odo's volte-face were, in fact, to preserve unity and to promote better government. In September 1087, just before he died, Pope Victor III publicly thanked Odo for his conduct at Capua, and he recommended him to be the next pope. When he succeeded Victor, Odo could, therefore, assert that he had been designated by both Gregory VII and Victor III; and he was able to claim and quickly win the loyalty of the partisans of both.[3]

Within the context of his policy of working with and conciliating all parties which furthered reform and helped the Papacy

[1] Practically nothing is known about Cardinal Odo's return from Germany and his subsequent activities up to the spring of 1087.

[2] Ps. 77: 9 (Vg.); Hugh of Flavigny, *Chron.* ii, *M.G.H. Scr.* viii. 467.

[3] *Ep.* ii, *P.L.* cli. 284-5. Urban II was elected pope, in March 1088, by all the cardinal-bishops, and their choice was confirmed by the cardinal-priests and deacons. The envoys of Countess Matilda of Tuscany and of the Gregorian party in Germany proclaimed their loyalty to him, and he enjoyed the support of the Normans. The extreme Gregorian party gradually became reconciled to his rule.

towards victory in the imperial schism, Urban II, as pope, sought and maintained close and cordial relations with Cluny. While these relations never received from Urban the intensity of expression which Gregory VII had given them, they were also not subject to the occasional crises and moments of disappointment which had punctuated Gregory's dealings.[1] Urban's support of Cluny was as unwavering as was its support for him.

Urban's consistent upholding of the liberty of Cluny itself has already been examined.[2] So far as other aspects of his dealings with regard to Cluny are concerned, two features of Gregory VII's use of it disappeared. First, Urban made no further use of Gregory's later practice of investing non-Cluniac monasteries with the 'libertas Romana' on the pattern of Cluny as Gregory VII idealized it. This implied no disapproval of Cluny. Rather, Urban's sober sense of political and social reality led him to abandon Gregory's attempt to import into Germany what was, in the long term, an impracticable model for the reformed monasteries. Instead, he worked towards a kind of monastic freedom which allowed for the inevitable claims of local lords and bishops, and yet owed much to the historical model of Cluny's own privileged position in the midst of feudal society.[3]

Secondly, so far as is known, Urban made no use of the Cluniacs as legates. This was, again, because he modified the methods of Gregory VII and not because he mistrusted the monks of his former monastery. Especially in France, he made less use than Gregory VII had done of such standing legations as that of Archbishop Hugh of Lyons. Under Gregory, Abbot Hugh's principal employment as a legate had been to serve with Hugh of Lyons and to act as a moderating influence upon him; under Urban II,

[1] For Urban's account of his election to Abbot Hugh of Cluny, in which he praised Hugh because 'sanctitatem vestram satis avidam exaltationis Romanae ecclesiae novimus', see *Ep.* ii, *P.L.* cli. 284–5; and for his still more insistent appeal to Hugh, as 'beati Petri privatiori filio', to come to Rome, see Ramackers, art. cit., no. xi, *Q.F.I.A.B.* xxiii (1931–2), 42–4.

[2] See above, pp. 58–61.

[3] See below, pp. 211–12. On this point, see the discussion by C. Violante, 'Il monachesimo Cluniacense di fronte al mondo politico ed ecclesiastico', *Spiritualità Cluniacense* (Todi, 1960), pp. 228–40.

Archbishop Hugh was less prominent and there was therefore little need for Abbot Hugh to fulfil his former function.[1] Urban did, indeed, often use temporary legates for *ad hoc* purposes; but for the most part they were either men who did not have the kind of local contacts with the localities to which they were sent which the abbot of Cluny so often had, or else they were much lesser men.[2]

However, there survives a little-noticed letter of Abbot Hugh which illustrates the close understanding which prevailed between Urban and the Cluniacs regarding French affairs and also Hugh's willingness for Cluny to be used as a papal agency in France. Hugh asserted that Urban in effect enjoyed the services of the Cluniacs as his own 'domestici' in helping the Papacy in France; and there is some evidence to suggest that he did, in fact, so use them.[3] But in general, it seems that whereas Gregory VII had sought to use Abbot Hugh and the Cluniacs in his active service, Urban II, as Abbot Hugh's 'filius et alumnus',[4] sought rather, upon the evidence of his letters, to be of service to his former monastery and to its abbot—partly from gratitude and partly because he saw in the Cluniac monastic family a principal

---

[1] He did, however, prompt Hugh of Lyons to hold the Council of Autun in 1094: Mansi, xx. 800–2.

[2] Schieffer, *Die päpstliche Legaten in Frankreich*, pp. 141–62; Becker, *Urban II*, i. 210–11.

[3] 'Amantissimo et reverendissimo patri, sanctae atque apostolicae sedis summo pontifici, domno papae Urbano, frater Hugo Cluniacensis cum tota congregatione nostra continuas et fidelissimas devotionis orationes et perpetuam pacem. Multi, o domine pater, iustis ac necessariis causis existentibus cupiunt dignam vestram adire praesentiam, sed impediuntur variis difficultatibus obsistentibus. Unde et aliqui eorum saltem ad nos veniunt, quasi ad domesticos vestros, si quo modo eis consulatur vel subveniatur illorum necessitatibus.' The letter goes on to refer to the complaints against the monastery of Marmoutier of Archbishop Manasses of Rheims (1096–1106), 'vester humilis filius, noster quoque devotus amicus': *Chronicon sancti Huberti Andaginesis*, 84, *M.G.H. Scr.* viii. 616–17; *P.L.* clix. 929. The date is 1096. One example survives of the performance by the Cluniacs of a specific service on behalf of Urban. In 1088, while he was still at Terracina and unable to establish himself at Rome, Urban wrote to Archbishop Lanfranc of Canterbury, asking that Peter's Pence should be sent as soon as possible to Cluny for safe-keeping, if it were not feasible to send them direct to Rome: *Ep.* iv, *P.L.* cli. 286–8.

[4] *Ep.* ii, *P.L.* cli. 285.

means for advancing the interests of the Papacy and of reform in France and elsewhere. Hence his continual vigilance for the rights of Cluny and its subject houses.

The greatest event of Urban's pontificate was the First Crusade. One of the most difficult of all the questions that arise in connection with the debt of the Papacy to Cluny, is the extent to which Cluny prepared the way for the success of Urban II's initiative at Clermont. An adequate discussion of this problem would require a full-length study. But in the light of the relationship between the Cluniacs and the concerns of the Papacy, it may briefly be suggested that Cluny was of importance both in the long history of Crusading origins and in the immediate circumstances in which Urban II preached at Clermont. Cluny did not initiate any of the developments that led to the Crusade; but it probably did more than any other single agency to define and mould the general factors in eleventh-century society that Urban galvanized into effectiveness in 1095.

In the longer perspective, Cluny played its part in preparing for the Crusade in a number of ways. First, Cluny had for many decades been associated with the campaigns in Spain, in which French knights had made war upon the Saracens. It is better not to describe these campaigns as 'Crusades'; this term should be reserved for enterprises which had the religious motives of a pilgrimage (*peregrinatio*) and clearly exhibited the characteristics which the later juridical tradition of the canonists attached to the Crusade.[1] But like the Crusades of later times the eleventh-century Spanish campaigns had the general character of holy wars, and those who waged them were more than once given the 'vexillum sancti Petri' to set upon them the stamp of papal blessing.[2] The chronicler

---

[1] For the problems of definition which arise in relation to the term 'Crusade', see esp. M. Villey, *La Croisade. Essai sur la formation d'une théorie juridique* (Paris, 1942). During the first century and a half of Crusading, there was no medieval Latin word for 'Crusade'; the nouns in common use were 'expeditio', 'iter', and (above all) 'peregrinatio': Mayer, *Geschichte der Kreuzzüge*, p. 21.

[2] For the 'vexillum sancti Petri', see esp. Erdmann, *Die Entstehung des Kreuz-zugsgedankens*, pp. 166–84. For a convincing argument, as against Erdmann, that a clear distinction should be drawn between the 'holy war' and the 'Crusade', see Villey, op. cit. The Spanish campaigns had the character of holy wars from the point of view of the French adventurers who took part in them; from that of the

Ralph Glaber, who began his work at Cluny, recorded that some of the earliest of the French knights who campaigned in Spain during the eleventh century, devoted much of their spoils to the enrichment of Cluny;[1] and the fact that so many of those who helped the Spanish kings in the days of King Alphonso VI of León-Castile came from Cluny's own neighbourhood in Burgundy, strongly suggests that the Cluniacs gave them their encouragement.[2]

Yet it is all too easy to overstate the probable extent of Cluny's sponsorship of the French expeditions. Such views as that, in France, the Cluniacs were among the 'promoters' of the 'Crusades' in Spain, and that 'legions' of black monks went in the time of Abbot Odilo, enflamed with apostolic zeal, to organize the monasteries of Catalonia, Aragon, and Navarre, go far beyond the evidence.[3] The knights to whom Ralph Glaber referred gave their spoils to Cluny because they sought the blessing of St. Peter and St. Paul upon their enterprises and because they desired the prayers of the monks after their deaths. Cluny at no time showed a tendency to advance beyond pre-Gregorian reformers like Cardinals Peter Damiani and Humbert in their reserve with regard to the waging of war by Christians in order to extend the boundaries of their faith. The Cluniacs did not share Gregory VII's new and more favourable attitude to Christian warfare, illustrated by his attempts to recruit a 'militia sancti Petri', in any way that might have led them to 'promote' military campaigns.[4] Yet their concern for Spanish affairs and their reputation for assuring spiritual benefits to members of the military classes who looked to them and who directed their arms towards objectives of which they approved, tended to encourage men in the waging of the holy war. By their ever-growing concern with Spain, the Cluniacs

Christians of Spain, they were merely incidents in the everyday hostilities between Christians and Moslems: see W. Kienast, 'Zur Geschichte des Cid', *D.A.* iii (1939), 103–4.

[1] *Historiarum*, iv. 7, ed. Prou, pp. 109–10.   [2] See below, p. 243.

[3] Cf. P. Boissonnade, *De Nouveau sur la Chanson de Roland* (Paris, 1923), esp. pp. 11–13; P. Rousset, *Les Origines et les charactères de la première croisade* (Neuchâtel, 1945), esp. pp. 31–5.

[4] Cf. Erdmann, op. cit., p. 60.

helped to build up a state of mind amongst the military classes in France which made possible, in due course, the preaching of a Crusade that was directed towards the defeating of the external enemies of Christendom, not only in Spain, but also in the East.

The Cluniacs also helped, in the long term, towards the development of the Crusade by their sponsorship of pilgrimages. Ralph Glaber made several references to their encouragement of pilgrimages to Jerusalem;[1] and part of their concern with Spanish affairs was owing to their enthusiastic encouragement of the cult of St. James at Compostela.[2] But if the eleventh century may fairly be called the heyday of pilgrimage, it would be easy to exaggerate the importance of the Cluniacs in preparing the way for that great armed 'peregrinatio',[3] the First Crusade, by their undoubted zeal for pilgrimage. The crucial period in the development of Compostela as a pilgrimage centre fell within the reigns of its Cluniac bishop, Dalmatius, (1094–1100) and, above all, its first archbishop, Diego Gelmirez (1100–39);[4] this was too late for its influence upon the First Crusade to have been a fundamental one. Moreover there is no evidence in a Cluniac source, save in the records about Urban II himself, of any tendency to depart from the general eleventh-century notion that the carrying of arms was altogether incompatible with the nature of a pilgrimage.[5] Until this notion had been revised, as it was by Urban II himself, the emergence of the Crusade as an armed pilgrimage was inconceivable. Cluny's preparation for the First Crusade by means of

[1] Ralph Glaber, *Historiarum*, i. 5, ed. Prou, p. 20; ii. 4, p. 32; iii. 1, p. 52; iii. 7, p. 71; iv. 6, p. 106.

[2] Cf. S. Runciman, *A History of the Crusades*, i (Cambridge, 1951), 38–50; Töpfer, *Volk und Kirche zur Zeit der beginnenden Gottesfriedensbewegung im Frankreich*, pp. 39–51.

[3] See e.g. the use of this term and its cognates in the *Gesta Francorum*, ed. R. Hill (London, 1962), pp. 8, 12, 28, 65, 72, 91.

[4] For Diego Gelmirez, see G.–M. Colombes, *D.H.G.E.* xiv. 441–4; R. Pastor de Togneri, 'Diego Gelmirez', *Mélanges Crozet*, i. 597–608. It was at his own request and after consultation with Abbot Hugh, who counselled hesitation in the matter, that in 1104 Pope Paschal II conferred the pallium upon Diego: *Historia Compostellana*, i. 16–17, *P.L.* clxx. 910–13.

[5] For the sense of impropriety which had earlier been generally felt at the suggestion that pilgrims might carry arms, see e.g. Lampert of Hersfeld's account of the German pilgrimage of 1064–5; *Annales, s.a.* 1065, *S.R.G.*, p. 94.

its encouragement of pilgrimage, though genuine, was diffused and indirect.

A third and again an indirect way in which Cluny prepared the ground for the Crusade, was by the connections with the church at Jerusalem, which it maintained through its southern French dependencies and especially Moissac. In 1088 Sergius, the legate of Patriarch Euphemius of Jerusalem, committed certain lands in France which belonged to this see 'in manu et providentia abbatum et seniorum Cluniacensium seu Moissacensium, scilicet domini Hugonis et omnium successorum ipsius in perpetuum'. The monks were to pass on the rents of the lands entrusted to their oversight into the hands of visiting representatives of the patriarch.[1] It is thus clear that the Cluniac network in south-western France was in close touch with affairs at Jerusalem and that it had a direct concern for the well-being of its church. At Moissac, in particular, this concern had its complement in the growth of a spiritual and artistic preoccupation with the theme of Jerusalem, which may well have helped to prepare the seed-bed for the preaching of Urban II on his journey in France.[2]

But it was by the impact that the Cluniacs made upon the feudal society of western Europe that they did most, in the long term, to prepare the way for a widespread response to Urban II's preaching. It is now widely agreed that the principal developments which led to the First Crusade must be sought, not outside western Europe, but within its feudal society and especially within that of France.[3] Here above all, Cluny had the ear of its contemporaries. It did much to insist upon the need to create better order, to raise the level of men's social conduct and sense of purpose, and to disseminate the need to perform whatever actions might lead to the remission of their sins. These were the general motives to which Urban appealed in his preaching. Cluny had for long sought to promote the Peace of God and the Truce of God

---

[1] A. Gieysztor, 'The Genesis of the Crusades: the Encyclical of Sergius IV (1009–12)', *Medievalia et Humanistica*, vi (1950), 25, n. 102, quoting Bibliothèque nationale, Coll. Doat, 128, fos. 216ᵃ–217ᵇ.

[2] Art. cit., *Med. et Hum.* v (1948), 3–23; vi (1950), 3–34.

[3] See Erdmann, op. cit., pp. vii–viii; C. Cahen, 'An Introduction to the First Crusade', *Past and Present*, vi (1954), 26–9.

amongst the feudatories of France;[1] Urban II is widely reported
to have included in his preaching an injunction that men should
cease to waste each other's lands at home and turn their arms,
instead, to the service of Christendom.[2] If the so-called 'Encyclical of Pope Sergius IV' was, indeed, a piece of propaganda for the
First Crusade which had its origin at Moissac, then the Cluniacs
there supported Urban by impressing upon all Christians the religious duty of seeking peace at home, in order that the resources
of the West might the better be marshalled for the warfare of
Christendom against the enemies of God.[3] More generally, the
attempts which the Cluniacs had always made, since the time of
Abbot Odo, to discipline the lives of the knightly classes and to
turn their weapons to the service of the needy, tended to make the
chivalric classes the more attentive to the preaching of Urban,
when he directed their minds to warfare in pursuit of religious
ends.[4] Above all, the incessant propaganda of the Cluniacs, that
laymen must take thought for the remission of their sins by the
doing of good works which would stand them in good stead
before St. Peter and St. Paul at the Day of Judgement, prepared
them to look for the remission of their sins by the specific good
work of Crusading, when it was directly recommended to them
by the vicar of St. Peter himself.

Cluny also made a contribution to the genesis of the Crusade
in more immediate ways. Among the charters of Cluny, there is
evidence that Abbot Hugh encouraged knights to take part in the
Crusades of 1095 and 1101, and that he afforded them material
help in doing so.[5] It was by making an itinerary which included

---

[1] See above, p. 135.

[2] Baudri of Dol, *Historia Jerosolimitana*, i. 4, *Recueil des historiens des Croisades,
historiens occidentaux*, iv. 12–15; Robert the Monk, *Historia Hierosolymitana*, i. 1,
ibid., iii. 727–8; Fulcher of Chartres, *Gesta Francorum Iherusalem peregrinantium*,
i. 3, ed. H. Hagenmayer (Heidelberg, 1913), pp. 130–8.

[3] Gieysztor, art. cit., *Med. et Hum.* vi (1950), 33–4.

[4] Erdmann, op. cit., pp. 78–9.

[5] In 1096 a knight pledged his goods to Cluny, saying that he wished to take
part 'in hac tam multa et permaxima excitatione vel expeditione Christiani populi
decertantis ire in Iherusalem, ad belligerandum contra paganos et Sarracenos pro
Deo, et ipse tali intentione permotus, cupiensque illo ire armatus . . .'; he pledged
his goods in return for two thousand Lyons shillings and four mules: Bruel, 3703.

a large number of Cluny's subject houses in France that Urban was enabled to preach the Crusade. On his way from Italy to Clermont, Urban visited Cluny and also Souvigny; afterwards he visited Sauxillanges, Saint-Flour, Limoges, Poitiers, and Moissac.[1] The close connection of Cluny with Urban's itinerary and his repeated granting of privileges to its subject houses,[2] suggest that Cluny may have played an important part in organizing Urban's journey, and thus in enabling him to acquaint the feudatories of France so widely with his Crusading plans.

Yet Cluny did not do more than prepare the ground for Urban. The Swabian chronicler Bernold was fully justified in representing the Crusade as essentially the personal work of the pope.[3] Nothing in Cluny's past history anticipated Urban's achievement in transforming current ideas about the holy warfare of Christian chivalry against the heathen into the ideology of the Crusade. It was part of Urban's distinctive achievement so to associate ideas about the holy war with ideas about pilgrimage that the unprecedented spectacle of an armed Crusade to the Holy Land might take shape.[4] Furthermore, there is evidence that, at Clermont, Urban acted no less decisively by relating participation in the armed pilgrimage

---

In the same year two brothers pledged a *mansus* for a hundred shillings, 'pro peccatorum nostrorum remissione cum ceteris in expeditione Hierosolimam proficiscentes': Bruel, 3712. Abbot Hugh's warm support for the Crusade of 1101 is clear from Bruel, 3737 and 3755.

[1] For Urban's itinerary, see esp. R. Crozet, 'Le Voyage d'Urbain II et ses négociations avec le clergé de France (1095-1096)', *Revue historique*, clxxix (1937), 271-310.   [2] See above, p. 60.

[3] 'Cuius expeditionis domnus papa maximus auctor fuit': Bernold, *Chron. s.a.* 1096, *M.G.H. Scr.* v. 464. One twelfth-century writer, however, ascribed Urban's eloquence at Clermont in no small measure to his training at Cluny: 'Qui vir magnus et urbanae elegantiae quis vel quantus esset apud Clarum Montem aperuit, et verbis suis orbem latinum fere totum movens ad Iherosolimam liberandam mirabili potentia misit. Quem nemo dubitet in Cluniacensi monasterio in quo prior extiterat scientiam illam et verborum affluentiam collegisse, quae universis fidelibus edocendis sufficeret, et ad comprimendos infideles Christianis audatiam daret. Et hoc tantum bonum ab eodem sancto loco processit, de cuius fonte vir ille apostolicus sanctae religionis et tantae facundiae fluenta bibit': Constable, 'The Letter from Peter of St. John to Hato of Troyes', *Studia Anselmiana*, xl (1956), 51.

[4] See esp. Erdmann, op. cit., pp. 284-325 and the criticisms of Mayer, op. cit., pp. 16-17.

to the gaining of the remission of sins in a special way: he attached
to it the value of a plenary indulgence for sins in the strict sense of
the term.[1] As it was preached by Urban, the Crusade thus had a
spiritual significance for Christians such as no previously existing
aspect of the Christian life had so strikingly possessed. This included Cluniac monasticism. Cluny's preaching of men's need to
seek the remission of their sins encouraged a climate of opinion in
which men were ready to hear the vicar of St. Peter, when he
preached the taking of the cross as a means to this end. But Cluny
had no significant part in the early history of indulgences. The
effect of Urban's preaching was to provide a 'novum salutis
promerendae genus' which did much to render the Cluniac way
old-fashioned, and so to reduce the predominant position that
Cluny under Abbot Hugh enjoyed in the Christian world. The
remission of sins was becoming available by other ways, in addition to the traditional way of gaining an association with the
prayers and alms of the cloister.[2]

But these developments belong essentially to the history of the
twelfth century. In the time of Abbot Hugh, Cluny did much to

[1] See esp. canon 2 of the Council of Clermont: 'Quicumque pro sola devotione,
non pro honoris vel pecuniae adeptione, ad liberandam ecclesiam Dei Jerusalem
profectus fuerit, iter illud pro omni poenitentia reputetur': Mansi, xx. 816; i.e.
the Crusaders were to receive a plenary indulgence in the precise sense of an
annulling of all penances which the Church had imposed for sins. In his letter of
1095 to the Flemings, Urban spoke more generally, saying that, in view of the
persecution of the eastern Churches and the enslavement of the holy city of Christ,
he had enjoined an expedition (*procinctus*) upon the princes of France and their
subjects 'pro remissione omnium peccatorum suorum': H. Hagenmayer, *Die
Kreuzzugsbriefe aus den Jahren 1088–1100* (Innsbruck, 1901), no. 2, pp. 136–7. To
the clergy and people of Bologna, Urban wrote in September 1096: 'Sciatis
autem eis omnibus, qui illuc [Jerusalem] non terreni commodi cupiditate sed pro
sola animae suae salute et ecclesiae liberatione profecti fuerint, poenitentiam totam
peccatorum, de quibus veram et perfectam confessionem fecerint, ... dimittimus':
ibid., no. 3, p. 137.

[2] Guibert of Nogents' words are particularly significant: '. . . instituit nostro
tempore praelia sancta Deus, ut ordo equestris et vulgus oberrans, qui vetustae
paganitatis exemplo in mutuas versabantur caedes, novum repperirent salutis
promerendae genus; ut nec funditus electa, uti fieri assolet, monastica conversatione, seu religiosa qualibet professione, saeculum relinquere cogerentur, sed sub
consueta licentia et habitu, ex suo ipsorum officio, Dei aliquatenus gratiam con-
sequerentur': *Historia quae dicitur Gesta Dei per Francos*, 1, *Recueil des historiens des
Croisades, historiens occidentaux*, iv. 124.

prepare the way for the Crusade by the kinds of religious motives which it encouraged and by the character of its impact upon feudal society. In this respect, as in so many others, its history during the eleventh century was one of genuine and effective harmony with the purposes of the Papacy.

PART IV

THE CLUNIACS OUTSIDE FRANCE

UNDER Abbot Hugh the circle of Cluniac influence widened beyond the borders of France and Burgundy to a hitherto unprecedented extent. For the most part this development did not happen by the planting of houses which were directly and permanently subject to Cluny, but in more indirect and diffused ways. Nevertheless in Germany, Spain, and Italy, in particular, the work of the Cluniacs was strong and positive, and it contributed significantly to the propagation of the Gregorian Reform in these lands.[1]

[1] The coming of the Cluniacs to Norman England after the foundation of Lewes in 1072–7 was virtually without direct implications for the Gregorian Reform. For the relevant evidence see W. Dugdale, *Monasticon Anglicanum*, v (new edn. by J. Caley, H. Ellis, and B. Bandinel, London, 1825), 1–215; G. F. Duckett, *Charters and Records among the Archives of the Ancient Abbey of Cluni from 1077 to 1534* (2 vols. (Lewes, 1888), esp. i. 43–57. Cluniac foundations in England were few in number, and the abbot of Cluny's authority over them was qualified and indirect: Knowles, *The Monastic Order in England*, pp. 151–8. William I enjoyed the confraternity of Cluny and he admired it greatly. Soon after the Conquest he applied to Abbot Hugh for monks who might administer and occupy sees and abbeys in his lands; he asked for six monks and, in return, promised generous annual payments to Cluny. Abbot Hugh replied that he could not receive money in exchange for souls which were committed to him, and that monasteries in the Anglo-Norman kingdom were too far away for him to govern properly: *Analecta*, iii, *P.L.* clix. 923–5; *Ep.* i, ibid., col. 927. That Hugh's real reason was his unwillingness to expand his monastic family to the north of the Loire is confirmed by evidence preserved in the *Carta fundationis* of Lewes, which records his reluctance to accede to William of Warenne's request 'propter longinquitatem alienae terrae et maxime propter mare': Dugdale, *Monasticon*, v. 12–13; cf. the charter for Thetford, ibid. pp. 151–3. (The Lewes Charter has been shown to be itself a fabrication of early thirteenth-century date, but the historical details which it embodies appear to rest upon a much earlier, and in all probability essentially reliable, foundation narrative: see *Early Yorkshire Charters*, ed. C. T. Clay, viii, *The Honour of Warenne* (Yorkshire Archaeological Society, Record Series, Extra Series, vi, 1949), pp. 59–62.) The firm royal control which William I established over the Anglo-Norman church also made it unlikely that its Cluniac houses would exhibit strongly Gregorian features.

I

THE CLUNIACS IN GERMANY

I. CLUNY'S DIRECT INFLUENCE IN GERMANY

In spite of the long history of imperial favour towards the Cluniacs and of the familiarity of the great abbots of Cluny with the imperial court,[1] Cluniac monasticism made little impact upon the German-speaking parts of the empire before the time of Abbot Hugh. There was just one known attempt to establish a Cluniac house. In 1014, after his imperial coronation at Rome, the Emperor Henry II encouraged Bishop Meinwerk of Paderborn to obtain from Abbot Odilo thirteen monks in order to set up a monastery at Abdinghof, near Paderborn. But Abdinghof soon gained, and for a long time kept, its independence of Cluny; and its foundation remained an isolated case.[2] The hardening of imperial policy in Germany against monastic exemption during and after the second quarter of the eleventh century, perhaps militated against the spread of Cluniac monasticism;[3] but the principal reasons for the absence of the Cluniacs from Germany arose from the contrasting characteristics of Burgundian and imperial monastic forms.

It emerges clearly from Hallinger's massive study of reform movements in the western Church during the tenth and eleventh centuries that there was, indeed, monastic reform in Germany, and on a massive scale; but it had stemmed from such Lotharingian houses as Gorze (reformed 933) and Brogne (founded 914),

---

[1] See above, pp. 157–9.
[2] *Vita Meinwerci episcopi Patherbrunnensis*, xxviii, ed. F. Tenckhoff, *S.R.G.*, p. 32. The assertion in the *Vita* that the Emperor Henry II and Bishop Meinwerk themselves visited Cluny, is not compatible with the known facts of the emperor's itinerary: see Tenckhoff's note, *ad loc.*; Hourlier, *Saint Odilon*, pp. 79–80. There are, however, no good reasons for doubting that Meinwerk obtained monks from Cluny for the foundation of Abdinghof. See also *Annalista Saxo, s.a.* 1030, ed. G. Waitz, *M.G.H. Scr.* vi. 678–9.   [3] See above, p. 29, n. 1.

which transmitted their reforming initiatives over the length and breadth of Germany by such intermediaries as St. Maximin, Trier; St. Emmeram, Regensburg; Niederaltaich; Lorsch; Fulda; Mainz; and Einsiedeln.

This reforming activity was not significantly indebted to Cluny or to Burgundian centres of reform. It kept more closely than they did to the reforms of St. Benedict of Aniane. In countless details of monastic dress, usage, and liturgy, Cluniac monasticism increasingly made new departures which stood in contrast with German ways. Trivial though they often were in themselves, they were sufficient to generate animosities which are reminiscent of those between Celts and Romans in the seventh-century Northumbrian church.[1] In addition, the constitutional position of German monasticism differed from that of Cluny. In general, the German reformers accepted episcopal and lay authority over their monasteries and churches. Up to the late eleventh century they showed no tendency to follow Cluny along the road to liberty upon the Roman model but were at home in the Imperial Church System. They differed from the Cluniacs in just those respects which most commended the Cluniacs to the Gregorians. Even when, towards the middle of the eleventh century, such reformers as Abbots Richard of Saint-Vanne (1004–46) and Poppo of Stablo (1020–48) introduced some borrowings from Cluny into the monasteries which they reformed, there was no thoroughgoing invasion of Germany by Cluniac Customs. In their circles as elsewhere, the traditional characteristics of German monasticism persisted; and these characteristics were sufficient to differentiate it sharply from Cluny.[2]

---

[1] The incipient interest of German monks in Cluniac monasticism, and also its utter strangeness to them, is illustrated by the letter of the monks of Monte Cassino in answer to an inquiry from Abbot Hartwig of Hersfeld (after 1072), in which the Germans were told that the Cluniac habit and tonsure 'nec nobis placent, nec cuiquam qui regulariter vivere voluerit iure placenda sunt, videntur enim omnino contra regulam': *Die ältere Wormser Briefsammlung*, no. 1, ed. W. Bulst, *M.G.H. B.D.K.* iii. 15. For the anger which was caused amongst German monks by the introduction of Cluniac dress, see e.g. *De unitate ecclesiae conservanda*, 42, ed. W. Schwenkenbecher, *M.G.H. L. de L.* ii. 276–7; Hallinger, *Gorze–Kluny*, pp. 702–24.

[2] Hallinger, op. cit., esp. pp. 280–1, 493–601. The topographical separation

Hallinger's critics have objected, with some justification, that he drew too harsh a contrast between Cluniac and German monasticism; and that he exaggerated the conscious hostility which, in his opinion, set them in antagonism. They have suggested that in many ways the differences between the two monasticisms arose from their contrasting political and social environments, rather than from any radical opposition on grounds of monastic principle.[1] But whatever may eventually emerge as the basis of the contrast between them, it can scarcely be gainsaid that, until the latter years of the pontificate of Gregory VII, Cluny and its Customs had made little real impact upon the German-speaking lands.[2]

Apart from Abdinghof there were, indeed, just a few indications at about the middle of the eleventh century that others in Germany besides the emperors were beginning to experience Cluny's attractive power. One or two Germans were becoming monks there, notably two men from Regensburg: Gerald, who later became grand prior of Cluny and cardinal-bishop of Ostia, and Ulrich, the future prior of Zell.[3] Again, Cluny's situation and growing importance with regard to the pilgrimage routes contributed to its becoming known by Germans.[4] On the impulse of

of the Cluniac and Gorzean reforms is made clear by the map in *Westermanns Atlas zur Weltgeschichte* (Brunswick, 1956), p. 87.

[1] See esp. the criticisms of Tellenbach and Schieffer referred to above, p. xvii, n. 2.

[2] Its influence was, perhaps, even less than Hallinger suggested. In his view, towards the end of the eleventh century, four monastic groups were working towards the dissemination of Cluniac monasticism in Germany: Anchin, near Douai; Siegburg, on the Rhine; and Hirsau and St. Blasien in the Black Forest: *Gorze-Kluny*, p. 418. But Anchin was of little importance until it had come under Bec's influence in 1087: ibid., pp. 474–5; and in a detailed monograph on Siegburg Semmler has established that it was less Cluniac in its way of life than Hallinger supposed: J. Semmler, *Die Klosterreform von Siegburg* (Bonn, 1959).

[3] *Vita sancti Udalrici prioris Cellae, vita prior*, 1, pp. 6–8, ed. R. Wilmans, M.G.H. Scr. xii. 251–3; and *vita posterior*, 11–12, ibid., pp. 256–7; another German Cluniac was Count Hermann of Baden, son of Duke Berthold of Zähringen: Berthold, *Annales, s.a.* 1073, M.G.H. Scr. v. 276; Bernold, *Chron. s.a.* 1074, ibid., p. 430. Cf. also Abbot Berno of Reichenau's cordial letter to Abbot Odilo, which may have been written at any date between 1008 and 1048: *Cluny im 10. und 11. Jahrhundert*, ed. J. Wollasch (Göttingen, 1967), no. 15, p. 48.

[4] See e.g. *Vita sancti Morandi confessoris, Bibl. C.*, cols. 501–6. Of German birth,

the moment, although not, perhaps, very deeply, two leading prelates, Archbishops Siegfried of Mainz (1060-84)[1] and Anno of Cologne (1056-75), also came under its spell. Anno was so favourably impressed by the monastery of Fruttuaria, near Turin, which the Cluniac William of Volpiano had founded, that he and other bishops sought to introduce monks and Customs from there and elsewhere, including Cluny, into Siegburg and other German monasteries.[2]

There were also attempts by lay families to establish and endow Cluniac houses. The first was in 1072, when Hesso of Üsenberg wished to give a church at Rimsingen, in the Breisgau, for colonization by monks from Cluny, and secured a royal charter to confirm his gift.[3] But Rimsingen did not prosper. The first viable Cluniac priory to be established in German-speaking lands was Rüggisberg (Rougemont, dioc. Lausanne), which was founded in 1073 by Count Lutold of Rümlingen; the German monk Ulrich came on a temporary visit from Cluny to establish its active life.[4] Ulrich returned to Cluny; but soon afterwards, in

Morand attended the cathedral school at Worms. On pilgrimage to Compostela, he visited Cluny and Abbot Hugh persuaded him to become a monk if he returned in safety. As a Cluniac monk he was first active in the Auvergne, but he later returned to Basle. In 1105 Frederick, son of Count Thierry of Montbéliard, entrusted him with the reform of St. Christopher's, Altkirchen: Bruel, 3835; A. Brackmann, *Germania Pontificia* (Berlin, 1911-35), ii, pt. 2, pp. 264-6. He died *c.* 1115.

[1] According to Lampert of Hersfeld, he visited Cluny in 1072: 'abdicatis . . . omnibus quae habebat, statuit ibi deinceps privatus aetatem agere atque ab omni saecularium negotiorum strepitu sub voluntariae paupertatis titulo inperpetuum feriari. Sed brevi perstitit in proposito': *Annales, s.a.* 1072, S.R.G., p. 139; cf. *Reg.* ii. 29, 4 Dec. 1074, pp. 161-2. According to Marianus Scottus, Siegfried was urged to return to Mainz by Abbot Hugh himself, in order to avoid a simoniacal election to his see: *Chronicon, s.a.* 1072, ed. G. Waitz, *M.G.H. Scr.* v. 560.

[2] Lampert of Hersfeld, *Ann. s.a.* 1075, pp. 244-5; Semmler, op. cit., esp. pp. 35, 255-7.

[3] *M.G.H. DD.* vi, pt. 1, no. 255, pp. 324-5; cf. Bruel, 3448. Abbot Hugh was at Worms when the former document was drawn up: Lampert of Hersfeld, *Ann. s.a.* 1072, p. 138.

[4] For its origins, see Brackmann, *Germania Pontificia*, ii, pt. 2, pp. 206-7. Its foundation is described in *Vita Udalrici, vita posterior*, 21, pp. 258-9. In a spurious diploma of Henry IV, dated 1076, it is said that Cardinal Gerald of Ostia was concerned with its foundation and that the king had issued a privilege for it: Brackmann, op. cit., p. 207. Gregory VII's confirmation of Cluny's privileges

1075 and 1076, he was sent by Abbot Hugh to Payerne, Cluny's dependency in the kingdom of Burgundy, where he resisted and sought to convert the loyal Henrican, Bishop Burchard of Lausanne (1073–89), in whose diocese Payerne lay.[1] He came back to Germany in 1078 or 1079 and collaborated with Abbot Bernard of Marseilles;[2] he returned permanently in the late 1080s, when his principal task was the firm implanting of Cluniac monasticism in Swabia. He settled, first, at Grüningen, on the lands of Duke Berthold I of Zähringen, for which the Cluniac endowments at Rimsingen were exchanged.[3] Then, in about 1087, Ulrich secured the further removal of the priory to Zell (dioc. Constance),[4] which was the property of the church of Basle with its staunchly Gregorian bishop, Burchard (1072–1106). In 1090 he imitated Abbot Hugh's foundation of Marcigny, of which he had been prior, by establishing a house for nuns nearby at Bollschweil.[5] He was soon after struck by blindness and died in 1093; up to his death he remained one of Abbot Hugh's most favoured and respected sons.[6] He was responsible for the introduction into Germany of Cluniac Customs;[7] and in his own work at Payerne and Zell as well as in his collaboration with his friend of Regensburg days, Abbot William of Hirsau, his alignments were always decisively with the Gregorian, not the imperialist, party. His work, and Abbot Hugh's commendation of it, demonstrate where Cluny's sympathies lay. But his importance within his very

(1075) included Rüggisburg (*cellam Montis Richeri*): Santifaller, Q.F., no. 107, p. 99.
[1] *Vita Udalrici, vita posterior*, 25, *M.G.H. Scr.* xii. 260.
[2] See *Constitutiones Hirsaugienses*, i, Prologue, *P.L.* cl. 927–9.
[3] *Vita Udalrici, vita posterior*, 27, pp. 260–1.
[4] Bruel, 3622. The first two witnesses of this charter were Duke Berthold I of Zähringen and Count Hermann of Baden, son of the Count Hermann who had become a monk at Cluny.   [5] *Vita Udalrici, vita posterior*, 32, p. 262.
[6] Upon his death Abbot Hugh asked Bishop Gebhard of Constance to attend to the translation of his body, 'asserens eum nequaquam fuisse de monachis sui temporis': *Vita Udalrici, vita prior*, 8, p. 253.
[7] *P.L.* cxlix. 635–778; see also *Vita Udalrici, vita posterior*, 33–4, pp. 263–4. Paul of Bernried named Ulrich, together with Bishop Altmann of Passau and Abbots William of Hirsau and Siegfried of Schaffhausen, as the four pre-eminent Gregorians in Germany: *Vita Greg. VII*, 118, *Pontificum Romanorum . . . vitae*, ed. Watterich, i. 543. For Ulrich, see E. Hauviller, *Ulrich von Cluny* (Münster, 1896).

limited sphere of work in Germany must not be exaggerated; and, with the exception of the first beginnings of the priory of Münchenwyler (Villar-les-moines, dioc. Lausanne),[1] it completes the tale of Cluny's immediate influence in Germany during and immediately after the pontificate of Gregory VII. Such as this influence was, it was authentically and positively Gregorian; but in its scope and in its effects, it was limited. When, towards the end of his life, Abbot Hugh passed in review the countries in which he had seen his monastic family spread, he saw no reason to mention Germany in the catalogue.[2]

II. HIRSAU

It is not, therefore, by the number and importance of its direct dependencies that the impact of Cluny upon Germany during the Investiture Contest must be measured, but by its indirect and derivative influence. The principal centre of this influence was the Black Forest monastery of Hirsau, which was situated to the north-west of Tübingen, midway between the Rhine and the Neckar. Hirsau was never subject to Cluny; but it owed a debt to its Foundation Charter, its Customs, its guidance, and its prestige. The precise nature and extent of this debt remain matters of controversy; and the detailed course of events at Hirsau will, perhaps, never be satisfactorily determined.[3] It is, however,

[1] Münchenwyler was given to Cluny in 1080 and the priory established in 1090: Brackmann, op. cit., pp. 205–6.

[2] *Imprecatio beati Hugonis abbatis*, P.L. clix. 951.

[3] On Hirsau, see esp. K. Schmid, *Kloster Hirsau und seine Stifter* (Forschungen zur Oberrheinische Landesgeschichte, ix, Freiberg, 1959); H. Jakobs, *Die Hirsauer* (Cologne and Graz, 1961); S. Greiner, 'Beiträge zur Geschichte der Grafen von Calw', *Zeitschrift für Württembergische Landesgeschichte*, xxv (1966), 34–58; H. Büttner, 'Abt Wilhelm von Hirsau und die Entwicklung der Rechtsstellung der Reformklöster im 11. Jahrhundert', ibid., pp. 321–38. Amongst older authorities, Hauck's account in *Kirchengeschichte Deutschlands*, iii. 866–76 remains of fundamental importance. See also Brackmann, *Zur politischen Bedeutung der kluniazensischen Bewegung*, and 'Gregor VII. und die kirchliche Reformbewegung in Deutschland', *S.G.* ii. 7–30; Hallinger, *Gorze–Kluny*, esp. pp. 428–42, 470–3, 564, 839–46; Mayer, *Fürsten und Staat*, pp. 58–133. For the general problem of monastic immunity in Germany, see H. Hirsch, *Die Klosterimmunität seit dem Investiturstreit* (2nd edn. with postscript by H. Büttner, Darmstadt, 1967), pp. 1–65, E.T. of pp. 26–65 in Barraclough, *Mediaeval Germany*, ii. 131–73.

possible to offer a tentative reconstruction of how reform was introduced there; and an estimate may be made of its services to the Gregorian cause, and of the extent to which these services were the consequence of its debt to Cluny.

Hirsau's rise to prominence was sudden. Its lay proprietor, Count Albert II of Calw, virtually re-founded the Carolingian monastery at the behest of his uncle Pope Leo IX. In due course, in 1065, monks came from Einsiedeln to revive the monastic life. Hirsau became a good example of the small proprietary monastery of a dynastic family, in this case, one of considerable local standing, whose proprietor claimed to exercise the rights of advocate by reason of his proprietorship. By the middle years of the eleventh century the impulse towards the freeing of monasteries from lay proprietorship, which had for long been operative in France, was also at work in Germany. It met with considerable resistance on the part of lay proprietors; and events at Hirsau well illustrate this resistance. In 1069 Count Albert of Calw summoned from Regensburg to be abbot of Hirsau a monk of St. Emmeram, named William. Upon his arrival William declared himself unwilling to consent to his election unless the liberty of Hirsau were conceded. Count Albert was reluctant; as a result, William had to devote the first phase of his rule, from 1069 to 1075, to imposing reform upon an unwilling proprietor. In 1071 the count and the abbot did, indeed, demonstrate that they had reached a *modus vivendi* by obtaining a charter from the king, now lost, which met some of Abbot William's demands;[1] and at some stage it was followed by a papal privilege,[2] which also has not survived. Afterwards, however, the count sought surreptitiously to go back upon his concessions. Abbot William therefore sought to deliver Hirsau completely and finally from the yoke of temporal authority.[3] The events which followed, by which Hirsau was drastically reformed, took place in three stages.

[1] For this first royal charter, see *Vita Willihelmi abbatis Hirsaugiensis*, 2–3, ed. W. Wattenbach, *M.G.H. Scr.* xii. 212; cf. *M.G.H. DD.* vi, pt. 1, no.*241, pp. 304–5.

[2] Referred to in Gregory VII's later Privilege and in the Hirsau Charter, see below, pp. 198–200.

[3] '. . . interpellabat Dominum, ut de terrenae potestatis iugo eriperet locum, quem pro suo amore susceperat regendum': *Vita Willihelmi*, 3, p. 212.

How Abbot William set about his task is known in great detail
from the most important document of German monasticism
during the Investiture Contest: the Hirsau Charter of 1075;[1]
the granting of which marks the first stage of William's reform.
This Charter did not embody, nor was it accompanied by, any
attempt to alter the internal life of the monastery. For the time
being its life continued on the traditional lines of German monasticism. The Charter was designed to transform and to settle the
external relationship between Hirsau and its lay proprietor. By
its terms the count of Calw renounced his proprietary rights
altogether. Hirsau was restored 'in potestatem et proprietatem' to
its patron saints, St. Aurelian and St. Peter. The monks were to
elect and to install their own abbot; he was to receive the abbatial
staff at the hands of the *decanus* from the altar of St. Aurelian, in
token of the saint's proprietorship of the monastery. Thus lay
investiture was abandoned and Hirsau stood under the exclusive
dominatio, ordinatio, and *potestas* of its abbot. The rights of the count
of Calw were reduced to the provision that, so long as some
member of his family was personally suitable for the office, the
monks must choose their advocate from it. Upon the abbot's
request, the advocate whom the monks elected was to receive his
jurisdiction (*Bann*) from the king. This provision made it clear
that the advocacy of Hirsau no longer depended upon the
proprietary rights of the count of Calw, but upon the public
authority of the king. The pope also came into the picture,
because an earlier placing of Hirsau under papal protection (*sub
Romanae ecclesiae mundiburdio et maiestate*), in return for the payment
to Rome of an annual *census*, was confirmed.

As regards its sources, this elaborate attempt to provide something for all the interested parties[2] was highly eclectic. One

[1] *M.G.H. DD.* vi, pt. 1, no. 280, pp. 357–62; cf. *Vita Willihelmi*, 3, p. 212. Its
authenticity was long in dispute; its editor in the *Monumenta*, D. von Gladiss,
marked it as spurious, and Brackmann, amongst others, concurred. It was, however, twice and independently vindicated in 1950, with convincing arguments,
by Hallinger, op. cit., pp. 564, 840–3; and Mayer, op. cit., pp. 50–82.

[2] Except, possibly, the diocesan bishop, the bishop of Speyer. But the provision
that the abbot's *ordinatio* must be performed 'canonice' may have safeguarded his
rights: Jakobs, op. cit., pp. 18–19.

element in it was that Hirsau was to enjoy *libertas* according to the understanding of this term in the Germany of immediately pre-Gregorian times: it was to become, in judicial matters, directly subject to the empire.[1] Yet it also placed Hirsau under papal protection. Furthermore, the proposals of 1075 exhibited a considerable, if perhaps an indirect, debt to the Cluniac charter of 909. They did so in such a provision as the self-investiture of the abbot, and still more in matters of vocabulary: terms like *dominatio, ordinatio*, and *potestas* were characteristically Cluniac and not German terms. In 1075 Abbot William had an eye to Cluniac precedents, if of a rather old-fashioned kind which centred on Cluny's Foundation Charter, when he defined the constitution of Hirsau as he then aspired to establish it.[2] Cluniac monastic forms were beginning to be implanted in Germany.

But William quickly changed his mind about the purpose of his reform at Hirsau and the Charter of 1075 did not come into effect. For the time being it became lost in the turmoil of the most tumultuous phase of the Investiture Contest; and a second stage of William's reform of Hirsau supervened. During the last months of 1075 and with the concurrence of Count Albert of Calw,[3] William went to Rome in order to secure a papal confirmation of the Charter. His arrival there coincided with the disintegration of relations between Gregory VII and Henry IV, which issued in the first excommunication of the emperor at Gregory's Lent Council of 1076.[4] In these circumstances Gregory was unlikely to confirm in all its details the Hirsau Charter with its emphasis upon the royal *Bannleihe*; yet it would have been impolitic to administer a rebuff to the count of Calw by condemning the

[1] Hirsch, op. cit., pp. 8–9; Mayer, op. cit., pp. 48–9.

[2] Von Gladiss indicates most of the borrowings in his edition. See also Jakobs, op. cit., pp. 18, 19, 21–2, 82–7, 98; Brackmann, *Zur politischen Bedeutung*, pp. 65–7; Mayer, op. cit., pp. 88, 93–9. For occasional earlier German uses of Cluniac formulas, see Hirsch, *Die Klosterimmunität*, pp. 19–22, 27, 220–3.

[3] If *Reg.* ii. 11, 26 Oct. 1074, pp. 142–3, was, as is probable, addressed to Count Albert of Calw and his wife Wiltrud, it illustrates Gregory VII's long-standing approval of the count as an ally in the cause of reform, of whose value Gregory took a characteristically enthusiastic view.

[4] The disintegration is illustrated by *Reg.* iii. 10, 8 Dec. 1075, pp. 263–7, and by the excommunication of the emperor: *Reg.* iii. 10*a*, pp. 268–71.

Charter outright. So Gregory provided William with a new and very carefully drafted privilege of his own.[1] In it he praised the count for first restoring and then freeing Hirsau, and he confirmed that it enjoyed the protection of St. Peter and St. Paul. He next referred to the count's work as follows:

> We decree that the provisions and forms of immunity and liberty (*constitutiones quoque et immunitatis et libertatis modos*) which the illustrious Count Albert included in the text of his conveyance (*scripto suae traditionis*) and which he caused to be confirmed with the king's seal, shall be diligently observed as a security in time to come and to ward off hostile attacks: those, that is to say, which are not against canonical sanctions, so that nothing of what is permissible may be omitted, and nothing of what is forbidden may be imposed (. . . *hos dumtaxat, qui canonicis sanctionibus non obsistunt, ut nec de permissis quidlibet negligatur nec de vetitis quidlibet irrogetur*).

This arresting and surprisingly little-discussed passage, for which there seems to be no earlier parallel or precedent,[2] first of all confirmed, in very broad terms, the Hirsau Charter of 1075, and so avoided offering any rebuff to the count and to Abbot William. Yet it did so with the all-important reservation, that the Charter

---

[1] For this papal privilege, which survives only in a fifteenth- or sixteenth-century copy and is undated, see Santifaller, *Q.F.*, no. 88, pp. 71–3. The chief source for Abbot William's attitude is the *Vita Willihelmi abbatis Hirsaugiensis*, *M.G.H. Scr.* xii. 209–25. His journey to Rome is introduced as follows: 'quo [the Hirsau Charter of 1075] ad votum completo, statuit etiam apostolicam sedem adire, et privilegium Hirsaugiensi coenobio secundum scita canonum acquirere. . . . Ibi a domno apostolico . . . Gregorio benigne susceptus, cognitis causis quarum gratia illo advenerat, libentissime prout competebat annuit. Nam privilegium apostolica auctoritate plenum sibi contradidit': 4, p. 213. This agrees with the earlier account by Berthold, according to which Abbot William went to Rome 'pro cuius institutionis liberrimae decretis, apostolicae auctoritatis privilegio roborandis, . . . et ad votum suum apud papam Gregoriam id efficaciter, pro quo exierat, perageret [et] . . . cum acquisitis apostolicae liberalitatis privilegiis et benedictionibus vix [because of his severe illness] repatriavit: *Ann. s.a.* 1075, *M.G.H. Scr.* v. 281. There is also a brief account of William in the *Historia Hirsaugiensis monasterii*, 3, ed. G. Waitz, *M.G.H. Scr.* xiv. 256–7.

[2] This passage seems to be decisive in ruling out any date earlier than the winter of 1075–6 for the document; only with the crisis that led up to the excommunication of the emperor is so radical a provision plausible; and it corresponds closely with the account of the privilege in the *Vita Willihelmi*: see above, n. 1.
It is not discussed by Mayer, op. cit., pp. 100–3, or Jakobs, op. cit., pp. 11–12.

held good only in so far as its provisions did not run counter to canonical sanctions. The reservation was not only made negatively, in the sense that whatever was against the canons must be a dead letter; but also positively, in the sense that whatever was canonically permissible must not be neglected in providing for the future of Hirsau. Gregory's language strongly suggests that he intended the 'constitutiones quoque et immunitatis et libertatis modos' henceforth to be understood as Rome understood them rather than as Germany did. The norm was to be canon law, not German law. Hirsau's liberty was to be liberty in a Roman sense. Gregory, in effect, claimed *carte blanche* to make of Hirsau whatever he would.

He did not particularize further. Perhaps at this early stage of the crisis between Papacy and empire, his own ideas of what was permissible in Germany were not precisely articulated; for they were certainly in process of drastic revision. A little over a year before, he had been so far willing to show his toleration of the state of affairs from which even the Hirsau Charter had delivered Hirsau, as to recognize the hereditary advocacy of the counts of Egisheim at Holy Cross, Woffenheim, just as Pope Leo IX had done.[1] But if the above interpretation be correct, the Hirsau Privilege is the first evidence that Gregory was abandoning his toleration of German practice and that, by the winter of 1075–6, he was seeking to introduce into Germany what he understood to be the norms of canon law. In a very general way, such a development with respect to the monastic order was foreshadowed by Gregory's letter of 22 January 1075 to Abbot Hugh of Cluny, in which he voiced his despair of bishops and secular princes, and his hopes for the collaboration of the monks in his plans for the Church.[2] Abbot William's visit to Rome in connection with his reform of Hirsau may well have seemed to present Gregory with

[1] *Reg.* ii. 4, 29 Oct. 1074, pp. 146–7.
[2] *Reg.* ii. 49, pp. 188–90; see above, pp. 152–3. The partial community of themes between the letter to Abbot Hugh and the letter which was probably written to the count and countess of Calw in Oct. 1074, illustrates the early stages of Gregory's quest for new allies in the cause of reform: *Reg.* ii. 11, pp. 142–3. But in 1074 he sought allies amongst the laity; in 1075 he turned to the monastic order.

an excellent opportunity for refashioning a German monastery as his active ally, by introducing Roman ideas about monastic liberty. If so, the Hirsau Privilege marks a kind of half-way house between his arrangements of 1074 for Holy Cross, Woffenheim, and his privilege of 1080, in which he entrusted All Saints', Schaffhausen, to Abbot William for reform on the model of Cluny's liberty.[1] In 1080 he did not hesitate to condemn as 'contra sanctorum patrum statuta' an earlier privilege of Alexander II's for Schaffhausen, which can have differed little from his own arrangements of 1074 at Woffenheim. Gregory asserted that by allowing the founder of All Saints', Count Eberhard of Nellenberg, to be its hereditary advocate as well as to appoint its abbot and generally to oversee its affairs, Alexander had been 'deceived by the craft of others'. Gregory expressly annulled the proprietary and other rights of the counts of Nellenberg which infringed the liberty of All Saints'. The abbot might name whatever advocate he chose, not necessarily from the Nellenberg family; and he might dismiss him at will. All Saints' was to enjoy immunity from all manner of external interference in temporal matters, whether its basis were proprietorship, hereditary right, advocacy, or investiture. It was expressly endowed with the 'Romanae sedis libertas' according to the models of Cluny and Saint-Victor, Marseilles.

In the light of these documents the aspects of the Hirsau Charter which Gregory condemned in his privilege, because they ran counter to canonical sanctions, may well have been not only the concessions that it made to the king in the matter of the *Bannleihe*, but still more, the local claims that infringed Hirsau's absolute immunity, such as the not inconsiderable rights as advocate which the Charter still normally reserved to the comital family of Calw. In the pursuit of his new policy of relying more and more upon the monastic order, Gregory was beginning to envisage the establishment of a relationship between Hirsau and the Papacy, utterly unimpeded by the claims of other parties, in which Hirsau was to enjoy 'libertas' in the Gregorian sense of

[1] See above, pp. 173–4; also K. Hils, *Die Grafen von Nellenburg im 11. Jahrhundert* (Freiburg, 1967), esp. pp. 82–6.

direct, complete, and exclusive subjection to Rome. Unlike the Schaffhausen document of five years later, the Hirsau Privilege of 1075 did not name Cluny. But Gregory's appeal to canon law opened the way for Hirsau to progress towards the kind of 'libertas Romana' that Gregory so greatly admired at Cluny and sought to reproduce at Schaffhausen. The old-fashioned points of similarity with the Cluny of 909 that characterized the Hirsau Charter were beginning to be replaced by a more up-to-date similarity to Cluny's developed liberty. The result was at once to inaugurate the refashioning of Hirsau as an apt instrument of Gregory VII's purposes in Germany, and at the same time to open the way for vital direct contacts between Hirsau and Cluny. The gradual establishment of these contacts marks the third stage of Abbot William's reform of Hirsau.

In the winter of 1075-6 a mutation of Abbot William's own outlook gave impetus to this process. In the course of his stay at Rome, which was prolonged by grave illness and which seems to have covered the Lent Council of 1076, he became an ultra-Gregorian. Upon his return to Germany Hirsau quickly became the nerve-centre of the cause of St. Peter and so fulfilled the function that Gregory VII had envisaged for the monasteries in his letter of 1075 to Abbot Hugh of Cluny. After his election as anti-king at Forchheim in the spring of 1077, Rudolf of Swabia kept Pentecost at Hirsau; and from October 1077 until October 1078 Gregory's legate in Germany, Abbot Bernard of Marseilles, made it the base for his operations.[1] Bernard took advantage of the possibilities which the large and as yet unmapped 'libertas Romana' of Hirsau presented, to encourage Abbot William to remodel its outlook and internal life in ways which corresponded to its new function as a bastion of Gregorianism. In order to propound the canonical basis of papal authority, he seems to have introduced from Rome the *Collection in LXXIV Titles*.[2] Abbot

[1] For Bernard's work at Hirsau, see esp. his letter to Archbishop Udo of Trier and others: *Briefsammlungen der Zeit Heinrichs IV., Die Hannoversche Briefsammlung*, no. 33, *M.G.H. B.D.K.* v. 69–72. For Henry IV's countermeasures, see *Vita Willihelmi*, 26, *M.G.H. Scr.* xii. 222; Berthold, *Ann. s.a.* 1077, *M.G.H. Scr.* v. 301.

[2] This collection is now widely ascribed to Cardinal Humbert: A. Michel, *Die Sentenzen des Kardinals Humbert* (Leipzig, 1943), pp. 136–41; 'Pseudo-Isidor, die

Bernard also turned to Cluny, to which he owed a recent debt because it was by the intervention of Abbot Hugh that he was delivered from the captivity at the hands of Count Ulrich of Lensburg, into which he fell after the assembly of Forchheim.[1] He pressed upon Abbot William the Customs of Cluny as being those most suitable to be adopted at Hirsau, where Abbot William had hitherto not ceased to follow the Customs of his own former monastery of St. Emmeram. Abbot Bernard was warm in his praise of Cluny as providing the best example to follow:

for there, the monastic life has grown to such a height of vigour and fame, because of the reputation of its excellent monks as well as because of its long continuance, that if the marks of sanctity seem nowadays to be found in other monasteries, there is no doubt that its individual streams have come from Cluny as from a living and inexhaustible source.[2]

He also did everything in his power to see that Abbot William followed his advice. On his way back to Rome in 1078 he visited Cluny and commended Hirsau to Abbot Hugh's reforming zeal. Soon afterwards the Cluniac monk Ulrich, Abbot William's friend from Regensburg days, came to Hirsau. In response to the abbot's questions, he wrote down the Customs of Cluny for his guidance;[3] and, on three separate occasions, Abbot William sent pairs of monks to Cluny in order to assist him by observing and reporting upon its way of life at first hand.

It was thus not until 1079 that the monastic life at Hirsau effectively received a Cluniac imprint; but in that year recourse to Cluny was deliberate and conscientious. The depth of the Cluniac imprint is not easy to determine and is a matter of current debate; the problem will not be resolved until the several versions of the Customs of Cluny have been satisfactorily edited.[4] Hirsau

Sentenzen Humberts und Burkard von Worms im Investiturstreit', *S.G.* iii. 149–61, esp. pp. 157–9.

[1] Bernold, *Chron. s.a.* 1077, *M.G.H. Scr.* v. 434.

[2] William of Hirsau, *Consuetudines Hirsaugienses*, Introduction, *P.L.* cl. 928–9.

[3] *P.L.* cxlix. 643–778, esp. 643–4, 731.

[4] For the problems involved, see Hallinger, 'Klunys Bräuche zur Zeit Hugos des Grossen', *Z.S.S.R. kan.* xlv (1959), 99–140.

was certainly not simply made into a copy of Cluny. Abbot Hugh himself characteristically advised Abbot William to make such modifications in the Customs of Cluny as were dictated by local custom and by Hirsau's situation and climate.[1] In due course Abbot William drew up his own statement of the Customs which now became established there.[2] Brackmann and Hallinger have argued that in many fundamental aspects of the monastic life these developments brought about a close assimilation of Hirsau to Cluniac norms.[3] Jakobs, on the other hand, has expressed doubts about this. For example, he points out how one of the most 'Cluniac' features of the Hirsau Charter of 1075 was the self-investiture of the abbot. Yet the Customs of Hirsau as recorded by Abbot William broke entirely with this: they gave the bishop a renewed prominence which stood in contrast with the usages both of Cluny and of the Hirsau Charter. On the basis of this and other evidence Jakobs comes to the paradoxical conclusion that Hirsau was never again so 'Cluniac' as it was in the Hirsau Charter of 1075, before there was any question of Cluniac Customs being introduced, and before Abbot William's conversion to extreme Gregorianism.[4]

There can be little doubt that the paradox is strained too far. The Cluny of Abbot Hugh was not the Cluny of 909; significant as are the correspondences between Cluny's Foundation Charter and the Hirsau Charter, they are of far less weight than was the wholesale transplantation to Germany of Cluny's 'libertas Romana' that Gregory VII expressly intended to effect when he laid down the lines upon which William of Hirsau was to order

[1] See the introduction to William's Customs.

[2] For William's Customs, see *P.L.* cl. 927–1146; for his sending of monks to Cluny, see the introduction and the account of how Gerung, later abbot of Paulinzelle, who become a monk under Abbot William, was 'adeo paternae traditionis in claustralibus disciplinis emulator, ut ab abbate Wilhelmo bis Cluniacum mitteretur, quo illic regularis vitae institutis subtilius imbueretur, ut quasi novae rei mercator avidus, rarae vel secretae mercis indagator novi aliquid reportaret et meliora solitis adiceret': Sigeboto, *Vita Paulinae*, xxxvii, ed. I. R. Dieterich, *M.G.H. Scr.* xxx. 928.

[3] Brackmann, *Zur politischen Bedeutung*, pp. 21–2, 68–70; Hallinger, *Gorze-Kluny*, p. 428.

[4] *Die Hirsauer*, pp. 82–7, 99–103, 104–18.

Schaffhausen. The gradual progress of reform at Hirsau itself tended towards a similar arrangement as regards its external relationships. So far as the shaping of its internal monastic life after 1079 is concerned, Abbot William warmly acknowledged his debt to Cluniac Customs in his introduction to his own; while his repeatedly sending monks to Cluny confirms his desire to imitate Cluniac ways. Across the Neckar at Lorsch, Hirsau's critics in the next century could, it is true, contrast its innovations into German monasticism with the salutary conservatism of both Gorze and Cluny.[1] But there is ample evidence that just as before 1079 Abbot Bernard of Marseilles had urged Abbot William to have recourse to Cluny, so afterwards close observers associated William of Hirsau with its monasticism. Ulrich of Zell's biographer said that it was at Abbot William's bidding that Ulrich first introduced Cluniac Customs into Swabian monasteries.[2] It was said of Gerung, one of the monks of Hirsau whom Abbot William sent to Cluny as observers of its Customs, that he went there after the manner of a merchant, who was greedy to seek out choice merchandise and to bring it home to Hirsau for the improvement of its monastic life.[3] In 1081 Archbishop Siegfried of Mainz introduced reformed monasticism from Hirsau at Hasungen, near Kassel. One of the early Hasungen charters, as revised soon after 1085, spoke of his taking Cluny as a model: 'Cluniacensis sanctissimae religionis ordinem elegimus, in quo cum mundi huius contemptu voluntaria paupertas principatur'; another described how he effected a change there from the canonical life 'in excellentiorem regulam monachorum secundum habitum venerabilem et sacrosanctum consuetudinem coenobii Cluniacensis atque Herisaugiae'.[4] It is sufficiently clear that both at Hirsau

---

[1] *Chronicon Laureshamense*, ed. K. A. F. Pertz, *M.G.H. Scr.* xxi. 430.

[2] *Vita Udalrici, vita posterior*, 34, *M.G.H. Scr.* xii. 263.

[3] See the reference to Gerung of Paulinzelle, above, p. 205, n. 2.

[4] M. Stimming, *Mainzer Urkundenbuch*, i (Darmstadt, 1932), nos. 358, 362, pp. 253–8, 261–3. For their origin and authenticity, see W. Heinemeyer, 'Die Urkundenfälschungen des Klosters Hasungen', *Archiv für Diplomatik*, iv (1958), 226–63; and for the reform of Hasungen, Stengel, 'Lampert von Hersfeld der erste Abt von Hasungen', *Abhandlungen und Untersuchungen zur mittelalterlichen Geschichte*, pp. 242–59.

and elsewhere Abbot William set especial store upon Cluniac monasticism. For him conversion to out-and-out Gregorianism and a close following of Cluny belonged naturally together. His indebtedness to Cluny, and the recognition of his debt by his reform-minded contemporaries, are sufficiently marked to warrant Hirsau's inclusion in a comprehensive account of what the Gregorian Papacy owed the Cluniacs.[1]

The Papacy's debt to Hirsau itself was a notable one. Gregory VII made his arrangements for Schaffhausen in face of Henry IV's rising fortunes in Swabia during 1079; at that time it seemed less vulnerable than Hirsau on account of its position and of Zähringer protection. In the event Hirsau was never seriously threatened by imperial forces, nor did it yield place to Schaffhausen; although under the authority of Hirsau, Abbot Siegfried of Schaffhausen (1080–96) was amongst the most prominent of German Gregorians, and his monastery was, like Hirsau, a bastion of the papal cause. During the remainder of Abbot William's lifetime[2] Hirsau remained without question the chief of the reformed and Gregorian monasteries of Swabia. Scanty though the detailed evidence is, it stands out that Gregory VII was zealously served by Abbot William: together with Bishop Altmann of Passau, he was especially charged by Gregory with responsibilities in connection with the anti-King Hermann of Salm; and Paul of Bernried praised William, together with Altmann of Passau, Ulrich of Zell, and Siegfried of Schaffhausen, as the champions who sustained the Gregorian cause in south Germany.[3] In the 1080s, too, Hirsau became a refuge for Gregorians from all over Germany, wherever the imperial cause prospered. This led to an unintended accession of numbers, which prompted the promoting of a widespread

---

[1] The fourteenth-century *Chronica Reinhardsbrunnensis*, which drew upon earlier material, also recorded that in 1085, when Count Louis of Thuringia founded Hirsau's dependency of Reinhardsbrunn, he 'de Hirsaugia viros religiosos... adduxit... qui secundum Cluniacensium vel Hirsaugiensium ordinem Dei inibi devotius deservirent': *s.a.* 1085, ed. O. Holder-Egger, *M.G.H. Scr.* xxx. 526.

[2] He died in 1091.

[3] *Reg.* ix. 3, Mar. 1081, pp. 573–7; cf. *Briefsammlungen der Zeit Heinrichs IV.*, *Die Hannoversche Briefsammlung*, no. 18, *M.G.H. B.D.K.* v. 41–3; Paul of Bernried, *Vita Gregorii VII*, 118, *Romanorum pontificum ... vitae*, ed. Watterich, i. 543.

extra-mural campaign of propaganda in Germany on behalf of the Gregorian cause; Hirsau emerged as the first part of the monastic order to include amongst its activities the sponsoring of itinerant preaching.[1] Moreover, after a slow start the number of Hirsau's dependent houses increased rapidly, until, by the end of the century, they formed a network of centres of opposition to Henry IV in wide areas of Swabia.[2] The papal cause had no more strenuous champions in Germany than the monks of Hirsau in the years after Abbot Bernard of Marseilles brought them under the influence of Cluny.

Outside the monasteries which were filiated to Hirsau, there were other monasteries which were at once drawn into the circle of Gregorian houses and also into a loose relationship with Cluny. An example is St. Blasien, which Bernold, who was a monk there, named with Hirsau and Schaffhausen as being pre-eminent amongst the Gregorian monasteries of Germany.[3] No evidence survives by which it is possible to trace any such deliberate planting there of 'libertas' in the Gregorian sense as may be seen at Hirsau and Schaffhausen. But the gradual building up of a network of formal monastic unions reveals how it gradually moved into relationship with other reformed monasteries: in 1077, while Abbot Bernard was at Hirsau, it formed a union with Saint-Victor, Marseilles; between 1086 and 1091 there were unions with Hirsau, Muri, and Schaffhausen; and in 1096 during a visit by Abbot Hugh, which further demonstrates his approval of the reformed monasticism of south Germany, there followed a union of St. Blasien with Cluny itself.[4] This progressive building up of ties with Hirsau and Cluny had gone far enough by 1082 for Abbots Siegfried of Schaffhausen and William of Hirsau to reform the Habsburg proprietary monastery of Muri by turning it into a priory of St. Blasien, and at the same time establishing its

[1] Jakobs, op. cit., pp. 204–15; Hauck, op. cit., iii. 876; Grundmann, *Religiöse Bewegungen im Mittelalter*, pp. 509–10; E. Werner, *Pauperes Christi. Studien zu social-religiösen Bewegungen im Zeitalter des Reformpapsttums* (Leipzig, 1956), pp. 89–100.

[2] Jakobs, op. cit., pp. 35–76.

[3] *Chron. s.a.* 1083, *M.G.H. Scr.* v. 439.

[4] J. Wollasch, 'Muri und St. Blasien', *D.A.* xvii (1961), 420–46, esp. pp. 445–6.

'libertas' and its right to choose its advocate on the pattern of Gregory VII's privilege for Schaffhausen in 1080.[1] The Cluniac connection in Germany was thus progressively widened, and the Cluniac kind of liberty was spread amongst the monasteries that were most conspicuous for their resistance to the emperor.

If the course of events in Germany between Abbot William of Hirsau's journey to Rome in 1075 and his death in 1091 be surveyed, and if account be taken of developments which had either matured or were well advanced by that time, the debt of the Gregorians to Cluny and the Cluniacs was a large one. It is true that Abbot Hugh played no strikingly independent role in Germany, and that his own subject houses there remained a negligible factor. But Hirsau implicitly, and Schaffhausen explicitly, were the beneficiaries of the 'libertas Romana' as Cluny itself epitomized it in the estimation of Gregory VII. The monks of Hirsau enjoyed Cluny's guidance in shaping their monastic life, and they followed Abbot Bernard of Marseilles's advice that they should imitate its Customs. In some circles at least the monks of Hirsau were deemed to be Cluniacs, and the Chronicle of Bernold demonstrates that reformed circles in south Germany were aware of Cluny, and that they regarded it as an interpreter of the will of Gregory VII.[2] As the Cluniacs elsewhere in outposts like Saint-Mont which were directly subject to Cluny, the monks of Hirsau promoted the authority of Rome by giving hospitality to papal legates and by spreading the cultus of St. Peter and St. Paul.[3] Abbot Hugh himself never failed to afford to the monks of Hirsau the help for which they asked, and it was from Cluny that William of Hirsau obtained relics of St. Peter for his new church.[4]

---

[1] Although there was no explicit mention of Cluny. For the relevant documents, see *Acta Murensia*, 10, ed. M. Keim, *Quellen zur Schweizer Geschichte*, iii (1883), pt. 3, 32–4; for a discussion, Mayer, op. cit., pp. 113–33.

[2] For Bernold's references to Cluny, see *Chron. s.a.* 1074, p. 430; *s.a.* 1093, p. 457.

[3] When Abbot William completed his new church at Hirsau in 1091, it was dedicated to St. Peter and St. Paul: Schmid, op. cit., pp. 70–1; Jakobs, op. cit., p. 3, n. 3; W. Irtenkauf, *Hirsau, Geschichte und Kultur* (2nd edn., Stuttgart, 1966), pp. 28–9. The name of St. Aurelian, on the other hand, disappears from the records.

[4] Abbot William sent his prior, Gebhard, to Urban II in order to obtain relics of St. Peter. Although Urban received him favourably, he was unwilling, or

In assessing Gregory VII's debt to the Cluniacs in Germany, it is important to remember that the monastic order there provided Gregory VII with no ready-made allies.[1] Even in 1075 he had few, if any, active supporters in German monasticism upon whom he could really count. He had therefore to make allies for himself; and he did this principally by cultivating the monks of Hirsau. As it was refracted through Hirsau and its monastic dependencies and allies, the contribution of Cluny to the cause of St. Peter in Germany was a substantial one.

III. GERMANY AFTER 1085

It remained considerable, even when Pope Urban II in some respects modified it. Urban had first-hand knowledge of Germany; for during the final disastrous winter of Gregory's pontificate, he was there as papal legate.[2] He spent the earlier part of his stay in the south, and brought encouragement to the monastic group which Abbot William of Hirsau led. Under his guidance Gebhard, a monk of Hirsau who was the brother of the Gregorian Duke Berthold of Zähringen, was established as bishop of Constance.[3] He also visited St. Blasien. Slight as is the evidence for his time as legate, it shows that he had an opportunity to learn who his allies in Germany were. As pope, he hastened to inform them of his commitment to the work of Gregory VII and to an unwearying continuance of the struggle against the emperor; he exhorted the

unable, to grant his request. Gebhard, therefore, obtained three of St. Peter's hairs from Cluny: *Historia Hirsaugiensis monasterii*, 4, *M.G.H. Scr.* xiv. 257. The same source records that much of the cost of the new church at Hirsau was borne by Judith, wife of the Count Hermann of Baden who had become a monk of Cluny in 1073: 3, *M.G.H. Scr.* xiv. 257.

[1] Either in German monasticism or by way of an earlier Cluniac penetration. The assertion to the contrary by G. Barraclough, *The Origins of Modern Germany* (2nd edn., Oxford, 1947), pp. 106–7, needs revision.

[2] Becker, *Urban II*, i. 62–77.

[3] Until after the death of Henry IV, Gebhard remained a leading figure in the papalist party in Germany: G. Meyer von Knonau, 'Gebhard III., Bischof von Constanz', *Allgemeine Deutsche Biographie*, xvii (Leipzig, 1878), 453–7. Abbot Hugh maintained touch with him: *Vita sancti Udalrici prioris Cellensis, vita prior*, 8, *M.G.H. Scr.* xii. 253, a passage which also illustrates Hugh's enthusiastic approval of the work of Ulrich of Zell.

Gregorians in Germany, in the words of Ezekiel, to stand fast in battle in the day of the Lord.[1] But he soon showed that he realized how, in Germany, the rights of laymen over the Church, particularly through the institution of advocacy, were much more deeply rooted than in the Latin lands; Gregory's attempt to make a thorough imposition of the principles of Roman canon law upon German society was, therefore, impracticable. He modified the relentless campaign that Gregory had inaugurated, and that Hirsau and Schaffhausen had so enthusiastically championed, against all lay rights. Gregory's campaign had been given its ultimate expression in terms of Cluny's 'libertas'; and its impracticability in Germany was demonstrated as soon as he was dead. In 1086 Muri had regained its independence of St. Blasien, and the Habsburgs had once again become its advocates on pre-Gregorian lines.[2] In Germany it was impossible to dispense with advocates who had real standing and powers in local lay society. After the death of Abbot William of Hirsau a number of Urban II's own privileges for monasteries both inside and outside the circle of Hirsau's dependencies, while in general following the lines of Gregory VII's Schaffhausen privilege, allowed advocacies to be perpetuated in the founders' families; although this was never permitted upon an expressly hereditary basis.[3]

It was no less unrealistic to suppose that advocates could in the long run exercise their rights without regard to the position of the king. Thus, Urban's prudent withdrawal from Gregory VII's extremism about advocates was the first step in a longer process. This process had its culmination under the Emperor Henry V (1106–25), who was more prepared than his father had been to meet half-way the aspirations of the south German aristocracy. Henry V sought to recruit supporters by reaching an understanding with the reformed monasteries and with the dynastic families which protected them. He therefore engineered a compromise, whereby the monasteries which had been the strongholds

---

[1] *Ep.* i, *P.L.* cli. 283–4.

[2] *Acta Murensia*, no. 11, *Quell. zur Schw. Gesch.* iii (1883), pt. 2, 34–6.

[3] See Hirsch, 'Studien über die Privilegien süddeutscher Klöster', *M.I.Ö.G.* vii, Ergänzungsband (1907), 498–500.

of the Gregorian cause might become indirectly subject to the empire, whilst still keeping their spiritual independence. The basis for this was the Hirsau Charter of 1075,[1] with its Cluniac language and provisions. It followed Cluny's Charter of 909 by eliminating lay proprietorship and lay investiture. But it went beyond it in leaving to the founder's family a right of advocacy which turned upon the exercise of secular jurisdiction on the monastery's behalf. This jurisdiction in its turn depended upon the royal *Bannleihe*. In the early twelfth century the Hirsau Charter provided a blueprint which, because it had been drawn up to satisfy many interests, offered something to the claims of both *sacerdotium* and *regnum*. Reformers could welcome the elimination of lay proprietary rights; Henry V and his successors stood to gain by the reformers' recognition of the royal *Bannleihe*.[2] In a series of charters, of which that for Muri in 1114 is the most-discussed example,[3] the provisions of the Hirsau Charter were pressed into service to justify the claim that the jurisdiction of monastic advocates was exercised by delegation from the king. Freed from lay proprietorship, the monasteries thus provided a means whereby the king could endeavour, with at least some tangible advantage, to restore his authority after the calamities of the late eleventh century;[4] while the central demands of the reformers regarding monastic freedom were conceded.

These developments went far beyond the scope of direct Cluniac activity; yet they were made possible by the ferment which the diffusion of Cluniac influences produced. They were consolidated, partly by the use of a Charter which was indebted to a Cluniac model, and partly by the example of a pope who followed the ways of Cluny in his willingness to look more realistically than

[1] See above, pp. 198–9.

[2] Although it is an open question how substantial the recognition of the royal *Bannleihe* in fact proved to be.

[3] *Acta Murensia*, no. 14, pp. 40–2. But there is a long list of such documents, from a wide range of dates in Henry V's reign: Hirsch, *Die Klosterimmunität*, pp. 53–5; E.T. in Barraclough, *Mediaeval Germany*, ii. 157–60; and Stengel has shown that the Hirsau Charter was drawn upon in the early charters of Hasungen: see above p. 206, n. 4.

[4] Mayer, op. cit., pp. 132–3, and *Nachwort* to H. Hirsch, *Die hohe Gerichtsbarkeit im deutschen Mittelalter* (2nd edn., Graz and Cologne, 1958), pp. 252–4.

did Gregory VII at the claims and the functions of lay authorities. During the crisis of the Investiture Contest in Germany in its various phases, the Papacy owed a considerable debt to the Cluniacs, both for being the upholders of the Gregorian cause during the lifetime of Abbot William of Hirsau, and afterwards for the way in which Cluniac institutions were a factor in leading to a reputable and viable compromise.[1]

[1] The continuing if diffused influence of Cluny in southern Germany during the early decades of the twelfth century is made clear by current historiography and hagiography. This is well illustrated by the circle of Paul of Bernried, biographer of Gregory VII, and a staunch propagandist for the Gregorian cause in general and for the extirpation of simony and nicolaitism in particular. His *Vita Gregorii VII*, written *c.* 1128, made clear the close association between Gregory and the Cluniacs: chs. 18–19, 58, 84, 118–19, *Pontificum Romanorum vitae*, ed. Watterich, i. 481, 506, 524–5, 543–4. Paul himself was profoundly influenced by the anchoress and zealot for reform, Herluca, whose Life he wrote: *Acta sanctorum, Aprilis*, ii (Antwerp, 1675), 552–6. Herluca had been directed in her youth by Abbot William of Hirsau and Abbot Theoger of St. Georgen, later bishop of Metz (1118–20), and her zeal owed much to them. Theoger was buried at Cluny: ibid. i. 11, p. 553; a fact which illustrates Cluny's continuing appeal amongst this circle. For a study of it, see W. Wache, 'Eine Sammlung von Originalbriefen des 12. Jh. im Kapitalarchiv von S. Ambrogio im Mailand', *M.I.Ö.G.* 1 (1936), 298–303.

II

THE CLUNIACS IN SPAIN

THE contribution of the Cluniacs to the progress of the Gregorian Reform in Spain has not usually been rated very high.[1] As it will be argued that Cluny's record of service to Gregory VII in Spain was in fact a conspicuous one, it is desirable at the outset to place matters in proportion, by insisting upon the very small scale of historical events in the Christian kingdoms, and upon the correspondingly small scale of Cluny's work. The eleventh century saw the establishment in Spain of only a few Cluniac subject priories. In the last quarter of the century the adopting of Cluniac Customs elsewhere than in these priories was a more pronounced feature of Spanish than of German monasticism, and more Cluniac monks were active in Spain than in Germany. Yet the direct monastic influence of Cluny upon the Spanish Church is easily exaggerated.[2] The number of Cluniac monks who worked in Spain was, in all likelihood, small; and in marked contrast with the Cluniac houses of south-western France, the Spanish monasteries did not receive visits from the abbots of Cluny.[3]

It is remarkable that a Cluniac deployment in far-distant Spain which was numerically small and constitutionally diffuse should,

[1] The fullest accounts of the events in northern Spain during the late eleventh century which are discussed in this chapter are P. David, *Études historiques sur la Galice et le Portugal du vie au xiie siècle* (Lisbon, 1947), 341–430; and J. F. Rivera Recio, *La iglesia de Toledo en el siglo XII (1086–1208)*, i (Rome, 1966). For a briefer treatment see M. Cocheril, *Études sur le monachisme en Espagne et au Portugal* (Paris and Lisbon, 1966), pp. 85–123.

[2] Even when the connections of Moissac with Spain are taken into account: A. Mundó, 'Moissac, Cluny et les mouvements monastiques de l'est des Pyrénées du xe au xiie siècle', *Annales du Midi*, lxxv (1963), 563–4.

[3] Abbot Odilo never visited Spain; Abbot Hugh visited King Alphonso VI of León-Castile for brief periods in 1077: Hildebert of le Mans, *Vita Hugonis*, ii, *P.L.* clix. 886–7; and 1090: Bruel, 3638. His visits were to the king, rather than to the Cluniac houses of his kingdom.

nevertheless, have had so emphatically Cluniac an identity and should have played so decisive a part in Spanish history. The reasons for this were many; and for the most part they arose from the general factors that characterized Cluny and its appeal in the eleventh century. From the Spanish side, these factors included the enthusiasm which the Spanish kings felt for Cluny, on the grounds of its immense prestige as a place of intercession and of the strength of the bond of confraternity with it. From Cluny's side there were the direct and personal interest in Spanish affairs which Abbots Odilo and Hugh took; the increasing domination by Cluny of the pilgrimage routes that led to St. James at Compostela; and the enormous sums of money which came from Spain by way of tribute, and which did so much to build and embellish Cluny's second and third churches. Above all, Cluny's role in Spain was determined by the mutual realization of Cluny and the Papacy that, in Spain as elsewhere, each stood in need of the other. They therefore settled into a habit of collaboration which advanced the interests of both.

I. CLUNY'S ACTIVITY IN SPAIN UP TO THE REIGN OF KING ALPHONSO VI OF LEÓN-CASTILE

It was by virtue of its prestige with the kings of Christian Spain that Cluny established itself as a factor of importance in Spanish affairs. Its first great patron was King Sancho the Great of Navarre (1000–35). Sancho took advantage of the waning of Moslem power after the death in 1002 of Almanzor to extend his sway over Aragon, Castile, and León. His reign witnessed the first significant contact between Cluny and Spain.[1] Under Sancho

---

[1] For the earliest contacts between Cluny and Spain, see esp. Mundó, art. cit., pp. 552–60. The very first were through Abbot Warin of Lézat, which Abbot Odo of Cluny ruled for a time after 940; Warin, in his turn, reformed Cuxá, across the Pyrenees, and communicated something of Cluny's spirit and methods to it: see also C. M. Baraut, 'Cuxá', *D.H.G.E.* xiii. 1128–37. In the early eleventh century Cuxá, together with the Catalan monastery of Ripoll, was ruled, from *c.* 1008, by Abbot Oliva. There is some evidence for liturgical borrowings by Oliva from Cluny. But there is no suggestion of any major debt to Cluny in the material assembled in *Esp. sag.* xxviii. 122–40, 265–90, or in the exhaustive account of Oliva by R. Beer, 'Die Handschriften des Klosters Santa Maria de Ripoll', *SB.*

the bond of intercession that was to link the Spanish kingdoms so intimately with Cluny was first established; and he and Abbot Odilo maintained close touch with each other by letter and through legates.[1] The principal figure amongst the reformers of Sancho's reign was Paternus, who himself, with a group of associates, paid a visit of some years' duration to Cluny. In about 1021 he returned to become abbot of the principal monastery of Aragon, San Juan de la Peña; and his reform extended to other monasteries in Sancho's realms.[2] In the absence of modern critical editions of the Spanish royal charters of this period it is impossible accurately to assess either the true extent of Paternus's work or the depth of the Cluniac imprint upon it. He certainly brought Cluniac Customs to San Juan de la Peña; but elsewhere twelfth-century interpolations in the charters that survive have probably led historians to exaggerate the earlier role of Cluny.[3] It would be hazardous to conclude that Paternus's reforms effected any widespread or lasting introduction of Cluniac Customs into Spain. The importance of Sancho's reign did not lie in any large-scale penetration of Spain by Cluny and its Customs, for which there is no firm evidence. Rather, it lay in the precedent that Sancho set for intimate contact between Cluny and the Spanish kings.

Upon Sancho's death his kingdom was divided amongst his sons. Despite their rivalries with each other the three of them who were of lasting consequence all gave evidence of their zeal for Cluny. Navarre fell to the eldest of them, Garsia III (1035–54).

Wien, clv (1907), 3 abh., 69–99. Under both Abbot Warin and Abbot Oliva, Cluny's influence in Spain was slight, indirect, and impermanent. There seems to be no warrant for David's statement that Cluny maintained an influence at Ripoll until *c.* 1070, when Saint-Victor, Marseilles, 'supplanted' it: op. cit., p. 357.

[1] Jotsald, *Vita Odilonis*, i. 7, *P.L.* cxlii. 902.

[2] See esp. J. Pérez de Urbel, *Sancho el Mayor de Navarra* (Madrid, 1950), pp. 297–321.

[3] See esp. Pérez de Urbel's comments on Bruel, 2891, Sancho's charter for the monastery of San Salvador, Oña: op. cit., pp. 314–16. During the earlier years of their contact with Spain, although not later, there is some evidence that the Cluniacs were tolerant of the Hispanic rite, at least in the case of Spanish monks who came to Cluny: Ralph Glaber, *Historiarum*, iii. 12, ed. Prou, p. 62. Nevertheless, the fact that at San Juan de la Peña the Hispanic rite was used until 1071, tells against this monastery's having been closely associated with Cluny: *Esp. sag.* iii. 300.

It is possible that, in 1052, he gave to Cluny his monastic foundation of Santa Maria de Nájera.[1] Contact with Cluny had certainly
occurred soon after 1035, when Abbot Odilo wrote to Garsia
reminding him of his father's and his own devotion to Cluny,
and soliciting gifts to relieve the distress that two years of famine
had occasioned at Cluny. In return he promised Cluny's intercessory support.[2] In Aragon, Sancho's son King Ramiro I (1035–
63) was also well known at Cluny: a letter, which Abbot Odilo
wrote to Abbot Paternus of San Juan de la Peña at the same time as
he wrote to King Garsia of Navarre, testifies to the existence of
contacts between Cluny and Aragon.[3] But the most powerful of
Sancho's sons was Ferdinand I of Castile (1035–65), who, in 1037,
added to his own inheritance the kingdom of León. It was he who
initiated the annual payments to Cluny from the kingdom of
Castile by paying an annual tribute of a thousand gold pieces.[4]
In return Cluny singled him out in its liturgical commemorations
as the most favoured of Sancho's sons.[5]

Up to the last quarter of the eleventh century, however, this
developing bond between the kings of Spain and the monastic
life of Cluny was not reinforced by any significant movement of
the Cluniacs into Spain, for which reliable evidence can be produced. Indeed, Abbot Hugh may well have showed with regard
to Spain his normal reluctance to over-extend his resources by

[1] Bruel, 3343. If the text be reliable, Garsia's brothers, Ramiro of Aragon and
Ferdinand of Castile, witnessed the charter. For its donation to Cluny in 1079 by
King Alphonso of Castile, see Bruel, 3540. The connection which may have been
established with Cluny in 1052 must, however, be treated with reserve. Garsia's
charter made no mention of Cluny, and Alphonso's charter referred to no earlier
relationship of Nájera with it.
[2] *Ep.* iii, *P.L.* cxlii. 942.
[3] *Ep.* ii, *P.L.* cxlii. 941–2. The letter also refers to Bishop Sancho of Pamplona,
the counsellor of King Sancho the Great, who had taken the habit at Cluny. Odilo
asked for the dispatch to Cluny of Sancho's liturgical ornaments for use there,
and of his silver and gold to complete the furnishing of the altar of St. Peter and
the high altar.
[4] *Historia Silense*, ed. J. Pérez de Urbel and A. G. Ruiz-Zorrilla (Madrid, 1959),
p. 206; cf. Bruel, 3638. The size of the tribute sets it in sharp contrast with the
nominal *census* paid to Rome by institutions which enjoyed the 'libertas Romana'.
[5] *Ordo Cluniacensis per Bernardum* i. 13, 51, ii. 32, *Vetus disciplina monastica*, ed.
Herrgott, pp. 158, 246, 355–6.

propagating his monastic family in distant lands. Apart from the far-from-certain case of Santa Maria de Nájera, there is no record of an effective gift of a Spanish monastery to Cluny before the accession in 1065 of King Alphonso VI. Even after this date, outside Alphonso's kingdom of León-Castile Cluny continued to receive few gifts of churches and monasteries; and there is no reason to suppose that it actively desired to receive them.[1]

The evidence for Cluny's place in Spain up to the reign of Alphonso VI and, indeed, up to the pontificate of Gregory VII, thus points to the conclusion that, with the exception of the bonds of intercession and financial subvention that were built up between Cluny and the kings, it was a marginal one. There is no evidence to suggest that Cluny desired to embark upon a monastic colonization of Christian Spain, or of any part of it. What happened in Spain during the middle decades of the eleventh century was in no way comparable with the building up of a network of subject houses, which Cluny then undertook in Burgundy and Aquitaine. It was akin to the more diffuse influence that Cluny had upon such monasteries as Saint-Victor, Marseilles, under Abbot Isarnus, or Farfa and La Cava in Italy. There was some communication of Cluniac Customs and a temporary establishing of close but informal contact between local monasteries and Cluny; but there was little, if anything, more.

Two consequences follow from this conclusion, which must not be lost sight of when considering Cluny's more active concern with Spain in the last quarter of the eleventh century. First, the greatest reserve should be adopted in face of the widely held view that Cluny was in any serious way in competition with Saint-Victor, Marseilles, over their respective expansions in Spain. Saint-Victor's Spanish dependencies were mostly in Catalonia, where Cluny at no time had any great direct interest, and where

---

[1] See Mundó, art. cit., pp. 561–3. In Catalonia the charters of Cluny record the gifts in 1066 of San Pedro de Ager: Bruel, 3409; and in 1074 of Santa Maria de Cubières: Bruel, 3456. Mundó does not give any authority for his statement that Abbot Hugh refused these gifts, and Cubières reappears in his own list of Moissac's dependencies: ibid., p. 564. In 1079 Cluny acquired the Catalan house of San Pedro de Casserres: Bruel, 3541; and in 1080 that of San Pedro de Clará: Bruel, 3554.

there is no evidence to suggest that it ever desired to expand.[1] During the early and middle decades of the eleventh century there was no such competition as might have presented an obstacle to the collaboration of Cluny and Saint-Victor which, in fact, took place during Gregorian times. Secondly, the attempts that the Papacy made after the middle of the eleventh century to advance its authority in Spain, did not, at first, have to take account of a significant Cluniac presence there. Apart from such influence as they gained from the bond with the kings which was formed by intercession and tribute, the Cluniacs could do little either to help or to hinder the popes, until they had themselves become effectively established in Spain. Equally, there was no question of a papal challenge to an entrenched Cluniac position, nor of Cluniac hostility to anything that could be regarded as a papal intrusion upon Cluny's preserves. The concern for Spanish affairs which came to be shown by the Papacy and the Cluniacs grew up concurrently. If anything, it was the Papacy that was first in the field.

II. THE REVIVAL OF PAPAL CONCERN WITH SPAIN

The revival of papal concern with Spain began as early as the time of Pope Alexander II (1061–73); and in the long perspective of Mediterranean history it was no novelty. It was the relative inactivity of the Papacy with regard to Spain during the second third of the eleventh century that had been exceptional. For ever since the Arab conquests the popes had often shown their concern for the defence of the western Mediterranean and, therefore, of southern Italy and Christian Spain, against the inroads of Islam.[2] By Alexander II's time the reform of the Papacy had served once

---

[1] For the expansion of Saint-Victor, see Schmid, 'Die Entstehung des Marseiller Kirchenstaats', *A.U.F.* x (1928), 176–207; J. Ainaud de Lasarte, 'Rapports artistiques entre Saint-Victor et la Catalogne', *Provence historique*, xvi (1966), 338–46; A. Pladevall-Font, 'Saint-Miquel-del-Fai, prieuré victorin catalan', ibid., pp. 347–60; E. Baratier, 'La Fondation et l'étendue du temporel de l'abbaye de Saint-Victor', ibid., pp. 395–441. For the existence of a monastic union between Cluny and Saint-Victor, see above, p. 172.

[2] Cf. P. F. Kehr, 'Das Papsttum und der Katalanische Prinzipat bis zur Vereinigung mit Aragon', *Abh. Ber.* (1926), no. 1, pp. 3–5.

more to widen its horizons. In particular, the Norman settlement in southern Italy and the acceleration of the Christian reconquest in Spain had emboldened it to take initiatives against Islam in both countries. In 1059, by the Treaty of Melfi, the Norman adventurer Robert Guiscard, duke of Apulia and Calabria, promised fealty to Pope Nicholas II and his successors, both for the lands that were already his and also for Sicily, which was still under firm Moslem control.[1] If the Papacy might thus claim feudal superiority over Italy as it was reconquered, it was a natural step for it to advance a like claim over Spain—particularly as, in either case, the 'Donation of Constantine' lent colour to it.[2] The readiness of early eleventh-century popes to confer privileges of exemption and papal protection upon Spanish monasteries,[3] foreshadowed the intensification of papal claims which began in earnest under Alexander II.[4] It was especially marked in 1068 when, during a visit to Rome, King Sancho Ramirez of Aragon (1063–94) acknowledged the feudal claims of the Papacy by making his kingdom a papal fief.[5] The renewal of papal concern for Spanish affairs was also made clear by Alexander II's dispatching of Cardinal Hugh Candidus as papal legate on three occasions.[6] Thus, the seven years or so before Gregory VII became pope saw the establishment of bonds between Rome and north-eastern Spain;

[1] C. Mirbt, *Quellen zur Geschichte des Papsttums und des Römischen Katholizismus* (6th edn., ed. K. Aland, Tübingen, 1967), i, no. 542, p. 281. For the circumstances see H.-G. Krause, 'Das Papstwahldekret von 1059 und seine Rolle im Investiturstreit', *S.G.* vii (1960), 126–7.

[2] Esp. by the words which conferred upon the pope 'omnes Italiae seu occidentalium regionum provincias, loca et civitates': *cap.* 17, Mirbt, op. cit., no. 504, p. 255.

[3] Kehr, art. cit.; 'Das Papsttum und die Königreiche Navarra und Aragon bis zur Mitte des XII. Jahrhunderts', *Abh. Ber.* (1928), no. 4, pp. 6–10.

[4] Ibid.; see also Alexander II's privilege for San Juan de la Peña: Kehr, 'Papsturkunden in Spanien', *Abh. Gött.* xxii (1928), 260–2.

[5] Kehr, 'Wie und wann wurde das Reich Aragon ein Lehen der römischen Kirche?' *SB. Berl.* (1928), pp. 196–223; Erdmann, *Die Entstehung des Kreuzzugsgedankens*, pp. 347–62.

[6] G. Saebekow, *Die päpstlichen Legaten nach Spanien und Portugal* (Berlin, 1931), pp. 13–17. Hugh's missions, which took place in 1065–7 or 8, 1071, and 1072, were intended to strengthen the bonds between the Papacy and Spain; to promote reform, especially by combating simony; and to seek the extirpation of the Hispanic rite.

and the making good in Aragon, at least temporarily, of a claim to feudal superiority that balanced papal lordship over southern Italy.

With Alexander II's work as a starting-point, the first four years or so of Gregory VII's pontificate saw him endeavouring to advance his authority in Spain with his habitual vigour and thoroughness. His claims fell most heavily, not upon the Castile of King Alphonso VI, but upon Catalonia and Aragon, where the precedent of creating papal fiefs had been set by Alexander II. Gregory sought to build up his authority over Spain by three principal means.

First, he tried to assert his claims to feudal superiority by using the French knights who had for long sporadically campaigned in Spain.[1] Alexander II had already supported them;[2] thus, towards the end of his reign, Count Ebolus of Roucy found favour at Rome for his plan to make a large-scale foray across the Pyrenees.[3] In 1073 Gregory VII lost no time in addressing himself to the knights who were to take part in it. In a letter to them he declared that the 'regnum Hyspaniae' had of old been the possession of St. Peter. Although it had for long been in the hands of the heathen, it rightfully belonged to no mortal man but to the Apostolic See alone. He concluded that such lands as Ebolus captured must be held by him and his knights as fiefs of St. Peter.[4] There is no evidence that Ebolus ever crossed the Pyrenees, and he certainly set up no new lordship in Spain. But his project is important for having elicited from Gregory VII this first explicit claim to the Petrine proprietorship of the whole Peninsula. It was a peculiarly ill-presented claim, which was grotesquely out of touch with the realities of the Reconquest. Gregory supposed that the invading knights would be content to have no say in the disposal of their conquests: that was to be a papal prerogative. Not only was this stipulation in itself imprudent,

---

[1] For French knights in Spain, see Erdmann, op. cit., pp. 88–91, 124–6, 267–9; M. Defourneaux, *Les Français en Espagne aux xi⁴ et xii⁴ siècles* (Paris, 1949), pp. 125–45.

[2] Notably in the campaign of 1063 against the town of Barbastro: Erdmann, op. cit., pp. 125–7.

[3] Ibid., pp. 140–1.   [4] *Reg.* i. 7, 30 Apr. 1073, pp. 11–12.

but it rested upon a misunderstanding of the motives of the French knights who fought in Spain during the eleventh century. As a rule they fought for booty, not land; they had no desire for permanent lordships of their own, whether as papal fiefs or not. Moreover, in speaking of the 'regnum Hyspaniae', Gregory VII made no reference to the Christian kings and princes of Spain. They were unlikely to take kindly to the ignoring of their existence; and they, not French knights out for booty, were the key to the Reconquest. Gregory's first attempt to assert papal lordship over Spain was misconceived, and it came to nothing.

So, in 1077, he tried a second way, that of a direct address to the kings of Spain and the indigenous lay magnates. Gregory wrote to them reiterating his claim, as propounded to Ebolus of Roucy, that the 'regnum Hyspaniae' had of old been conferred upon St. Peter and the Roman Church 'in ius et proprietatem'. Gregory declared that, after the long years of heathen tyranny, God had at last given victory to the Christian kings of Spain. He reminded them that in the hour of triumph they should be mindful of the rights of St. Peter and obedient to the direction of the pope.[1] This direct address to the Spanish kings had at least the advantage of being an approach to those with whom political authority lay. But in 1077 their number was reduced to two. If they indeed received Gregory's letter, and there is no evidence that they did, they were both too secure in their kingdoms to have had any need to respond. Alphonso VI of León-Castile had by this time wrested power from his brothers. In 1076 Sancho Ramirez of Aragon had added the kingdom of Navarre to his realms; now that he was strong he gave no sign of remembering that he had once made Aragon a papal fief. Gregory therefore met with no response to his pressing of his own feudal superiority upon the Spanish kings; only a single count, Bernard of Besalù, far away in eastern Catalonia, at this time made his lands a fief of St. Peter.[2]

Thirdly, Gregory sought at various times to advance papal authority by continuing to send legates. In 1073 Cardinal Hugh

[1] *Reg.* iv. 28, 28 June 1077, pp. 343–7.

[2] Kehr, 'Das Papsttum und der katalanische Prinzipat bis zur Vereinigung mit Aragon', *Abh. Berl.* (1926), no. 1, pp. 34–5.

Candidus was sent back to Spain to see that Ebolus of Roucy and his companions respected the rights of St. Peter.[1] Soon afterwards Cardinal Gerald of Ostia was also active there.[2] In 1077, when Gregory addressed his claims to the Spanish kings, he sent Bishop Amatus of Oléron and Abbot Frotard of Saint-Pons de Thomières as his legates to act as mentors of the kings.[3] Of these four legates it was only the sometime Cluniac, Gerald of Ostia, who succeeded during this time in commending himself to a Spanish king. Alone of the four he was not sent, so far as is known, to propound Gregory's claim to feudal superiority. And it was with Alphonso VI, the devotee of the Cluniacs, that he found favour.

In respect of these three ways by which Gregory VII sought to assert papal authority over Spain during his early years as pope, the Cluniacs, apart from Cardinal Gerald, played a negligible part. The principal reason for this was probably the simple one, that Cluny's presence in Spain was insignificant, save far to the west in León-Castile.[4] Gregory for his part was well aware of Cluny's prestige with the French feudatories to whom he looked in 1073; and he may also have known of its connections with the Spanish kings, although there is nothing in the evidence to prove this. He was, therefore, anything but unwilling for the Cluniacs to become involved in the papal plans; indeed, he did his best to bring them in. The evidence for his doing so throws light upon his dealings with Abbot Hugh. When Gregory became pope, Abbot Hugh and his monks were at loggerheads with the legate Hugh Candidus, whom they had accused of simony at the Lateran Council of Lent 1073. Eight days after his election, Gregory wrote to his legates in France, Gerald of Ostia and the subdeacon Rainbald, urging them to patch up matters between Abbot Hugh and Hugh Candidus. He also recalled how he had charged the two legates to work with Abbot Hugh in support of Ebolus of Roucy. He said that he had called upon Abbot Hugh to join them

---

[1] *Reg.* i. 6, 30 Apr. 1073, pp. 8–10.
[2] Bruel, 3441; *Reg.* i. 64, 19 Mar. 1074, pp. 92–4.   [3] *Reg.* iv. 28.
[4] David's observation that Gregory VII 'sait bien que sans Cluny, à plus forte raison contre Cluny, rien n'est possible en Espagne', op. cit., p. 347, exaggerates Cluny's probable significance in Spain before it established itself in the dominions of Alphonso VI during the 1070s.

in sending envoys to correct the errors of the Spanish Christians,[1] and to see that Ebolus and his associates were mindful of St. Peter's proprietary rights. Gregory said that if these plans were maturing, they were to continue. If not, with the counsel of Cardinal Gerald and Abbot Hugh, Hugh Candidus was to go to Spain and attend to the interests of St. Peter. In this eventuality Gregory charged Gerald and Rainbald to seek from Abbot Hugh suitable companions who might travel with him.[2] Whatever happened with regard to Spain, it was thus Gregory's intention that Cluny should be as fully involved in his plans as was possible.

Not surprisingly, in view of the chimerical nature of the whole matter of Ebolus's campaign and Gregory's championship of it, nothing came of the arrangements that were outlined in this letter. There is no direct evidence for Abbot Hugh's reactions to Gregory's proposals; but he seems never to have allowed Cluny to become associated with the pope's extravagant attempts to assert direct Petrine proprietorship of the 'regnum Hyspaniae'. There is no record of his having expressed himself either for or against Gregory's plans. But his shrewd knowledge of men and his habitually prudent statesmanship make it improbable that he did not hold aloof from them; even though the result may well have been that he thereby temporarily incurred Gregory's acute displeasure.[3] If the principal reason for Cluny's small part in

[1] i.e. who would put down the Hispanic rite. For Gregory's exaggerated condemnation of it as heretical, see e.g. *Reg.* i. 64, 19 Mar. 1074, pp. 92–4; Santifaller, *Q.F.*, no. 215, 1084–5, pp. 258–60.

[2] *Reg.* i. 6. Abbot Hugh had been associated with Hugh Candidus's earlier work, and was present at his Councils at Toulouse and Avignon in 1068: Mansi, xix. 1065–6; Kehr, art. cit., *Abh. Berl.* (1926), v. 78–9. The allegation of simony against Hugh Candidus was referred to by Bonizo of Sutri, *Liber ad amicum*, vi, *M.G.H. L. de L.* i. 600, at the Lateran Council of Lent 1078. When Hugh Candidus had long since apostatized from Gregory, the pope implied that the charge had been just: *Reg.* v. 14a, pp. 369–70.

[3] For a later, and highly unfavourable, judgement upon the campaign, and upon the character of Ebolus, see Suger, *Vie de Louis VI le Gros*, v, ed. Waquet, pp. 24–8. Gregory VII's querulous letter to Abbot Hugh of 19 Mar. 1074, *Reg.* i. 62, pp. 90–1, reads, when it is compared with *Reg.* i. 6, as though it was written in a mood of disappointment at the fiasco of Ebolus's expedition. Gregory's displeasure with Hugh himself may well have been a consequence of his wholly understandable reserve regarding the expedition. If so, there is no need to see evidence in the letter of lasting differences between Gregory and Abbot Hugh.

Gregory VII's Spanish plans during the early years of his pontificate was its own very limited presence in Spain, a secondary reason appears to have been Abbot Hugh's prudent unwillingness to become involved in Gregory's more extravagant endeavours.

III. KING ALPHONSO VI AND REFORM
IN LEÓN-CASTILE TO 1079

It was well for all concerned, in the long run, that Cluny did not forfeit its freedom of action but that it remained aloof from Gregory's claims and plans as he at first proposed them. For in due course its mediatorial role in Spain was no less useful to Gregory, and no less advantageous to itself, than was the case elsewhere in western Europe.

Its mediating influence was particularly called for because, when he claimed a hegemony over the whole Peninsula, Gregory VII was not without a potential rival. While he was pressing the claims of the Papacy and calling upon the Spanish kings to observe the proprietary rights of St. Peter, King Alphonso VI of León-Castile was beginning to call himself 'imperator totius Hispaniae'; he thereby implied that he himself had a superiority over all the Christian kingdoms of Spain and over all the reconquered lands.[1] There are no grounds for supposing that Alphonso was deliberately issuing a challenge to Gregory, or even that he had heard of his claims: whereas the legates who brought Gregory's letter of 28 June 1077 to Spain are known to have been active in Catalonia and Aragon, there is no record of their ever having reached Castile.[2] In any case, they could only have arrived at a late date in 1077, by which time Alphonso was already using his imperial title. This title had sufficient precedent in Spanish history for it to be

---

[1] For the use of imperial titles by Alphonso and his successors, see H. J. Hüffer, *La idea imperial española* (Madrid, 1933), pp. 20–30; R. Menéndez Pidal, *La España del Cid* (4th edn., Madrid, 1947), ii. 725–31; R. Folz, *L'Idée d'empire en occident du ve au xive siècle* (Paris, 1953), pp. 64–9. Alphonso first used the full title in a charter of 26 Mar. 1077, which was referred to by P. de Sandoval, *Historia de los reyes de Castilla y de León* (Pamplona, 1613), fol. 38ʳ. The title *imperator* appears alone as early as 1075, e.g. in Alphonso's *fuero* for Burgos: T. Muñoz y Romero, *Colección de fueros municipales y cartas pueblas*, i (Madrid, 1847), 256–8. [2] David, op. cit., pp. 354–5.

accounted for by the desire of a victorious king to signalize his own paramount power in the Peninsula. Nevertheless, if Gregory VII had pressed his claims to Petrine proprietorship of the 'regnum Hyspaniae', and if he or his legates had come face to face with Alphonso's claims to an independent *imperium*, there might well have arisen a grave and lasting antagonism between pope and king. But after 1077 Gregory never pressed them. In the case of Alphonso VI as in that of William I of England, Gregory proved willing to reach a *modus vivendi* with a strong and reforming ruler.[1] The history of papal relationships with León-Castile during the remainder of Gregory VII's pontificate concerns the progress of this *modus vivendi*, which well served the interests of both pope and king. Up to 1079s the establishment of the Cluniacs in Alphonso VI's kingdom did much to make it possible; while in the early 1080s the Cluniacs advanced it still further by helping to bring the Church in his realms under a direct papal authority that was willingly accepted.

The Cluniac colonization of León-Castile was recent: it was a work of the 1070s. The way was prepared by a turning-point in Alphonso's political fortunes, which came in the year 1072. In 1065, when King Ferdinand I died, his lands had been partitioned amongst his sons, and the kingdom of León had fallen to Alphonso. In January 1072 Alphonso was defeated in the Battle of Golpejera by his brother, King Sancho II of Castile, who deposed him and put him in prison at Burgos. But soon afterwards Sancho was prompted, by the appearance in a dream of St. Peter, to release him. St. Peter's intervention marked the beginning of the events which culminated in Alphonso's assumption of the imperial title. He first went into exile amongst the Moors at Toledo, and found security there until, in October 1072, Sancho of Castile was murdered. Then Alphonso returned from Toledo and assumed the kingship of both León and Castile, which he ruled with conspicuous success. He ascribed this reversal of his fortunes, and especially his deliverance from prison by the intervention of

---

[1] Particularly as, in 1076, Gregory had high hopes of promoting reform throughout north-western Spain by collaboration with the Castilian Bishop Simeon of Oca-Burgos: *Reg.* iii. 18, May 1076, pp. 283–4.

St. Peter, to the intercession of St. Peter's monks at Cluny.[1] Thereafter he never wavered in his gratitude and devotion to them. The monks themselves responded by greatly increasing their intercessory support for him, so that the bond between the royal house of León-Castile and Cluny became stronger than that with the Saxon and Salian emperors had ever been.[2]

During the years that immediately followed, there occurred, as a result of Alphonso's gratitude for his deliverance, a succession of gifts of monasteries to Cluny, which was without earlier parallel in Spain. The monasteries became subject to the abbot of Cluny and adopted its Customs. In his own lands, the king gave Cluny San Isidoro de las Dueñas (1073),[3] San Juan Battista de los Eremitas (1077),[4] and San Coloma de Burgos (1081).[5] In 1079, when events following the partition of Navarre brought into his hands the monastery of Santa Maria de Nájera, he made it subject to Abbot Hugh.[6] Cluny also received gifts of monasteries from Alphonso's magnates. In 1075 San Salvador de Bilarfreda was given to Cluny by its proprietor, Enego Bermundus;[7] and in 1076 Countess Tarasia gave it San Zoil de Carrión.[8] King Alphonso also increased his financial generosity to Cluny. In 1077, the year in which he first met Abbot Hugh, he doubled his father's *census* to Cluny as a token of gratitude to St. Peter for his deliverance from prison[9] and for his place in Cluny's liturgical commemorations.[10] The Cluniacs also became his mentors at Court. From 1076 Alphonso had with him a Cluniac monk named Robert, who was his principal adviser in ecclesiastical matters, and who was soon to play an all too prominent part in the affairs of León-Castile.[11]

---

[1] For versions of this frequently recorded story, see Hugh, *Vita Hugonis, Bibl. C.*, cols. 443–4; Anonymus secundus, *Alia miraculorum quorumdam sancti Hugonis . . . relatio*, ibid., cols. 452–3; *Chronica de Nájera*, 10, ed. J. Cirot, *Bulletin hispanique*, xi (1909), 273; Gilo, *Vita Hugonis*, L'Huillier, *Saint Hugues*, p. 584; Hildebert of le Mans, *Vita Hugonis*, ii, *P.L.* clix. 866; *Epitome vitae [sancti Hugonis]*, 5, *P.L.* clix. 912.

[2] C. J. Bishko, 'Liturgical Intercession at Cluny for the King-Emperors of Leon', *Studia Monastica*, iii (1961), 53–76.

[3] Bruel, 3452. [4] Ibid., 3508. [5] Ibid., 3582.

[6] Ibid., 3540. [7] Ibid., 3481. [8] Ibid., 3492, 3507.

[9] Ibid., 3441, 3509; Hildebert, *Vita Hugonis*, ii. 10, *P.L.* clix. 866–7.

[10] Bishko, art. cit., pp. 63–5. [11] Bruel, 3441, 3492, 3509, 3582.

Cluny thus became entrenched in Alphonso's realms just at the time when Gregory, on the one hand, was asserting his claims to feudal superiority over Spain, and Alphonso, on the other, was proclaiming his imperial title. It has been suggested that, as a result of their collaboration in these circumstances, both Alphonso and the Cluniacs disregarded Gregory's authority; and that there followed a time of open hostility between Gregory and the Cluniacs, so far as Spain was concerned.[1] In the course of events up to 1079 there is not the slightest concrete support for such a supposition. It is in any case doubtful whether there was ever a confrontation in Spain of the extremer papal and royal claims. There was certainly no echo of it at Cluny. If Cluny seems to have stood aloof from Gregory's more extravagant positions about papal suzerainty, it also at no time, in any document that emanated from it, countenanced Alphonso's imperial pretensions: he was studiously called king, not emperor. Cluny prudently avoided giving such offence as it might have caused to either side by recognizing the other's claims. On the other hand, in matters that were of the utmost concern to Gregory, the Cluniacs worked in León-Castile with a willing king to serve the pope. In particular, the pope, the king, and the Cluniacs worked together to bring about the replacement of the Hispanic by the Roman rite.[2] King Alphonso testified that Abbot Hugh 'ordered' him to adopt the Roman rite;[3] and he worked resolutely to propagate it in face of much resistance from his subjects.[4] In 1077 he went so far as to

---

[1] Thus, Erdmann wrote that Gregory VII had 'auf der Halbinsel zeitweise eine ausgesprochen clunyfeindliche Politik getrieben': *Die Entstehung des Kreuzzugsgedankens*, p. 354; cf. Schmid, art. cit., *A.U.F.* x (1928), 186–7, 193–4.

[2] Cf. *Reg.* iii. 18.

[3] Bruel, 3441; Alphonso wrote to Abbot Hugh 'de Romano officio, quod tua iussione accepimus . . .'.

[4] For discussions, see esp. David, op. cit., pp. 391–405; Menéndez Pidal, op. cit. i. 237–43; L. de la Calzada, 'La proyección del pensamiento de Gregorio VII en los reinos de Castilla y León', *S.G.* iii (1948), 52–87. After its formal acceptance at San Juan de la Peña, in 1071, the Roman rite had been quietly adopted in Aragon. It was soon being promoted in Navarre and Castile in obedience to Gregory VII: *Reg.* i. 64, 19 Mar. 1074, pp. 92–4. After the partition of Navarre in 1076, Alphonso VI's attitude was crucial. His friendship with Cluny and the convenience of pilgrims passing through his lands to Compostela made the general adoption of the Roman rite expedient. That he soon made clear his decision in its

call upon Abbot Hugh to intercede with the pope for the return to Spain of Cardinal Gerald of Ostia, in order to press on with the reform.[1]

His request led to a two-year period of all-round collaboration. Cardinal Gerald died in December 1077. In May 1078 Gregory wrote Abbot Hugh a most cordial letter about the collaboration of the Cluniacs with him in Spanish affairs, which places beyond doubt the unity of purpose of Gregory and the Cluniacs. Gregory said that he had sent to Spain Cardinal Richard, the brother and, in 1079, the successor of Abbot Bernard of Saint-Victor, Marseilles. He revived the soundest of the arrangements that he had proposed in 1073,[2] by asking Abbot Hugh to aid Richard in his legatine mission, and to furnish him with a suitable companion.[3] Cardinal Richard's first legatine visit to Alphonso, in 1078-9, appears to have been altogether successful. No details of it are known. However, when Richard got back to Rome in the autumn of 1079, Gregory wrote Alphonso a cordial letter and sent him a relic of St. Peter's chains. He said that Richard had spoken well of Alphonso's zeal to correct the errors of his kingdom. He was sending the legate back, and he looked with confidence for the king's continuing collaboration with him in the business with which he was charged.[4]

In this whole sequence of events there is not the slightest hint of hostility towards Cluny on Gregory's part. On the contrary, he took for granted and warmly welcomed the place of the Cluniacs in his dealings with Alphonso VI. He sought and up to the autumn of 1079 obtained the full collaboration of all parties;[5] until this

---

favour is indicated by the stories about the judicial duel of 1077 at Burgos which was staged to settle the matter. Although the champion of the Hispanic rite vanquished that of the Roman, the king was said to have reversed the judgement of battle, saying, 'Ad libitum regum flectat cornua legum': *Chronicon Burgense, sub era* 1115, *Esp. Sagr.* xxiii. 309; *Chron. de Nájera*, 19, ed. Cirot, p. 277.

[1] Bruel, 3441: '. . . vestram deprecor paternitatem, quatinus faciatis ut domnus papa nobis suum mittat cardinalem, videlicet domnum Giraldum, ut ea quae sunt emendanda emendat, et quae sunt corrigenda corrigat'. For the date, see Bishko, art. cit., p. 63.

[2] *Reg.* i. 6. [3] *Reg.* v. 21, 7 May 1078, pp. 384-5.
[4] *Reg.* vii. 6, 15 Oct. 1079, pp. 465-7.
[5] Including, it may be noted, the collaboration of both Cluny and Marseilles.

time, if Gregory made no headway with his extremer claims to feudal superiority, he nevertheless began to secure a satisfactory and constructive *modus vivendi* with Alphonso in the cause of ecclesiastical reform. His legates were welcome in his realms, and with Cluniac aid they began to order the Church there as Gregory desired.

IV. THE CRISIS OF 1080

Then, suddenly and unheralded there broke a crisis of the first magnitude in relations between Gregory VII and Alphonso VI. The evidence concerning it is incomplete; but it is sufficient to warrant the conclusion that it was an utterly untypical exception to the general rule of their collaboration, both before and after. It should be compared with Gregory's dealings with Abbot Hugh, at about the same time, over the affair of Saint-Sernin, Toulouse.[1] Like these dealings, it above all illustrates the difficulties which Gregory had in following the course of distant events and in assessing novel situations; and which Gregory and Hugh alike had in controlling the activities of distant subordinates. But like the troubles at Toulouse, the crisis was transient: once the storm had subsided it had the ultimate effect of uniting the Papacy and the kingdom of León-Castile more closely than ever before. Moreover, although the Cluniac monk Robert, who was Alphonso's principal ecclesiastical adviser, was at the centre of the storm, Cluny itself was to emerge more decisively than ever as Gregory's ally in Spain.

It is not possible to say exactly when the crisis began, although it was probably after Cardinal Richard left for Rome in 1079. King Alphonso took two steps which served to precipitate it; both of them were calculated to consolidate Cluny's position in his realms.[2] First, he married, as his second wife, Constance of

---

[1] See above, pp. 114–18.

[2] David's suggestion that Cardinal Richard knew of both these matters, op. cit., pp. 407–9, depends on his dating of the conversion of Sahagún to Cluniac customs to May 1079. This is too early: see below, p. 231; and it is difficult to explain either his favourable report to Gregory in Rome, or his surprise at developments in Spain when he returned in 1080, if he knew very much about them before he left.

Burgundy.[1] Constance was not only a daughter of a ducal house which was steadfast in its support of Cluny, but she was also a niece of Abbot Hugh himself; and her former husband, Count Hugh of Châlon (died 1078), belonged to a family which had long-standing relationships with Cluny. The marriage was thus likely to strengthen the bonds between the kingdom of León-Castile and both the monasticism and the feudal society of Burgundy.

Secondly, Alphonso determined to establish in his realms a reforming centre which, although it would not be constitutionally subject to Cluny, would nevertheless follow Cluniac Customs and propagate them in other monastic houses. His choice for this purpose was the ancient royal monastery of St. Facundus and St. Primitivus at Sahagún, which was situated some sixty kilometres to the south-west of the town of León.[2] Early in 1080 he issued a charter to inaugurate its reform. He laid down that for the future the Benedictine life was to be lived there according to the Customs of Cluny. He nominated the Cluniac monk Robert, his ecclesiastical counsellor, to be its abbot and to supervise its conversion to Cluniac ways.[3] Some of the monks of Sahagún did not accept

[1] His first wife, Agnes of Poitou, died in 1078. It is, of course, likely that negotiations for the second marriage began before Cardinal Richard left Spain: some part of his later annoyance may have been occasioned by his not being informed of them.

[2] The principal source for the history of Sahagún remains R. Escalona, *Historia del real monasterio de Sahagún* (Madrid, 1782); on matters considered in this book, J. Puyol y Alonso, *El abadengo de Sahagún* (Madrid, 1915), adds little to it. See also F. Fita, 'El concilio nacional de Burgos en 1080', *Boletín de la real academia de la historia*, xlix (1906), 337–84; and Puyol y Alonso, *Las crónicas anónimas de Sahagún* (Madrid, 1920).

[3] Fita, art. cit., no. 2, pp. 341–6. It is the earliest surviving document in which Queen Constance's name appears together with his own. Its date presents great difficulties. Fita gave the date as 9 Jan. 1080, filling out the dating clause of the charter as 'feria vi^a, v idus ia[nu]a[r]ii. Era M.ª C.^a XVIII.^a.' But he himself noted that the original reads 'ii idus Maii', which, as he noted, was a Saturday not a Friday. David confirmed this, and proposed the date 9 or 10 May 1079, while conceding that the date in the Cartulary is 1080: op. cit., p. 408. From this evidence it may be concluded that the date 1080 is probable, but that the day and month are uncertain. The month of May is, however, impossible, as Robert, who is named as abbot of Sahagún, is known to have been superseded before 24 Apr. 1080: Fita, art. cit., no. 5, pp. 349–51. The strongest argument for placing the conversion of Sahagún in the month of Jan. 1080 is that, if the names of those who confirmed and witnessed the charter be compared with those in two other

the royal fiat, and left the monastery.[1] But the reform was proceeded with, and it quickly began to be propagated elsewhere. A lay donor made the monastery of San Pedro de Mazuecos subject to Sahagún;[2] and the king himself charged its monks with the reform of the women's house of San Pedro de las Dueñas: the Cluny of Spain was to have its Marcigny.[3]

It would appear that Cardinal Richard had not been informed of or consulted about these two developments, for they took him by surprise on his return to Spain in 1080. He took deep offence against the king because he had followed another counsel than his own, and also because of the unseemly reception which he received. He at once sent a letter of complaint to Gregory VII which has not survived; although its sharpness of tone can be inferred from the violence of the pope's reaction to it. This reaction can be judged from three letters which Gregory drafted, with all the marks of his own dictation, on 27 June 1080, to Abbot Hugh, to King Alphonso, and to Cardinal Richard.[4] In the first and most important of these letters Gregory told Abbot Hugh to read for himself Cardinal Richard's letter of complaint, a copy of which he enclosed; and he bitterly accused the Cluniac monk Robert, who was the king's principal adviser:

> You can see for yourself from the letter of our legate Richard, abbot of Marseilles, how great an outrage against religion (*impietas*) has come from your monastery through the presumption of your monk, Robert.

charters which are securely dated in January, many of them appear in common. Thus, in Fita, art. cit., no. 3, dated 22 Jan. 1080, the two bishops who confirmed also appear in no. 2; of six laymen who confirmed, four appear; and of five witnesses, three seem to appear. In Fita, art. cit., no. 4, of similar date, the three bishops who confirmed appear in no. 2; of six laymen, four appear; and of five witnesses, two have the same names as those in no. 2. This creates a presumption that all three documents were of approximately the same date. Although Robert became the nominal abbot of Sahagún, he remained at court, and Sahagún was ruled by a deputy named Marcellinus: Fita, art. cit., no. 3, p. 346. The recent attempt of Rivera Recio to spread the events of 1080 over the years 1080 and 1081 is open to the objections that its redating of documents is somewhat arbitrary, and that it extends the crisis over too protracted a period: *La iglesia de Toledo en el siglo XII*, i. 131–3.

[1] This may be inferred from the penultimate sentence of *Reg.* viii. 2, p. 518.

[2] Fita, art. cit., no. 3, pp. 346–7.   [3] Ibid., no. 4, pp. 347–9.

[4] *Reg.* viii. 2–4, 27 June 1080, pp. 517–21.

Robert, Gregory continued, had resisted the authority of St. Peter, as had Simon Magus of old:

This Robert has become the imitator of Simon Magus by not fearing to rise up against the authority of St. Peter with all the crafty wiliness that he could. At his prompting, a hundred thousand men who, by our diligent labour, had begun to return to the path of truth have been led back into their former error.[1]

This last hyperbole, and Gregory's later reference to a consequent 'Hispaniensi ecclesiae tantum periculum', can only have been occasioned by the cardinal's reporting to him that by Robert's agency Alphonso's kingdom had lapsed from the Roman rite to the Hispanic. In view of Alphonso's zeal for the Roman rite since Robert became his adviser, the report of a sudden volte-face is implausible, and it becomes the more so in the light of Gregory's second draft letter, that to the king himself. In it Gregory again made a clear if oblique allusion to the lapse of Alphonso's kingdom from the 'right way' of the Roman observance; and he now said that the king had been misled, not only by the rebellion of Robert, but also by the misdoings of an 'abandoned woman' who, like a new Eve, was leading him and his kingdom to perdition:

But now I find out that the devil, envying, as is his wont, your own salvation and that of all who depend upon you for theirs, has used his own member, the false monk Robert, and his ancient helper, an abandoned woman, to drag down your manly courage from the right way.

Gregory did not name the woman; but his condemnation, later in the letter, of Alphonso's second marriage, leaves no escape from the conclusion that he referred to Queen Constance herself.[2] However, it is even less plausible that the queen should have championed the Hispanic rite than that Robert should have done so. She is known to have sent at this very time to la Chaise-Dieu

---

[1] The charge against Robert was not one of simony in the specific sense, but of disobedience offered directly to St. Peter.

[2] None of the ingenious attempts that have been made to find an alternative identity for the woman has any plausibility: see David, op. cit., pp. 414-17, for a review and criticism of these attempts.

for St. Lesme to come and propagate the Roman rite in what she described as a rude and backward land to which the apostles' teaching had scarcely come.[1] Gregory's associating her with an attempt to restore the Hispanic rite casts added doubt upon the truth of the allegation that Cardinal Richard had so hastily made. Possibly the cardinal had listened too readily to mendacious allegations of the monks who had fled from Sahagún. They had certainly been in contact with him; for at the end of his letter to Abbot Hugh, Gregory charged the abbot to procure their restoration to their monastery.

In his draft letter to Alphonso, Gregory also made the king's marriage to Constance itself a further ground of offence against the king. Gregory had some canonical pretext for doing so, which had no connection with the question of rites; for Constance was related to Alphonso's first queen, Agnes of Poitou, within what were then the prohibited degrees.[2] In the matter of Constance as of Robert, Gregory did not mince his words. After reminding Alphonso of the example of the most wise King Solomon, whom incestuous love of women had shamefully cast down and who, by provoking the judgement of God, had almost entirely alienated the kingdom of Israel from his posterity, Gregory exhorted him to repent and to renounce his illicit marriage with a kinswoman of his first wife's. He was to put away Constance, while Robert (*nefandissimum Rodbertum monachum, seductorem tui et perturbatorem regni*) must be banished from the kingdom, excommunicated, and sent back to Cluny to do penance for his offences.

---

[1] Fita, art. cit., pp. 375–8; *Vita sancti Adelelmi*, 12–13, *Esp. sag.* xxvii. 857–60. The historian Roderic of Toledo later represented Constance as having always encouraged Alphonso to press on with the replacement of the Hispanic by the Roman rite: *De rebus Hispaniae*, vi. 25, in A. Schott, *Hispaniae illustratae scriptores*, ii (Frankfurt, 1603), 106.

[2] Gregory's vehemence is reminiscent of certain outbursts when an earlier Agnes of Poitou had married the Emperor Henry III in 1043: see the letters of Abbot Siegfried of Gorze, printed by W. von Giesebrecht, *Geschichte der deutschen Kaiserzeit*, ii (3rd edn., Brunswick, 1863), 679–85; and the tirade in the *De ordinando pontifice*, ed. E. Dümmler, *M.G.H. L. de L.* i. 13. In 1043 as in 1080 the marriage was favoured by the Cluniacs; and in both cases the storm rapidly died down, leaving situations which were to their advantage.

Gregory did not stop short at the threat of spiritual sanctions. In his covering letter to Abbot Hugh he wished him not only to forward this letter to King Alphonso but also to write and warn the king of the dangers to himself if he further provoked the wrath of St. Peter, and of the succession of measures that Gregory would take if he were disobedient. Gregory set out these measures in detail to Abbot Hugh: first, the king would be excommunicated; if this had no effect, Gregory would call out the 'fideles sancti Petri' in Spain against him; finally, if necessary, Gregory would himself come to Spain and personally lead a military campaign against him (*dura et aspera moliri*), as an enemy of the Christian religion.[1]

Such were the contents of the first two of Gregory's letters. Occasioned in large measure by the real or supposed delinquencies of Robert who was a Cluniac monk, the anger that Gregory expressed in them is the most plausible evidence that can be cited for the tension, if not the hostility, that is sometimes alleged to have prevailed in Spanish affairs between Gregory VII and the Cluniacs. Yet these letters were dictated only some four months after Gregory's eulogy of Cluny at his Lent Council of 1080; and his letter to Abbot Hugh twice echoed his eulogy in terms of warm praise, ending with the assertion that 'eadem enim via eodem sensu eodem spiritu ambulamus'.[2] Read against this background, Gregory's forceful opening to his letter was meant to stimulate him to action against a subject whose unauthorized actions Gregory did not doubt that he would punish. Gregory went on confidently to expect that Hugh would forward his letter to Alphonso and communicate his sanctions to him; that he would bring about the return to Sahagún of the monks whom Robert had forced to flee; and that he would collaborate in ensuring that

---

[1] Gregory's threat is the more astonishing when it is remembered that the Council of Brixen took place two days before it was written. But the expedition to Spain was no more bizarre than Gregory's scheme of 1074 for an expedition to the East: *Reg.* i. 46, 2 Feb. 1074, pp. 69–71; *Reg.* i. 49, 1 Mar. 1074, pp. 75–6; *Reg.* ii. 31, 7 Dec. 1074, pp. 165–8; *Reg.* ii. 37, 16 Dec. 1074, pp. 172–3; *Briefsamm- lungen der Zeit Heinrichs IV.*, ed. Erdmann and Fickermann, *M.G.H. B.D.K.* v, *Die Hildesheimer Briefe*, no. 43, pp. 86–7.

[2] See above, p. xx.

for the future no reforms were to be introduced in Alphonso's realms if they lacked the legate's approval.[1] Accordingly, in the remarkably restrained third letter that Gregory VII dictated on 27 June 1080 to Cardinal Richard, he exhorted him to patience, and assured him that he was working in harmony with Abbot Hugh to secure the recall of the offending Robert:

We will in no wise fall short of your own zeal in sending your letter of complaint to the abbot of Cluny together with our own, so that he may compel the false monk Robert to return to his monastery as quickly as may be, cut him off from the communion of the Church, and visit him with such a protracted infliction of heavy penance, that he may indeed feel the retribution of penitence for the evil deed that he has done against you, or rather against God.

In all three letters Gregory was confident of Abbot Hugh's sympathy and collaboration, and regarded him as a trusted agent of his purposes.

It may be doubted whether Abbot Hugh in fact forwarded Gregory's hasty letter to Alphonso; it would be hard to account for the speedy *rapprochement* that took place between Gregory and Alphonso, if the king had known of Gregory's references to Queen Constance or of his threats against himself. Hugh's prudence is likely to have restrained him from acting without further consultation with Gregory, and he may well have been better informed than Gregory was about what was really happening in Spain.[2]

There, for some weeks before Gregory drafted his three letters, events had already rendered his threats otiose so far as the matter of the Hispanic rite was concerned. If upon his return to Spain

[1] It is here that Gregory's attitude to Cluny in this crisis particularly foreshadowed his attitude soon afterwards over Saint-Sernin, Toulouse, when he did not blame Abbot Hugh for the high-handed actions of Abbot Hunald of Moissac, but looked with confidence for the co-operation of Abbot Hugh, to whom he looked as a distant, detached, and blameless authority, in disciplining an unruly subject. See above, pp. 114–18.

[2] It is noteworthy that, in Gregory's Register, *Reg.* viii. 3 and 4, unlike *Reg.* viii. 2, are undated. It would be unwarranted, in view of the vagaries of papal chancery practice, to conclude from this that they were never dispatched to the addressees; but it is likely that Abbot Hugh was allowed to use his discretion about forwarding them, and that he did so by suppressing at least the letter to the king.

Cardinal Richard had allowed himself to be persuaded that Alphonso had lapsed with regard to it, he quickly learnt that he had been misinformed. He can scarcely have anticipated the violence of Gregory's reaction to his report, for he soon resumed his quiet and amicable collaboration with the king to secure the liturgical reform that Gregory considered to be so vital. During the late spring of 1080 Alphonso and Richard together held the Council of Burgos, at which the king finally accepted the Roman rite as the universal observance in his realms.[1]

Thus it would appear that, even before Gregory drafted his three letters, the crisis was beginning to be resolved. The Council of Burgos not only settled the liturgical question, but it also began to ease the way towards an agreement concerning the king's marriage. This emerges in an undated letter of 1081, in which Gregory VII replied to a letter from Alphonso which has not survived, in which the king had informed him about the work of the Council and had made suggestions about his marriage and about other matters.[2] Gregory's letter was cordial, and it contained no reference whatsoever to the existence or to the contents of his compositions of 27 June 1080. Instead he was fulsome in his praise of Alphonso's work at Burgos in restoring the Roman rite, and he extolled him as a pattern of righteous kingship:

We renew our joy in your wisdom the more abundantly, when we remember, at the same time, the good report of your humility, and the virtue which lives so seldom and with such difficulty under the same roof as royal power, but which we perceive to rule in your heart.

---

[1] Fita, art. cit.; also 'El monasterio toledano de San Servando en la segunda mitad del siglo xi', *Bol. real acad. hist.* xlix (1906), 280–331; *Crónica del Obispo Don Pelayo*, ed. B. Sanchez Alonso (Madrid, 1924), p. 80, where the date 1085 is incorrect. Fita discusses the question of the date, about which there now seems to be general agreement. Its dating to the late spring of 1080 is especially supported by Fita, 'El concilio nacional de Burgos', no. 6, *Bol. real acad. hist.* xlix (1906), 351–6; and confirmed by *Reg.* ix. 2. The *terminus ante quem* is the date of the former of these documents—8 May 1080; the *terminus a quo* is the return of Cardinal Richard. April 1080 is the probable month.

[2] *Reg.* ix. 2, pp. 569–72. The first two paragraphs, which are obscure, are probably to be understood, not of Spanish affairs, but as Gregory's vindication of his own unswerving righteousness in his contest with Henry IV of Germany, against slanderous rumours which he feared had reached Alphonso's hearing.

With regard to requests that Alphonso had addressed to him about his marriage and about the monastery of Sahagún, Gregory said that they might better (*competentius*) be answered on the spot through his legate, Cardinal Richard, and Bishop Simeon of Burgos.[1] Warned by his experiences of the previous year, Gregory evidently now wished to avoid settling at a distance matters about which it was so easy to be misinformed, and to make possible an amicable resolution of them by those who were at hand. After dealing in no less tactful and conciliatory terms with certain other problems,[2] Gregory thanked Alphonso profusely for a gift, which stood as a pledge of his devotion to St. Peter, and which was 'tam amplum et magnificum . . . ut et te regem dare et beatum Petrum recipere convenienter decuerit'. In return Gregory conferred upon Alphonso and his subjects an apostolic blessing that would bring them victory over their enemies both visible and invisible.

Alphonso's restoration to Gregory's favour was complete, and no more was heard of the marriage problem. Past events were buried, and Gregory seems tacitly to have let drop his graver charges against the Cluniac monk Robert, once he ceased to be abbot of Sahagún.[3] Alphonso's loyalty to the Papacy was

---

[1] The choice of Simeon was in itself a conciliatory gesture. As well as having local knowledge, the bishop enjoyed the king's favour; on 25 Dec., perhaps in return for his part in resolving the marriage crisis, Alphonso gave him for a residence part of the royal palace at Burgos: L. Serrano, *El obispado de Burgos y Castilla primitiva*, iii (Madrid, 1935), 61–2. The *lapsus calami* in *Reg.* ix. 2, p. 571, where Sahagún is referred to as 'abbatia sancti Secundi', betrays Roman unfamiliarity with affairs in León.

[2] These included consultations about an appointment to the see of Toledo after its projected reconquest. For a recent, and somewhat speculative, discussion, see Rivera Recio, *La iglesia de Toledo en el siglo XII*, i. 63–6.

[3] It seems that, after he stepped down from being the nominal abbot of Sahagún, which he did by 24 Apr. 1080 (Fita, art. cit., no. 5, pp. 349–51), Robert was not further punished nor permanently kept at Cluny, but that he returned to Spain. In ibid., no. 6, p. 353, he was referred to as 'Robertus prior', and this may indicate the capacity in which he remained at Sahagún; for the *fuero* of 1085 for the town of Sahagún was attested, among others, by a 'Robertus prior', whose name followed Abbot Bernard's, and by a 'Marcellinus', in whom it is tempting to see the monks of these names who were prominent in the reform of 1080: Muñoz y Romero, *Colección de fueros*, i. 306. The monk to whom Alphonso referred in 1081 as 'dilectissimus meus atque fidelissimus vester frater Rodbertus', Bruel, 3582, may also be the same person; if so, his exculpation was indeed a thorough one.

confirmed, and Gregory's letter of 1081 ushered in a period of close and cordial contact between Rome and León-Castile, which marked a considerable advance upon the *modus vivendi* that had already grown up during the 1070s.

V. SAHAGÚN

The resolution of the crisis of 1080 had the further effect of leaving Cluny in a stronger position than ever before in the kingdom of León-Castile. Not only did it advance to a still higher place in Alphonso's regard, but through the agency of Cardinal Richard the Papacy itself now collaborated with the Cluniacs to set up Sahagún as the Cluny of Spain. While it remained free from immediate and formal subjection to the abbot of Cluny, it was left under a Cluniac abbot and observed Cluniac Customs; above all, it became expressly endowed with the 'libertas Romana' upon the model of Cluny itself.

The assimilation of Sahagún to Cluny was a gradual process which extended over some three years. It began in January 1080 when, in the absence of Cardinal Richard, Alphonso and Constance had first begun to develop Sahagún on Cluniac lines. But at this date Sahagún fell far short of the model of Cluny. While it received a Cluniac abbot and Cluniac Customs, it did not receive even the kind of autonomy and freedom from outside claims, which was the birthright of Cluny in its Foundation Charter of 909.[1] Its abbot, Robert, was chosen by the king. Moreover, while Robert had authority 'ad gubernandum', and while Sahagún was made immune from the temporal claims of lesser men, the king

---

[1] Cluny's own earlier attitude to advocacy in Spain seems to have been one of indulgence towards the rights of donors, and it seems to have allowed bishops to keep their jurisdiction. Thus, in 1077, the king's rights as advocate were safeguarded at San Juan Battista de los Eremitas: Bruel, 3508. This charter made no reference to the bishop; but the relevant episcopal charter, issued in the same year in favour of four monasteries at Burgos called 'de Hermedes', prescribed that, while the purpose of their reform was 'ut sit in eis regula sancti Benedicti et mos Cluniacensis coenobii', it was to take place 'salva tamen obedientia vel subiectione nostrae episcopalis ecclesiae quam sancti canones commendant habere': Serrano, op. cit., iii. 54. Alphonso's reservation of his rights in 1080 was thus in keeping with earlier practice.

studiously reserved his own right 'ad regendum et defendendum'.[1] The Cluniac character of Sahagún was, therefore, to depend simply upon its observing the Customs of Cluny; in respect of lay control it was denied the freedom with which the duke of Aquitaine had initially endowed Cluny.

When Cardinal Richard returned to León, important changes quickly followed. Robert was replaced as abbot of Sahagún by another Cluniac monk by the name of Bernard.[2] Furthermore, after the Council of Burgos, King Alphonso and Queen Constance made some new provisions for Sahagún in a charter dated 8 May 1080.[3] This charter stated that Sahagún's internal life had already been regulated 'per quosdam religiosos viros ad instar Cluniacensis normae monasticae ordinis sancti Benedicti docte eruditos'. It went on to revise the constitutional arrangements of the previous winter, in a direction that was a first step on the road to genuine liberty on the Cluniac model. Whereas in the earlier arrangements Alphonso himself had sent (*mittimus*) Robert to be the abbot, in the May charter the new abbot, Bernard, was said to have been elected by the monks. Only after this election was he given his office by the king in the presence of the legate (*per electionem fratrum ibidem commorantium Bernardum in eodem praefato monasterio abbatem constitui in praesentia Ricardi Romanae ecclesiae cardinalis*). By this revision, the free election of the abbot by the monks was foreshadowed. The new charter also augmented Sahagún's liberty at least in a negative way, because Alphonso confirmed its immunity without any longer claiming a royal prerogative 'ad regendum et defendendum'.

Another, and this time a positive, step forward was taken in a further document of Alphonso's, dated 12 December 1080, when the king described recent changes at Sahagún in novel terms of death to an old order of subjection and resurrection to a new life of liberty:

You know that I have, with all pious zeal, been much concerned to advance the venerable house of St. Facundus and St. Primitivus by the mercy and aid of God in the worship of our holy religion. Whereas it

---

[1] Fita, art. cit., no. 2, pp. 341–6.   [2] Ibid., no. 5, pp. 349–51.

[3] Ibid., no. 6, pp. 351–6.

was buried beneath the power of men, it has been as it were raised up by me from the dead and devoted to the liberty that is proper for the Church (. . . *quatinus qui humana erat sub potestate sepultus per me quasi a morte resuscitaretur, ecclesiasticae libertati donandus*).[1]

Alphonso's omission, in May, of any reference to royal rights was thus not fortuitous, but a step towards the building up of Sahagún's liberty according to Gregorian reforming ideals of which this latest document made an authentic statement.

The gradual progress towards liberty in the course of the year 1080 is the only indication of what may have been the king's proposals to Gregory in his letter written during the crisis and of what Cardinal Richard may subsequently have advised.[2] But Richard's work and still more that of Abbot Bernard of Sahagún came to its fulfilment in 1083. Abbot Bernard then travelled to Rome and there received, together with his consecration as abbot at Gregory VII's own hands, a privilege which was designed fully, finally, and expressly to make Sahagún the Cluny of Spain.[3] Sahagún was endowed with the 'libertas Romana', on the pattern of Cluny, which Gregory had already introduced at Cardinal Richard's own monastery of Saint-Victor, Marseilles, and then at All Saints', Schaffhausen. Sahagún was given the protection of the Papacy and it owed in return an annual *census* of two shillings. It was confirmed in its right freely to elect its abbot. For his consecration or for the ordination of his monks, the abbot might resort to Rome or to any catholic bishop; while no bishop might administer the sacraments within its walls without the abbot's leave. Gregory spoke in unequivocal terms of the Cluniac model upon which these arrangements were based:

. . . we take this monastery into the safekeeping of our perpetual defence and of Roman liberty, and we lay down that it is to be free from the yoke of every ecclesiastical or secular power.... It is especially to cleave to the Apostolic See after the pattern and form of Cluny which, in God's providence and under Roman liberty, shines more clearly than daylight through almost all parts of the world, because of the fame of its religion, reputation, and dignity. It is likewise to enjoy

[1] Ibid., no. 7, pp. 356–9. [2] See *Reg.* ix. 2, p. 571.
[3] Santifaller, *Q.F.*, no. 209, pp. 243–6.

a perpetual and an inviolable security. Thus like Cluny in France, Sahagún may be illustrious in Spain for its prerogative of liberty. As by the grace of God it will be its peer in religion, so let it be its equal in the confirmation of its rights by the Apostolic See.[1]

King Alphonso's own dealings with Sahagún fell into line with this programme: his ever-increasing devotion to Cluny found its complement in a no less intense following of Rome. Thus in 1085, when he founded the town of Sahagún for the benefit of the monastery, he declared in the *fuero* by which he did so that

... I have made it free from every burden to the royal fisc and from every ecclesiastical obligation; for I have given it to the Roman Church and to St. Peter in Roman liberty (*dedi enim eam Romanae ecclesiae et beato Petro in libertate Romana*).[2]

Alphonso, that is, named St. Peter, rather than St. Facundus and St. Primitivus, as the beneficiary of his gift. He gave the town into St. Peter's proprietorship and into that of the Apostolic See of Rome. Its subjection to St. Peter was full and absolute.

Taken together the documents concerning the monastery and town of Sahagún are eloquent of the victory that Gregory VII had won, through the Cluniacs, in Spain. Since his letter of 1077 he had not pressed his extravagant claims to a Petrine proprietorship of the 'regnum Hyspaniae'. But in 1083 his privilege for Sahagún, the Cluny of Spain, implanted the 'libertas Romana' in the realms of a willing king; and in 1085 Alphonso could surrender to the proprietorship of St. Peter and of the Roman Church the town which he founded on Sahagún's behalf. As a pledge of Spanish loyalty to Gregory and to Gregorianism, these developments were significant. Gregory's original intentions in Spain had

[1] With this may be compared Roderic of Toledo's statement that Alphonso intended that 'sicut in Galliis illud monasterium [Cluny] praecellebat, ita et istud [Sahagún] omnibus monasteriis eiusdem ordinis in Hispaniis praesideret': *De rebus Hisp.* vi. 25, in Schott, *Hisp. illus.scr.* ii. 106. For the cordiality of Bernard's reception at Rome, see also *Crónicas anónimas de Sahagún, primera crónica*, 4, ed. Puyol y Alonso, p. 29; where reference was made to Gregory's privilege, 'el qual previlegio con nos oi dia tenemos con gran guarda e consolaçion'.

[2] Muñoz y Romero, *Colección de fueros*, i. 302–3; the full text of the *fuero* occupies pp. 301–6. For the subsequent revolts of the citizens against these arrangements, see the *Crónicas anónimas*, esp. *prim. crón.* 13, pp. 32–4.

been chimerical; but the introduction of Cluniac monasticism to Sahagún culminated in a naturalization of Gregorian claims in terms which satisfied all parties. It represented a solid and useful victory for the Gregorian cause, which won for Gregory what was soberly attainable in Spain.

Sahagún was not only important as an institution, and for its continuing work as a centre of monastic reform.[1] It was also important in the person of its abbot, Bernard, who procured the privilege of 1083. During the next forty years he worked to secure the fruits in Spain of the reform of Sahagún. He ranks with the greatest of the sons of Cluny, and the reformed Papacy owed him a considerable debt with respect to the internal life of the Spanish Church and to the building up of papal authority over it. In 1086 he became the first archbishop of Toledo after Alphonso VI had recaptured it from the Moors in the previous year. He did so with the cordial support of Abbot Hugh; when he was chosen to be archbishop, Bernard wrote to his former abbot to seek advice, and Hugh's reply to him has survived. Abbot Hugh made it clear that he had actively sought his appointment; and in warmly counselling his acceptance, Hugh urged him to remember his obedience to his former monastery and to his spiritual father.[2] Until his death in 1126 Archbishop Bernard remained an outstanding servant of both papal and Cluniac interests in Spain. He succeeded to the position of Amatus of Oléron as papal legate in Spain and Narbonne.[3] He also worked, not without success, to

---

[1] There is no adequate study of the extent of Sahagún's reforming influence in late eleventh-century Spain. But Alphonso VI's gift to it, in 1100, of the monastery of San Salvador de Villaverde illustrates his continuing favour: Bruel, 3735. Pope Urban II confirmed Gregory VII's privilege to it in 1095: see P. Ewald, 'Reise nach Spanien in Winter von 1878 auf 1879', *N.A.* vi (1881), 352. In 1132 Pope Innocent II made it formally subject to Cluny: *Ep.* cxxiv, *P.L.* clxxix. 166–7.

[2] M. Férotin, 'Une Lettre inédite de saint Hugues, abbé de Cluny, à Bernard d'Agen, archevêque de Tolède (1087)', *Bibliothèque de l'école des chartes*, lxi (1900), 339–45; 'Complément de la lettre de saint Hugues, abbé de Cluny, à Bernard d'Agen, archevêque de Tolède', ibid., lxiii (1902), 682–6. For Bernard, see J. Pérez de Urbel, 'Bernard Ier de Sedirac', *D.H.G.E.* viii. 755–6; and Rivera Recio, *La iglesia de Toledo en el siglo XII*, i. 125–96. Rivera Recio also refers to and quotes at length Abbot Hugh's letter of 1087, but overlooks Férotin's earlier article: op. cit., pp. 67–9.

[3] For Bernard as a papal legate under Urban II, see Ewald, 'Reise nach Spanien

maintain the collaboration in Spain between the monks of Saint-Victor, Marseilles, and the Cluniacs, which had done much to overcome the crisis of 1080. Thus in 1088, when the Toledan monastery of San Servando was made subject to Saint-Victor, with a full grant of the 'libertas Romana', Archbishop Bernard was amongst those who confirmed its charter.[1]

As abbot of Sahagún, and then as archbishop of Toledo and papal legate, Bernard demonstrates the harmony of interest which was established in León-Castile between the Papacy, the Cluniacs, and the king, during the last troubled years of Gregory VII's pontificate. In a distant corner of Christendom it did something to relieve the burden of disaster that elsewhere overtook the Gregorian cause.

VI. CLUNY AND LEÓN-CASTILE AFTER 1085

During the last fifteen years of the eleventh century this fundamental harmony was not seriously shaken. Cluny's own position in Alphonso's realms was consolidated. The beginning of the Almoravid attacks made the king increasingly dependent upon Cluniac intercessions and upon Burgundian military support.[2] Abbot Hugh's second visit to Spain in 1090 saw the king's confirmation to Cluny in perpetuity of the royal *census* at the double rate that was promised in 1077.[3] The intercessory bond between Cluny and Alphonso was further strengthened.[4] Urban II followed

im Winter von 1878 auf 1879', *N.A.* vi (1881), 299–300; Urban II, *Ep.* lxiv, *P.L.* cli. 346; and Rivera Recio's discussion, op. cit., pp. 141–3. For the exceptional liturgical commemorations of him at Cluny after his death, see *Pontii abbatis praeceptiones piae*, *P.L.* clxvi. 841–2.

[1] Fita, art. cit., pp. 281–3.

[2] After the Almoravid invasion of 1086 and Alphonso's severe defeat at Sagrajas (Zallaca), the loss of tribute to the Castilian fisc caused the king to default in his annual payments to Cluny. Abbot Hugh sent his chamberlain, Seguin, to Spain with a letter in reply to which Alphonso protested his unique affection for Cluny, promised his continued help towards the building of the third church, and sent Seguin back with a gift of ten thousand talents. He urged Hugh to come to Spain: 'Deum enim, cui omnia nuda et aperta sunt, testor, non est homo in mundo quem adeo diligam; non est locus sub caelo cui tam familiaris adhaeream vel in quo tantam confidentiam habeam': Bruel, 3562 (wrongly dated).

[3] Bruel, 3638.

[4] *Statuta sancti Hugonis pro Alphonso rege Hispaniarum*, *P.L.* clix. 945–6.

Gregory VII in his concern for Spanish affairs, and he used the Cluniacs as Gregory had done. His early letters show his interest and pleasure in the rehabilitation of the see of Toledo. He wrote to Archbishop Bernard[1] and the Spanish bishops[2] in confirmation of its primacy. He also communicated with Abbot Hugh about it; after referring to Hugh's support for Bernard as a candidate, he expressed his pleasure at his appointment.[3] He wrote in the same sense to Alphonso VI.[4] In this letter he exhorted Alphonso in the practice of Christian kingship according to the older Gelasian formulas, not those of Gregory VII; he in no way echoed Gregory's claim to papal superiority over Spain.

Amongst the practical issues with which Urban dealt in this letter, there was one serious and new point of difference between the pope and the king which, if it had been less prudently handled, might have upset the collaboration of all parties in Alphonso's lands.[5] It concerned the see of Compostela. In 1087 the king had imprisoned its bishop, Diego Pelaez, probably for his complicity in a rising of Galician nobles. At the Council of Husillos (1088) he used Cardinal Richard to secure his deposition and replacement by Abbot Peter of Cardeña. Urban called upon Alphonso to release Bishop Diego from prison. He declared that Cardinal Richard's action was null and void because of his excommunication by Pope Victor III. He reserved the bishop's case for his own jurisdiction at Rome. Urban followed up this letter by means of a new legate, Cardinal Rainer of San Clemente,[6] whom he sent to replace Cardinal Richard.[7] But although, in 1091, Cardinal Rainer secured Bishop Peter's deposition, he failed to effect the restoration of Bishop Diego Pelaez. In 1094 the matter was settled after negotiations in which Abbot Hugh was involved, by giving the see of Compostela so Dalmatius, a Cluniac monk who

---

[1] *Ep.* v, *P.L.* cli. 288–9.   [2] *Ep.* vii, *P.L.* cli. 290–1.
[3] *Ep.* viii, *P.L.* cli. 291.   [4] *Ep.* vi, *P.L.* cli. 289–90.

[5] For a general account of Spanish affairs, see Becker, *Urban II*, i. 227–54. For Urban II's strong reaction to this matter, see Loewenfeld, *Epistolae pontificae Romanorum ineditae*, nos. 123–4, p. 60; *Historia Compostellana*, i. 3–4, *P.L.* clxx. 899–901.

[6] Rainer was the future Pope Paschal II (1099–1118).

[7] Urban characteristically sought to heal the breach with Richard by confirming the privileges of Saint-Victor: *Ep.* xiii (1089), *P.L.* cli. 296.

S

had oversight of the Cluniac monasteries in Spain. Dalmatius was appointed at the instance of the king and of his son-in-law and vice-regent in Galicia, Count Raymond of Burgundy; but he was also *persona grata* to the pope.[1] The compromise and the part played in it by the Cluniacs suggest that, during a decade in Spanish history for which there is little evidence, Cluny continued to maintain conciliation and collaboration between the Papacy and the kingdom of León-Castile.[2]

VII. CLUNY AND THE KINGDOM OF ARAGON-NAVARRE

During the last quarter of the eleventh century, Cluny also exerted a comparable influence in the neighbouring kingdom of Aragon-Navarre. In part this was the consequence of the help that, during the late 1070s, French feudatories who had connections with Cluny brought to King Sancho Ramirez. In 1077–8, and so just before he became a monk at Cluny, Duke Hugh of Burgundy led an expedition to Aragon. Soon afterwards Duke William of Aquitaine was fighting there. They were followed by Count Hugh of Châlon.[3] At very much the same time Abbot Frotard of Saint-Pons-de-Thomières who, unlike his fellow legate, Amatus of Oléron, spent some years in Aragon after Gregory VII sent him there in 1077, was promoting Cluniac interests.[4] In particular, in 1084, he obtained the see of Pamplona for a monk of

[1] *Historia Compostellana*, i. 5, *P.L.* clxx. 901–2.
[2] Abbot Hugh's concern for the stability of Alphonso's realms is further illustrated by the letter in which Count Raymond of Burgundy and Count Henry of Portugal reported the treaty of friendship which they contracted with each other: D'Achéry, *Spicilegium*, iii (Paris, 1723), 418–19. For a discussion of the history of the see of Compostela, see Rivera Recio, *La iglesia de Toledo en el siglo XII*, i. 181–93.
[3] For Hugh of Burgundy, see *Historiae francicae fragmentum*, F. Du Chesne, *Historiae Francorum scriptores*, iv (Paris, 1639), 88; for Duke William of Aquitaine, *Historia pontificum et comitum Engolismensium*, 33, *Bibliothecae novae*, ed. P. Labbe, ii (Paris, 1657), 258; and for Count Hugh of Châlon, the first husband of Queen Constance of León-Castile, E. Petit, *Histoire des ducs de Bourgogne*, i (Paris and Dijon, 1885), 215. For accounts of French knights in the service of the Spanish kings of this time, see esp. David, op. cit., pp. 383–6; Erdmann, op. cit., pp. 267–9; Defourneaux, op. cit., pp. 143–5.
[4] For Frotard, see Kehr, art. cit., *Abh. Berl.* (1928), pp. 23–5.

Thomières, Peter of Roda. Peter became a staunch supporter of
Cluny; through his endeavours, successive kings of Aragon and
Navarre were brought into closer association with it while, at the
same time, they drew nearer to the Papacy. In 1088 or 1089 King
Sancho Ramirez renewed his tribute to Rome,[1] and Pope Urban
II conferred a privilege of exemption upon San Juan de la Peña.[2]
The papal privilege made no reference to Cluny; but in his *fuero*
King Sancho Ramirez named Cluny as the pattern of its liberty.[3]
His successor, King Peter I (1094–1104), enjoyed confraternity
of an exceptional kind with Cluny, and Bishop Peter of Pamplona
was ultimately accorded like benefits with the king's.[4]

Thus in the kingdom of Aragon-Navarre as well as in that of
León-Castile, the last decades of the eleventh century saw the
spread of devotion to Cluny; and in both kingdoms the Cluniacs
served to advance the position and authority of the Papacy. Events
in Spain were small in scale and remote from the greater theatres
of the history of the time. Yet Spain was of deep concern to the
Papacy as well as to Cluny. The debt to Cluny in Spanish affairs
that the Papacy both owed and acknowledged, must be given its
full weight in assessing the relationship between the Cluniacs and
the Gregorian Reform.

[1] Kehr, art. cit., *SB. Berl.* (1928), iii, iv, pp. 218–19.

[2] Kehr, art. cit., *Abh. Gött.* xxii (1928), no. 7, pp. 269–71.

[3] '. . . prae caeteris aliis monasteriis quae sunt in omni regno meo hunc volo esse
liberiorem, et eminentiorem, tam rebus quam etiam legibus: videlicet, ut sicut
Cluniacense monasterium est liber ab omni censu humano ita iste et ingenuus sit ab
omni iugo regali seu episcopali': Muñoz y Romero, *Colección de fueros*, i. 324.

[4] Ramackers, art. cit., *Q.F.I.A.B.* xxiii (1931), no. 17, pp. 48–9.

III

THE CLUNIACS IN ITALY

DURING the crisis of the Investiture Contest, Cluny also exerted an appreciable influence in promoting the Gregorian cause in Italy. It played a subordinate but definite part in assisting the Italian allies of Popes Gregory VII and Urban II.

It was only in the last quarter of the eleventh century that Cluny began to have monastic dependencies in Italy and to attract endowments there on any considerable scale; during the middle decades of the century in particular, its support there was negligible. At an earlier period it had, indeed, played a sporadic part in Italian history. Abbot Odo had been called to Rome in 936 by Alberic, prince and senator of the Romans. Between 936 and his death in 942 he visited Rome on six occasions and reformed many of its monasteries, but with little permanent result.[1] Later in the century Abbot Majolus collaborated with the Empress Adelaide to found the monastery of San Salvatore at Pavia in 971, and he reformed that of San Pietro Ciel d'oro in the same city in 983.[2] The abbey of St. Majolus at Pavia, at first founded in honour of the Blessed Virgin, had an association with Cluny which began in 967, and it persisted as a centre of Cluniac life throughout the eleventh century.[3]

This century also saw the introduction of Cluniac Customs into certain other leading monasteries of Italy. One of these was the imperial abbey of Farfa, which lay some fifty kilometres to the north of Rome. Under the reforming Abbot Hugh I (997–1038),

[1] For Odo's work at Rome, see esp. Sackur, *Die Cluniacenser*, i. 99–114; B. Hamilton, 'Monastic Revival in Tenth-century Rome', *Studia Monastica*, iv (1962), esp. pp. 47–9.

[2] Sackur, op. cit., i. 224, 236; *Italia Pontificia*, ed. Kehr, vi, pt. 1, *La Lombardia* (Berlin, 1913), 191–4, 203.

[3] Sackur, op. cit., i. 237, 340; C. Manaresi, 'La fondazione del monastero di San Maiolo di Pavia', *Spiritualità Cluniacense*, pp. 274–85.

contacts were established with Abbot Odilo of Cluny, which led to the adopting of Cluniac Customs at Farfa at some time between *c.* 1030 and 1048. Farfa did not, however, become in any way subject to the abbot of Cluny; during the Investiture Contest its sympathies lay with the emperor.[1] With it may be contrasted the abbey of La Cava, near Salerno.[2] Its first abbot, Alferius (1011–50), had been instructed in the monastic life at Cluny by Abbot Odilo, who met him at the Piedmontese monastery of San Michele, Chiusa.[3] Under its third abbot, Peter (1079–1123), who had spent upwards of five years at Cluny and had for some time been one of Abbot Hugh's familiar monks, a more rigid discipline according to Cluniac usages was introduced. This caused some resistance amongst the monks; but it also led to a series of papal privileges by Gregory VII, Urban II, and Paschal II, which invested it with the 'libertas Romana' and established it as a centre of monastic reform in south Italy.[4] A yet closer link between the adopting of Cluniac Customs by an Italian monastery and its receiving the approval of Gregory VII, is provided by the Tuscan monastery of San Benedetto, Polirone. Polirone had been founded, in 1007, by Count Tedald of Tuscany, grandfather of Countess Matilda, who was Gregory VII's staunchest partisan in northern Italy, and at whose castle of Canossa the Emperor Henry IV submitted to Gregory VII in January 1077.[5] Immediately after Canossa, Gregory gave Polirone a privilege by which he took it into papal protection.[6] He also wrote to Abbot Hugh, whom he addressed as 'dilectissime frater et abbas venerande', a letter in which he recorded that Abbot Hugh had provided him with a monk from Cluny named Guy to be abbot of Polirone and to introduce

---

[1] Sackur, op. cit., i. 349–52; *Consuetudines Farfenses*, in *Consuetudines monasticae*, ed. Albers, i; H. Schuster, 'L'Abbaye de Farfa et sa restauration au xie siècle', *Revue bénédictine*, xxiv (1907), 17–35, 374–402.

[2] See P. Schmitz, 'Cava', *D.H.G.E.* xii. 21–5.

[3] *Vita quattuor priorum abbatum Cavensium*, ed. L. M. Cerasoli, *Rerum Italicarum scriptores*, ed. L. A. Muratori, new series, vi, pt. 2 (Bologna, 1941), 6.

[4] Ibid., p. 17; *Italia Pontificia*, viii, *Regnum Normannorum-Campania* (Berlin, 1935), 309–24; Santifaller, *Q.F.*, no. 25, p. 9.

[5] For Matilda, see esp. L. Simeoni, 'Il contributo della Contessa Matilde al papato nella lotta per le investiture', *S.G.* i (1947), 353–72.

[6] Santifaller, *Q.F.*, no. 125, p. 125.

Cluniac Customs there. He further stipulated that to ensure the permanence of this reform, the abbots of Cluny should have the regular duty of overseeing on the pope's behalf the election of the abbots of Polirone and of ensuring the continuance of reforming zeal.[1] As a result, Cluniac Customs were introduced at Polirone, though with much local adaptation.[2] Gregory's employment of Abbot Hugh just after Canossa to reform the principal family monastery of Countess Matilda provides evidence of his confidence in Abbot Hugh as an agent of reform, and of his regarding the Cluniacs as an appropriate monastic body to set their stamp upon a region which was crucial for his maintaining contact with Lombardy and Germany.

But it was in Lombardy that the spread of the Cluniacs became most marked and of particular importance.[3] Its first patron there seems to have been the Gregorian bishop, Opizo of Lodi (1061– ?), who in 1064 gave it the church of San Marco, which was to become a Cluniac priory.[4] Cluny soon afterwards found a zealous adherent in Bishop Anselm II of Lucca who, while he acted as papal vicar in Lombardy from 1081 to 1086, himself wore the habit of a Cluniac monk.[5] With the founding in 1079 of the

---

[1] Santifaller, *Q.F.*, no. 126, pp. 125–7. The continuing relationship between Cluny and Polirone is illustrated by Bruel, 3552 (1080).

[2] S. A. van Dijk, 'The Customary of St. Benedict's at Polirone', *Miscellanea liturgica in honorem L. Cuniberti Mohlberg*, ii (Rome, 1949), 451–65; H. Schwarzmaier, 'Das Kloster S. Benedetto di Polirone in seiner cluniacensischen Umwelt', *Adel und Kirche*, ed. Fleckenstein and Schmid, pp. 280–94.

[3] See esp. P. Zerbi, 'Monasteri e riforma a Milano', *Aevum*, xxiv (1950), 44–60, 166–78; and 'I monasteri cittadini di Lombardia', *Monasteri in alta Italia dopo le invasioni saracene e magiare (sec. X–XII)* (Turin, 1966), pp. 285–314.

[4] Bruel, 3415. In 1075 Opizo was referred to by Gregory VII as a zealous opponent of simony: *Reg.* ii. 55, 3 Mar. 1075, pp. 200–1. It is possible that, much later, he abandoned his support of the Papacy: see Zerbi, art. cit., *Monasteri in alta Italia*, p. 305.

[5] Anselm may possibly have first become a monk at Polirone: Bardo, *Vita Anselmi episcopi Lucensis*, ed. R. Wilmans, 40, *M.G.H. Scr.* xii. 24; but, if so, he did so before it became Cluniac. In 1075, however, when he left his see in perplexity of mind because he had been invested by Henry IV, he became 'regulae sancti Benedicti et Cluniacensium subiectus': ibid., 4, p. 14; and the metrical 'Life' of him by Rangerius establishes that this took place at Saint-Gilles, which was currently under the reforming hand of Abbot Hugh: *Vita Anselmi Lucensis episcopi*, ed. E. Sackur, G. Schwartz, and B. Schmeidler, 1001–4, 1025–30, 1065–72,

Cluniac monastery of San Giacomo di Pontida, near Bergamo,[1] there appears the first major landmark in a remarkably numerous series of gifts of churches and other endowments to Cluny in the part of Italy which had hitherto been least amenable to Gregorian ideals. This was particularly true of Milan, where the Cluniacs played a small but assured part in the developments whereby the proud Ambrosian metropolis turned from its old impatience of Roman intervention to be under Urban II the champion of the cause of St. Peter in Lombardy.[2] The setting up of Cluniac houses in its vicinity began in 1081, with the gift to Cluny of the church of Santa Maria di Laveno;[3] it continued in 1086 with the foundation of the women's house of Santa Maria di Cantù;[4] and under Archbishop Anselm III (1086–93) the gift to Cluny of Santa Maria di Calvenzano provides particularly striking evidence of the penetration of Cluniac ideas about the surrender of lay proprietorship into the cathedral of Milan, the erstwhile stronghold of opposition to all manner of reform.[5] A further Cluniac dependency which was set up in the time of Urban II was San Elia di Viggù.[6] Besides these Cluniac houses, there were numerous other gifts of churches and land in Lombardy.[7] This remarkable Cluniac expansion in northern Italy and especially around Milan took place at a time when the cause of St. Peter was

1275–8, *M.G.H. Scr.* xxx. 1178, 1179, 1183–4. After Gregory VII had recalled him to his see, he continued to regard himself as a monk: Bardo, *Vita*, 4, p. 14; *Die Hannoversche Briefsammlung*, 21, *Briefsammlungen der Zeit Heinrichs IV.*, ed. Erdmann and Fickermann, *M.G.H. B.D.K.* v. 50. When Anselm died in 1086, his biographer recorded his desire to be buried at the (by then) Cluniac monastery of Polirone, 'unde frater ipse ac monachus fuit': Bardo, *Vita*, 40, p. 24. For Anselm, see esp. G. B. Borino, 'Il monacato e l'investitura di Anselmo vescovo di Lucca', *S.G.* v (1956), 361–74; C. Violante, 'Anselmo da Baggio', *Dizionario biografico degli Italiani*, iii (Rome, 1961), 399–407.

[1] *Italia Pontificia*, vi, pt. 1, 392–3; cf. Bruel, 3618.
[2] For a fuller discussion see Cowdrey, 'The Papacy, the Patarenes and the Church of Milan', *T.R.H.S.* xviii (1968), 25–48.
[3] Bruel, 3583.　　　　　　　　　　　　　　　[4] Bruel, 3612.
[5] Bruel, 3793.
[6] D. Sant'Ambrogio, 'L'antica obbedienza cluniacense di San Elia di Viggù', *La scuola cattolica*, xxxv (1907), 122–4; quoted by Zerbi, art. cit., p. 57 n. 1.
[7] e.g. Bruel, 3425, 3489, 3494, 3519, 3536, 3543, 3548, 3581, 3584, 3591, 3593, 3600, 3603, 3606, 3611, 3616, 3617, 3618, 3631, 3642, 3643, 3644. See the map of Cluny's Italian possessions, Schwarzmaier, art. cit., *Adel und Kirche*, p. 294.

making much headway there. The Cluniacs helped to create a concern for reform, which enabled Urban II to recruit the support that came to him in Lombardy with surprising readiness.[1]

[1] They also appear in connection with Urban's encouragement of the Crusade in north Italy. In 1096, when he was negotiating about it with Count Humbert II of Savoy, the count made a gift to the priory of Bourget, in order that he might have the benefit of Abbot Hugh's support: S. Guichenon, *Histoire généalogique de la royale maison de Savoye*, iv (Lyons, 1660), 27.

EPILOGUE

AFTER ABBOT HUGH

THE Cluny of Abbot Hugh was in many respects the spiritual centre of Europe, and Abbot Hugh saw his monastic family spread into many lands. Yet his death in 1109 left Cluny facing great problems so far as its own affairs were concerned, at a time when the monastic order as a whole was undergoing a period of reappraisal, if not of crisis.[1]

So far as Cluny itself is concerned, the protracted personal dominance of Abbot Hugh itself created certain difficulties. The government of Cluny and of the whole monastic body which owed allegiance to it depended entirely upon the abbot himself. Despite the expansion which the sixty years of Hugh's reign had witnessed, the Cluniacs developed no constitutional structure. They had no general chapters nor was there any such interchange of monks amongst their priories as served to maintain the vitality of the twelfth-century monastic orders. The abbot's powers were not in any way delegated to or shared by his subordinates.[2] As Abbot Hugh grew older, the limitations of advancing years made it increasingly difficult for him effectively to exercise the authority

[1] See esp. Knowles, *The Monastic Order in England*, pp. 191–226, *From Pachomius to Ignatius*, pp. 16–40, 'Cistercians and Cluniacs', *The Historian and Character, and Other Essays* (Cambridge, 1963), pp. 50–75; J. Leclercq, 'La Crise du monachisme aux xie et xiie siècles', *Bulletino dell'istituto storico italiano per il medio evo e archivio Muratoriano*, lxx (1958), 19–41; Cantor, 'The Crisis of Western Monasticism', *American Historical Review*, lxvi (1960), 47–67; M.-D. Chenu, *La Théologie au douzième siècle* (2nd edn., Paris, 1966), pp. 225–73.

[2] A striking example of the idiosyncrasy of Abbot Hugh's personal rule during his latter years is provided by his decree of c. 1107, when he admitted Abbot Geoffrey of Vendôme to the confraternity of Cluny. Geoffrey recorded that Hugh 'decrevit generali praecepto, ut quamdiu vixero, si in eius absentia venero Cluniacum, capitulo et mensae toti ordine vice illius praesim': *Cartulaire de l'abbaye cardinale de la Trinité de Vendôme*, ed. Métais, ii, no. 416, pp. 179–80. The wholly personal nature of the abbot of Cluny's rule over his subject priories is strikingly expressed in King Louis VI of France's privilege for Cluny of 1119: *Bibl. C.*, cols. 575–8.

that was vested in himself alone. After his visit to Burgos in 1090, his itinerary seldom took him far from the vicinity of Cluny, and the visits to his subject houses which were so necessary for their governance became infrequent.[1] The consequences of this relaxation of control which continued through the troubled years of Abbot Pons (1109–22) and the brief episode of the two-months' abbacy of the aged Hugh II (1122), were made clear in the legislation of the next great abbot, Peter the Venerable (1122–57). For example, it became a widespread practice for Cluniac monks to be professed without the abbot of Cluny's leave; this led to many unsuitable persons being received. Again, novices who were admitted away from Cluny delayed for up to thirty years before they came to the mother house for their blessing or profession.[2] Under Abbot Hugh the Cluniac body became too vast and unwieldy to be ruled by a single man, however saintly, respected, and capable. It is not surprising that the rule of Abbot Pons should have issued in a grave, if to the modern observer enigmatic, crisis amongst the Cluniacs themselves.[3] The times called for some new way of securing the good government of the Cluniac body.

The slowing down in the building of Abbot Hugh's third church also illustrates the gathering problems with which Cluny was faced. The church which Abbot Hugh designed was large enough to accommodate the whole Cluniac body if it had ever assembled; and Abbot Hugh hoped to finance his grandiose design very largely from the tribute which he received from King Alphonso VI of León-Castile. By 1095 it was possible for Urban II to consecrate the altars of the church, and its eastern end came into use. But with Alphonso's death in 1109 and with the waning of Castilian power in the twelfth century, the chief supply of money for the church was reduced. Although Pope Innocent II was able to dedicate the building as a whole in 1130, it was not

---

[1] See his itinerary, *Neue Forschungen*, pp. 369–76.

[2] *Statuta congregationis Cluniacensis*, xxxv, xxxviii, *P.L.* clxxxix. 1035–6.

[3] See esp. de Valous, 'Cluny', *D.H.G.E.* xiii. 56–9; H. V. White, 'Pontius of Cluny, the *Curia Romana* and the End of Gregorianism in Rome', *Church History*, xxvii (1958), 195–219; G. Tellenbach, 'Der Sturz des Abtes Pontius von Cluny und seine geschichtliche Bedeutung', *Q.F.I.A.B.* xlii (1963), 13–55.

until *c.* 1225 that the western extremity of the narthex could be completed and that the whole building could stand as Abbot Hugh had envisaged it.[1]

The slow progress with the construction of third church reflected Cluny's wider economic problems. Up to *c.* 1080, when the third church began to be projected, Cluny had enjoyed a comfortable prosperity, based upon the produce of its ever-increasing domains which was well supplemented by the profits of its lands, justice, and other sources of revenue. Then changes set in. Cluny acquired new kinds of cash income which during the next thirty years or so transformed its economy. They were largely the consequence of its expansion in the south of France, in Italy, and in Spain. The massive annual tribute paid by Alphonso VI is the most considerable example; but the annual *census* paid by Cluny's subject houses, although small in each individual case, also provided in aggregate a considerable revenue. Such cash income was not for the most part capitalized in economically productive ways but was used for building and liturgical embellishment. Besides meeting the cost of the third church, it was used to buy corn and other necessities for the multitude of workmen, guests, and others, for whom Cluny had increasingly to provide. Cluny thus developed as a considerable economic centre. But the new sources of its finance made it sensitive, not only to ordinary fluctuations of produce and exchange, but also to political factors in distant lands over which Cluny had no control but which might have a damaging effect upon it. Cluny's situation was the more insecure because the decades of change in Cluny's economy saw no great modification of the way in which its lands were managed.

Thus, whereas at the apogee of Abbot Hugh's reign Cluny was economically secure, by his death it was at best in a state of fragile equilibrium, and at worst it was dangerously vulnerable to the vagaries of economic change and of political developments in far-off lands.[2] By 1109 the dangers of the situation were already clear in shortages of cash and food. At a time when gifts to Cluny

---

[1] Conant, 'Medieval Academy Excavations at Cluny', *Speculum*, xxix (1954), 10.

[2] See esp. the *Dispositio rei familiaris Cluniacensis facta a domno Petro abbate*, Bruel, 4132.

were tending to fall off,[1] there is no evidence that its rulers had any new ideas about how to put matters right.[2]

In the context of feudal developments, too, the Cluny of 1109 was beginning to be ill at ease. Under Abbots Odilo and Hugh, Cluny had owed a large part of its influence to its appropriateness to the feudal society of the eleventh century. This may be seen in its skill in meeting the religious needs of this society, and in its network of relationship with the lay feudatories of the time. It is no less clear in the well-known parallels between the forms of Cluny's monastic life and those of contemporary feudalism: thus, for example, the personal bond between Cluniac monk and Cluniac abbot was like that of feudal vassal to feudal lord; while the prior of a subject house expressed his submission to the abbot by a ceremony which corresponded closely to feudal homage.[3] But round about 1100 the fabric of feudal society was itself changing. The personal bonds between lord and vassal of which Cluniac conventions are reminiscent, were becoming less important than the material bonds of the fief. Lands, jurisdiction, and services were coming to the fore, and with them an increasing importance attached to institutions and constitutional structures.[4] In the Church, too, the work begun by Gregory VII and Urban II was not only adding a new weight to papal authority, but was also equipping this authority with a structure of courts, canon law, and institutions. In face of such changes in feudal society and in the Church alike, Cluny was in danger of keeping to personal and non-institutionalized ways of thought and action which were appropriate to a vanishing age.

The problem of adjustment was the harder because this same time saw profound changes in patterns of thought and feeling in

---

[1] See above, p. xviii.

[2] For the above paragraphs, see G. Duby, 'Le Budget de l'abbaye de Cluny entre 1080 et 1155', *Annales, Économies, Sociétés, Civilisations,* vii (1952), 155–71.

[3] Knowles, *The Monastic Order in England,* pp. 146–8, *From Pachomius to Ignatius,* pp. 11–13.

[4] Cf. Marc Bloch's contrast between the first and second feudal ages: *La Société féodale,* i, *La Formation des liens de dépendance* (Paris, 1939), 95–190; H. Mitteis, *Der Staat des hohen Mittelalters* (5th edn., Weimar, 1955), pp. 3–6; T. Mayer, *Mittelalterliche Studien* (Lindau and Constance, 1959), pp. 470–2.

both religious and secular life, which also tended to leave Cluny high and dry.[1] In their most general character, the changes have been epitomized as having been from epic to romance. In religious terms, the twelfth century saw a gradual turning away from the preoccupation with the Last Judgement and with the hieratic Christ in Majesty of the Apocalypse, which dominated Romanesque art and found such a complete expression in the Cluny of Abbot Hugh. Instead, twelfth-century piety was to centre upon the human Jesus and to be concerned with the approach of the individual to him upon a human plane. Such was to be the emphasis of Cîteaux (founded 1098) and of its offshoot, Clairvaux (founded 1115), as of St. Bernard himself. It was part of the conscious opposition of the Cistercians to the Cluniacs, and its effect was to make Cluniac religion somewhat old-fashioned. The new age was also unsympathetic to the elaboration of Cluniac worship and to the richness of its spiritual and material life. To an older age, and in the time of Cluny's greatest fervour, these things had spoken of the majesty of Christ and of the glories of heaven. Now, they easily seemed to stand in contrast to the simplicity of the Rule, and behind it of the Gospel itself, and, instead, to savour of worldliness and empty pomp and show. When, in addition, the Crusades were providing a 'novum promerendae salutis genus', and when a new penitential discipline was about to emerge based upon the contrition of the individual, great adjustments were called for if Cluny was to meet the changed circumstances of the new century.

Indeed, the contrast between Cluny and Clairvaux suggests that Cluny's problems upon the death of Abbot Hugh lay deeper still, and that there was a crisis at the heart of the monastic order itself. The three centuries which separated Hugh of Cluny from Benedict of Aniane had witnessed the pre-eminence of a kind of monasticism which, in adhering to the Rule of St. Benedict of Nursia, sought to remain in vital and physically close contact with

---

[1] Besides Bloch's discussion, some particularly valuable treatments of this change are W. P. Ker, *Epic and Romance* (London, 1896); C. S. Lewis, *The Allegory of Love* (Oxford, 1936); G. L. Prestige, *Fathers and Heretics* (London, 1940), pp. 180–9; Southern, *The Making of the Middle Ages*, pp. 219–57.

the centres of secular life and settlement. Its houses were usually in or near towns, and its manner of life allowed ample scope for corporate wealth and the building of elaborate monasteries; indeed, as at Cluny, these were the hallmark of its excellence.

But there was another monastic tradition with its roots in the very origins of Christian monasticism in the Egyptian desert, which was by nature eremitical. It sought places of solitude not of human habitation, and the basis of its life was extreme austerity and mortification. This was true of its corporate life, no less than of its individual observance. The eleventh century which witnessed the apogee of Cluny, also witnessed the revival of this kind of monasticism. Its heralds were men like St. Romuald and his disciple Peter Damiani. It found expression in the hermit groups of Fonte Avellana and Camaldoli, and in the style of life which St. John Gualbertus established at what he called the 'eremus' of Vallombrosa. Such developments gradually percolated into France and gave rise there to such things as the foundation of the Carthusians in 1084. The insistence of the Cistercians upon founding their monasteries in places of solitude, the unadorned severity of their architecture, and above all their desire to strip away the accretions of time and to return to the stark letter of the Benedictine Rule (*Regula ad apicem literae*), all illustrate the challenge which more austere standards of monasticism were presenting to Cluny within the western monastic order which Cluny had dominated for so long. By 1109 it was already beginning to be posed.[1]

However, this monastic challenge was itself only part of a still wider challenge concerning the basis of the Christian life itself. During the eleventh century there had grown up a widespread and multifarious insistence upon the need to accomplish the reform of the Church or some part of it, 'ad formam primitivae ecclesiae'. This signified the establishment of a way of life which corresponded to the 'vita apostolica' of the earliest days of the Church.[2] Those who followed it aspired to a life in common, marked by a primitive simplicity of dress, food, and behaviour, and

---

[1] See esp. Knowles, as referred to above, p. 252, n. 1.

[2] See esp. Miccoli, *Chiesa gregoriana*, pp. 225–99.

with no external magnificence of buildings or ritual. Its keynote
was humility of individual and common life. Few aspects of
eleventh- and twelfth-century Church life were untouched by the
ramifications of this insistence. In 1059 no less a person than
Archdeacon Hildebrand sought to establish the Apostolic See
itself upon such a basis,[1] and Urban II accorded the canonical life
according to the Rule of St. Augustine an equal esteem with
monasticism.[2] This quest for apostolic simplicity had its place
amongst the aims of the Cistercians, for it fitted in with their zeal
for a simpler mode of life.[3] By contrast, it could easily lead men
to pass adverse judgements upon the most exalted institutions of
the Church. Cluny was especially vulnerable. One of its defenders, the conservatively minded Abbot Rupert of Deutz (1120–
9), represented an imaginary adversary as passing in review the
rise and fall of the great empires of antiquity; so, the adversary
said, it would be with the great monastic empires of his day, and
he named Cluny in particular. They would fall in their turn, and
give way to new and more humble forms of the monastic life.[4]

At its most radical, the quest for a life 'ad instar vitae apostolicae' threatened to cut the ground from under the older monasticism of Cluny. In Abbot Hugh's day such figures as Robert of
Arbrissel foreshadowed the popular religious movements which
were to pullulate in the twelfth century, giving rise to such

[1] A. Werminghoff, 'Die Beschlüsse des Aachener Concils im Jahre 816', *N.A.*
xxvii (1901–2), 669–75.

[2] 'Non minoris aestimandum est meriti, hanc vitam ecclesiae primitivam
aspirante et prosequente Domini spiritu sustentare, quam florentem monachorum
religionem eiusdem spiritus perseverantia custodire': Urban's privilege for the
church of Raitenbuch, 1092, *Ep.* lviii, *P.L.* cli. 338.

[3] 'Quod a primitiva ecclesia communis vitae traditio coeperit, et quod hinc
monasticae religionis institutio principium sumpserit': *Exordium magnum ordinis
Cisterciensis*, ii, *P.L.* clxxxv. 997.

[4] 'Dixisti enim "Postquam regnum Babylonium crevit in immensum, crescere
desiit et succrevit aliud, scilicet regnum Persarum atque Medorum, et deinde super
hoc aliud, videlicet regnum Macedonum." . . . Subiunxisti, "Sic futurum esse,
iamque fieri debere, ut magnitudo sive altitudo illorum, qui hactenus in conversatione monachica viguerunt, maximeque Cluniacensium", de quibus nescio
utrum aliquod unquam dixeris amabile verbum, "deprimeretur, atque minueretur
admodum, atque humilibus suborientibus fieret aliud principium" ': *In regulam
Sancti Benedicti*, iv. 13, *P.L.* clxx. 535–6.

religious orders as those of Fontevrault and Prémontré; to such
movements as the Humiliati and the Waldensians; and eventually
to the mendicant orders of the thirteenth century.[1] Such movements were to find their support in social classes which the Cluny
of Abbot Hugh scarcely touched at all. Their character and
aspirations throw into even sharper relief than do the Cistercians
the deeply old-fashioned character of Cluniac monasticism, and
the time of crisis into which it had come.

The developments which have just been summarized show that
in 1109 Cluny faced an uncertain future. It is not too much to say
that it found itself at the centre of a crisis in western monasticism,
which its very pre-eminence in the eleventh century placed it at a
disadvantage in seeking to weather. It would be beyond the scope
of the present discussion to investigate fully how Cluny tried to
meet the crisis, and what measure of success it achieved. It is
enough to say that, during the twelfth century, the crisis was at
least weathered, and to discuss two aspects of the manner in which
this was done.

First, as regards most of the points which have been noticed, the
Cluny of Peter the Venerable managed to adapt itself adequately,
if not usually with conspicuous success.[2] It increasingly accepted a reduced role in the Church at large, and settled into a
firm and honoured position in the Church of France. So far as
its constitutional problems were concerned, the abbacy of Peter
the Venerable restored a fair, if not conspicuous, level of stability
and wisdom after the uneasy years of Pons and his aged and short-
lived successor Hugh II. The third church took shape according
to Abbot Hugh's grandiose design, albeit slowly; for other
sources of revenue were found which did something to make good

[1] Grundmann, *Religiöse Bewegungen im Mittelalter*, remains the fundamental
study. See also Knowles, *From Pachomius to Ignatius*, pp. 42–3; but in many
respects, the 'new religious climate' began to be apparent before the second half
of the twelfth century. For a general survey, see C. N. L. Brooke, 'Heresy and
Religious Sentiment: 1000–1250', *Bulletin of the Institute of Historical Research*, xli
(1968), 115–31.
[2] For Peter the Venerable, see de Valous, 'Cluny', *D.H.G.E.* xiii. 59–72;
J. Leclercq, *Pierre le Vénérable*, (Saint-Wandrille, 1946); *Petrus Venerabilis*, ed.
G. Constable, *Studia Anselmiana*, xl (1956); *The Letters of Peter the Venerable*,
ed. Constable, 2 vols. (Cambridge, Mass., 1967).

the decreasing help from Spain.¹ Peter the Venerable made an attempt, of which the details are largely preserved in his Statutes,² to make such economic retrenchments as would enable Cluny to overcome its financial problems. In this he was not altogether successful; but with the help of a prudent policy of securing credit, Cluny's economy was placed upon a viable basis.³ Peter the Venerable also did much to pilot Cluny through the wider monastic crisis which he inherited. He was helped by the fact that even in the eleventh century, Cluny had shown its awareness of the eremitical life as represented by Fonte Avellana and Vallombrosa, and Peter Damiani's enthusiasm for Cluny is a reminder that the contrast between the different forms of monasticism should not be pressed too far. Peter the Venerable himself sought to accommodate some of the values of the eremitical tradition in ways which show both Cluny's capacity to absorb other ideas and the limits within which such an absorption was feasible. For example, in his Statutes he normally reserved some parts of the new church for the exclusive use of the monks, so that they could find a place 'velut in eremo' for private devotions and austerities.⁴ His sheltering of Peter Abelard when he was a fugitive from the zeal of St. Bernard is a reminder of Cluny's traditional insistence upon the great mercies of God and its availability to all men as an 'asylum poenitentium' with its doors ever open to the righteous and sinners alike: as such it still had a place amidst the changes of the twelfth-century world. Cluny was not without a capacity for self-renewal and for employing its traditional ways to meet the demands of a different age. To see Cluny through the eyes of

¹ e.g. King Henry I of England contributed very substantially to the building of the third church (Bruel, 4183, an endorsement of which speaks of him as 'basilicae novae nostrae praecipuo constructore post regem Hispaniae'). For Peter the Venerable's building, see K. J. Conant, 'Cluniac Building during the Abbacy of Peter the Venerable', *Studia Anselmiana*, xl (1956), 121–7.
² *P.L.* clxxxix. 1025–48. For the unfavourable verdict which they led Knowles to pass on Peter's work, see *The Historian and Character*, pp. 69–75; also Knowles's study, 'The Reforming Decrees of Peter the Venerable', *Studia Anselmiana*, xl (1956), 1–20.
³ Duby, art. cit., *Annales*, vii (1952), 166–71.
⁴ *Statuta*, liii, *P.L.* clxxxix. 1039–40. Cf. Leclercq, 'Pierre le Vénérable et l'érémitisme clunisien', *Studia Anselmiana*, xl (1956), 99–120.

a Rupert of Deutz or a Peter of St. John, or even through those of
the mature St. Bernard, is to understand that there were those for
whom the fame of Clairvaux did not blind men to Cluny's
virtues.[1] Nor did Cluny cease to stand for monastic values which
Clairvaux itself did not so fully exhibit.

Secondly, Cluny continued to rely upon and to renew the bond
with the Papacy that had been established during the eleventh
century. Abbot Pons secured from Popes Paschal II, Gelasius II
(1118–19), and Calixtus II (1119–24) confirmations of Cluny's
privileges and possessions as they had been built up in earlier
centuries.[2] After Pons had been deposed in 1122, Peter the Venerable lost no time in safeguarding his own position by having his
election confirmed by Calixtus II.[3] Whatever may have been
the circumstances of his succession to the Papacy, Honorius II
(1124–30) also confirmed Cluny's privileges.[4] Furthermore, until
Pons's death at Rome in 1126, Honorius repeatedly intervened to
defend Cluny and its possessions against him; particularly in 1125,
by insisting upon Peter the Venerable's authority over Cluny's
principal subject houses,[5] and in 1126, when he marshalled the
French bishops to support his legate, Cardinal Peter, against Pons
as the 'invasor' of the monastery of Cluny.[6]

But still more than these events, the renewed disputes between
Cluny and the churches of Mâcon and Lyons which broke out
with their old bitterness after Abbot Hugh died, made it clear that
the bond between Cluny and the Papacy was by no means a thing
of the past. During his latter years as bishop, Berard of Mâcon
sought to assert his spiritual claims against Cluny. At first Paschal
II temporized, and so far accommodated the bishop's demands as

---

[1] For Rupert, see esp. *In regulam sancti Benedicti*, iv. 13, *P.L.* clxx. 535–8; for
Peter, see Constable, 'The Letter from Peter of St. John to Hato of Troyes',
Studia Anselmiana, xl (1956), 49–52; for St. Bernard, see Knowles, *The Historian
and Character*, pp. 64–6.

[2] Paschal II, *Ep.* cclxxx, *P.L.* clxiii. 260–1; *Ep.* cclxxxiii, ibid., col. 262; *Epp.*
cccxcvii–viii, ibid., cols. 358–9. Gelasius II, *Ep.* viii, *P.L.* clxiii. 492, cf. *Ep.* xxvi,
ibid., cols. 509–10. Calixtus II, *Ep.* lxxvii, *P.L.* clxiii. 1164–6. Gelasius died and was
buried at Cluny: *Bibl. C.*, col. 463.

[3] *Epp.* clxxxix–cxc, *P.L.* clxiii. 1256–7.

[4] *Ep.* vi, *P.L.* clxvi. 1225–7.   [5] *Epp.* vii–x, ibid., cols. 1227–30.

[6] *Epp.* xliv–vi, xlviii, ibid., cols. 1258–61, 1265–8.

to prohibit Abbot Pons from having chrism consecrated in his
monastery.[1] Calixtus II, however, returned to the ways of earlier
popes by suspending Berard from his episcopal office until he
ceased from vexing Cluny and made amends for the wrongs that
he had done.[2] At about this time Berard enjoyed the support of
his metropolitan, Archbishop Humbald of Lyons; in or soon
after 1119, Abbot Pons wrote a letter to his monks in which he
referred to the archbishop's 'nefanda scripta' and appealed to the
rulings of the earlier popes in language which almost certainly
echoes Gregory VII's eulogy of 1080.[3] Calixtus II was himself
present at the Council of Rheims (1119), at which the old battles
of the eleventh century were fought again.[4] So far as Cluny is
concerned, a lengthy account of the Council is provided by
Ordericus Vitalis.[5] His sympathies were deeply engaged upon the
Cluniac side; but if they coloured his narrative, there is no doubt
that he discloses the issues that were discussed. According to his
account, Archbishop Humbald complained on behalf of his suf-
fragans about the wrongs that Cluny's exemption inflicted upon
the church of Mâcon. Abbot Pons answered him by making an
appeal to Cluny's direct subjection to the Apostolic See and by
insisting upon the pope's function of protecting it against all who
would attack it. He did so in such a way as to elicit an exercise of
papal as against episcopal authority which was charged with
meaning in the light of the claims of the eleventh-century French
bishops.[6] Calixtus adjourned the Council until the next day, when

---

[1] *Ep.* cccviii, *P.L.* clxiii. 281.

[2] Cf. his vigorous action against Bishop Berard of Mâcon: *Ep.* ccxlvi, *P.L.* clxiii.
1304. For the date see Tellenbach, art. cit., *Q.F.I.A.B.* xlii (1963), 33.

[3] 'Si [Humbald] intellexisset scita sanctorum conciliorum sacrorumque canonum,
quibus sanctae Romane ecclesiae auctoritas innititur et declaratur, non in
coelum posuisset os suum, sed digito buccam suam compressisset': Bruel, 3952.
The words 'buccam suam' seem to be a clear echo of Gregory's words in 1080.

[4] For a general account of the Council and its wider significance, see Fliche,
La Réforme grégorienne et la reconquête chrétienne, pp. 381-3.

[5] Ordericus Vitalis, *Hist. eccles.* xii, ed. Le Prévost, iv. 385-9.

[6] 'Cluniacensis ecclesia soli Romanae ecclesiae subdita est et papae propria, et
ex quo fundata est a Romano pontifice obtinuit privilegia quae proclamatores isti
sua nituntur abolere et frustrari violentia. Notum autem sit vobis, beati patres qui
adestis, omnibus, quod ego et fratres nostri monasticas res, quas iure servandas sus-
cepimus, sicut eas venerabilis Hugo aliique sancti predecessores nostri habuerunt,

he called upon John of Crema, cardinal-priest of San Crisogono, to speak in Cluny's defence. The cardinal began by insisting in general terms upon the daily obedience that all bishops owed to papal authority and upon the pope's right to intervene in their dioceses to defend his own churches and possessions.[1] Then he eulogized Cluny itself in language which, like that of Pons's letter, echoed Gregory VII's in 1080; he praised both its liberty and its excellence in the monastic life.[2] Finally, he dwelt upon the relationship between the function of the Apostolic See as 'cardo et caput omnium ecclesiarum', and Cluny's status as an abbey which was wholly committed to Roman authority.[3]

The French bishops heard John of Crema with an ill grace, and the dispute between Cluny and Mâcon did not cease to smoulder on.[4] But so far as Cluny's relationship to the Apostolic See is concerned, the cardinal's speech as Ordericus Vitalis presents it

servare contendimus. . . . Ecclesiam suam dominus papa, si vult, defendat, et ecclesias decimasque cum aliis possessionibus quas ipse mihi commisit patrocinetur et custodiat': ibid., pp. 386–7.

[1] 'Sicut iustum est ut dominus papa clamores vestros solerter audiat, vobisque sicut pater filiis sine fictione omnimodis subveniat, talique vobis obsequi famulatu non semel sed quotidie debeat, sic nimirum decet ac iustum est ut ipse idem in parrochiis vestris aliquid proprietatis possideat, ecclesiamque seu domum vel aliquam possessionem sua electione sive fidelium oblatione liberam habeat': ibid., p. 387.

[2] 'Ducenti et eo amplius anni sunt ex quo Cluniacensis ecclesia fundata est, et ab ipso primordio fundationis suae Romano papae donata est, a quo utilibus privilegiis in Romana synodo coram multis arbitris diversae dignitatis evidenter insignita est. Ratum est, et in cartis insertum legentibus liquido patescit quod Geraldus Aquitanicus Cluniacense coenobium in alodio suo construxit, et illud, Romam pergens, Romano pontifici devotissime commisit. . . . Praefata ergo ecclesia nulli principum seu praesulum usque nunc nisi papae subiacuit. . . . unde bonus odor laudabilis famae longe lateque per orbem fragravit ': ibid., pp. 387–8.

[3] 'Omnis credentium multitudo credit ac perhibet quod qui apostolicae sedi, iubente Deo, praesidet, ligandi atque solvendi potestatem habet. . . . Ergo apostolica sedes cardo et caput omnium ecclesiarum a Domino et non ab alio constituta est. Et sicut cardine ostium regitur, sic apostolicae sedis auctoritate omnes ecclesiae, Domino disponente, reguntur. . . . Igitur cum Cluniacensis abbatia soli papae subiciatur, et ille qui praecipiente Deo in terris super omnes est ipsam patrocinetur, Romana auctoritas Cluniacensium privilegia corroborat, et in virtute Dei omnibus ecclesiae filiis imperat ne quis eos temere pristina libertate privet, nec possessionibus olim habitis spoliet, nec insolitis exactionibus praegravet': ibid., pp. 388–9.

[4] Letonnellier, *L'Abbaye exempte de Cluny et la Saint-Siège*, pp. 105–7.

shows that, well into the twelfth century, Cluny remained to the more conservatively minded high Gregorians everything that Gregory VII had proclaimed it to be. The monastic pre-eminence and the esteem in the eyes of the Papacy which Cluny achieved under its great eleventh-century abbots clearly left behind a long afterglow. It is a final reminder of the closeness in which, by virtue of the universality of its appeal, the Cluny of Abbot Hugh had stood to the Gregorian Reform.[1]

[1] In a brief epilogue, I have not attempted to discuss comprehensively all the issues that Tellenbach has raised in his masterly study of the fall of Abbot Pons: art. cit., *Q.F.I.A.B.* xlii (1963), 13–55, referring to White, art. cit., *Church History*, xxvii (1958), 195–219. Tellenbach argues that Pons's supersession in 1122 must be understood partly in the light of his unyielding insistence upon the monastic privileges which had been vindicated at Rheims, and partly of the impact within the Cluniac body of the more austere notions of the newer monasticism. It was occasioned when, in 1122–3, the Roman Curia and with it Calixtus II, the first non-monastic pope since Alexander II, reappraised the whole matter of monastic liberty. The evidence for this reappraisal may, for example, be seen in canons iv, xvii, and xix of the First Lateran Council: Mansi, xxi. 282–6. I have little doubt that Tellenbach's view is basically correct. Nevertheless, Tellenbach in my opinion does not sufficiently demonstrate that the issues of the Lateran Council of 1123 were already active in the spring of 1122, although he establishes a likelihood that they were. Further, the question of monastic exemption in 1122–3 must be discussed in the light of a fuller appraisal of the question in the eleventh century, and of the general European context. Against a wider background, the events of 1122–3 lose much of the significance that White and Tellenbach accord them. I hope to return to the subject in a future study.

CONCLUSION

THE conclusion to which this study points is that it is not easy to remain satisfied with the prevailing opinion regarding the relation of the Cluniacs to the Gregorian Reform. The Cluniacs were by no means altogether conservative in their attitude; they did not stand in sharp contrast to Gregory VII; nor did they remain essentially superior to party during the ecclesiastical revolution of the eleventh century, nor act as a kind of 'third force' in the Church, poised in cautious neutrality between pope and emperor.

No simple formula will suffice to define their standpoint. Their relationships with their contemporaries were not of a uniform colour but presented a very broad spectrum indeed. The massive researches of Tellenbach's school have clearly demonstrated how at one end of this spectrum the Cluniacs, especially in France, merged into the ecclesiastical and feudal societies of the pre-Gregorian age. Furthermore their especial perceptiveness and skill in answering the need for the 'remissio peccatorum' which their contemporaries of all outlooks and states of life experienced, served to ensure Cluny's acceptability in many and often highly contrasting parts of the eleventh-century world.

Yet it was a notable consequence of Cluny's universal appeal that the Gregorians themselves, and Gregory VII above all, were second to none in the value that they set upon its specifically monastic work of offering prayers and performing alms for the benefit of all Christians. As for Cluny itself, it was uniquely committed to the Apostolic See of Rome. Its most pressing needs, particularly in face of the local pressure of the bishops of Mâcon and of the episcopal order in general, made it utterly and repeatedly dependent upon papal support. To the Papacy Cluny owed and acknowledged an incalculable debt for its liberty as it had evolved up to the time of Abbot Hugh, and it was to this liberty that Cluny was indebted for the possibility of developing so many of the characteristic features of Cluniac monasticism at its apogee.

In return Cluny's liberty furnished the Papacy with the quint-essential example of the liberty that it aspired to realize in the Church. As Cluny's monastic family spread, it tended, in spite of its considerable variations from region to region, to propagate in its dependencies the characteristics of the mother house. It therefore often called into play the exercise of papal authority on high Gregorian lines. In Germany, Spain, and Italy, the Cluniacs were in various ways of cardinal significance for the dissemination of Gregorian ideas and for the promotion of the cause of St. Peter. There can be little doubt that Tellenbach's school has displayed only one end of a very broad spectrum. At the other end of it, as the popes and reformers of the Gregorian age were tireless in proclaiming, Cluny was indissolubly bound to the Gregorian Papacy, deeply committed to many of its objectives, and habitually faithful in its collaboration with it.

The evidence that has been presented in this study seems more than sufficient to justify the contention that it is upon the Gregorian end of the spectrum of Cluniac attitudes and activities that especial emphasis should be laid. In all aspects of their work, whether as concentrated upon Cluny itself or as diffused amongst those who in any significant way drew their inspiration from it, it was the general rule that the Cluniacs collaborated whole-heartedly and intimately with successive popes. In so doing, they were true to the purposes which the Cluny of Abbot Hugh set itself. Thus the reforming popes were understandably at one in their praise of Cluniac monasticism, and of its services to the Apostolic See and to the apostles to whom Cluny and the Papacy had a common dedication.

When Gregory VII wrote to Abbot Hugh that 'eadem enim via eodem sensu eodem spiritu ambulamus', he meant what he said; in all essential respects, Cluny's position in the Church and its services to the Papacy gave him good reason to say it.

APPENDIX

In 1680 Pierre Simon, a monk of Cluny, published a collection of papal privileges and other documents under the title *Bullarium sacri ordinis Cluniacensis*. Most of the early documents which Simon collected in this exceedingly rare volume have been reprinted in Migne's *Patrologia Latina* and elsewhere. Three of them, however, are difficult to obtain and are included in this appendix.

(i) *Pope John XIX's general letter in support of the Cluniacs*

Date: 28 March 1027.

Original: lost.

Copy: Paris, Bibliothèque nationale: Nouv. acqu. lat. 2262, Cartul. C, p. 21, no. 24, early twelfth century.

Printed: *Bull. C.*, pp. 9–10; L. Santifaller, 'Chronologisches Verzeichnis der Urkunden Papst Johanns XIX.', *Römische historische Mitteilungen*, i (1958), no. 44, pp. 55–6.

J.L. 4079.

The text which follows is as printed by Santifaller.

Johannes episcopus servus servorum dei omnibus cuiuscumque ordinis vel dignitatis tam presentibus quam futuris gratiam dei et copiam apostolicae benedictionis. Coenobium Cluniacense quod olim a Uuilelmo Aquitanorum principe constructum est in partibus Burgundie in comitatu Matisconensi et nunc videtur esse sub dilectissimi filii nostri abbatis Odilonis provisione, ita constat deo et sanctis eius apostolis Petro et Paulo atque Romanae ecclesiae eb eodem seniore delegatum speciali donatione, a predecessoribus quoque nostris apostolicae sedis praesulibus Formoso,[1] Johanne,[2] Benedicto, item Benedicto,[3] Gregorio,[4]

---

[1] There was no pope by the name of Formosus in the early tenth century; the dates of the only Formosus in the list of popes are 891–6. John XIX does not refer to Agapetus II's privilege of 949 (see above, p. 16): this may be an erroneous reference to it, or to a lost papal confirmation in the time of Abbot Berno: see above, p. 16, n. 1.

[2] John XI: see above, p. 16.

[3] There is no evidence that Benedict V (974–83), Benedict VI (973–4), or Benedict VII (974–83) issued a general privilege in Cluny's favour. In 978 the last of them gave the island of Lérins and the monastery of Arluc to Abbot Majolus: *Ep.* xiii, *P.L.* cxxxii. 332.   [4] Gregory V: see above, pp. 20–1.

Appendix 269

Silvestro,[1] meo etiam non modo spirituali patre, sed et carnali fratre Benedicto[2] multiplicibus privilegiis apostolicae auctoritatis roboratum et confirmatum, ut ad nullum alium respiciat locus ille sive habitatores eius, nisi ad deum et sanctum Petrum et apostolicae sedis pontificem summum. Quorum sequens exemplum fultus apostolico vigore ego Johannes apostolice sedis presul cum ceteris coepiscopis et fratribus meis in conventu Romae congregatis in presentia domni Conradi regis divi augusti nuper a deo et nobis in imperium Romani orbis electi et coronati statuta, quae supra memorati antecessores mei de libertate predicti loci sanxerunt et habitatores ipsius per centum et eo amplius annos sine alicuius contradictione tenuerunt, laudo et auctoritate dei sanctorumque apostolorum Petri et Pauli perpetua stabilitate mansura confirmo. Preterea pervenit ad nos, quod quidam episcoporum temere et sine aliqua rationabili causa consultu pravo excommunicant sibi subiectos non solum seculares perversa agentes, sed et religiosos sobriam et deo placitam vitam ducere cupientes, quod de monachis Cluniacensibus omnino fieri prohibemus. Sed si quelibet querimonia episcoporum adversum illos exorta fuerit et aliter finiri non potuerit, apostolicae sedis examini reservetur, ut per eius iudicium quod iustum est decernatur. Quod si huic nostrae institutioni quilibet cuiuscumque ordinis vel dignitatis contraire voluerit, timeat illud, quod meretur, qui contra divinum preceptum catholicorum et apostolicorum patrum terminos temerario ausu sive ambitionis cupiditate transgredi presumpserit. Si vero episcopus aut cuiuslibet aecclesiasticae dignitatis fuerit, noverit se omnino potestate aecclesiasticae auctoritatis carere, quia matri sue contradicit aecclesiae videlicet Romane, a qua si quam videtur habere aecclesiasticam potestatem accepto anathemate apostolicae auctoritatis colligatus et a liminibus sanctae dei aecclesiae repulsus per perpetuam excommunicationem nisi resipuerit a societate fidelium separabitur. Qui vero observator et custos ipsius extiterit, gratiae dei et benedictionis apostolicae compos existat. Bene valete. Dat. V. kal. aprilis per manum Petri episcopi sanctae Praenestinae aecclesiae et bibliothecarii sanctae apostolicae sedis, anno pontificatus domni Johannis sanctissimi noni decimi papae tertio, indictione decima.

[1] Silvester II (999–1003). Silvester issued no confirmation of Cluny's privileges which has survived. There was a tacit, if perhaps rather reluctant, countenancing of the beginnings of Cluny's exemption in his letter to Abbot Odilo about the regularity of ordinations by a bishop who had become a monk: *Ep.* xii, *P.L.* cxxxix. 283–4.

[2] Benedict VIII: see above, p. 21.

(ii) *Pope Clement II's letter to the bishops and magnates of France and Aquitaine*[1]

Undated.

Original: lost.

Copy: Paris, Bibliothèque nationale, Nouv. acqu. lat. 2262, Cartul. C, p. 15, no. 16, early twelfth century.

Printed: *Bull. C.*, p. 12.

J.L. 4136.

The text which follows is that of the Paris Manuscript; variant readings in *Bull. C.* are indicated (S).

CLEMENS episcopus servorum dei servus[2] omnibus episcopis galliae seu aquitaniae principibus[3] et magnatibus gratia et pax a deo patre et domino nostro Ihesu Christo. Scitis fratres dilectissimi quia tempus est ut incipiat iudicium de domo domini. Ergo si tempus iudicii adpropinquat, praeparet se unusquisque qualiter tam tremendae maiestati rationem de suis actibus reddat. Est enim deus cuius irae nemo potest resistere, sub quo curvantur qui portant orbem. Quod ad vos pertinet quibus commissa est cura ecclesiae dei, et causa populi christiani. Requirite pacem, augete studium honestae vitae, et incepto bono perseverantes ad meliora tendite, ut deum deorum in syon videre possitis felici exultatione. Obsecro vos confratres et dilectissimi filii per misericordiam domini dei nostri, ut illud sacrum cenobium cluniacum et praedia eius cellas vel monasteria in vestris partibus posita cum tali amore et diligentia custodiatis, ut senioribus et fratribus nulla molestia inseratur. Si quis ergo hanc nostram ammonitionem observaverit, habebit ut spero[4] confido dei gratiam et benedictionem apostolicam. Si aliquis[5] pro nihilo duxerit, certe praedico feriendus est districtae[6] anathematis vinculo. Vos vestraque deus in pace custodiat.

(iii) *Pope Gregory VII's conciliar allocution in praise of Cluny*

Date: during the Lent Council at the Lateran, early March 1080.

Original: lost.

---

[1] For information about this and the following document I am indebted to Mlle M.-T. d'Alverny and M. Pierre Gasnault, of the Bibliothèque nationale.

[2] 'servus servorum Dei' (S).   [3] 'principibusque' (S).

[4] S adds 'et'.   [5] S has 'Si autem quis'.

[6] 'districti' (S).

Copies: Vatican Library, Codex Vaticanus latinus, 1208 (olim 186), fos. 125^v–26^v, twelfth century; Bibliothèque nationale, Collection Moreau, 283, fos. 39^v–40^r, transcript made by Lambert de Barive in 1773 of a lost fifteenth-century copy.[1]

[1] The eighteenth-century copy was made by Lambert de Barive from a document which he found at Cluny, giving as its reference 'Abbaye de Cluny—Grand Tresor. Tiroir portant pour inscription: Anglettêre. Liasse 7ème—Cotte 127'. The full text occupies fos. 39^r–40^v of Bibl. nat., Coll. Moreau, 283. On the last folio, Lambert de Barive described his Latin documents as

contenu sur une demie feuille de grand Papier portant douze pouces de hauteur sur onze pouces de largeur, compris les marges, icelle lacérée aux 7. et 8e. lignes à droite, mais lisibles, le tout de l'Écriture du quinzième siécle, par copie sans signature à nous représentée par le Tresorier du monastére de Cluny et par lui retirée, Ledit extrait fait et revû par moy soussigné ayant charge pour le Roy sous les ordres de Monsgr Bertin Ministre et Sécretaire d'État, aux archives de L'abbaye de Cluny le 30. novembre 1773.

His first document is a letter of Pope Innocent IV (1243–54) to King Henry III of England (1216–72), dated 23 May 1249 (*Bull. C.*, p. 119, cf. Bruel, 4912; Duckett, *Charters and Records . . . of Cluni*, ii. 206; not in E. Berger's edition of Innocent IV's Register nor listed in A. Potthast, *Regesta pontificum Romanorum*):

Innocentius episcopus servus servorum dei carissimo in Christo filio regi anglie illustri salutem et apostolicam benedictionem. Sua nobis dilecti filii abbas et conventus cluniacensis petitione monstravit, quod cum super reddendis eis maneriis redditibus et aliis bonis ipsorum que in tuo regno sasiri fecisti, celsitudini tue pluries direxevimus [*sic*] scripta nostra, tu id facere denegas nisi dictus abbas ad presentiam tuam accedat tibi fidelitatem et hommagium prestaturus. Quia vero ab eodem abbate seu predecessoribus eius a te vel aliis regibus in quorum regnis habent bona hactenus petita huiusmodi non fuere, serenitatem regiam duximus attente rogandam consideratis clementer quod hoc propter aliorum exemplum in grave ipsius monasterii preiudicium redundaret, ab eodem abbate novum quid non exigent [*sic*], predicta sibi pro divina et apostolice sedis reverentia ac nostra sine difficultate qualibet facias liberari; ita quod accrescat tibi meritorum cumulus apud deum et nos regalem manificenciam [*sic*] dignis in domino laudibus commendemus. Datum Lugduni x. Kalendas junii pontificatus nostri anno sexto.

Gregory's allocution was next introduced by the rubric 'Sequitur certa statuta in Concilio generali Lateranensi presidente domino Gregorio papa vij°. super exemptione monasterii Cluniacensis'. The allocution seems thus to have been used by the Cluniacs in their long resistance to Henry III's attempts to inhibit Cluny's taxation of its English possessions by papal authority. For aspects of this dispute, see Cal. Close Rolls, 24 Henry III, 174–5; 28 Henry III, 147; 30 Henry III, 381, 386; 35 Henry III, 466. In the light of these references, and of Innocent IV's presence at Lyons on the date concerned, Duckett's ascription of the letter to Pope Innocent VI (1352–62), and his association of it with the problem of alien priories, are mistaken.

272 *Appendix*

Printed: *Bull. C.*, pp. 21–2; G. F. Duckett, *Charters and Records from among the Archives of the Ancient Abbey of Cluni from 1077 to 1534*, ii (Lewes, 1888), 206–8 (from Lambert de Barive's transcript).
J.L. 7 March 1080.
References: Cited by Pope Urban II in *Ep.* ix, *P.L.* cli. 291–3 ;[1] Urban also referred to Gregory VII's exemption of Cluny 'in Romano synodo' in *Ep.* cxxxvii, *P.L.* cli, 410–12. A text of the allocution was seen by J. Severt in a Manuscript *Chronicon Cluniacense*, from which he made a brief quotation of it: *Chronologia historica hierarchicae antistitum Lugdunensis archiepiscopatus* (Lyons, 1607), p. 430.

The text which followed is that of the Vatican MS.(V); variant readings in Lambert de Barive's transcript are indicated (B), and in Simon's printed version (*Bull. C.*).

DOMNUS[2] ac beatissimus papa Gregorius VII anno pontificatus sui septimo[3] in basilica Lateranensi quae et Constantiniana dicitur in honore Salvatoris et beati Iohannis Baptistae consilium generale celebrans, indicto cunctis silentio surrexit et dixit:[4] Noveritis, fratres et consacerdotes nostri, immo tota[5] haec sancta synodus cognoscat et sciat, quia cum ultra montes multa sint monasteria ad honorem Dei omnipotentis et beatorum apostolorum Petri et Pauli[6] nobiliter et religiose fundata, inter omnia[7] quoddam[8] in illis[9] partibus habetur, quod quasi[10] peculiare et proprium beato Petro et huic ecclesiae speciali iure adheret, Cluniaticum[11] videlicet, ad honorem et tutelam huius sanctae et apostolicae sedis ab[12] ipsis primordiis principaliter adsignatum, et faciente[13] divina clementia sub religiosis et sanctis abbatibus ad id usque dignitatis et religionis pervenit, ut ceteris monasteriis, quamvis multis antiquioribus, quantum ipse cognosco, in Dei servitio et spirituali[14] fervore precellat, et nullum in terra illa quod ego sciam, huic omnino[15] valeat adaequari. Nullus enim abbas umquam ibi fuit qui sanctus non fuisset.

For Lambert de Barive's work in the Cluny archives, see L. Delisle, *Inventaire des manuscrits de la Bibliothèque nationale, fonds de Cluny* (Paris, 1884), pp. xii–xiii.

[1] See above, p. 59, n. 2. [2] 'Dominus' (B).
[3] The seventh year of Gregory's pontificate ran from 29 June 1079 to 28 June 1080.
[4] B adds 'in hunc modum'. [5] B omits 'tota'.
[6] B omits 'Petri et Pauli'. [7] 'cuncta' (B).
[8] B adds 'monasterium quod'. [9] 'illis in' (B, *Bull.C.*). [10] 'quia' (B).
[11] 'Cluniacum' (B); Cluniacense (*Bull. C.*). [12] 'et' (*Bull. C.*).
[13] 'favente' (B, *Bull.C.*). [14] 'speciali' (B). [15] 'anno' (B).

Qui[1] abbates[2] et monachi huius semper ecclesiae filii in nullo[3] degenere[s][4] extiterunt[5] nec curvaverunt genua sua ante Bahal nec[6] Bahalim:[7] nec Geroboam,[8] sed huius sanctae Romanae sedis libertatem dignitatemque imitantes,[9] quam[10] ab origine traxerunt, nobiliter sibi per successionis seriem auctoritatem servavere.[11] Non enim alicui umquam[12] alienae vel terrenae potestati colla subdiderunt, in sola beati Petri et huius ecclesiae subiectione defensioneque[13] permanentes. Et idcirco volumus atque apostolica auctoritate firmamus et contradicimus,[14] ut nulla umquam persona, parva vel magna, sive potestas aliqua, non archiepiscopus, non episcopus, nullus regum, ducum, marchionum, principum, comitum, nec etiam aliquis legatus meus supra[15] illum locum et monasterium umquam buccam suam aperiat, aliquamve exerceat potestatem. Verum iuxta tenorem privilegii nostri et antecessorum nostrorum auctoritatem, et libertatis immunitatem sibi ab hac sede concessam integram perpetuamque omnino possideat, ut[16] tantummodo sub alis apostolicis ab omni aestu et turbine impugnationis respiret, et in gremio huius[17] sanctae[18] ecclesiae, ad honorem omnipotentis Dei et beatorum apostolorum Petri et Pauli in perpetuum dulcissime quiescat. Et ita vertens se domnus[19] papa ad dextram partem[20] synodalis conventus, percunctatus est[21] eos dicens, Placet ita vobis? laudatis? Responderunt,[22] Placet, laudamus. Vertens se iterum in[23] sinistram[24] eodem [modo interrogavit].[25] Eodem quoque modo responsum est a sancto conventu, Placet, laudamus. Post haec verba stando in throno pontificali perorata domnus papa assedit.[26]

[1] 'Quin' (*Bull. C.*).　　[2] 'abbas' (B).　　[3] 'nullo modo' (*Bull. C.*).
[4] 'degenere' (V); 'degeneres' (B, *Bull. C.*).　　[5] 'exstiterunt (B).
[6] 'et' (*Bull. C.*).　　[7] Cf. 1 Kgs. 19: 18.
[8] 'ne hieroboam' (B); B underlined the two words with dots to indicate an uncertain reading. Cf. 1 Kgs. 12: 25–33.
[9] In B, the first part of this word is made deliberately illegible and underlined with dots.
[10] 'quas' (B).　　[11] 'servaverunt' (B, *Bull. C.*).　　[12] B omits 'umquam'.
[13] B omits 'defensioneque'.　　[14] 'contendimus' (B).
[15] 'semper' (B).　　[16] 'et' (*Bull.C.*).　　[17] 'huiusmodi' (B).
[18] B and *Bull. C.* add 'matris'.
[19] 'dominus' (B).　　[20] B omits 'partem'.　　[21] *Bull. C.* omits 'est'.
[22] B adds 'tunc'.　　[23] 'ad' (B).　　[24] 'sinistrum' (*Bull. C.*).
[25] 'eodem interrogatum' (V); 'eodem modo interrogavit' (B, *Bull. C.*).
[26] B omits the final sentence; 'sedit' (*Bull. C.*).

SELECT BIBLIOGRAPHY

Note. This is not a full bibliography of the subject, but an indication of the sources and secondary works which have principally been considered.

I. SOURCES

Acta Murensia, ed. M. Keim, *Quellen zur Schweizer Geschichte*, iii (1883), pt. 3.

ALBERS, B., *Consuetudines monasticae*, 5 vols. (i, Stuttgart and Vienna, 1900; ii–v, Monte Cassino, 1905–12).

ANONYMUS PRIMUS, *Epitome vitae* [*sancti Hugonis*] *ab Ezelone atque Gilone monachis Cluniacensibus proxime ab obitu sancti scriptae, per anonymum excerpta, P.L.* clix. 909–18.

ANONYMUS SECUNDUS, *Alia miraculorum quorumdam sancti Hugonis abbatis relatio, Bibl. C.*, cols. 447–62.

BERNARD OF CLUNY, 'Ordo Cluniacensis per Bernardum', in Herrgott, *Vetus disciplina monastica*, pp. 134–364.

Bibliotheca Cluniacensis, ed. M. Marrier (Paris, 1614).

BRACKMANN, A., *Germania Pontificia*, 3 pts. in 5 vols. (Berlin, 1911–35).

Bullaire de l'abbaye de Saint Gilles (685–1777), ed. É. Goiffon (Nîmes, 1882).

Bullarium sacri ordinis Cluniacensis, ed. P. Simon (Lyons, 1680).

Cartulaire de l'abbaye de Saint-Chaffre du Monastier, ed. U. Chevalier (Paris, 1884).

Cartulaire de l'abbaye de Saint-Sernin de Toulouse, ed. C. Douais (Toulouse, 1887).

Cartulaire de Sainte-Foi de Morlaas, ed. L. Cadier (Pau, 1884).

Cartulaire de Saint-Vincent de Mâcon, ed. M. C. Ragut (Mâcon, 1864).

Cartulaire du chapitre de l'église métropolitaine Sainte-Marie d'Auch, ed. C. Lacave la Plagne Barris (*Archives historiques de la Gascogne*, Paris and Auch, 1899).

'Cartulaire du prieuré de Notre-Dame de Barbezieux', *Archives historiques de la Saintogne et de l'Aunis*, xli (1911).

Cartulaire du prieuré de Paray-le-Monial, ed. U. Chevalier (Paris, 1890).

Cartulaire du prieuré de Saint-Flour, ed. M. Boudet (Monaco, 1910).

Cartulaire du prieuré de Saint-Mont, ed. J. de Jaurgain (*Archives historiques de la Gascogne*, Paris and Auch, 1904).

Cartulare monasterii de Domina, ed. C. de Monteynard (Lyons, 1859).

Cluny im 10. und 11. Jahrhundert, ed. J. Wollasch (Historische Texte, Mittelalter, no. 6, Göttingen, 1967).

Consuetudines Farfenses, in Albers, *Consuetudines monasticae*, i.

De Gallica Petri Damiani profectione et eius ultramontano itinere, ed. G. Schwartz and A. Hofmeister, *M.G.H. Scr.* xxx. 1034–46.

FÉROTIN, M., 'Une Lettre inédite de saint Hugues, abbé de Cluny, à Bernard d'Agen, archevêque de Tolède (1087)', *Bibliothèque de l'école des chartes*, lxi (1900), 339–45.

—— 'Complément de la lettre de saint Hugues, abbé de Cluny, à Bernard d'Agen, archevêque de Tolède', ibid., lxii (1902), 682–6.

GILO, *Vita sancti Hugonis*, in L'Huillier, *Vie de saint Hugues*, pp. 574–618.

Gregorii VII epistolae collectae, in *Monumenta Gregoriana*, ed. P. Jaffé, *Bibliotheca rerum Germanicarum*, ii (Berlin, 1865), 520–76.

Gregorii VII Registrum, ed. E. Caspar, 2 vols. (*M.G.H. Epp. Sel.*, Berlin, 1920–3).

HERRGOTT, M., *Vetus disciplina monastica* (Paris, 1726).

HILDEBERT OF LE MANS, *Vita sancti Hugonis*, P.L. clix. 858–94.

Histoire et cartulaire de Saint-Denis de Nogent-le-Rotrou, ed. C. Métais (Vannes, 1895).

HUBERT, E., 'Recueil historique des chartes intéressant le département de l'Indre (vie–xie siècles)', *Revue archéologique historique et scientifique du Berry* (1899), pp. 81–268.

HUGH, monk of Cluny, *Hugonis abbatis Cluniacensis vita*, Bibl. C., cols. 437–48.

KEHR, P. F., 'Papsturkunden in Katalonien', *Abh. Gött.* xviii (1926).

—— 'Papsturkunden in Navarra und Aragon', *Abh. Gött.* xxii (1928).

Las crónicas anónimas de Sahagún, ed. J. Puyol y Alonso (Madrid, 1920).

Le Cartulaire de Marcigny-sur-Loire (1045–1144), ed. J. Richard (Dijon, 1957).

Le Cartulaire de Sauxillanges, ed. H. Doniol (Clermont-Ferrand and Paris, 1864).

Le Cartulaire du prieuré de Notre-Dame de Longpont (Lyons, 1879).

MUÑOZ Y ROMERO, T., *Colección de fueros municipales y cartas pueblas*, i (Madrid, 1847).

PAUL OF BERNRIED, *S. Gregorii VII vita*, in *Pontificum Romanorum . . . vitae*, ed. Watterich, i. 474–546.

Pontificum Romanorum, qui fuerunt inde ab exeunte saeculo IX usque ad finem saeculi XIII, vitae ab aequalibus conscriptae, ed. J. M. Watterich. 2 vols. (Leipzig, 1862).

RALPH GLABER, *Historiarum*, ed. M. Prou (Paris, 1886).

RAYNALD OF VÉZELAY, *Vita sancti Hugonis*, P.L. clix. 893–910.

Recueil des chartes de l'abbaye de Cluny, ed. A. Bruel, 6 vols. (*Documents inédits sur l'histoire de France*, Paris, 1876–1903).

Recueil des chartes et documents de Saint-Martin-des-Champs, i, ed. J. Depoin (Paris and Ligugé, 1912).

RODERIC OF TOLEDO, *De rebus Hispaniae*, in *Hispaniae illustratae scriptores*, ed. A. Schott, ii (Frankfurt, 1603), 28–148.

SANTIFALLER, L., *Quellen und Forschungen zum Urkunden- und Kanzleiwesen Papst Gregors VII.*, 1 Teil, *Quellen: Urkunden, Regesten, Facsimilia* (*Studi e testi*, cxc, Vatican City, 1957).

SCHMITT, F. S., 'Neue und alte Hildebrand-Anekdoten aus den *Dicta Anselmi*', *S.G.* v (1956), 1–18.

Statuta sancti Hugonis pro Alphonso rege Hispaniarum, P.L. clix. 945–6.

Ulrich of Cluny, *Antiquiores consuetudines monasterii Cluniacensis*, P.L. cxlix. 635–778.

Vita sancti Morandi confessoris, Bibl. C., cols. 501–6.
Vita sancti Udalrici prioris Cellae, ed. R. Wilmans, *M.G.H. Scr.* xii. 249–67.
Vita Willihelmi abbatis Hirsaugiensis, M.G.H. Scr. xii. 209–25.
Vitae quattuor priorum abbatum Cavensium, ed. L. M. Cerasoli, *Rerum Italicarum Scriptores*, ed. L. A. Muratori, new series, vi, pt. 2 (Bologna, 1941).
WILLIAM OF HIRSAU, *Consuetudines Hirsaugienses, P.L.* cl. 927–1146.

II. SECONDARY WORKS

A Cluny. Congrès scientifique (Société des amis de Cluny, Dijon, 1950).
Adel und Kirche. Festschrift für Gerd Tellenbach, ed. J. Fleckenstein and K. Schmid (Freiburg, 1968).
AMANN, E., and DUMAS, A., *L'Église au pouvoir des laïques (888–1057) (Histoire de l'église*, ed. A. Fliche and V. Martin, vii, Paris, 1948).
APPELT, H., 'Die Anfänge des päpstlichen Schutzes', *M.I.Ö.G.* lxii (1954), 101–11.
ARQUILLIÈRE, H.-X., *Saint Grégoire VII. Essai sur sa conception du pouvoir pontifical* (Paris, 1934).
BARRACLOUGH, G., *Mediaeval Germany, 911–1250*, 2 vols. (Oxford, 1938).
BECKER, A., *Studien zum Investiturproblem in Frankreich* (Saarbrücken, 1955).
—— *Papst Urban II.*, i (*Schriften der Monumenta Germaniae Historica*, 19/1, Stuttgart, 1964).
BECQUET, J., 'Saint Hugues sur les chemins de Moissac', *Annales du Midi*, lxxv (1963), 365–72.
BISHKO, C. J., 'Liturgical intercession at Cluny for the King-Emperors of Leon', *Studia Monastica*, iii (1961), 53–76.
BRACKMANN, A., 'Die Anfänge von Hirsau', *Festschrift für Paul Kehr zum 65. Geburtstag* (Munich, 1926), pp. 215–32; repr. *Zur politischen Bedeutung der kluniazensischen Bewegung*, pp. 49–75.
—— 'Die politische Wirkung des kluniazensischen Bewegung', *Historische Zeitschrift*, cxxxix (1929), 34–47; repr. *Zur politischen Bedeutung der kluniazensischen Bewegung*, pp. 9–27.
—— 'Die Ursachen der geistigen und politischen Wandlung Europas im 11. und 12. Jahrhundert', *Historische Zeitschrift*, cxlix (1934), 229–39; repr. *Zur politischen Bedeutung der kluniazensischen Bewegung*, pp. 31–46.
—— 'Gregor VII. und die kirchliche Reformbewegung in Deutschland', *S.G.* ii (1947), 7–30.
—— *Zur politischen Bedeutung der kluniazensischen Bewegung* (Darmstadt, 1955).
BREUILS, A., *Saint Austinde archevêque d'Auch (1000–1068) et la Gascogne au xime siècle* (Auch, 1895).
BÜTTNER, H., 'Abt Wilhelm von Hirsau und die Entwicklung der Rechtsstellung der Reformklöster im 11. Jahrhundert', *Zeitschrift für Württembergische Landesgeschichte*, xxv (1966), 321–38.

CANTOR, N. F., 'The crisis of western monasticism', *American Historical Review*, lxvi (1960), 47–67.

CASPAR, E., 'Gregor VII. in seinen Briefen', *Historische Zeitschrift*, cxxx (1924), 1–30.

COCHERIL, M., *Études sur le monachisme en Espagne et au Portugal* (Paris and Lisbon, 1966).

COTTINEAU, L. H., *Répertoire topobibliographique des abbayes et prieurés* (Mâcon, 1935).

COUSIN, P., 'L'Expansion clunisienne sous l'abbatiat de Saint Odilon', *A Cluny*, pp. 186–91.

COWDREY, H. E. J., 'Unions and confraternity with Cluny', *Journal of ecclesiastical history*, xvi (1965), 152–62.

CROZET, R., 'Le Voyage d'Urbain II et ses négotiations avec le clergé de France', *Revue historique*, clxxix (1937), 271–310.

DAVID, P., *Études historiques sur la Galice et le Portugal du vi^e au xiie siècle* (Lisbon, 1947).

DE CATEL, G., *Mémoires de l'histoire du Languedoc* (Toulouse, 1633).

DEFOURNEAUX, M., *Les Français en Espagne au xe et xiie siècles* (Paris, 1949).

DE LA CALZADA, L., 'La proyección del pensamiento de Gregorio VII en los reinos de Castilla y Aragón', *S.G.* iii (1948), 52–87.

DELARUELLE, E., 'L'Idée de croisade dans la littérature clunisienne du xie siècle et l'abbaye de Moissac', *Annales du Midi*, lxxx (1963), 419–40.

DEVIC, C., and VAISSETE, J., *Histoire générale du Languedoc*, 16 vols. (Toulouse, 1872–6).

DIENER, H., 'Das Itinerar des Abtes Hugo von Cluny', *Neue Forschungen*, pp. 355–426.

—— 'Das Verhältnis Clunys zu den Bischöfen vor allem in der Zeit seines Abtes Hugo (1049–1109)', *Neue Forschungen*, pp. 221–352.

DUBY, G., 'Recherches sur l'évolution des institutions judiciaries pendant le xe et xie siècle dans le sud de la Bourgogne', *Le Moyen Age*, lii (1946) 149–94; liii (1947), 15–38.

—— 'Le Budget de l'abbaye de Cluny entre 1080 et 1155', *Annales, Économies, Sociétés, Civilisations*, vii (1952), 155–71.

—— *La Société aux xie et xiie siècles dans la région mâconnaise* (Paris, 1953).

EGGER, B., *Geschichte des Cluniazenser-Klöster in des Westschweiz (Freiburger Historische Studien*, iii, Freiburg, 1907).

ERDMANN, C., *Die Entstehung des Kreuzzugsgedankens* (Stuttgart, 1935).

ESCALONA, R., *Historia del real monasterio de Sahagún* (Madrid, 1782).

FABRE, P., *Étude sur le Liber Censuum* (Paris, 1892).

FAZY, M., 'Le Rôle du prieuré clunisien de Souvigny dans la formation et le développement de la seigneurie de Bourbon', *Revue Mabillon*, xxvi (1936), 180–96.

FEINE, H. E., *Kirchliche Rechtsgeschichte*, Band 1: *Die katholische Kirche* (3rd edn., Weimar, 1955).

FITA, F., 'El monasterio toledano de San Servando en la segunda mitad del siglo xi', *Boletín de la real academia de la historia*, xlix (1906), 280–331.

—— 'El concilio nacional de Burgos en 1080', ibid., pp. 337–84.

FLICHE, A., *La Réforme grégorienne*, 3 vols. (Louvain and Paris, 1924–37).

—— *La Réforme grégorienne et la reconquête chrétienne (1057–1123) (Histoire de l'église*, ed. A. Fliche and V. Martin, viii, Paris, 1946).

GANSHOF, F. L., 'L'Immunité dans la monarchie franque', *Les Liens de vassalité et les immunités (Recueils de la société Jean Bodin, i, 2nd edn., Brussels, 1958), pp. 171–216.

GIEYSZTOR, A., 'The genesis of the crusades: the encyclical of Sergius IV (1009–12)', *Medievalia et humanistica*, v (1948), 3–23; vi (1950), 3–34.

GOETTING, H., 'Die klösterliche Exemtion in Nord- und Mitteldeutschland vom 8. bis zum 15. Jh.', *A.U.F.* xiv (1935–6), 105–87.

GOIFFON, É., *Saint Gilles, son abbaye, sa paroisse, son grand prieuré* (Nîmes, 1882).

HALLER, J., *Das Papsttum. Idee und Wirklichkeit*, ii (2nd edn., Darmstadt, 1962).

HALLINGER, K., *Gorze–Kluny. Studien zu den monastischen Lebensformen und Gegensätzen im Hochmittelalter (Studia Anselmiana*, xxii–v, Rome, 1950–1).

—— 'Zur geistigen Welt der Anfänge Klunys', *D.A.* x (1953–4), 417–45.

—— 'Klunys Brauche zur Zeit Hugos des Grossen', *Z.S.S.R. kan.* xlv (1959), 99–140.

—— 'Cluny', *Enciclopedia Cattolica*, ii (Vatican City, 1949), 1883–93.

HAUCK, A., *Kirchengeschichte Deutschlands*, 5 vols. (3rd and 4th edns., Leipzig, 1914–20).

HAUVILLER, E., *Ulrich von Cluny. Ein biographischer Beitrag zur Geschichte der Cluniacenser im 11. Jahrhundert (Kirchengeschichtliche Studien*, iii. 3, Münster, 1896).

HESSEL, A., 'Cluny und Mâcon. Ein Beitrag zur Geschichte der päpstlichen Exemtionprivilegien', *Zeitschrift für Kirchengeschichte*, xxii (1901), 516–24.

HIRSCH, H., 'Untersuchungen zur Geschichte des päpstlichen Schutzes', *M.I.Ö.G.* liv (1942), 363–433.

—— *Die Klosterimmunität seit dem Investiturstreit* (2nd edn., with postscript by H. Büttner, Darmstadt, 1967).

Histoire des institutions françaises au moyen âge, ed. F. Lot and R. Fawtier, iii, *Institutions ecclésiastiques*, by J.-F. Lemaringnier, J. Gaudemet, and G. Mollat (Paris, 1962).

HOFFMANN, H., 'Von Cluny zum Investiturstreit', *Archiv für Kulturgeschichte*, xlv (1963), 165–209.

HOURLIER, J., 'Cluny et la notion d'ordre religieux', *A Cluny*, pp. 219–26.

—— 'L'Entrée de Moissac dans l'ordre de Cluny', *Annales du Midi*, lxxv (1963), 353–61.

—— *Saint Odilo, abbé de Cluny* (Louvain, 1964).

HUNT, N., *Cluny under Saint Hugh, 1049–1109* (London, 1967).

HUYGHEBAERT, N., 'Un Légat de Grégoire VII en Flandre, Warmond de Vienne', *Revue d'histoire ecclésiastique*, xl (1944–5), 187–200.

JAFFÉ, P., *Regesta pontificum Romanorum*, i (2nd edn., Leipzig, 1885).

JAKOBS, H., *Die Hirsauer* (Cologne, 1961).

JORDAN, K., 'Die päpstliche Verwaltung im Zeitalter Gregors VII.', *S.G.* i (1947), 111–35.

KLEWITZ, H.-W., *Reformpäpsttum und Kardinalkolleg* (Darmstadt, 1957).

KNOWLES, D., *The monastic order in England* (Cambridge, 1949).

—— *The historian and character, and other essays* (Cambridge, 1965).

—— *From Pachomius to Ignatius. A study in the constitutional history of the Religious Orders* (Oxford, 1966).

LADNER, G. B., 'Two Gregorian letters on the sources and nature of Gregory VII's reform ideology', *S.G.* v (1956), 221–42.

—— *Theologie und Politik vor dem Investiturstreit* (2nd edn., Darmstadt, 1968).

LAMMA, P., *Momenti di storiografia cluniacense* (Rome, 1961).

LASTEYRIE, C. de, *L'Abbaye de Saint-Martial de Limoges* (Paris, 1901).

LECLERCQ, J., *Saint Pierre Damien, ermite et homme d'église* (Uomine e dottrine, 8, Rome, 1960).

—— 'Pour une histoire de la vie de Cluny', *Revue d'histoire ecclésiastique*, lvii (1962), 385–408, 783–812.

LEMARIGNIER, J.-F. *Étude sur les privilèges d'exemption et de jurisdiction ecclésiastique des abbayes normandes depuis les origines jusqu'en 1140* (*Archives de la France monastique*, xliv, Paris, 1937).

—— 'L'Exemption monastique et les origines de la réforme grégorienne', *A Cluny*, pp. 288–340.

—— 'Hiérarchie monastique et hiérarchie féodale', *Revue historique de droit français et étranger*, xxxi (1953), 171–4.

—— 'Structures monastiques et structures politiques dans la France de la fin du Xᵉ et des débuts du XIᵉ siècles', *Settimane di studio del centro italiano sull'alto medioevo, 1956* (Spoleto, 1957), pp. 357–400.

—— *Le Gouvernement royal aux premiers temps capétiens (987–1108)* (Paris, 1956).

LERCHE, O., 'Die Privilegierung der deutschen Kirche durch Papsturkunden bis auf Gregor VII.', *A.U.F.* iii (1911), 125–232.

LESNE, E., *Histoire de la propriété ecclésiastique en France*, i (Lille, 1910), ii (Lille, 1922–8).

LETONNELLIER, G., *L'Abbaye exempte de Cluny et la Saint-Siège* (*Archives de la France monastique*, xxii, Paris and Ligugé, 1923).

L'HUILLIER, A., *Vie de saint Hugues, abbé de Cluny* (Solesmes, 1888).

MAGER, H.-E., 'Studien über das Verhältnis der Cluniacenser zum Eigenkirchenwesen', *Neue Forschungen*, pp. 169–217.

MAGNOU, E., *L'Introduction de la réforme grégorienne à Toulouse* (*Cahiers de l'association Marc Bloch de Toulouse*, iii, Toulouse, 1958).

—— 'Le Chapitre de la cathédrale Saint-Étienne de Toulouse', *La vita comune del clero nei secoli xi e xii*, ii (Milan, 1962), 110–14.

MAYER, H.-E., 'Die Peterlinger Urkundenfälschungen und die Anfänge von Kloster und Stadt Peterlingen', *D.A.* xix (1963), 30–129.

MAYER, T., *Fürsten und Staat* (Weimar, 1950).

Mélanges offerts à René Crozet, ed. P. Gallais and Y.-J. Riou, 2 vols. (Poitiers, 1966).

MENÉNDEZ PIDAL, R., *La España del Cid* (4th edn., Madrid, 1947).

MEYER VON KNONAU, G., *Jahrbücher des Deutschen Reichs unter Heinrich IV. und Heinrich V.*, 7 vols. (Leipzig, 1898–1909).

MICCOLI, G., *Pietro Igneo, Studi sull'età gregoriana* (Rome, 1960).

—— *Chiesa gregoriana* (Florence, 1966).

MOLLAT, G., 'La Restitution des églises privées au patrimoine ecclésiastique en France du ixe au xie siècle', *Revue historique de droit français et étranger*, lxvii (1949), 339–423.

MORGHEN, R., *L'origine e la formazione del programma della riforma gregoriana* (Rome, 1959).

MUNDÓ, A., 'Moissac, Cluny et les mouvements monastiques de l'est du Pyrénées du xe au xiie siècle', *Annales du Midi*, lxxv (1963), 551–73.

Neue Forschungen über Cluny und die Cluniacenser, ed. G. Tellenbach (Freiburg, 1959).

PÉREZ DE URBEL, J., *Los monjes españoles en la edad media*, 2 vols. (Madrid, 1934).

—— *Sancho el Mayor de Navarra* (Madrid, 1950).

PHILIPPEAU, H. R., 'Pour l'Histoire de la coutume de Cluny', *Revue Mabillon*, xliv (1954), 141–51.

RAMACKERS, J., 'Analekten zur Geschichte des Reformpapsttums und der Cluniazenser', *Q.F.I.A.B.* xxiii (1931), 22–52.

RIVERA RECIO, J. F., *La iglesia de Toledo en el siglo XII*, i (Rome, 1966).

RONY, —, 'Un Procès canonique entre S. Jubin, archevêque de Lyon, et S. Hugues, abbé de Cluny', *Revue Mabillon*, xviii (1928), 177–185.

RUNCIMAN, S., *A history of the Crusades*, i, *The First Crusade* (Cambridge, 1951).

SACKUR, E., *Die Cluniacenser in ihrer kirchlichen und allgemeingeschichtlichen Wirksamkeit bis zur Mitte des elften Jahrhunderts*, 2 vols. (Halle an der Saale, 1892–4; repr. Darmstadt, 1965).

SAEBEKOW, G., *Die päpstlichen Legaten nach Spanien und Portugal* (Berlin, 1931).

SCHIEFFER, T., 'Cluniazensische oder Gorzische Reformbewegung?' *Archiv für mittelrheinische Kirchengeschichte*, iv (1954), 24–44.

—— 'Cluny et la querelle des investitures', *Revue historique*, ccxxv (1961), 47–72.

SCHMID, K., *Kloster Hirsau und seine Stifter* (Forschungen zur Oberrheinische Landesgeschichte, ix, Freiburg, 1959).

—— and WOLLASCH, J., 'Die gemeinschaft des Lebenden und Verstorbenen in Zeugnissen des Mittelalters', *Frühmittelalterliche Studien*, ed. K. Hauck, i (Berlin, 1967), 365–405.

SCHMID, P., 'Die Entstehung des Marseiller Kirchenstaats', *A.U.F.* x (1928), 176–207.

SCHMITZ, P., *Histoire de l'ordre de Saint-Benoît*, i (2nd edn., Maredsous, 1948).

SCHREIBER, G., 'Cluny und die Eigenkirche', *A.U.F.* xvii (1942) 359–418; repr. *Gemeinschaften des Mittelalters*, i. 81–138.

—— 'Gregor VII.', Cluny, Cîteaux, Prémontré zu Eigenkirche, Parochie, Seelsorge', *Z.S.S.R. kan.* xxxiv (1947), 31–171; repr. *Gemeinschaften des Mittelalters,* i. 283–370.

—— *Gemeinschaften des Mittelalters,* i (Regensburg and Münster, 1948).

SCHUSTER, H., 'L'Abbaye de Farfa et sa restauration au xiᵉ siècle', *Revue bénédictine,* xxiv (1907), 17–35, 374–402.

SCHWARZ, W., '*Jurisdicio* und *Condicio.* Eine Untersuchung zu dem *Privilegia libertatis* der Klöster', *Z.S.S.R. kan.* xlv (1959), 34–98.

SEMMLER, J., *Die Klosterreform von Siegburg* (Bonn, 1959).

—— 'Traditio und Königsschutz. Studien zur Geschichte der königlichen monasteria', *Z.S.S.R. kan.* xlv (1959), 1–34.

SEVERT, J., *Chronologia historica successionis hierarchicae antistitum Lugdunensis archiepiscopatus* (Lyons, 1607).

SMITH, L. M., 'Cluny and Gregory VII', *E.H.R.* xxvi (1911), 20–33.

—— *Cluny in the eleventh and twelfth centuries* (London, 1930).

SOUTHERN, R. W., *The making of the Middle Ages* (London, 1953).

Spiritualità Cluniacense (Convegni del centro di studi sulla spiritualità medievale, ii, 1958, Todi, 1960).

STACPOOLE, A., 'Hildebrand, Cluny and the Papacy', *Downside Review,* lxxxi (1963), 142–64, 254–72.

—— 'Hugh of Cluny and the Hildebrandine miracle tradition', *Revue bénédictine,* lxxvii (1967), 341–63.

STEINDORFF, E., *Jahrbücher des Deutschen Reichs unter Heinrich III.,* 2 vols. (Leipzig, 1874–81).

STENGEL, E. E., *Diplomatik der deutschen Immunitätsprivilegien vom 9. bis zum Ende des 11. Jahrhunderts* (Innsbruck, 1910).

—— *Abhandlungen und Untersuchungen zur mittelalterlichen Geschichte* (Cologne and Graz, 1960).

Studi Gregoriani, ed. G. B. Borino, 7 vols. (Rome, 1947–61).

SYDOW, J., 'Cluny und die Anfänge der apostolischen Kammer', *Studien und Mitteilungen zur Geschichte des Benediktordens und seiner Zweige,* lxiii (1951), 45–66.

SZAIVERT, W., 'Die Entstehung und Entwicklung der Klosterexemtion bis zum Ausgang des 11. Jahrhunderts', *M.I.Ö.G.* lix (1951), 265–98.

TELLENBACH, G., *Church, State, and Christian society at the time of the Investiture Contest* (E.T. by R. F. Bennett, Oxford, 1940).

—— 'Die Bedeutung des Reformpapsttums für die Einigung des Abendlandes', *S.G.* ii (1947), 125–49.

—— 'Zum Wesen der Cluniacenser', *Saeculum,* ix (1958), 370–8.

—— 'Der Sturz des Abtes Pontius von Cluny und seine geschichtliche Bedeutung', *Q.F.I.A.B.* xlii (1963), 13–55, cf. *Annales du Midi,* lxxvi (1964), 355–62.

TÖPFER, B., *Volk und Kirche zur Zeit der beginnenden Gottesfriedensbewegung* (Berlin, 1957).

ULLMANN, W., *The growth of papal government in the Middle Ages* (London, 1955).

VALOUS, G. de, *Le Monachisme clunisien des origines au xv*^{e} *siècle*, 2 vols. (*Archives de la France monastique*, xxxix, Ligugé and Paris, 1935).

—— 'Cluny', *D.H.G.E.* xiii (Paris, 1956), 35–174.

VILLEY, M., *La Croisade. Essai sur la formation d'une théorie juridique* (Paris, 1942).

VIOLANTE, C., 'Il monachesimo cluniacense di fronte al mondo politico ed ecclesiastico (secoli X e XI)', *Spiritualità Cluniacense* (Todi, 1960), pp. 155–242.

WATTENBACH, W., and HOLTZMANN, R., *Deutschlands Geschichtsquellen im Mittelalter*, new edn., ed. F.-J. Schmale, 2 vols. (Darmstadt, 1967).

WERNER, E., *Pauperes Christi. Studien zu sozial-religiösen Bewegungen im Zeitalter des Reformpapsttums* (Leipzig, 1956).

WHITNEY, J. P., *Hildebrandine essays* (Cambridge, 1932).

WOLLASCH, J., 'Königtum, Adel und Klöster im Berry während des 10. Jahrhunderts', *Neue Forschungen*, pp. 19–165.

—— 'Muri und St. Blasien', *D.A.* xvii (1961), 420–46.

—— 'Ein cluniacensisches Totenbuch aus der Zeit Abt Hugos von Cluny', *Frühmittelalterliche Studien*, ed. K. Hauck, i (Berlin, 1967), 406–43.

ZEMA, D. B., 'Economic reorganization of the Roman See during the Gregorian Reform', *S.G.* i (1947), 137–68.

ZERBI, P., 'Monasteri e riforma a Milano', *Aevum*, xxiv (1950), 44–60, 166–78.

INDEX

PRINTED IN GREAT BRITAIN
AT THE UNIVERSITY PRESS, OXFORD
BY VIVIAN RIDLER
PRINTER TO THE UNIVERSITY